Sexuality in Islam

Abdelwahab Bouhdiba

Sexuality in Islam

Translated from the French by
Alan Sheridan

Saqi Books

British Library Cataloguing-in-Publication Data
A catalogue record for this book is available from the British Library

ISBN 0 86356 086 5 (pbk)

This paperback edition first published 1998

Saqi Books
26 Westbourne Grove
London W2 5RH

Contents

Preface

This book is an attempt to think through the mutual relationship of the sexual and the sacral within the Arabo-Muslim societies. In pursuing this I am not following fashion. The dialectic of sexual ecstasy and religious faith, which is coextensive in the human being, is unaffected by variations of a socio-economic kind.

Indeed one is struck by the way in which sexual and religious behaviour all too often assumes the character of a flight from the modern world. Without wishing to overdramatize a situation that is already disturbing enough, it would certainly be true to say that the crisis of faith is not unconnected with the crisis of consciousness that affects modern society. For a balanced society produces a balanced sexuality – and not the reverse! Now the Islamic model is offered as a harmonious synthesis and a permanent adjustment of sexual ecstasy and religious faith. But has this synthesis ever been achieved except in theory? Is it not rather a regulatory harmony, a norm to be attained rather than a practical model? These are some of the questions that I raise and hope to resolve in this book.

Situating sexuality in the Arabo-Muslim societies involved at the outset the drawing up of a sort of inventory. As I pursued my research I tried to understand the place and function of sexuality in our society past and present. From the Quran to the 'agony columns' of women's magazines there is no shortage of evidence. There is a remarkable continuity both in the problems that arise and in the positions defended.

Of course, in a totalizing society like ours, the impact of Islam could not fail to be world-wide. Islamic ethics are certainly at the centre of discussion. Rediscovering the meaning of things also involves questioning the functions attributed to the sacred and the sexual in a particular civilization. And it is not so much a question of showing that the sexual is in essence sacral or that the sacred is sexual in origin as of establishing the ways and means by which the social may profit both from the majesty of the sacred and from the power of the libido. Islam in no way tries to depreciate, still less to deny, the sexual. On the contrary, it attributes a sublime significance to the sexual and invests it with such a transcendental quality that any trace of guilt is removed from it. Taken up in this way sexuality flows freely and joyfully. Sexuality is the reference and its content is a full positivity. Islamic life becomes an alteration and complementarity of the invocation of the divine Word and the exercise of physical love. The dialogue with Being and the dialogue of the sexes punctuate our daily lives. The social becomes a permanent attempt to integrate the religious and the sexual. What history reveals, then, is a three-term dialectic. In no way does this prevent economic and cultural factors from interfering with domestic ethics and from inflecting both the religious and the sexual in the direction of the survival of the group.

There are no isolated sociological 'sequences'. The phenomena are to be found in every century and every section of society; they are total, both social and psychological. An understanding of the sexual and the religious involves something beyond the phenomenon that only an interdisciplinary approach can grasp. The investigation then becomes a mobilization of all the resources of knowledge and research. So ambitious a programme requires indulgence – and modesty.

One must set out from the Quran. It is the revealed source: the primary source, chronologically and ontologically, and the ultimate source for the Muslim consciousness. My first task was to disentangle the place of sexuality in the traditional Islamic view of the world, at least in so far as it is revealed in Scripture. I tried to clarify the ethics inherent in the fiqh and in Islamic thought. The traditional idea of Eros cannot but be compared with actual experience and behaviour. The aim of the second part of this book is to locate everyday life in the great economic, social, cultural and political axes on which this *Weltanschauung* is based, to elucidate certain processes of socialization and counter-socialization of the Islamic Eros and faith. All research is a gamble. This research is an adventure and a process. But will man on the inside be forgiven for objectifying a collective subjectivity in the light of which he could not but engage his own subjectivity?

PART I

The Islamic view of sexuality

Tradition is a permanent element in the basic Arabo-Muslim personality. Quran, hadiths and fiqh are pre-eminently the invariants. Their value lies not so much in their historical import as in their revealed character. They are Revelation, that is to say, uncreated, eternal discourse. Even if Revelation is situated here and now, the content is perceived as an eternal and extra-temporal message. It lays down the model that God has chosen for his community; and this divine choice cannot undergo change. That is the basic intuition on the basis of which tradition proposes series of stereotyped forms of behaviour that at any given moment must be restored – at least as far as possible – in their entirety and in their original purity. The Quran is the divine Word, *kalāmu Allah*, the universal logos, pure idea. The Sunna of the Prophet is the practical model, the ideal behaviour that conforms to the sacred Word; behaviour embodied in a living being, of course, but which, though historical, is nevertheless the privileged echo of transcendence. In Islam, tradition is an ideal cultural set of rules. To conform to them strictly ensures that we are in the ways of God. Departure from them is tantamount to straying into error. Islam is essentially an orthodoxy. Hence the continual, 'regressive' temptation of 'fundamentalism'.

Of course one will find in the Sacred Texts innumerable passages marked by an indubitably historical and existential will. Nevertheless the dominant tendency bears the mark of the eternal. The great debate between the ancient and the modern, the *qadīm* and the *jadīd*, is at the very heart of Islam: 'Among the Arabs the *qadīm*, so vilified by the advocates of *jadīd*, might be another name for the "organic". The traditionalists like to oppose living tradition to rotten tradition. Let us define *qadīm* as the rotten side of something that might be called archetypal.'[1] There is a fundamentalism inherent in Arabo-Muslim culture. Hence the nostalgia for an absolute order that the Quran, the uncreated Word, reveals in a permanent way, which Muslim ideology will never be able to explain adequately and to the realization of which Muslim consciousness has never ceased to strive.

Let us be attentive, as generation after generation of Muslims have been, to these Quranic positions: 'And We sent Messengers before thee, and We assigned to them wives and seed; and it was not for any Messengers to bring a sign, but by God's leave. Every term has a Book, God blots out, and He establishes whatsoever He will; and with Him is the Essence of the Book.'[2] While possessing its own value historical existence is strictly dependent on the scriptural archetype. The very nature of Prophecy embodied in a living community symbolized here by wife and seed inscribes the meaning of the divine in the very hollow of historicity. The sign of Prophecy may be produced only on the order of God who, alone and sovereignly possessing the archetypal absolute, *Umm al-Kitāb*, may efface and confirm what He wishes. The phrase 'every term has a book' (*li kulli ajalin kitāb*), so controversial in both traditional and modern theology, certainly allows a historicizing understanding of the Word of God. This Word is embodied in different formulations, suited to different centuries. But the trans-historical meaning remains the same: the word pronounced here and now always refers back to the ineffable Word. And outside the archetype there are merely shadows or, rather, renewal is a plunging back into the absolute.

The Sunna of the Prophet and, later, the fiqh are ultimately merely a continuous commentary upon the absolute. The effort of understanding, of exegesis, of penetration of the divine Word are so many successive points of view of a meaning that remains profoundly identical to itself. Although the viewpoint is historical, the meaning envisaged is eternal.

So we must not be afraid of the non-historicity of Tradition. On the contrary, a rigorous analysis of Islamic culture requires that we situate ourselves at the very heart of that tradition and grasp it as a whole. For the overall corpus of the Quran, of hadith, of exegesis, of fiqh defines a total science (*'ilm*) whose purpose is to apprehend a non-temporal command defined by the *ḥudūd Allah*. It is also intended to be understood as such.

It would, of course, have been highly interesting to carry out a historical and comparative study of the development of this corpus. One might even have been able to uncover a veritable 'archeology' of Islamic views of the world, although neither could nor ought to have been my main concern. Firstly, too many of the stages in such a development are missing: there is too much ignorance and too little knowledge of the matter. Secondly, and more importantly, to project historical preoccupations on to Tradition really would have been to sin by anachronism. For Tradition specifically rejects historicity. And what matters in my undertaking is to grasp Tradition as a whole, made up certainly of contributions from different ages, but forming an ethics that claims to be non-temporal. The fact is that, not so long ago, whole generations did not see Tradition in any other way.

But there is more to it than that. For the traditional image of Tradition operated a veritable inversion of history.

The historical Model embodied by the Prophet and described by the Sunna is an 'ancient' model. This means that, the more history moves forward, the more Muslims move away from that Model, the more the collective image that they have of it becomes degraded. The Companions of the Prophet were truly privileged men: they lived in constant and close contact with the ideal Model, concerning which, through their questions, they could at any moment bring down Revelation, *waḥy*. The Companions of the Companions, the *Tābi ūn*, are necessarily less privileged. But at least they were able to consult the men of the heroic generation who lived in contact with the prophetic Model. This ability declined as the years passed, so that the image that the group has of the Model is thus in a state of decline. Far from being a bearer of progress, history is a retreat, a gradual moving away from the original Model, which will necessarily be more and more enveloped in a halo, enlarged, mythified. In the end, history, prophecy, legend and myth merge together.

As a result the entire Arabo-Muslim cultural system is centred on the need to identify, analyse and understand Tradition. Education, philosophy, politics, the arts, even science are no more than so many ways of learning to conform to this revealed ideal Model. It may be, of course, that there are objective explanations to account for this arrested history. But what really matters to us is to observe the extent to which the basic Arabo-Muslim personality was to be indelibly marked by this prior condition: to seek in all things conformity with the past. Exemplary behaviour will always be a restriction and a restoration. All original creation occurring after the Prophecy will be seen as innovation and perhaps even as culpable innovation (*bid'a*). Authentic effort, on the other hand, will always be directed towards identifying oneself with the perfect example. It will be a matter of re-creation.

In these circumstances one can see the extent to which the problem of sexuality was in a sense to be simplified by the Arabo-Muslim tradition. The understanding of sexuality would begin therefore not with the internal demands felt by the individual and by the community. It would start from the will of God as revealed in the Sacred Book. And in order to understand it better one must refer to the model realized by God's Messenger. To begin with, then, I shall try to grasp the sacred representation of sexuality. From the traditional corpus conceived as a whole there emerges a *Weltanschauung* the permanence of which, right up to our own day, defines a set of 'invariants' in the Arabo-Muslim personality. The first part of this book will be an attempt to grasp those 'invariants'. It will be devoted almost exclusively to the traditional corpus, which has formed a veritable super-ego presiding over all Islamic cultural development. I shall try to grasp the totality of impressions left by these collective ideals. I shall then try to analyse the different ways in which this sacred representation was understood by the Arabo-Muslim communities.

Then only, indeed, will the dialectic of the erotic and sacral in Islamic social practice appear in all its majesty and all its clarity, and will enable us, I am convinced, to understand the nature and profound meaning of the present crisis in love and faith within the Arabo-Muslim societies.

CHAPTER 1

The Quran and the question of sexuality

Everything is double and that is the sign of the divine miracle. Bivalence is the will of God, and sexuality, which is the relating of male and female, is merely a particular case of an absolutely universal divine wish. Many verses sing of it in triumphal fashion. The Sura known as 'the Greeks' especially so.[1]

A view of the world based on bivalence and dual relations emerges from the Quran: opposition of contraries, alternation of the various, the coming into being of all things, love, causality, surrection and resurrection, order and call and, in the last analysis, prayer (*qunūt*). One cannot but be struck by the central place given to human love. Sexual relations, which are correlative to it, are mediators in this universal process that begins with opposition, continues through alternation and becoming, and culminates in prayer.[2] It is no accident that the quranic text is placed under the sign of the Sign and that the word *āya* should recur in it so frequently. This is because all signs (*āya*) taken together sing the praise of the Lord by describing the miracle of opposition and relation, order and call. It may even be said that sexuality, by virtue of the central, universal position that it occupies in this process of the renewal of creation, is a sign of signs, an '*āyāt al-āyāt*'.

Everything is centred on the notion of *zawj*, which assumes considerable importance. The *Lisān al'Arab*[3] emphasizes the fact that the duality included in the concept refers both to the parity and the opposition of the sexes. *Azwāj* is the unity of that which has a *qarīn*. *Azwāj* is two. Diversification and its corollary, copulation, are at the centre of the analysis here and Ibn Mandhūr himself refers us to the Quran. 'Allah created the two *zawj*, the male and the female';[4] 'of every thing we have created a *zawj*, a couple'.[5] The letter and the spirit thus agree in saying that copulation is a universal law in the world. The sexual relationship of the couple takes up and amplifies a cosmic order that spills over on all sides: procreation repeats creation. Love is a mimicry of the creative act of God. The Quran, therefore, abounds in verses describing the genesis of life based on copulation and physical love.

This is because sexual relations are relations both of complementarity and pleasure. 'Your Lord', says the Quran, 'created you of a single soul, and from it created its mate, and from the pair of them scattered abroad many men and women.'[6] Elsewhere the Quran declares: 'They are a vestment for you, and you a vestment for them. . . . So now lie with them, and seek what God has prescribed for you.'[7]

Not only is the working of the flesh lawful, in accordance with the will of God, and with the order of the world, but it is the very sign of divine power. It is miracle, ever-renewed and permanent. It is also both a source of life and a sum of contradictions. Being is formed out of dust, ejaculation, abject water. But this emergence into existence is the very sign of human greatness and of divine majesty. The breath of life that runs through the Quran links biological dynamism with the movement of matter. The sense of this becoming sustained by the divine will is what creates in man repose, relaxation and pleasure. The original unity evolves towards duality by bipartition. But bipartition is not an end in itself. It is the springboard towards the continuous, ever-renewed search for an ultimate unity. Sexuality, then, is merely a variation on the one and the many. 'He created you a single soul, then from it He appointed its mate. . . . He creates you in your mothers' wombs, creation after creation is threefold shadows.'[8] It is in the threefold secret of the abdominal wall, the womb and the placenta that stage by stage life develops and man undergoes his mutation. The Sura, 'the believers', provides a more specific description of the process:

> We created man of an extraction of clay,
> then We set him, a drop, in a receptacle secure,
> then We created of the drop a clot
> then We created of the clot a tissue
> then We created of the tissue bones
> then We garmented the bones in flesh;
> thereafter we produced him as another creature.
> So blessed be God, the fairest of creators!

> Then after that you shall surely die,
> then on the Day of Resurrection you shall surely be raised up.[9]

The quranic embryogenesis constituted, for many centuries, the essence of Muslim knowledge of the chronological origins and the processes of appearance of foetal life. So great, so informed, so lucid a mind as Raghib Bāsha gives us the following valuable indications as to the way in which, on the basis of the quranic tradition, people in the Muslim world still conceived, not so long ago, of the genesis of the embryo.

> Learned men declare that sperm, when placed in the uterus, is first transformed into a small, round ball, while keeping its original white colour. And this lasts for six days. At the centre of this ball then appears a spot of blood. This spot will be the confluence of the souls (*multaqā al arwāh*). When the creation is completed this will be the heart. Two spots of blood then appear: one above the preceding spot, which will become the brain; the second to the right of the first spot will be the liver. These three spots will develop perfectly. These various transformations require three more days. That makes a total of nine days from the beginning of conception, give or take one or two days. Six days later, that is to say, on the fifteenth day after adherence, the blood invades the whole of the ball, which becomes an *'alaqa*, again give or take a day or two. The *'alaqa* becomes a *mudhgha*. This means that the coagulated blood becomes a piece of flesh as big as a spoonful. . . . This second stage requires twelve more days. These three organs (heart, brain and liver) become differentiated from one another. . . . Nine days later, the head separates from the arms and the limbs from the ribs and torso. This differentiation is sometimes noticeable and sometimes not after forty days. . . . The Messenger of God . . . said: 'Each of you lay in your mother's womb for forty days, first in *nutfa*, then in *'alaqa*, then in *mudhgha*. Allah then sends an angel who breathes the soul into it. The angel is given the order to pronounce four words that will decide its level of fortune, date of death, mode of action and lastly fortune or ill fortune. . . .'[10]

One can speak of a spermatic odyssey that prefigures in a sense the human odyssey. Embryonic life situates us in the midst of human becoming. On the other hand, in the quranic view of the world, physical love impinges directly on the social order. The social acquires meaning through the biological or, to put it another way, physical love is called upon to become spiritual by transcending itself towards the social. Indeed as soon as a couple is formed there appears immediately and necessarily the fundamental distinction between the public and the private through which we enter life separately. Sexuality is presence to my body, but also presence to the bodies of others. Sexuality is a transcending of solitude. It is a call to others, even at the carnal level. Being essentially social the sexual relation must be regulated as far as its real practice is concerned. This social meaning of sexuality, as apprehended in the Quran, is to be found in the myth of the primal couple. 'It is He who created you out of one living soul, and made of him his spouse that he might rest in her. Then, when he covered her, she bore a light burden and passed by with it; but when it became heavy they cried to God their Lord, "If Thou givest us a righteous son, we indeed shall be of the thankful." '[11] Adam and Eve form, therefore, the original dyad whose mutual meeting creates security, *sakīna*, which is the prelude to all procreation.

Strictly speaking, the procreative act was not immediately revealed to man. It is the result of a long quest that began only with the expulsion from Eden. Chased out of paradise in the company of Eve, Adam was to seek for a long time more or less illusory and temporary compensations. We know that on this point the quranic version differs appreciably from the biblical one. Indeed the temptation of Iblis concerns the truth that had hitherto been concealed from the primary couple by a veil of light. Having tasted of the tree of Immortality and Eternal Power, the couple became immediately aware of the nakedness 'of their shameful parts' (sū-ātihima).[12] This truth, which cost them so dear, turned out in the end to be sexual truth!

We should note the remarkable concordance between the notions of disobeying God, awareness of nakedness and shame. I shall come back later to the key concept of *'aura*, but it is already clear that the interhuman relationship involving shame bears within itself the key to the fundamental distinction between the public and the private!

At the very outset, the primary couple 'invented' clothing: in other words, the descent on to Earth, which is the entry into social life, is accompanied *ipso facto* by the feeling of shame. The notions of guilt and sin in the Christian sense are non-existent here. No curse is involved. On the contrary: God took pity on man and gave him the ability to dress himself. Clothing effaces shame, but it introduces man to social life.

The diversity of the social does not necessarily imply an equality of roles and a similarity of status, for the quranic view is also developed in accordance with another axis, namely, that of the hierarchy of the sexes. Indeed the primacy of man over woman is total and absolute. Woman proceeds from man. Woman is chronologically secondary. She finds her finality in man. She is made for his pleasure, his repose, his fulfillment. There is a certain 'primacy' of the male and this explains verse 38 of Sura IV, the meaning of which is as enigmatic as its import is crucial.

> Men are the managers of the affairs of women
> for that God has preferred in bounty
> one of them over another, and for that
> they have expended of their property.
> Righteous women are therefore obedient,
> guarding a secret for God's guarding.
> And those you fear may be rebellious
> admonish; banish them to their couches,
> and beat them. If they then obey you,
> look not for any way against them; God is
> All-High, All-great.[13]

Married life, then, is hierarchized. The Islamic family was to be essentially male-worshipping. And the division of labour is clearly drawn up in law in favour of the woman. For *noblesse oblige*: the right to beat one's wife also implies the duty to maintain her and work for her. A great deal could be said about the 'degree' that men have over women.[14] Many commentators would like to see this as a difference of nature.

Nevertheless the reciprocity of the two points of view remains total and dialectical. For man finds his fulfillment only in woman. Man transcends himself only through femininity. If marriage is a major canonical obligation it is for that very reason! A famous hadith declares that 'the man who marries takes possession of half of his religion'. The relationship between couples is a relationship of complementarity. Despite appearances to the contrary, one would seek in vain for the slightest trace of misogyny in the whole of the Quran. I shall come back to this crucial point.

It is enough for our purpose here to remember that the quranic view of sexuality is total and totalizing. The cosmic and the sociological, the psychological and the social rest on the union of the sexes. Sexuality is creation and procreation. It is affirmation and complementarity. The way of plenitude passes through sexual peace. Eros traverses all human behaviour, every stage in human experience, every level of the real and imaginary. The erotic drive reigns everywhere. Where there is life there is desire and where there is desire there is Eros. As soon as man was chased from paradise, he was thrown into a world in which Eros found meaning. The life of the world is a life devoted to Eros. The fundamental bond is essentially erotic. Becoming, alternation, opposition, diversity and all other forms of relation have, in one way or another, an erotic significance. It is Eros, therefore, that governs the entire universe. Sexuality is diversity in unity. Hence its importance and purificatory power. Biology occupies a special place in the Quran. This is because man is a being of desire and because the lightning flash of desire trans-poses the body and re-poses the spirit. There is no break: only unity and totality. Life is a search for immortality.

The biological schema offered by the Quran is merely an image whose profound meaning brings us to full consciousness. The biological reflects consciousness. Its truth cannot be denied and the terms by which the Quran designates the various embryonic stages are as much psychological as biological. 'The threefold shadows' in which being is formed imply an astonishingly symbolic view of the mother's womb. The very act of the animation of the *janīn* (embryo) by God is one in which a spirituality becomes incarnate and inscribed in the biological, but reveals itself to the psyche. The biological has no autonomy: it is a reflection of the psychical. The *sūra*, a form of the human body, is understood through the psyche.

Hence the initial, radical rejection of every form of asceticism. Contempt for the body is ultimately contempt for the spirit. Islam is first of all a naturalism and Islamic spirituality is full naturalness.

Furthermore quranic biology is duplicated by sociology, since the meaning of the organism is to be found in social life. Love has its finality in procreation, which is the gift of existence, the promotion to existence of a new being. Of course, sexuality cannot be reduced to procreation. Nevertheless procreation is primarily the transmission of existence in the form of an immanent thrust in which God himself participates. There is carnal pleasure immanent in the being who experiences it. Genetic power is immanent in the act of generation and in the generator himself. Creation, then, is a growth of the species and a movement of life. The sacred mission of sexuality is to propagate life, to multiply existence. In assuming it, man takes part in a divine work whose majesty is enough to give a new meaning to his existence. Sexuality is a deployment of the intensity of life.

So the act of generation is highly commendable. 'Couple and multiply,' the Prophet was to order. And the exercise of sexuality is a pious obligation. One must marry off one's slaves and children.

> Marry the spouseless among you and your
> slaves and handmaidens that are righteous;
> if they are poor, God will enrich them
> of His Bounty.[15]

Muhammad himself is berated by the Quran for swearing to go on sexual strike against his nine wives as a result of certain marital difficulties. 'O Prophet, why forbiddst thou what God has made lawful to thee, seeking the good pleasure of thy wives?'[16] And, anyway, does not the sūra 'The Table' invite us to partake of 'earthly food' without prohibition: 'O believers, forbid not such good things as God has permitted you; and transgress not; God loves not transgressors.'[17]

It is hardly surprising, then, if love arouses the wonder of God himself. The mystery of sexuality is like the completion of his work, of which it is both the support and the meaning. The wonder of God, who is love of love, gives some idea of the exceptional place accorded to sexuality by the Quran.

CHAPTER 2
Sexual prohibitions in Islam

The quranic exercise of sexuality assumes, therefore, an infinite majesty. It is life conveyed, existence multiplied, creation perpetuated. The sexual function is in itself a sacred function. It is one of those signs (*'āya*) by which the power of God may be recognized. To accept one's sex is to accept being a witness to Allah. So the relation of the sexes was to be the object of very special attention on the part of the Quran: it must be regulated so that it may be used in the right way. The Quran does not itself lay down prohibitions; it merely regulates sexual practices.

To begin with, Islam rejects the notion of the impurity of women. The opposition of the pure and impure is in no sense synonymous with the opposition of the sexes. It is the sexual relation itself that produces impurity in men as well as in women. Not in itself, but by virtue of the excreta that it produces. Soiling is bound up with *ḥadath*, that is to say, with all evacuation of organic waste: sperm, menstrual blood or cleansings. This theme of impurity consequent on the organic exercise of sexuality is central to Islam and the whole of Chapter 5 of this book is devoted to the subject.

But in addition to these prohibitions concerning the state of the man or woman who has indulged in sexual activity of any kind (with one's legal spouse, with a concubine or prostitute, homosexuality, masturbation, nocturnal emission, etc.), there are others that organize sexual relations within the Muslim community and which form what amounts to a body of sexual law. Islam distinguishes not only between lawful (*ḥalāl*) and unlawful (*ḥarām*) relations, but lays it down that lawful relations create specific taboos of the *iḥṣān*, violation of which constitutes the capital sin of *zinā*.

Coitus is not penetration into the world of evil, but into the world of the dark forces of the sacred. As a transference of existence, it gives rise to a series of taboos that constitute the state of *iḥsān*, which is, according to the fuqahā, which are unanimous on this point, the *de facto* status of any free Muslim man or woman who, having contracted a legal marriage (*nikāḥ*), is bound by strict marital fidelity.

The *muḥṣana* is the person who, by virtue of legal marriage (*nikāḥ*) is exclusively reserved to his or her spouse. Any sexual relation outside marriage or concubinage is reprehensible. Premarital relations are condemned. Nevertheless this kind of sin is quite minimal beside that committed by a married man with a woman who may have a husband. The penalty incurred for this crime is maximal: stoning to death. Of two fornicators who have committed the same sexual offence (sodomy, for example, or rape of a non-nubile girl), the legally married individual would incur the maximum penalty, but the non-married one the minimum. What is at issue is not a penal offence or a contravention of the law, but a formal, absolute taboo.

Nikāḥ creates *iḥsān*. Hence the very special importance attached to it by Islamic tradition, which distinguishes between marriage (*nikāḥ*) and coitus (*waṭ*).

However, we should not lose sight of the strictly sociological sense of *nikāḥ*. It involves a vow, a public acknowledgment, and therefore cannot be reduced simply to a legitimation of the sexual bond. Marriage is the act that gives a concrete form to the order of existence and gives sexuality a new significance. *Nikāḥ* is coitus transcended.

Has anyone noticed, for instance, the importance of publicity in Islamic marriage, which in order to be valid must be accompanied by a feast (*walīma*), with singing, dancing and shouts of joy? 'What distinguishes the lawful from the unlawful, the Prophet was fond of saying, was the drum and shouts of the *nikāḥ*.'[1] The aim of the ritual of marriage was precisely to surround the sexual relationship with the maximum publicity. The function of *nikāḥ* is not to remove taboos, but to make them known. Beyond all possible forms of sexual relationship, *nikāḥ* sanctifies one of them.

The antithesis of *nikāḥ*, which is *zinā*, is affected by a particularly violent prohibition: at least twenty-seven verses are devoted to it in the Quran.[2] 'And approach not fornication (*zinā*); surely it is an indecency and evil as a way,' declares verse 34 of the Sura 'Isra' or 'The Night Journey'. The third verse of the Sura 'Light' compares it quite simply with a form of paganism, to *ishrāk*, the association of false gods with Allah: 'The fornicator (*zāni*) shall marry none but a fornicatress (*zānia*) or an idolatress, and the fornicatress none shall marry her but a fornicator or idolator.' In the final analysis, *zinā* is a break with the Muslim community.

Indeed, *nikāḥ* is defined not only in opposition to *zinā*. 'Legal impediments' (*al mawāni' al shar 'ya*) define a set of incestuous relations and in the case of a triple repudiation a temporary declaration of unlawfulness that can be lifted only by remarriage, followed by a break, with a third person. Indeed a valid *nikāḥ* cannot be declared in the framework of the broad familial constellation defined by the Quran. It rests on links of blood, on those of suckling and even on the magical links of *ḍhihār* or *īlā*.

Now these links are specific to *nikāḥ*. The kinship system that determines lawful sexual relations is not necessarily the same as that which determines rules of succession. Indeed inheritance is strictly divided up in terms of blood relations. Magical relations do not provide *de jure* access to patrimony. Without being totally independent the sexual and the economic do not quite correspond: this emphasizes once again the privileged character of intersexual relations in the Islamic view of the world.

Islamic kiiship may be conceived in terms of consanguinity, but it cannot be reduced to them.

Islam offers the widest possible view of incest: the father's wives enjoy the same status as blood relations. Blood relationships prohibit *nikāḥ* with ascendants, descendants, laterals, collaterals, nephews and nieces. The prohibition is even extended to kinship through women.[3] For alliance through marriage equals consanguinity and it is just as unlawful to marry mothers-in-law, daughters-in-law or sisters-in-law. Parents and parents-in-law are identified definitively in the first degree and temporarily in the second degree, account being taken of the implications of polygamy.

Relations of suckling are hardly less important. The same impediments to marriage are created by suckling between infants on the one hand and the nurse on the other, and the whole of her family. Infants suckled by the same nurse are regarded as brothers and sisters, even if they have not suckled together. The Prophet is supposed to have said: 'Prohibitions of suckling are identical with prohibitions of blood!'[4] And Razi comments: 'By calling the nurse mother and the co-suckled infants brothers and sisters, Allah gave suckling the same importance as consanguinity.'[5] Through this theory of suckling the notion of the *maḥārim* assumes a mystical, affective quality in Islam.

Recognition by Islam of kinship through suckling and the role that it is made to play in defining the family constellation within which any form of sexual relation is severely prohibited confirms us in our view of *nikāḥ* as an instigator of taboos and as a specific form of relation with the sacred through the sexual. Kinship through suckling is a kinship of pleasure[6] and, assuming the same significance of blood, lactic fluid ultimately plays the same role as seminal fluid. So much so that the mother's pleasure appears as exclusive in the human relations of sexual pleasure. The analogy between the blood, milk and sperm takes us at once into the magico-religious spheres of life and gives a good idea of the sacralizing character of *nikāḥ*.

What seems at first sight curious is the fact that Islam, which takes such a broad, magical view of incest, radically rejects the very notion of adoption. Whereas it has maintained the mythical, physical character of the notion of kinship, it seems to be concerned exclusively with consanguinity. The Quran recognizes only two types of children, the legitimate and bastards (*laqīṭ*). No one may recognize an illegitimate child[7] and he does not even have recourse to adoption: '*alwaladu lil firāsh wal lil'āhir al ḥajar*,' said the Prophet.[8] 'The child is he who is designated by the marriage bed, and may the adulterer be stoned!'

This is because adoption creates conflicts between the kinship of blood and the kinship of milk. Now, in Muslim law, where a conflict of values is concerned, it is always the least important value that gives in. In this instance, blood has the primacy over milk and milk eliminates adoption.

The sacralizing virtue of *nikāḥ*, and the prohibitions that it brings with it, also allow one to grasp the disapproval of the two magical practices of *ḍhihār* and *īlā*. *Ḍhihār* consists in the speaking of magical phrases that identify the wife with the subject's mother. As the Quran puts it: 'Those of you who say, regarding their wives, "Be as my mother's back," they are not truly their mothers; their mothers are only those who gave them birth, and they are surely saying a dishonourable saying, and a falsehood.'[9]

It is significant that the curse is not declared purely and simply null and void. Its effect is recognized and admitted. It can only be annulled by the *kaffāra*,[10] that is to say, by a pious act of substitution whose mystical significance cannot be in doubt. In any case, we should remember the possible equivocation, within the most legal marriage, of the wife's sex and the mother's back. The fear of incest even by metaphor gives another key to *nikāḥ*.

An *īlā* is an oath by which the husband makes his wife unlawful for a given period. The Quran accepts the validity of such an oath, but limits its duration to four months, at the end of which the husband who does not return to the marriage bed, is *ipso facto* separated definitively from his wife.

This is another aspect of *nikāḥ*, the obligation to satisfy one's spouse. *Nikāḥ* and unconsummated marriage are mutually exclusive. Abstinence of a hundred and twenty days is a maximum not to be exceeded in any circumstances.

Sexual intercourse is one of the pillars of *nikāḥ*. What is now understood is that the parallel between the sacral and the sexual is beyond question. This becomes clear when analysing the profound meaning of the ritual practices of repudiation and *muḥallil*. We know that this is acquired simply by saying certain phrases even if they are not deliberately intended. In the Maghreb the most common phrase is the famous *bil ḥarām* (by the taboo). The phrase is sufficiently magical to be effective in itself. The very saying of the word dissolves the *nikāḥ*. A husband who has spoken the words a little too hastily will have to marry his own wife again.

However, one must not repudiate the same partner more than three times. A third repudiation is always final and the spouses may no longer cohabit together, unless the wife has been married, then repudiated by a third party. This operation is called *taḥlīl*: a declaration of sexual lawfulness. Of course this marriage involving *taḥlīl* must be a true marriage, not one of convenience. It must be consummated and Muhammad even lays it down that 'each of the two partners must have tasted of the little honey of the other'.[11]

So it can be said that, although the purpose of *nikāḥ* is to make sexual relations lawful, these relations also have the effect of justifying *nikāḥ* and even in certain extreme cases of making it possible.

But in any case, by virtue of the various prohibitions that accompany it, *nikāḥ* is as much a magical operation. It implies a veritable sacralization of man, who has become conscious of his body and of his soul and of the mystical links that unite him, beyond the human community, with nature and with God. *Nikāḥ*, therefore, is the legal form of the sexual relation.

CHAPTER 3
The eternal and Islamic feminine

Male supremacy is fundamental in Islam. Nevertheless the Quran does not ignore the eternal feminine. After all the man/woman difference is no more than a single poor, small degree (*daraja*)! A feminist breath sometimes blows through the most sacred texts. It is even said that 'some women in the first Islamic community, such as the ancient warrior Nusaybah, were ardent feminists. She asked Muhammad why, in the Quran, God always addressed himself to men and never to women. The legend has it that God recognized the validity of her question, for thereafter Revelation referred to "believers" in both genders.'[1]

Are these apocryphal rationalizations? Almost certainly. Nevertheless the folk image of women enslaved by Islam requires some qualification. The Quran, like the Sunna, presents women in terms of 'stereotypes' that are charged with meaning. Certainly Islam has no woman-prophet. But all the men-prophets bask in a female world that is richly evoked in the sacred texts. Eve,[2] of course, the mother of all of us; but also the disturbing Bilqis,[3] queen of Sheba and Solomon's conquest; Mary[4] daughter of Imran, the Virgin of the Immaculate Conception, to whom two Suras are almost exclusively devoted; Lot's wicked wife[5] and his abusive daughters;[6] Noah's wife, who is strangely condemned;[7] Zachariah's noble lady, who wins our respect;[8] Asia,[9] so virtuous, though the pharaoh's wife; the beautiful Zuleikha,[10] titular wife of Putiphar, but the illustrious temptress of Joseph. . . . These and other ladies, who enjoy the privilege of being mentioned in the Quran, constitute the Muslim sample of an eternal feminine that has never ceased to haunt men's minds. Moreover, the account of the Prophet's private life, which took place so frequently in a feminine environment, is studded with innumerable highly coloured descriptions.

The fifteen women with whom he had sexual intercourse, the nine others who tempted him, his four daughters, his own mother Amina and nurse Halima – these legendary figures give rise to much chronicle and legend and form a veritable Islamic 'review' of woman.

Some particularly stand out. Khadija,[11] the first lady of Islam, a noblewoman and businesswoman, protective, maternal and loving. But there is also Aysha, the artless redhead; the beautiful Zaynab, with her incomparable finery; Hafsa, daughter of the faithful companion Omar; Um Salāma, the inconsolable widow of a martyred cousin; Safya, the beautiful Jewess; the charming Maymūna, sister-in-law of the all-powerful uncle 'Abbas; the lonely Khawla, who sought and found refuge in the prophet's harem; Rayḥāna, the beautiful captive, who hesitated for so long about being converted to Islam and who finally preferred the status of non-Muslim concubine to that of a Muslim wife and mother of believers. . . . An innumerable sacred harem!

Despite the extreme variety of the feminine myths and of the poetic fascination they exert, two types of woman have assumed symbolic value in Islam: Aysha, the 'virtuous' coquette, and Zuleikha, Joseph's enigmatic temptress: Aysha, so much a woman but always without reproach, and Zuleikha, driven mad by desire!

The Quran gives us a very powerful description of the temptation of Joseph[12] that differs on certain essential points from the biblical version. The version in the Bible is purely and simply an account of the temptation, which, when finally unsuccessful, is transformed into petty vengeance.

> Now Joseph was handsome and good-looking. And after a time his master's wife cast her eyes upon Joseph and said, 'Lie with me.' But he refused and said to his master's wife, '. . . my master . . . has put everything that he has in my hand; . . . nor has he kept back anything from me except yourself, because you are his wife; how then can I do this great wickedness and sin against God?' And although she spoke to Joseph day after day, he would not listen to her, to lie with her or to be with her. But one day, when he went into the house to do his work and none of the men of the house was there in the house, she caught him by his garment, saying, 'Lie with me.' But he left his garment in her hand, and fled and got out of the house. And when she saw that he had left his

> garment in her hand, and had fled out of the house, she called to the men of her household and said to them: 'See, he has brought among us a Hebrew to insult us; he came in to me to lie with me, and I cried out with a loud voice; and when he heard that I lifted up my voice and cried, he left his garment with me, and fled and got out of the house.' Then she laid up his garment by her until his master came home, and she told him the same story. . . . When his master heard the words which his wife spoke to him . . . his anger was kindled. And Joseph's master took him and put him into the prison.[13]

The grandeur of the biblical text derives from its unvarnished style, from its straightforward narration of the main points. Joseph resists temptation. He emerges victorious. He prefers to be unjustly accused rather than commit adultery with Putiphar's wife. The temptation fails abysmally: Joseph rejects it immediately, categorically, definitively. The word 'temptation' is somewhat inappropriate. The dishonest proposition, repeated insistently, is not even examined by Joseph. Putiphar's wife, obsessed with her desire, is hardly subtle in her approach: 'Lie with me'!

The quranic vulgate, on the other hand, unfurls a veritable 'film' of temptation. With penetrating psychological analysis, it gives us the real secrets of the love-prophecy dialectic.

> And when he was fully grown, We gave him
> judgement and knowledge. Even so We recompense
> the good-doers.
> Now the woman in whose house he was
> solicited him, and closed the doors on them.
> 'Come,' she said, 'take me!' 'God be my refuge,'
> he said. 'Surely my lord has given me
> a goodly lodging. Surely the evildoers
> do not prosper.'
> For she desired him; and he would have taken her,
> but that he saw the proof of his Lord.
> So was it, that We might turn away from him
> evil and abomination; he was one of
> Our devoted servants.
> They raced to the door; and she tore his shirt
> from behind. They encountered her master
> by the door. She said, 'What is the recompense
> of him who purposes evil against thy folk,

but that he should be imprisoned, or
a painful chastisement?'
Said he, 'It was she that solicited me';
and a witness of her folk bore witness,
'If his shirt has been torn from before
then she has spoken truly, and he is
one of the liars;
but if it be that his shirt has been torn
from behind, then she has lied, and he is
one of the truthful.'
When he saw his shirt was torn from behind
he said, 'This is of your women's guile; surely
your guile is great.
Joseph, turn away from this, and thou, woman,
ask forgiveness of thy crime; surely thou art
one of the sinners.'
Certain women that were in the city said,
'The Governor's wife has been soliciting her
page; he smote her heart with love, we see her
in manifest error.'
When she heard their sly whispers, she sent
to them, and made ready for them a repast,
then she gave to each one of them a knife.
'Come forth, attend to them,' she said.
And when they saw him, they so admired him
that they cut their hands, saying 'God save us!
This is no mortal; he is no other
but a noble angel.'
'So now you see,' she said, 'This is he you
blamed me for. Yes, I solicited him, but
he abstained. Yet if he will not do what I
command him, he shall be imprisoned, and be
one of the humbled.'
He said, 'My Lord, prison is dearer to me
than that they call me to; yet if Thou
turnest not from me their guile, then I
shall yearn towards them, and so become
one of the ignorant.'
So his Lord answered him, and He turned
away from him their guile, surely He is
the All-hearing, the All-knowing.[14]

Zuleikha is a sensual wife, who is irresistibly attracted to her adopted son. This son, however, is a prophet. Nothing could be more natural than that women should love a prophet. But can a prophet fall in love with women who already have husbands? To ask the question is not only to examine the exact nature of the prophet, but also to understand the complex mutual interpenetration of sacral and sexual. A veritable arabesque of motifs and themes sets up a passionate dynamic within the quranic Sura. He who sets out in the way of the unlawful cannot find an honourable outcome. Not so much because Joseph is an adopted son, as because it is quite simply a matter of *zinā*.

Joseph is only an adopted son. As such, and taking into account the values of kinship in Islam, there is no question of incest. The quranic drama is quite unlike Racine's *Phèdre*. The human drama is rather one of adultery, of *zinā*. At no point, then, are we plunged into the tragic.

Zuleikha's behaviour is not entirely inexcusable. The commentators of the Quran have been happy to find her some excuses. To begin with Putiphar, the *'azīz*, the 'all-powerful', was, by a cruel twist of faith, sexually impotent and incapable of having children.[15] He is a highly complaisant husband and the neglected Zuleikha seeks some natural compensation from Joseph. Now Joseph is handsome, young, strong, wise, learned. He has everything to attract a woman seeking his favours. She wants, therefore, to seduce him.

On the one hand, then, is a husband, an officer, the pharaoh's great steward, an *'azīz*, but also an *'ajiz*, an impotent powerful man. On the other hand is the handsome youth, full of promise and vigour, who has been instructed by Allah in person in the interpretation of riddles, wisdom and absolute knowledge. Between the two a woman whom the Quran refrains from making antipathetic. And were it not for a divine miracle, passion might well have triumphed over the prophet who, departing from the biblical model, begins to give in to the idea of adultery! 'For she desired him; and he would have taken her'[16] (*Wa la qad hammat bihī wa la qad hamma bihā*), the Quran explicitly states. Some commentators, including the imam Ali, have seen here the beginning of a fall. He even wrote: '*ṭama'a fiha*'.[17] Indeed, burning with desire, Joseph lost his head and began to undo the belt of his trousers. Ibn 'Abbas interprets the *hamma bihā* thus: 'He undid his trousers, adopting the posture of traitors.' Another tradition declares that

Joseph had already taken up position between Zuleikha's thighs and was beginning to remove her garments.[18]

Of course Razi and the orthodox exegetes do not believe a word of this 'pseudo-tradition', which however does not stop them reporting it, not without a certain honest complaisance; *a priori* it is impossible that a prophet should forget himself to such an extent and initiate the process of adultery. Nevertheless the miracle takes place and an image of Jacob, Joseph's father, appears. From then on the temptation comes up against a brick wall. Concupiscence is extirpated! Razi prefers to admit that it was the angel Gabriel who, taking Joseph in hand, rid his heart of all trace of unhealthy desire.[19] But it is worth noting that it is the image of the father that blocks the upsurge of desire. Should we call this the Joseph complex? Certainly it is no accident that the miracle takes place through the image of Jacob or that of Gabriel! The end of the temptation and Joseph's 'awakening' is the reality principle defeating the pleasure principle!

So the help of Allah, translated into the image of the father, allows the sacred to triumph: Joseph remains pure. But that purity must be paid for. Joseph takes hold of himself. He wants to flee. He is caught. In the event his garment is torn from behind. The reversal of roles changes the temptation into an attack on purity that is saved just in time. We cannot but admire the displacement of meaning, from the body to the garment; that is to say, from the inside to the outside and, correlatively, from the front to the back. We must admire, too, the verbal poetry: *qudda min duburin*. Such, indeed, is the price that Joseph must pay to keep his virginal virtue intact.

How can one not be struck by the abundance of sexual symbols? The symbolism of the door could not be clearer. There is a closed door towards which one runs, but behind which there is a husband, an *'azīz*, lying in wait. Everything turns around doors, that is to say, the prohibition, the secret, the taboo of the *ḥurumāt*. Joseph refused to cross his master's matrimonial door. Zuleikha, however, wanted to reveal to him the innumerable secrets that lay behind her door. But, in the end, entry remained closed and when she opened she found a great officer lying jealously in wait behind it, who surprised the young man in a state of undress and whom only the image of Jacob his father stopped at the threshold of the great door of prohibited sin!

It is an ironic inversion, too! A man undressed by a woman and, what is more, from behind! It is an admirable dialectic of passion: the snatched garment ought in principle to excite still further the woman's desire. It suddenly changes into a weapon in her hands, proof that will bring punishment down upon the far-too-insensitive Joseph. But this was to ignore the divine miracle, for God does not abandon his servant. Innocence will be vindicated. The police investigation was not invented yesterday and the clues suggesting guilt are also part of the divine mystery.

It all ends in the expected way. Innocence is revealed and the temptress confounded. Furthermore it is an essential feature of the eternal feminine that the Quran wishes to bring out: '*Inna kaidahunna 'adhīm.*'[20] This 'your guile is great' is addressed beyond Zuleikha, to the whole female sex.

Certain misogynists have seen this incident as proof of the eternal damnation of women. One really must be deaf to the poetry of the language not to feel the tender emotions at work in the quranic account. Zuleikha certainly constitutes the prototype of the female temptress, intriguing, false, lying. But how sly and playful she is! Wickedness, artifice, trickery and false innocence, the *kaid* is all these things at once!

The second act of the quranic version gives the temptation its true dimension, which is social. Indeed persistence in *murāwada* (temptation) is expressed by the active participation of the entire community of women.

Indeed the news is not slow to spread and the passion for Joseph, which had taken place on the enclosed theatre of the Powerful One's house, becomes in the end a subject of gossip in the streets: the passion itself becomes social. All the woman are summoned to a feast at which, according to tradition, oranges and knives were served. Joseph comes in and all the women 'slash their hands'. They think he is 'wonderful', *akbarnahu*, as the Quran puts it. The word itself also means the menstrua, and if one follows the interpretation of al-Azhari, quoted by Razi,[21] we should translate the passage as 'they had their periods'. Indeed the emotion felt at the sight of Joseph was so great that the charming assembly was seized by a collective physiological pain. One can imagine all the women of the town gathered together at the house of the great al-Azīz, all having their periods at the same moment. But the menstrual blood has its corollary and counterpart in the blood shed on their own hands. Their admiration for Joseph was such that they could no longer distinguish between either the fruit and their hands, or the blades and the handles of their knives! The symbolism could not be more transparent: the oranges and knives are substitutes for an act of love so desired by the women, but refused by Joseph, the mere sight of whom brings on a collective orgasm on their part. The eroticism here derives from the divine, angelic character of Joseph. Love and prophecy are identified: the beautiful reveals the sacred. And it is no accident if Islamic tradition has always insisted on the exceptional character of Joseph's beauty: 'When he walked through the streets of Egypt,' writes Razi, 'the reflections from his face shone on the walls like sunlight lighting up the sky.'[22] Marvellous beauty combined with exemplary virtue – this is the very essence of prophecy. One cannot help but fall passionately in love with a prophet, but one is unable to seduce him. The prophet is the unsinning seducer.

Faithful to himself, therefore, Joseph persists in his indifference and is cast into prison. Note the irony here: he was rescued from the well into which his brothers had thrown him only to go back to prison. The entire trial is ultimately no more than an interlude between one hole and another. Indeed is this not the profound meaning of initiation? Having been initiated by Allah in person, Joseph did not need to be initiated by women. There are two types of initiation: by God and by love. The first, of course, is preferable and Allah provides Joseph with 'wisdom' and 'knowledge'. In such circumstances the revelation that love might bring him would cut a very poor figure. It is nothing but intrigue, error, cunning, danger: in a word, feminine *kaid*.

Nevertheless the Quran refrains from condemning in an irremediable absolute way the attempts by Zuleikha and her companions on Joseph's virtue. Side by side with divine wisdom there is room for feminine guile. But one must be on one's guard against it and at any price avoid *zinā*. With Zuleikha female initiative in sexual matters finally acquires its letters patent of nobility! Indeed the way the theme is treated reveals a whole area of Arabo-Muslim dream life. Can a *faqih* fail to identify himself with Joseph? Certainly one wants to emerge triumphant from temptation. At least one must be tempted: one can see why this Sura is so popular with Muslims. It encourages mistrust of the female sex, while providing considerable compensations. Delighting in the words of the Quran, one can dream without sinning. Sexual pleasure is all the purer for its sacred context, for exalting the ultimate triumph of virtue. Temptation can do nothing against the *ḥisān*. But what Muslim, providing of course that he remains pure, would not have loved to meet the beautiful Zuleikha?

As it happens, Islamic tradition imagined a sequel to the story of Joseph and Zuleikha. Indeed, could so much love really lead nowhere? Was there not some frustration at the sight of so much beauty, so much judgment and so much passion going to waste? The quranic version was to find a significant extension in legend.

This is what Abu Nasr al Hamadhāni says of the matter in his essay *Kitābal: sab'iyyāt*:

> The death of the pharaoh's *'azīz* (officer) left Zuleikha poor, old and blind. But her love for Joseph and her passion for him went on increasing from day to day in her heart. Her patience was exhausted. Her condition became very serious.
>
> Now up to that day she still worshipped idols. One fine day she threw her idols to the ground, became converted and began to believe in the Living Eternal God. One Friday night she said many prayers to God: 'My God,' she said, 'I am no longer well and I have lost all my charms. I am no more than a poor, old, humiliated woman, without a penny to her name. You certainly tested me when you aroused in me such a passionate love for Joseph, may Salvation be upon him. Grant me the joys of union with him, or turn me away from that passion and inspire in me indifference!'
>
> The angels heard this voice and in turn addressed this prayer to God: 'Lord and Master! This day Zuleikha addresses Thee and invokes Thee in the name of her faith and sincerity!' God the Most High replied: 'My angels, the moment has come to save her and to free her.'
>
> Now one day Joseph, still as pure as ever, was walking through the streets of the town. Zuleikha set out to meet him and, when he was near her, she cried out: 'Glory to Him whose Clemency transforms slaves into kings!' Joseph stopped and asked her:
>
> 'Who art thou?'
>
> 'I am she who wanted to buy thee with gold and precious stones, silver and pearls, musk and benjamin! I am she who ceased to feed her belly till it was full from the day she loved thee, she who has not slept a single night since she saw thee!'
>
> 'Art thou Zuleikha, then?' Joseph asked.

'I am!'

'But where are thy beauty, thy fortune, thy riches?'

'My passion for thee has ruined everything I had!'

'But how is thy passion now?'

'As it always was! What am I saying? It has not ceased to grow with every hour, with every moment!'

'What dost thou desire now?'

'Three things: beauty, riches and union with thee!'

Joseph was about to pass on, but God said this to him: 'Joseph, thou hast asked Zuleikha what she desired. Why now dost thou refuse to answer her? And knowest that God now marries thee to her. He has carried out in heaven all the formalities of canonic marriage.'

Joseph said unto Gabriel:

'But Zuleikha has nothing: neither wealth, charm, nor youth!'

'God has asked me to tell thee,' said Gabriel, 'that although she has neither wealth, charm, nor youth, she has strength and majesty, power and good actions!'

Then God gave back Zuleikha her youth and beauty so that she became even more beautiful than she was before. She became like a fourteen-year-old girl. God then cast love and passion into Joseph's heart, may He be praised. The beloved became the lover and the lover became the beloved.

Joseph returned to his house and wished to retire with Zuleikha . . . but Zuleikha first prepared herself for the *ṣalāt*. Joseph waited while she completed her *ṣalāt*. . . . His patience at an end, he finally tugged at her shirt, which he tore. Gabriel then descended from heaven and said: 'Shirt for shirt. You are now quits. I remove any reproach that might still separate thee from Zuleikha.'[23]

Though certainly apocryphal, this text seems so much to be part of the most authentic quranic tradition that it seems to complement it perfectly. For the death of the *'azīz* makes Zuleikha available for a new *nikāḥ*. With widowhood the question of *zinā* no longer arises. Lastly, the conversion to monotheism removes any other barrier. Indeed it is as if the realization of the *wiṣāl* (carnal union) was achieved through spiritual conversion and we find once again the dialectic of the sacral and the sexual noted above. The union, therefore, is consecrated in heaven by God himself before it is realized on earth.

As for the exchange concerning the woman's passing charms, the ravages of old age, these are so typical of quranic narrative that the final touch, 'shirt for shirt', represents a veritable reemergence of the symbolism of clothing and it is now Zuleikha who is *quddat min duburin*. In a word Zuleikha is the archetype of the excessively amorous woman who nevertheless arouses our sympathy on account of her suffering, her passion and her all-too-lovable 'vice'.

The Islamic tradition is marked by a very high degree of sensitive feeling; the archetype of the eternal feminine, of which Putiphar's wife represents only one, albeit deliciously pernicious aspect, emerges at every stage. There are chosen women as there are chosen men; and the men as well as the women may be condemned. Or perhaps one should say that they are tested, but hardly ever condemned when they love to excess. Muhammad himself underwent this trial by love more than once, first with Khadija, then with Aysha, then with the beautiful Zaynab. . . .

CHAPTER 4
The frontier of the sexes

The Islamic view of the couple based on the pre-established, premeditated harmony of the sexes presupposed a profound complementarity of the masculine and the feminine. This harmonious complementarity is creative and procreative. By that is meant that the extension of life, which is happiness and appeasement of tension, but also satisfaction and legitimate pleasure, may take place only within the framework of *nikāḥ*, whose global, total and totalizing character we have already stressed. Indeed Islam conceives of both the separation of the sexes and their union, their differentiation and their mutual adjustment. Hence the unique value attributed to each of the two sexes.

The bipolarity of the world rests on the strict separation of the two 'orders', the feminine and the masculine. The unity of the world can be achieved only in the harmony of the sexes realized with full knowledge. The best way of realizing the harmony intended by God is for the man to assume his masculinity and for a woman to assume her full feminity. The Islamic view of the world removes any guilt from the sexes, but it does so in order to make them available to one another and to realize a 'dialogue of the sexes' in a context of mutual respect and *joie de vivre*.

Anything that violates the order of the world is a grave 'disorder', a source of evil and anarchy. That is why *zinā* arouses such strong, unanimous condemnation. However, in a sense, *zinā* still remains within the framework of order. It is a disorder in order: it does not strictly speaking violate the fundamental order of the world; it violates only its modalities. It is, in its own way, a form of harmony between the sexes. It is a false *nikāḥ*, it is not an anti-*nikāḥ*. It recognizes the harmonious complementarity of the sexes and its error lies in wishing to realize it outside the limits laid down by God.

Islam remains violently hostile to all other ways of realizing sexual desire, which are regarded as unnatural purely and simply because they run counter to the antithetical harmony of the sexes; they violate the harmony of life; they plunge man into ambiguity; they violate the very architectonics of the cosmos. As a result the divine curse embraces both the boyish woman and the effeminate man, male and female homophilia, auto-eroticism, zoophilia, etc. Indeed all these 'deviations' involve the same refusal to accept the sexed body and to assume the female or male condition. Sexual deviation is a revolt against God.

'God has cursed those who alter the frontiers of the earth.'[1] In these terms the prophet condemns any violation of the separation of the sexes. Tradition has it that four categories of person incur the anger of God: 'Men who dress themselves as women and women who dress themselves as men, those who sleep with animals and those who sleep with men.'[2] Homosexuality (*liwāṭ*)[3] incurs the strongest condemnation. It is identified with *zinā* and it is advocated that the most horrible punishment should be applied to those who indulge in it.

In the final analysis, *liwāṭ* even designates all forms of sexual and parasexual perversion. Nevertheless, in Islam, male homosexuality stands for all the perversions and constitutes in a sense the depravity of depravities. Female homosexuality (*musāḥaqa*), while equally condemned, is treated with relative indulgence and those who indulge in it incur only the same reprimand as those condemned for auto-eroticism, bestiality or necrophilia.[4]

Lot, as we shall see, has a quite different significance in Islam and in Christianity.[5] Indeed, in Genesis there is an extension of the myth[6] that does not exist in the Quran. Held alone in a cave with their father, Lot's two daughters get drunk and sleep with him in turn in order to perpetuate the race threatened with extinction by the destruction of Sodom.

The Quran,[7] unlike the Bible, makes no mention of Lot's incest, let alone justifies it. So a veritable change of meaning in the approach to sexual questions takes place in the movement from the Bible to the Quran. A modern dictionary can declare:

> The biblical account is our first tradition of incest, extrapolations from the Egyptian civilization forming only

part of our culture and Oedipus being no more than a poetic idea. Indeed the difference between the three incestuous states is quite considerable. The incest of the pharaohs belonged to a sort of sacred biology to which they submitted themselves. Oedipus's incest is an involuntary drama worked out by fate. Only Lot's incest with his daughters is a willed act, at least on the part of the two women; even if we do not ignore that the purpose was to perpetuate the race, incest, willed and willing, is nevertheless present.[8]

For a Muslim, on the other hand, it would be unthinkable that Lot, the virtuous prophet, the man spared from the destruction of Sodom, could, even unknown to himself, sink into incest. This is because the meaning of Lot's paradigm has been displaced in Islam from incest to homosexuality. Not that incest is less serious. It is an abominable depravity and strictly prohibited. There is no legal *nikāḥ* between ascendants and descendants, between laterals and collaterals, between uncles and nieces, and between aunts and nephews. But the crime of incest is never actually mentioned in the fiqh. It is not differentiated, not even linguistically, since there is no word in Arabic to designate it specifically. Indeed we have already noted that the notion of incest is quite different in Islam and in Christian canon law. This is because the great sexual taboo of Islam is not so much failing to respect a kinship relation as violating the order of the world, the sexual division and the distinction between male and female. In addition to being a depravity, a search after refined pleasure, homosexuality is a challenge to the order of the world as laid down by God and based upon the harmony and radical separation of the sexes.

So much so indeed that the segregation of the sexes almost ends up embracing the segregation of the age groups, and by affecting beardless boys whose virility is not yet sufficiently marked to discount any wicked temptation of homophilia. The mere sight of pretty boys is regarded by the fiqh as disturbing and terribly tempting. According to one hadith there are three sorts of male homosexual: 'those who look, those who touch and those who commit the criminal act'.[9]

'Grown men', comments Alūssi, 'have behaved in an exaggerated fashion in turning away from beardless boys, in refraining even from looking at them and sitting next to them. Al-Hassan Ibn Dhakwām said: "Do not sit next to the sons of the rich and noble: they have faces like those of virgins and they are even more tempting than women." '

Thus we pass imperceptibly from a world based on the dichotomy of the sexes to a world based on the dichotomy of ages, since youth is quite simply projected on to the feminine side – and duly repressed! This is because the frontier between the masculine and the feminine was to be so carefully marked in terms of the *ḥudūd Allah*. After all the temporary devirilization of the *fityān* and *murd* constitutes no more than an additional precaution arising from the laying down of rigid frontiers between masculine and feminine.

The sexual dichotomy ought quite naturally to be marked at the level of clothing. It is hardly surprising, then, that the books of the fiqh regulated the ways in which each of the two sexes were to dress right down to the slightest detail. The collection of Bokhari's hadiths represent an entire book on correct dress.[10] Of course, the Muslim is left free to dress as he wishes providing he respects everything that serves to differentiate the sexes, while covering the shapes of the body. What it amounts to is a substitution of the anatomical forms of the body by a sexual symbolism of clothing. Clothes fulfill, therefore a very precise function over and above their universal utilitarian one: that of transcending the biological towards the theological. Clothes cease to be a mere custom and become a system of ethics, even of theology. Thus the toga (*izār*) must reach the ankles. Clothes must not be tight or cling to the body. Canonical clothing consists of: a loose *burnous*, very loose-fitting trousers for those who do not have cloth, sandals, a turban, a night cap and a flannel belt, which may be decorated. The way the clothes must be worn is also laid down. One must not wrap oneself in a single garment, thus allowing the sexual organs to be exposed in whole or in part. The prophet also advised against touching other men's clothes or pulling on them violently lest they be accidentally removed.[11]

The colours green, red and white are strongly advocated for men to the exclusion of any other colours. What is more, men must not wear clothes made of silk: 'Silk is made for women', '*al ḥarīr lil nisā*'.[12] Gold jewellery is strictly forbidden for '*al khātem lil nisā*'.[13]

The beard is a male prerogative. It must be the object of scrupulous and continuous attention. Indeed five things are defined as 'natural' (*mianl fiṭra*): circumcision, mourning, shaving of the armpits, cutting of the fingernails and wearing a beard.[14] Another hadith adds shaving of the pubic hair and the trimming of the moustache.[15] On the other hand, men must not have tattoos.[16]

In this set of prescriptions, the beard enjoys a privileged position. It is indeed the symbol of virility, just as the veil is the symbol of feminity. But whereas the veil, as is normal, must conceal femininity, the beard is intended on the contrary to draw attention to itself and in some sense exhibit virility. The beard is a form of masculinity. There is therefore a canonical duty to wear a beard.

It must be worn long, but trimmed, brushed, combed and smoothed down.[17] One grasps it in the fist and only that part of it that protrudes from the fist must be cut. It is recommended to scent it.[18] It may also be dyed, henna being particularly recommended. One may ask one's wife or concubine to assist one in this matter.[19]

The Prophet set the example by taking meticulous, patient, loving care of his beard.[20] He recommended 'to trim the moustache and to let the beard flow free'.[21]

But he himself combed his beard forty times on the top and as many times underneath and said that this increased one's vivacity and intelligence and eliminated phlegm.[22] Aysha was fond of taking an oath by using the following words: 'Not by him who has adorned heroes with beards.' Another hadith 'makes a link between the fullness of the beard and the breadth of the intelligence.' There is, therefore, a definite connection between the beard and intelligence! There is a close correspondence between the beard and authority, wisdom, power and judgment.

An Arabic treatise on physiognomy informs us that 'the superior man, reasonable, intelligent, philosophical, enlightened, aware, learned, a good judge of men, has hair (*khamūti*) between the dark and the red, neither hard nor sparse, neither abundant nor thin, neither excessively long nor too hard, neither too thick nor too fine. . . .'[23]

At a more general level, one recognized, in traditional Arab society, the social rank of a man by the length, shape and colour of his beard. 'Thus a bourgeois sported a fine beard of average length, dyed either blue, yellow, green or red. A workman or a slave could be recognized by a small beard cut fairly short. Notables and men practising the liberal professions, doctors, qadis, teachers, imams, wore very long beards, white as snow, while those of soldiers were divided into two tufts of the finest black.'[24]

It is understandable, then, that facial hair should be a matter of pride for youths who have waited for it so long and for mature men who wear it as an aesthetic attraction, an instrument of seduction and as a sign of prestige.

The female point of view must not be ignored, for it is crucial on this subject, as Shahrazād makes quite clear in *The Thousand and One Nights*. To a woman who expresses a preference for youths without prickly moustaches and beards, she replies caustically:

> My sister, you are a fool. . . ! Do you not know that a tree is beautiful when it has leaves. . . ? A beard and moustaches are to a man what long hair is to a woman. . . . And yet you tell me to choose a beardless boy for a lover? Do you think that I would ever stretch myself out for love below a youth who, hardly mounted, thinks of dismounting; who, hardly stretched, thinks of relaxing; who, hardly knotted, thinks of unknotting; who, hardly arrived, thinks of going away; who, hardly stiffened, thinks of melting; who, hardly risen, thinks of falling, who, hardly laced, thinks of unlacing. . . . Undeceive yourself, poor sister! I will never leave a man who enlaces as soon as he sniffs, who stays when he is in, who fills himself when he is empty, who begins again when he has finished, whose moving is excellence, whose jerking is a gift, who is generous when he gives, and, when he pushes, pierces!'[25]

Generally speaking, it can be said that there is an undeniable fetishism of hair in Islam, the significance of which is both sexual and religious. If Kairwan is regarded as a very holy city it is not so much because it was the first city to be founded in Africa by the Arab conquerors or because so many martyrs of the Islamic faith died there and still have their graves there, but rather because of the presence there of the remains of the Prophet's companion, Abu Zama'a al-Balawi, buried in the city with the three hairs that he pulled one day from the Prophet's beard and which he always kept on him.[26]

Behind the fetishism of the beard stands the wider fetishism of clothing based on the separation of the sexes. Clothes, an instrument of modesty, must conceal the body and at the same time reflect the sexual dichotomy of the world. This function was to be assumed on the female side by the veil, whose value goes well beyond its merely utilitarian purpose and springs from a veritable theology of the maintenance of female purity.

The veil appears to have been 'invented' by Omar[27] and he was no less proud of the fact because it was God himself who had given it to him. The ultimate limit of the separation of the sexes, the ever-renewed, tenacious symbol both of Islam and of Muslim woman, the veil, is to be found at the centre of a powerful mythology that derives its letters patent of nobility and its justification from the Quran itself.

> Say to the believers, that they cast down
> their eyes and guard their private parts;
> that is purer for them. God is aware of
> the things they work.
> And say to the believing women, that they
> cast down their eyes and guard their private
> parts, and reveal not their adornment
> save such as is outward; and let them cast
> their veils over their bosoms, and not reveal
> their adornment save to their husbands,
> or their fathers, or their husbands' fathers,
> or their sons or their husbands' sons,
> or their brothers, or their brothers' sons,
> or their sisters' sons, or their women,
> or what their right hands own, or such men
> as attend them, not having sexual desire,
> or children who have not yet attained knowledge
> of women's private parts; nor let them stamp
> their feet so that their hidden ornament
> may be known. And turn all together
> to God, O you believers; haply so
> you will prosper.[28]

So there is a double recommendation to lower one's eyes and to conceal one's private parts. There is a psycho-sociology of the look here, but one that apprehends it as the beginning of 'transgressing' the limits laid down by God.

The veil, then, places the Muslim woman in the most utter anonymity. To be a Muslim woman is to live incognito. And to make doubly sure, Arab society places the female sex behind bars. The Arab house was to become a stone veil enclosing the cotton or woollen veil. Misogyny is not far away. A subtle lover of femininity, Ibn Ḥazm, himself the author of the treatise on love known as *The Pigeon's Necklace*, does not hesitate to make the following comment on the quranic verses:

> Now if Allah the Powerful and the Great did not know the subtlety with which women play with their eyes to try to attain their lovers' hearts, the subtlety of their strategems when they use craft to arouse passion, certainly he would not have laid such stress on that vast and profound idea, infinite in its implications. These are cases when one remains outside the limit of the danger of seduction. What then can be said of cases in which one finds oneself within that limit?[29]

The look, the last entrenchment of the frontier of the sexes, was to become the object of strict religious recommendations. If one remembers Sartre's fine observations on the look, the various descriptions of the fiqh and Sunna take on a striking significance. The confrontation of the sexes, as conceived by Islam, transforms each sexual partner into an '*être-regard*', being-as-a-look, to use Sartre's term.[30]

The 'upsurge of the other's look'[31] has been so clearly felt by Islam that one may speak quite literally of a subtle dialectic of the encounter of the sexes through the exchange of looks. How to look and how to be looked at are the object of a precise, meticulous apprenticeship that is an integral part of the socialization of the Muslim. To be a Muslim is to control one's gaze and to know how to protect one's own intimacy from that of others.

However, the concept of intimacy is far-reaching, for we are confronted here by the concept of *'aura*, which tradition divides into four categories: what a man may see of a woman, what a woman may see of a man, what a man may see of a man, what a woman may see of a woman.

Between men and women and also men before their own wives, the part to be concealed from the eyes of others stretches from the navel to the knees exclusively, with a greater or less tolerance for the lower part of the thighs, especially in the case of youths. A woman must reveal only her face and hands. Between husband and wife sight is permitted of the whole of the body except for the partners' sexual organs, which one is advised not to see for 'the sight of them makes one blind'.[32] However, this is allowed in cases where it is necessary, for juridical or medical purposes, to examine the sexual organs of the *zānī* or woman in confinement.

Certain fuqaha authorize the partners to look at one another's sexual organs during intercourse. Zayla'i, armed with the opinion of Ibn 'Omar and Imam Abu Hanifa, even affirms that it increases one's ability to reach the quintessence of ecstasy.[33] Could it be that in every Muslim there is a sleeping voyeur? One is tempted to think so when one reads a hadith reported by Zayla'i himself: 'The sight of the sexual organs engenders oblivion.'[34] For Razi the look is an aphrodisiac so powerful that the temptation it arouses is irresistible.[35]

Indeed the root *'aur* is very rich. To begin with it signifies the loss of an eye. The qualificative adjective *'aura* came to mean the word or the act, for, as the *Lisān al'-arab* explains, it is as if 'the obscene word or act put out the eye and prevented it from carrying the look very far and with great clarity'.[36] A powerful conjoint mythology of the look and the sexual organ!

Other significant hadiths bear witness to the canonical and oneiric importance of the *'aura*. 'The man who looks with concupiscence at the attractions of a woman who is not his will have lead poured into his eyes on the Day of Judgment.'[37] 'The man who looks at the forms of a woman beyond her clothes to such an extent that he is able to make out the form of the bones (*sic*) will not smell the odour of paradise.'[38] 'The man who touches the hand of a woman who is not his will have burning coals put into his hand on the Day of Judgment.'[39]

Zayla'i adds this admirable commentary: 'If the woman in question is very beautiful, of course. But if she is simply an undesirable old woman there is at first sight no harm in shaking her hand and touching it: she could not arouse temptation.' And he adds at once, almost correcting himself, by way of conclusion: 'But if it is a young man shaking the hand of an old woman, he will certainly not feel desire rising within him. But the old woman herself may very well be excited when the young man touches her hand. She has known the pleasure of intercourse and touching a man's hand, therefore, arouses desire in her. It is therefore permitted only to two children, or two old people sheltered from any temptation, to touch one another's hands.'[40]

Total nudity is very strongly advised against, even when one is 'alone'. This is because absolute solitude does not exist in a world in which we share existence with the djinns and angels. 'Never go into water without clothing for water has eyes,' Daylami observes.[41]

This set of prescriptions defines the Muslim conception of the 'lawful look' (*al-naḍhar al-mubāḥ'*) and *a contrario* the *zinā* of the eye (*zinā al 'aini*).[42] The Prophet said: 'The *zinā* of the eye is the look; the *zinā* of the tongue is the word; the *zinā* of the hand is the touch; the *zinā* of the foot is to walk towards our desires.'[43] He also said: 'God the Sublime said to me: "The look is an arrow of Iblis. The man who looks away out of fear of Me, I transform that look into an act of faith the sweetness of which he will savour in his heart." '[44]

On the other hand: 'Whoever looks at a woman when he is fasting in such a way that he can see the form of the bones (*sic*) of that woman, his fast is broken.'[45]

One should add that similar prescriptions apply to the auditory function. This is because the frontiers between the sexes may be crossed, even if the visual function is limited and regulated, by the hearing of a word, a song or even the sound of a footstep or the movement of hips! The quranic verse quoted above lays down precise recommendations for the sound produced by ankle bracelets (*khalkhāl*). The *zinā* of the ear (*zinā al-udhuni*) is hardly less reprehensible than the *zinā* of the eye.[46] It is therefore 'forbidden to the Muslim to take pleasure in the harmonious voice of a woman who is not his'.[47]

The voice of a Muslim woman is also *'aura*. Not only because the sweet words coming from her mouth must be heard only by her husband and master, but because the voice may create a disturbance and set in train the cycle of *zinā*. When one knocks at the door of a house and there is no man or little boy or little girl to answer 'Who is there?', a woman must never speak: she must be content with clapping her hands.

Hence that love at a distance based almost exclusively on hearing or hearsay and which is fed on fantasy. 'Sometimes the ear falls madly in love before the eye,' as the libertine poet Bashshar Ibn Burd nicely puts it, but perhaps we should remember that Bashshar was blind.

Yet in a sense does not the whole of Arabo-Muslim society suffer more or less consciously from a 'blindness' imposed by the law of the inexorable separation of the sexes? After all, in practice, a good half of society spends its time hiding itself from the other half, while trying to imagine it or surprise it! Voyeurism is a refuge and a compensation. Arabic poetry became a hymn to the eyes and a symphony of the gaze. Love may be born from a description, a portrait. Fantasy and reality overstimulated one another. Can one ever become blind to others?

Thus rigid, hermetic frontiers define femininity and masculinity, by laying down strict rules governing status and role. It might well be expected that any ambiguity on the matter would have disappeared from Muslim society. However, that would be to ignore human reality. Moreover, there is a great problem of 'travesty' in Arabo-Muslim life. The masculine woman and the effeminite man are accursed.[48]

This is because travesty is a constant and because the veil took some time to catch on and indeed never became an absolute rule. In the countryside of the Maghreb, for example, it never became accepted. Ḥabib Zayyat is not afraid to declare that the masculine woman has a widespread occurrence before the Revelation and after it.[49]

It is because the sexual dichotomy is itself essentially anxiety-inducing. How far we are from the magnificent harmony practised by the beautiful, vigorous quranic conception of sexual accord as the source of life and existence! In this context travesty is merely a sign of psychological hermaphroditism aggravated by the cultural context. It indicates a profound disturbance in sexuality. Taking refuge in the clothes of the opposite sex is a refusal to assume one's own sexual condition. It is to play the role of the opposite sex. The virilization of woman, the need to dress as a man, that is to say, the search for the external forms of masculinity, are a more or less satisfied revolt against femininity and the status accorded the weaker sex.

This is the significance of those innumerable masculine women (*ghulāmiyyāt*) in Islam. *The Thousand and One Nights*, the *kitāb al-aghāni*, for example, has left us, among others, innumerable delightful examples.

The embarrassment of the fuqaha when faced with the extreme cases of true hermaphroditism is even greater. What is a hermaphrodite, a *mukhannath*? A man? A woman? Something else? Is it a malformation of nature? In a world in which the pre-established, premeditated, but hierarchized and dichotomized harmony of the sexes is the rule, what exactly is its place and what is its status? Does the hermaphrodite inherit as a male (double) or as a female (half). Does he/she wear the veil? Where does he/she pray, with the men or with the women? What in fact is he/she?

Al-Washtāni defines the hermaphrodite thus: 'He resembles

women in his moral qualities, his way of speaking, his way of walking. The name comes from the word *takhannuth*, which is a way of associating gentleness and a break. Indeed the *mukhannath* is gentle of speech and broken of walk. It may be as a result of creation, but it may also be a mode of behaviour deriving from a perversion.'[50] To the ambiguity of intersexuality is added that of authenticity! Hermaphroditism is a pole of ambiguity.

The question was already posed even during the lifetime of the Prophet, who advocated removal to a safe distance.

The incident of the Hermaphrodite of Medina is interesting on more than one count. One day, when the Messenger of God was at home, Um Salma, one of the Prophet's wives, was visited by a hermaphrodite who said to her: 'If God assures you victory at Taif tomorrow, I shall take you to the daughter of Ghailān: seen from the front she has four folds on her belly, but seen from behind she has eight! Her mouth? A veritable poppy! When she walks, she folds herself in two! When she speaks, she enchants! The space between her legs is an upturned jar. . . .' The Messenger of God, who was there, then said to her: 'You allowed your eyes to dwell long upon her!' And he decided to exile him.[51] Indeed the rest of the hadith informs us that the hermaphrodite in question was really a woman, since in the end she married one of the Prophet's companions.

Ibrahim Ḥalbi's *Multaqa al-abḥur* devotes a whole chapter to the question and provides a perfect summary of it.[52] The hermaphrodite has two sexes, male and female. He is to be characterized by the sexual organ from which he urinates most. Where there are equal quantities, there is an ambiguity, for the quantity of urine emerging from both sexual organs can no longer serve as a positive criterion. One will then wait until puberty and the appearance of some feature of masculinity. If his beard grows, if he is able to make love, if he has nocturnal emissions, he is a man. If, on the other hand, he menstruates, gets pregnant, has fairly voluminous breasts and can give milk, if one can have sexual intercourse with him, he is a woman. But if none of these characters appears, or if, on the contrary, they appear, but in a contradictory way, then there is a fundamental ambiguity . . . and one is dealing with a true hermaphrodite. When the ambiguity is obvious one must 'decide on the most prudent course'. He will say his prayers veiled, but will take up his position between the men and the women. If ever he says his prayers in the rows reserved for the men, those who were his immediate neighbours on the left, on the right, in front and behind, must say their prayers again.[53] If he has said his prayers in the rows reserved to the women, then *he* must say his prayers again.[54] He must wear neither silk clothes nor jewellery. On his pilgrimage to Mecca he must not wear sewn clothes and he must unveil neither before men nor before women. He must not travel without a veil. He will be circumcized neither by a man nor by a woman. But a female slave will be bought for him at his own expense or at the expense of the Bait el Māl and she will circumcize him. If he dies before his sex is determined, he will not be washed.[55] But he will be given simply a pulveral lustration (*tayammum*). He will be wrapped in five winding sheets. When he reaches adulthood, he will never attend any ceremony of funeral washing of man or woman. It is advisable to cover his grave with a veil as his body is being lowered into the grave.[56] If the funeral prayers are collective, one places the just man in front of the Imam, then the hermaphrodite and lastly the woman,[57] and they all say the prayer together. In the case of an inheritance he must have the smallest share. If his father dies and he has a brother, that brother inherits, according to Shafei, two shares and the hermaphrodite only one. According to Abu Yussef, he will have the arithmetical average, that is, three-sevenths. If he is found guilty of theft, his hand will be cut off and if ever the law of retaliation is applied to him he will be treated as a woman, whether he is the victim or the author of the original damage.

The theoretical importance accorded extreme cases does not derive as one might think from a gratuitous casuistry. On the contrary it expresses a real concern to establish as precisely and strictly as possible the limits of the sexes, for these are in fact, limits laid down by God. This concern to go as far as possible into detail shows how much the intersexual frontiers are difficult to draw up and the importance they have in the eyes of the Muslim consciousness which, having decided to limit sexual relations to *nikāḥ*, finds itself led more and more to set up an impenetrable wall between the sexes.

CHAPTER 5
Purity lost, purity regained

The innumerable Islamic prescriptions concerning purification have always been a source of surprise. Analysed correctly, these long chapters may however tell us a great deal about the profound meaning of sexuality in Islam, about the biological and psychological conditioning of the Muslim man, all of whose energy is literally caught up in a permanent experience of his own body. Islam teaches the art of remaining pure as long as possible and of expelling impurity as soon as one becomes aware of it. The life of the Muslim is a succession of states of purity acquired then lost and of impurity removed and then found again. Man is never ultimately purified. Nor is he condemned to permanent impurity. Purity is a state that may be achieved and purification is a technique that may be acquired, the aim of which is to enable the good Muslim to face God.

The nature of the purificatory act is of a metaphysical order. It is the art of sublimating the body, of removing pollution and of placing it at the service of the soul and spirit. A material, physical, psychological or moral pollution is never final in Islam and the purpose of the purificatory techniques is to restore man to his original purity.

The original, essential purity of man may be affected simply by living. Indeed to exist is to maintain with the world a set of processes of exchange, borrowing and rejection that sully one's initial purity: eating, drinking and breathing; and eliminating, too. Whatever the body eliminates is impure and sullies the body. And that pollution must be cleansed each time. It is not sin that creates impurity, but man's very life involves pollution. This pollution concerns the functions of elimination and excretion, and nothing else.

Pollution has nothing to do with sin and it may derive just as easily from lawful acts as from an unlawful act. Even sexual relations within the legitimate framework of *nikāḥ* produce pollution. But, conversely, an act of *zinā* that does not involve ejaculation produces no pollution if one of the two partners is impotent or if the act is abandoned prior to ejaculation. It is ejaculation, a physiological and material phenomenon, that produces pollution, not *zinā*. The fiqh poses, for example, the problem of the validity of the fast of a man who practises sexual intercourse with a boy or an alien woman in broad daylight. The answer is unanimous: no orgasm, no breaking of the fast. Which is not the same as to say that there is no sin!

Purifying oneself from pollution is a technique, a pleasure, an art, a practice – and, sometimes, an obsession. *Tahāra* is that which gives man back his original status. It is a total, solemn act. And although purity necessarily results from cleanliness, cleanliness cannot be reduced to purity. One cannot be too much on one's guard against hygienic or medical interpretations of the Islamic religion. *Tahāra* is essentially magico-religious: it wipes out pollution, it does not eliminate dirt and one should distinguish it carefully from *naḍhāfa*, which is hygiene or cleanliness. Indeed one can be perfectly clean and remain impure, and conversely, though it is more difficult and more unusual to be very pure and very dirty at the same time.

It is the *ḥadath*, the event, rather than the 'product' that makes impure and it is the devil, the *Shaiṭān*, that presides at the *ḥadath*. The impure man comes dangerously close to evil. In him existence precedes essence, making essence secondary, denying it in some sense, if only temporarily. The angels who normally keep watch over man and protect him leave him as soon as he ceases to be pure. So he is left without protection, despiritualized, even dehumanized. He can no longer pray, or recite sacred words, still less say the Quran. The prohibition applies equally to reading the Bible, the Gospels, the Pentateuch and the Tora, even in translation.

From the outset the impure man is exposed to every kind of danger: devils may do a great deal to him and he doesn't even have the ability to pronounce the quranic words that might protect him, precisely because he is impure and the Quran may be touched only by the 'most pure', *al-muṭahharūn*. His security, his *ḥasana*, is seriously in question. It is important, then, to reestablish the system of protection and this is the role of the ritual, which is a social, magical and religious purification, at once. Purification is a security system. Indeed death itself is followed by a precise ritual of ultimate purification. On the deathbed many impurities may be produced and one must meet the Face of the Lord only in a state of absolute purity. Only the *juthmān al-ṭāhir* is worthy of the *liqā ma wajh Allāhi*.

The fuqaha[1] traditionally distinguish between two kinds of impurity (*ḥadath*). Major impurity (*janāba*) results from any emission of sperm, menstruation and lochia or cleansings. Minor impurity is contracted as a result of any excretion by 'one of the two principal ways' (*aḥad al-sabīlain*).

Whatever emerges from the human body, gas, liquid or solid, is perceived by the fiqh as impure. What we have here is the universal horror[2] at the sight of any rottenness, putrefaction or defecation. The body's excreta are all impure and disgusting: gas, menstrual blood, urine, faecal matter, sperm, blood, pus.

There are two fundamental forms of purification: *wuḍū* (minor purification) and *ghusl* (major purification). To these two forms one should add *tayammun*, or pulveral lustration, which occurs in cases where there is a lack of the water required by the two previous forms of purification. Lastly the two ways of bodily excretion must be kept pure. Hence two other forms of ritual associated with natural needs: *istinjā* and *istibrā*, which are the art of maintaining the anus and the urinary *meatus* in a state of ideal purity.

It is not without interest to note the linguistic richness of the Arab terminology. *Wuḍū*, minor purification, also means embellishment. The *Lisān al-'Arab* makes this quite clear: 'The origin of the word is *waḍhā-a*, which means beauty'.[3]

Ghusl is the total major purification of the body and must follow the sexual act. But the word came to mean the working of the flesh itself. An ardent, indefatigable man in love is called a *ghussāl* – which is logical enough as the *Lisān al-'Arab* points out: '*Ghasala* means to have sexual intercourse, for the man who sleeps with his wife obliges her to wash.'[4] Throughout the entire Arab world today such expressions as 'to wash', 'to bathe', 'to go to the hammam' have come to mean 'to make love'.

The same sliding of meaning occurs in the case of the word *istinjā*, which covers the whole of the ritual intended to keep the anus pure. The etymology of the word goes back to the word *khalāṣ*, deliverance. Hence the derived meaning of defecation. It involves eliminating all trace of excrement by means of water.[5]

Istibrā is the entire ritual concerned with urine. Ibn Mandhūr defines it thus: 'It is a way of emptying the urinary tract of all trace of urine, of purifying the place and the tract in order to restore them to their former state, as one pays back a debt. *Istibrā* is the way of purifying the penis of urine by shaking it, pressing it, striking it sharply and other procedures.'[6] Major impurity, *janāba* is in the strict sense a form of 'alienation', a state in which one becomes 'beside oneself'.[7]

The purificatory techniques are well worthy of our interest. They are precise and rigorous and they involve constant attention to the body. In the rearing of the Muslim, they occupy a place of particular importance; even if in everyday practice one tends to simplify the ritual, to skimp it in a sense, the prescriptions are very frequently observed especially in stricter communities, notably those in the cities. In any case they reflect a climate, a way of life, a civilization that in a word rests on an ethical view of the body apprehended in terms of the categories of the pure and impure. A non-Muslim is regarded by a Muslim as being incapable of purifying himself and therefore the prisoner of the servitudes of his own body. In this very precise context purification is a permanent attention to the body and to its physiological functioning. There is a specific perception of the body as a whole, but more especially of the strictly sexual zones. To paraphrase Ferenczi we might say that the entire fiqh postutales an 'ethics of the sphincters'.

This is how the technique of *istibrā* is presented in the *fatāwā hindiyya*:

> One purifies oneself of urine by taking the penis in the left hand and by rubbing it several times against a wall or a stone. . . . One must not take the penis in the right hand, or the stone in the right hand, or the penis in the right hand and the stone in the left hand.
>
> If this cannot be done one must grasp securely between both heels a piece of well-dried mud and rub the penis on it, holding it in one's left hand. If this cannot be done, one must take the stone in one's right hand, but without moving it. . . . *Istibrā* must be continued until one is certain that nothing remains in the tract. . . . Some say that *istibrā* must take place only after one has taken a few steps. . . . Others say that one

must strike the ground with one's foot, cough violently, wrap one's right foot around one's left foot, descend and rise. In fact, it may vary from one individual to another. The essential thing is to proceed with the *istibrā* as long as possible and until one is certain that the urinary tract has been entirely emptied.[8]

Anal purification (*istinjā*) is carried out by means of water:

One uses the left hand. One must become as supple as possible. One raises one's middle finger in such a way that it may be slightly pushed ahead of the other fingers and one washes the place [of the anus] thus touched. Then one begins the same operation again with the little finger. One goes on washing until one is certain that a definite or probable purity has been achieved. In *istinjā*, one should not use more than three fingers. One must use the sides, not the ends of the fingers. Water must be poured gently and one must not beat oneself violently. . . . One should stroke oneself gently. . . . Most of our learned men think that a woman should sit down with her thighs well apart; she then washes what appears [of her vagina] with the palm of her hand; she does not have to put her fingers inside. . . . One purifies the hand at the same time as the place on which the *istinjā* is taking place. But one must wash it afterwards. . . . When one washes in summer one tends to continue the action for a long time, for one likes to cool oneself in this way. But it is in winter that one must really persist in order to achieve a better state of cleanliness. This is particularly so if the water used is cold. But if it is warm the same thing happens as in summer [with cold water]. But the merit in the after-life (*thawāb*) thus gained is less than if one uses cold water.[9]

What emerges without any doubt from the two texts quoted above is that purification is a meticulous, precise, complex and sometimes arduous technique. And the words of Salmān take on a new meaning: 'The Prophet of God taught us everything, even how to defecate.'[10]

This very special attention to the functioning of the body is just as apparent in the legal definitions of the boundary between the states of purity and of lawful impurity. The chapters concerning the *nawāqiḍ al-wuḍū* and the *nawāqiḍ al-ghusl* (the facts that break *wuḍū* and *ghusl*) reveal the same concern: to lay down, with all due care, God's boundaries, *ḥudūd Allah*, between the two states. And it is no accident if the boundary between *ṭāhir* and *khabīth* is fixed with such precision.

> Ablutions are interrupted by anything that emerges from the two ways of excretion, urine, stools, wind emitted from behind, sperm and other seminal fluids,[11] worms, stones. Stools, urine and wind emitted from behind require us to purify ourselves whatever the quantity. . . . Wind emitted by the penis or vagina does not interrupt ablutions. . . . If the urine only arrives in the urinary tract of the penis, it is not necessary to carry out new ablutions; but these are necessary if the urine reaches the glans. . . . If urine flows into the woman's uterus, but does not reach her vagina, ablutions are annulled. . . . When it is proved that a hermaphrodite is in reality of the male sex the second sexual organ is regarded as a wound and what emerges from it does not annul the ablutions. . . . Thus a man who has a wound on his penis so that the latter has two extremities: the first through which flows what normally follows the urinary tract, and the second through which flows what does not normally follow the urinary tract; it is the first that counts and stands as the urethra. When urine appears at its end it is time to renew the ablutions, even if the urine has not actually left the penis. And if the urine appears at the end of the secondary extremity, one does not have to purify oneself until the urine has left the penis.
>
> If a man fears that urine may spread [because he cannot contain himself] there is no harm in placing cotton inside the urethra so as to prevent the urine from emerging; he does not have to renew his ablutions until the urine appears on the cotton. . . . If a man tries to put his anus, which has come out, back in place, directly with his hand, or by using a piece of cloth, once the anus is in place his purification has been annulled, for he has certainly soiled his hand with some excrement. For others . . . it is the emergence of excrement from the anus itself that annuls the ablutions.[12]

I have already shown the extent to which the obsession with the boundaries laid down by God underpinned the fiqh. The conception of the pure does not escape the rule. The frontier between the pure and impure must be laid down, circumscribed precisely, strictly, scrupulously, meticulously. The Muslim owes it to himself to be pure for as long as possible. It is therefore of the utmost importance that he should know exactly when the state of impurity begins for him. Hence this 'lying in wait' for the body, this continuous self-observation of the slightest details of physiological life. To be a Muslim is also to know how to be aware of the slightest details of physiological life in order to confront them with the demands of purity.

Of course this way of spying on one's own body is an admirable training in will and self-control. The training of the sphincters is carried very far, more perhaps than in any other culture. Some people manage to control themselves when in continuous pain. For it is not easy to spy on one's own organism without falling into excess. Ghazali is quite right to warn against the *waswās* of obsession. However the Islamic doctrine of purity seems to me to be fundamentally anxiety-inducing.

So far we have dealt only with the minor purifications applicable to the needs of the digestive system. Where major purification, *janāba*, is concerned, even greater care must be devoted to the delimitation of the field of purity.

Once again I shall refer to the *fatāwā hindiyya*, which provide the most relevant details on this question: they also enjoy the greatest authority throughout the entire Muslim world, independently of any Sunnite or Shi-'ite obedience.

There are two conditions for *janāba*. The first is constituted by the emission of sperm by effusion and desire even without intromission, as a result of a touch, a look, a dream or masturbation. . . .

Desire comes into play at the moment when the sperm leaves its source and not when it appears at the end of the glans. . . . If a man dreams or looks with concupiscence at a woman and if the desire is [so strong that the sperm leaves its source] or if the man grips his penis so firmly that the desire disappears and if immediately there is [nevertheless] emission of sperm, one must proceed to major ablutions. . . . If a man proceeds to major ablutions before urinating or before going to sleep,[13] then says his prayers and if then some portion of sperm flows, he must do his ablutions over again but not his prayers. . . . In the case of a dream, if the sperm leaves its source, but without reaching the end of the glans, no washing is necessary. . . . If a woman washes after her husband has made love to her, if then her husband's sperm flows out of her vagina, she must proceed to the minor, not to the major ablutions. If a man wakes up and finds dampness on his couch or bed and remembers a nocturnal dream, if he is certain that it is sperm, or seminal fluid, or if he does not know if it is one or the other, he must wash. If he is certain that it is some other liquid he does not have to wash. If the bed is found to be damp and if the husband attributes this to his wife and the woman to her husband they must both wash. . . .

The second condition of *janāba* is intromission. When intromission takes place in one of the two partner's openings to the extent that the glans disappears entirely, *ghusl* becomes an obligation both for the active and for the passive partner, whether or not there is ejaculation. If the man's glans has been cut off, *ghusl* becomes obligatory as soon as the length of the penis equivalent to the glans is introduced. . . . Intromission in the vagina of an animal, a corpse or a child not normally capable of intercourse, does not make *ghusl* obligatory. . . . If a woman has been penetrated elsewhere than in her vagina, if the sperm nevertheless reaches her vagina and if she is a virgin or widow she does not have to wash, for in this case there has not been an intromission of a length equal to that of a glans, nor emission of sperm.[14] If a woman recognizes that she has a djinn [as lover] who visits her and makes her feel what she feels when her husband lies with her, this woman does not have to wash. . . . If a ten-year-old boy has sexual intercourse with a pubescent woman, the woman must wash but not the boy; however it is advisable to get him to do so, so that he may acquire good habits [*sic*]. Intercourse with a castrated man involves an obligation of *ghusl* for the active and for the passive partner. . . . In the case of a man who surrounds his penis with a rag and practises intromission without ejaculation, there is a divergence of opinion. . . . The safest course is that if the rag is fine enough for one to feel the warmth of the partner's penis and derive pleasure from it, one should wash, otherwise not. In the latter case it is more prudent to wash all the same. . . . A man who practises intromission in the sex of a true hermaphrodite must wash himself. . . .[15]

Behind the evident and sometimes complaisant casuistry appears the clear concern to draw up strict boundaries for the state of *janāba*. A single concern emerges from the chapter traditionally devoted by the fiqh to the premature interruption of the month-long fast of ramadhan. This occurs when, accidentally or not, one eats or drinks something. But sexual pleasure is also a form of breaking the fast, in so far as fasting also involves an exercise in sexual abstinence. Let us turn once again to the *fatāwā hindiyya* on the question. We learn with a mass of details and specific examples the limits assigned to the exercise of sexuality during the fast.[16]

Thus purity and impurity are not automatic. They result from a dialectic of the psychical and the biological. Indeed all the tests previously mentioned involve considerations of a psychological order (the intention of ejaculating, fasting, or simply 'playing', by indulging in foreplay) and of a very biological order (partial or total intromission, mechanical ejaculation or complete coitus, masturbation, etc.). As one can see ethics has nothing to do with the question, for ethics is concerned only with the lawfulness or unlawfulness of the act. An unnatural act perpetrated on a boy, while being condemned and regarded as a terrible sin, does not break the fast if it is not followed by ejaculation!

For the woman coitus followed by orgasm is not the only case of impurity. *Janāba* also derives from the menstrua, lochia and pseudo-menstrual emissions.

The fiqh merely passes on here an almost universal, in any case very widespread, attitude among ordinary people. Menstrual blood arouses considerable revulsion. More or less everywhere in the world popular tradition accuses it of aborting serious projects, of turning milk sour and food rotten.

The fuqaha have defined in great detail the notion of the menstrua by distinguishing between the lawful impurity (*ḥaiḍ*) of the woman and evident impurity (*istiḥāḍha*).

> The menstrua are made up of blood that emerges from the woman's vagina at other moments than during childbirth. The blood that emerges from the anus is not menstrual. The menstrua are lawful if certain conditions are fulfilled. First if they take place between the ages of nine and fifty-five. . . . According to the greatest authorities, the blood that appears beyond that age does not constitute lawful menstruation. . . . The blood must flow outside the vagina, even if that condition is fulfilled only by abstaining from the use of a cotton tampon. If this tampon prevents the menstrual blood from passing from the uterus into the vagina, there is no menstruation. If a pure woman observes on the tampon or on her underwear some trace of blood, she is said to have

> menstruated. A menstruating woman who does not see any trace of blood on the tampon is said to have completed her menstrual period. . . . Menstrual blood must be one of the six following colours: black, red, yellow, lemon yellow, green and grey-green. One considers the colour of the cotton at the very moment when it is removed, not when it has dried. . . . The legal duration of the period is a minimum of three days and three nights, and a maximum of ten days and ten nights. . . . The period of purity between two menstrual periods must be at least fifteen days.[17]

The legal duration of the lochia (*nafās*) is forty days. Childbirth involves an obligation to proceed to major ablutions unless the birth occurs without the shedding of blood. In that case one has only to proceed to minor ablutions. There is lawful childbirth when the greater part of the newborn child has emerged. Supposing that for some reason or another the child is cut up into several pieces, a legal birth is said to have occurred when a normally formed part of the body (a foot, a head) has emerged; otherwise only menstruation has taken place. When the delivery has taken place through the navel (in the case of a caesarian operation), there is a lawful childbirth only if at the same time some blood flows from the vagina.

Children are said to be twins when two births occur less than six months apart. If the interval is greater, there are two separate childbirths and therefore a double prescription where purification and fasting are concerned. (Menstruation and the lochia, of course, annul the woman's fast.) The minimum duration for a childbirth is one hour, with a maximum of forty days.

The blood that flows after the lawful duration of childbirth or of the menstrual period or what appears between two lawful menstrual periods or two lawful childbirths or between a legal menstrual period and a legal childbirth is regarded as an apparent menstruation. The same applies to blood emissions occurring before the age of nine and after the age of fifty-five.

Of course the lawful impurity of the woman does disturb her order and confers on her a status that places her outside the ordinary norms. *Ipso facto* she is dispensed from prayer and fasting. If she is performing either, she must break off at once. She will take them up again at a later date, when she is once more pure. She must not enter a mosque, unless there is an absolute need for her to draw water in a well placed within the sacred precincts. The same tolerance is applied in case of danger: if, for example, one has to flee a wild beast, a bandit, or if one wants to take refuge against cold, hail or lightning. Similarly it is prohibited to carry out the *tawāf*, or circumambulation around the *ka'ba*, or sacred black stone of Mecca. Similarly she is forbidden to read, to recite, to copy out or to touch the Quran, the Gospels, the Bible or the Tora. If she is obliged to do so, she must pronounce the words one by one, spacing them out.

Lastly, intercourse is forbidden with a woman during her period or lawful confinement: 'The husband may embrace her, lie next to her and enjoy her whole body except the part comprised between the navel and the knees.'[18]

Furthermore, purification is not an end in itself. It is merely a way of returning to the ritual practices: prayer, fasting, profession of faith, reading of the Quran pilgrimage. Purification is not gratuitous. It is a state that makes possible a dialogue with the sacred. It cannot be substituted for it. That is why Ghazali denounces the carrying out in either a mechanical or an exaggerated way of what after all is merely a preparation.

For him the ultimate aim of purification is the peace of the soul and mastery over the body.[19] He attacks the tendency, which was fairly widespread among his contemporaries and which is in fact a permanent feature of Arabo-Muslim societies, of cleaning the body in order to conceal the sinfulness of the soul. The purificatory technique then becomes a form of deceit, of deceiving others and deceiving oneself. This is why Ghazali lays such stress on the famous verse: 'God does not desire to make any impediment for you; but He desires to purify you.'[20] And Ghazali maintains that what is most important is to purify the mysteries of the private being; it is the heart, the mind, the entire soul that must first of all be purified, not the body.

The true aim of purification, therefore, is to be able to see God. Now, knowledge of God is exclusive and can be attained only if one has first prepared oneself by abolishing in oneself any other viewpoint. But one cannot reach that state if the heart has not itself been previously purified. One must first furnish it with virtues, faith and noble beliefs. One must rid it of vices and false beliefs. It is in this sense that, for Ghazali, purity constitutes 'half of faith'.[21] Purity of heart rests in turn on cleansing the sense of concupiscence, desire, jealousy, cowardice and cupidity. But all this requires, by way of preparation, the purification of the body, *ṭahāra*, in the ordinary sense of the word.

Thus purification is an ascesis, the various stages of which support one another. The purification of the body is merely a preparation for the true purity of the spiritual being. It is not an end in itself.

> Of course man has become so blinded that he is no longer aware of this hierarchy of levels and of all these stages of purity keeps only the last. But this last is merely bark, exteriority, appearance; the bottom step in a scale of values; a springboard to a centre that, alone, is the target to be reached. One sets out on a hopeless quest for exteriority! One spends all one's energy on it! One devotes all one's time to cleaning one's anus, washing one's clothes – cleaning the outside, looking for plentiful supplies of running water. And this obsession (*waswasa*) and these fantasies (*takhayyul*) lead us in the end to believe that the noble *ṭahāra* being pursued is no more than these practices alone! If one does so one is ignorant of the conduct of the ancients, who devoted all their efforts, all their power to purifying their hearts and who, on matters of mere appearance, were on the contrary full of tolerance![22]

And Ghazali remarks not without a touch of humour and disenchantment:

> But the ultimate today is reached by those who confuse popular medication (*ra-wana*) with cleanliness and who regard it as the foundation of religion. They spend most of their time polishing their fingernails as a beauty specialist might for a bride preparing for her wedding night! While the inside is stuffed with vices. Pride, infatuation, ignorance, ostentation, hypocrisy do not shock them, do not stir them up to any condemnation. But if someone is content to practise *istinjā* with stones, if he walks barefoot, if he says his prayers on the ground or on the bare earth of a mosque without a carpet, if he does his ablutions with water taken from the recipient of some good old woman or of a man whose piety cannot be guaranteed, they will seek a quarrel with him, track him down, call him every bad name they can think of, excommunicate him, cease to share their food with him and even to see him.[23]

In the history of Islamic ethics, Ghazali succeeded in reviving the question of purification in an admirable way. With authority and using the most sacred texts as support, he put an end to the dichotomic, Manichean opposition of the pure and the impure. He substituted for it an ascending, Platonic dialectic of progressive ascent to ever purer states.

Purification is not a technique of physical cleanliness, but a permanent, private quest for spirituality. Without expatiating too long on the historical character of Muslim thought, it should be pointed out how far we are from the sterile opposition of ultimate good and ultimate evil.[24] To pose the problem in terms of a quest is to say that purification has a meaning and that this meaning is to be sought in a transcending of one's own body. This notion is quite crucial if we are to situate correctly the Islamic conception of *ṭahāra*.

Of course, purification involves bodily elements of all kinds,[25] but it cannot be reduced to mere hygiene. Again it comprises a level that might be called that of cleanliness. And it is quite normal for a physician to make use of Islamic 'hygienism', which postulates from the outset the integration of faith and cleanliness. 'Cleanliness is part of faith. Dirt is the work of the devil,' says a popular saying. But if cleanliness is at the service of faith, it is not coextensive with it.

It is also true, of course, that the particular care with which the fiqh tries to define the rules of lawfulness, lawful purity, is directly related to social life. This is because it involves the very organization of the historically embodied community. Paternity, widowhood and inheritance are directly involved. It involves an affirmation of the limits that God places on his community, which is made up of men and women who have relations between themselves that involve their most vital temporal interests. The chapters of the fiqh that deal with these questions confront explicitly, therefore, a series of facts perceived in their totality. It may be said without hesitation that, in Islam, purification is a total phenomenon, at once social and psychical.

But this total vision should not blind us to the fact that what is in question, above everything else, is the relationship of two forces: that of the sexual and that of the sacred.

Islam is a constant attention paid to one's own body. A Muslim upbringing is a training that makes one permanently aware of the functioning of the physiological life. Eating, drinking, urinating, farting, defecating, having sexual intercourse, vomiting, bleeding, shaving, cutting one's nails. . . . All this is the object of meticulous prescriptions, of which we have provided only a few examples. There are formulas to be recited before, during and after each act. There are ways in which the acts are to be performed, certain gestures to be carried out, a style to be respected. It comes very close to obsession, as Ghazali saw very clearly when he recommended, at each step of the monumental summa that makes up the Iḥyā, a sense of balance (*i'tidāl*), which is alone capable of banishing obsessional *waswās*.[26]

Perhaps more than any others, Muslim societies have produced men and women who are sick with cleanliness. The meat that is bled, then washed by certain people as many as seven times, sometimes even in soapy water; the receptacles that are washed seven times; the long, frequent visits to the Moorish baths; this unhealthy fear and mistrust of uncleanliness in every form and especially the meticulous and excessive attentions that one lavishes on one's body in the form of minor purification, all this points directly to anality. Like orality, anality seems to me to be an essential part of Arabo-Muslim upbringing. *Istinjā* is, among other things, an eroticization of the anal zone. One may apply to the fiqh Ferenczi's term 'morality of the sphincters'. Is it not a matter of rigorously supervising the movement of everything that emerges from the body, solid, liquid or gas, to be aware of it and to behave as a consequence in a canonically adequate fashion?

This leads to a total, complete and absolute cathecting or investment of the body. The fiqh is a way of experiencing one's body, of apprehending it, of assuming it positively and fully. Islam is a way of taking charge of one's physiological life, the art of living one's corporality and of continually resacralizing it. The fulfillment of each physiological action is immediately and unfailingly followed by a set of techniques that reestablish the purity that Ghazali sees as the natural, normal, truthful state of things. Purity is not the conquest of some deep, original impurity. It is a restoration of and return to an originally positive situation. In this sense the fiqh is in itself liberating. It appeases our scruples and gives us back our confidence. Through an adequate attitude to his body the Muslim achieves security.

Where sexuality in the strict sense is concerned, this role of purification becomes even more marked. Sexuality is desacralizing: it brings into play forces that have always appeared to man as alien, mysterious and necessarily involving a break with the sacred.

Purification is precisely the resacralization and reconciliation of man with himself.

We know the famous theory of Georges Bataille, largely borrowed, it is true, from Durkheim, that this is one of the origins of life. The great problem is to overcome anxiety.

'Anxiety, it seems, constitutes humanity: not anxiety itself, but anxiety overcome, the overcoming of anxiety.'[27]

Now, we can say quite clearly that *ghusl* has metaphysical implications: it is precisely an overcoming of anxiety; the mysterious forces of orgasm, menstrual blood and childbirth are, as it were, reabsorbed by this 'resumption of control' over my own body. These forces are forces of delusion, mystery, overflowing, ecstasy. Purification captures them, canalizes them, integrates them. Organic life is loss, despiritualization. Ritual purity is restoration and resacralization. The way of assuming one's body will assuage anxiety, and anxiety will be replaced by peace of mind, the necessary condition for complete internal balance. *Ghusl*, then, has both a compensatory and an integrating function.

We can see in actual cases how the sexual is placed at the service of the social and how the social serves the sexual. Muslim society exploits for its own ends the drives of the sexual mystery and integrates them into normal, stereotyped behaviour. What might have been an unconscious, destructive drive both for society and individuals alike is transformed into ritual and myth, and thus loses its morbid, alien and supposedly dangerous characteristics. Purification is in the full sense of the word an end to that most dangerous of alienations: *janāba*.

CHAPTER 6
Commerce with the invisible

For Islam man exceeds in dignity the whole of creation and contains within himself the wonders that bear witness to the divine majesty. Second in relation to God, he is first in relation to every other creature. He is the link between *natura naturata* and *ens naturans*. And it is no accident if he possesses at once a soul, a sex and responsibility. For the Quran, responsibility is grounded in love. So much so that the traditional exegesis is not afraid to give a sexual meaning to the famous quranic verse concerning the 'remembrance' offered by God to the heavens and the earth, which rejected it, and that only man accepted. Sexuality is a precious 'remembrance' or gift entrusted to man's safe keeping.[1] This great juvenile lead of creation lives in a world peopled by the invisible. And relations with the invisible are also of a sexual order.

Islamic theology distinguishes between four sorts of creatures: the *malā-ika* (angels), the *ins* (men), the *jānn* (djinns) and the *shaiṭān* (devils). All are animated, responsible (mukallafa)[2] and, with the exception of angels, sexual beings.

Only the angels have no sex. Razi remarks that they have no femininity. 'No femininity, no progeniture.'[3] They do not know physical love; they are beings without desire. 'They know neither hunger nor sexual appetite.'[4] They have only spiritual desires: to sing the praises of God, for example. They reflect deeply rooted tendencies in Muslim man to aspire to cross the boundaries of his being. Indeed they express a permanent desire for transcendence and for a sublimation that is all the more ethereal in that the angels, who are essentially a-sexual, are outside our grasp. Angelic oneirism is an oneirism of sublimation, which is not the case with oneirism of the devil and oneirism of the djinns, with whom sexual intercourse is possible *de jure* and . . . *de facto*.

The devil is an angel, but a rebel one. Jealous of man, he swore to bring about his perdition by every means. He obtained from God the power to lead men into error. In Islam he is the tempter who urges man to disobey God, but above all to fornicate and transgress the sexual taboos. Indeed man has received, among other gifts from God, that of distinguishing between good and evil, a faculty that is at the disposal neither of the angels nor of the djinns, who are quite incapable of choice. In Islam temptation does not have the same meaning and significance as it has in Christian theology. It does not derive from human culpability, since Islam has no conception of original sin. The corollary of human responsibility, the ability to be tempted, is a logical consequence of freedom.[5]

The devil does not enjoy total power over man. And if the devil likes to tempt men, it is above all to prove to God that they can sin and that the faculty of choosing that was given to them is used by them for evil, not for good ends. Iblis seized upon this as proof of his superiority over Adam and over his descendants and to justify his own refusal.

Henceforth all human sin is a justification of Iblis. The evil that it makes us do enables him to recover the power given to our race. Iblis is not pure negativity.

Nevertheless, for orthodox Islam, Adam remains the being of Eden and Iblis the infernal being. Iblis is anti-man and as such he reveals man to himself. He is the other that enables us to place ourselves. Without Iblis there may not have been humanity. He is the underside of ourselves and as such he expresses our own essence.

The power of the devil is certainly very varied. Nevertheless it is the sexual appetite that is at the centre of the archetype. Iblis, the fallen angel, the a-sexual being, is everywhere a highly eroticized and eroticizing character. One hadith commented upon by Qortobi provides a key to the mystery. 'After making Adam the Blessed in Eden, God the Most High left him alone there for some time. Iblis then began to walk around the creature and examine him well. When he saw that Adam was hollow and bellied (*ajwaf*), he realized that he had been made in such a way that he could not control his sexual appetite.'[6] There is a continuity from the idea of sexuality, a remembrance or token of God's trust, to that of Adam, bellied and hollowed and handed over to the power of Satan from the outset.

Indeed to keep to the chronological order of his making, man was first of a single sex. According to a tradition reported by Abdullah Amr-Ibn El 'As, 'the first thing that God created of man was his sexual organ. He then said: "I entrust you with this gift. Use it only according to the truth. If you look after it, it will look after you. The sexual organ is a gift, the ear is a gift". . . .'[7] It was certainly this gift that made Iblis jealous of Adam and his descendants. What the non-sexed devil was jealous of was human sexuality. Depravity, *zinā* and other perversions are temptations of the jealous devil.

Of course this in no way excludes the syncretism and the clearly sexual signification of the character of Iblis is an extension of other, earlier Arab or universal beliefs. Gaudefroy-Demombynes observes,

> In ancient Arabic, Shaytan had the sense of 'serpent', which was the animal form that the djinns most readily adopted . . . according to the Muslim tradition . . . Iblis got back into Paradise in the belly of a four-footed animal, like a Bactrian camel, in order to trick the angels who were guarding paradise: Allah cursed this fine animal, which became a serpent crawling on its belly.[8]

Iblis is the Serpent of the Bible. He is at once the general principle of evil, the archetype of the lower soul within us, symbolized by Satan, the serpent and the scorpion, to take up the trilogy dear to Mme Maryse Choisy.[9]

So much does the devil express this underside of himself for the Arabo-Muslim that he is constantly in dialogue with himself and not only in his dreams! From Ma'ariis's *Message of Pardon* to Qazwīni's *Marvels of Creation*, to Abderrahman Shukri, to Taufiq al-Hakīm, to the Arabic-speaking Brazilian poet Shafiq Ma-lūf,[10] what we have, in the final analysis, are so many variations on the extraordinary dialogue imagined by al-Hallaj between Moses descending the mountain where he had received the Tablets of the Law and Iblis the challenger, with his face blackened by divine curse. We have only to turn to the magnificent researches of Massignon.[11]

But there is a less well-known text in which Muhammad in person enters into dialogue with Iblis. This anonymous text traditionally appears after Muh'y iddin Ibn Arabi's *The Cosmic Tree*.[12] It is a compilation in dialogue form of authentic hadiths reported by Bokhāri and Muslim.[13] One day the Prophet was surrounded by a group of believers at Medina when Iblis appeared among them. Ordered to do so by God, he had come to reveal to the Prophet the absolute truth about himself.

So Satan talked with Muhammad the Messenger of God and revealed to him certain truths. He unveiled to him his greatest secrets. This confession ordered by God himself constitutes in a sense an exercise of exegesis and a warning. Hence the injunction addressed by Muhammad to his companions: 'Understand well what he says to you; listen to what he is about to tell you.' Omar's first, spontaneous response was 'to kill the devil', but the Prophet advised him to begin by understanding the Evil One, in order to outwit his cunning. We are to understand by this that temptation is a 'mechanism', which it is up to us to take apart if we are to overcome it. Knowledge, even when revealed by the Spirit of Evil, is a way of purification. Evil and sin are reduced here to an action that is in some sense mechanical, though insidious on the part of the Tempter, who wishes to lead the most just, most virtuous, most holy men into error.

Despite the power that he exerts over men the devil is, in the last resort, presented here in a rather reassuring guise and the image that is given of him is far from terrifying, even if on reflection he turns out to be terrible. 'He was a one-eyed old man with a thin beard. In his beard there were seven hairs like those of the Mare. Both his eyes were split [vertically]. His head was like that of a big elephant. His teeth protruded like those of a wild boar and his lips were like those of an ox.'[14] The character is certainly ridiculous. He is ugly, of course, but he is not excessively monstrous. How far we are from medieval Christian fantasy, from the strange monsters of Vézelay Abbey, for instance! How far we are from diabolical hubris! What we are confronted with is almost a 'de-demonized' devil. A Spirit of Evil, no more, a rebel against God. A continual temptation, nothing more.

However, when looked at more closely and as a whole Iblis's features constitute a clever symbolic arabesque. The tempter, who is capable of assuming a thousand and one shapes, chooses that of an old man (*shaikh*) and therefore in principle and according to the stereotypes of Arabo-Muslim society, he assumes the features of a mature, adult man, who, being beyond the age of love-making, whether lawful or unlawful, ought to have no other thoughts than those of piety and fear of God. Then, little by little, by successive touches, the features shape the character and situate him.

For this old man is one-eyed. Iblis justifies his reputation: he is often rightly called the *a'war*. From pre-Islamic times Arab society, like many others, was ill disposed towards the one-eyed, who were supposed to bring misfortune: they symbolized the more or less deserved loss of the essential instrument of contact with light! God punishes wicked, indiscreet voyeurs, by depriving them of the sight of one or two eyes. The one-eyed is the half-condemned. Psychoanalysis has shed light on this theme of symbolic punishment by the loss of an eye.

Furthermore, this single eye is split vertically. This is almost as if to stress the sexual signification of this eye. The word *shaqq* (slit or vulva) certainly designates the female sexual organ in Arabic, whereas the word *'ala al ṭūl* stresses still further the excessive elongation of the thing. The vaginal symbol is obvious. A certain cruelty is also present in it, for it is a diabolical eye that sees everything, lays in wait for everything, watches man's slightest gestures, observes his slightest weaknesses in order to exploit them and, taking advantage of weak points in our psychical armoury, strikes at the most unexpected moment.

In this portrait there is a deliberate desire not only to de-demonize the devil, but also to de-virilize him; this is what is meant by the feature of the thin beard. Iblis is not quite beardless (*amrad*), which would have given his portrait a sodomistic touch. The word used here is *kausaj*:[15] without hair on the cheeks. Just a short, thin goatee with exactly seven mare's hairs. This last detail demeans Iblis still further, animalizing him and devirilizing him still more.

The mission of the devil is here a mission of truth and Iblis is ordered to show himself as he really is:

> The Lord orders you to go and find Muhammad, to make yourself small, humble and modest before him and to tell him how you trick the descendants of Adam and inspire wicked thoughts in them. You will answer truthfully whatever questions he asks you. By My Power and Majesty, if you lie once and conceal the truth from him, I shall reduce you to ashes, which will be scattered to the winds, and all your enemies will rejoice at your ill fortune. 'Here I am, Muhammad,' said the devil, 'I have come as I was ordered to.

Ask whatever questions you will. If I lie, my enemies will rejoice in my misfortune, and nothing is more difficult to bear for me than that.'[16]

Iblis speaks and presents his view of things, which in reality is merely the perfect antithesis of the Islamic image of the world. The holiest being, the Prophet, becomes, in Iblis's eyes, the most hateful of beings and, conversely, the most impious is seen by Iblis as the most likeable. The world of the devil is hierarchized; it contains many different levels, as does our own, and is presented as an anti-world. The devil does not care, then, either for Muhammad or for his four companions, who will be his successors, nor for anyone who imitates his holy example: piety allied with youth, humility allied with knowledge, masculinity allied with purity, poverty allied with endurance, wealth allied with gratitude for the gifts of God, prayer in common, fasting at ramadhan, the pilgrimage to Mecca, reading the Quran, the giving of alms, without forgetting the coming together of learned men. Indeed Iblis describes in great detail his own world, his own ritual and gives much useful information on satanic behaviour. This is how he answers the detailed questions put by Muhammad:

The Prophet: Tell me, Accursed one, with whom do you share your table?
Iblis: The man who eats from usury!
The Prophet: And your companion?
Iblis: The fornicator!
The Prophet: And who shares your bed?
Iblis: The drunkard!
The Prophet: And who is your guest?
Iblis: The thief!
The Prophet: And your messenger?
Iblis: The sorcerer!
The Prophet: Who is the apple of your eye?
Iblis: The man who is always swearing by the repudiation of his wife!
The Prophet: Who is your friend?
Iblis: The man who has given up Friday prayers!
The Prophet: Accursed One! What can break your back?
Iblis: The neighing of horses taking part in Holy War!
The Prophet: And melt your body?
Iblis: The return to God of the sinner who repents!

The Prophet: And burn your liver?
Iblis: To hear night and day those who ask God to pardon their misdeeds!
The Prophet: And what makes you blush?
Iblis: To see alms given in secret!
The Prophet: And what pierces your eye?
Iblis: Prayers at dawn!
The Prophet: And what strikes you violently on the head?
Iblis: To see people praying together!
The Prophet: Who for you is the happiest of men?
Iblis: He who has voluntarily given up his prayers!
The Prophet: And the most unfortunate?
Iblis: The misers!
The Prophet: What, then, can turn you away from your activity?
Iblis: The meetings of learned men!
The Prophet: How do you eat?
Iblis: With the fingers of my left hand!
The Prophet: Where, then, do your sons seek shade in the heat of the day and when the warm, poisoned wind blows from the south?
Iblis: Under men's nails!
The Prophet: How many things have you asked of God?
Iblis: Ten!
The Prophet: What are they, then, Accursed One?
Iblis: I asked him to let me associate with the sons of Adam, and with their goods and progeniture, and he associated me with them. And he revealed it in his Holy Book. 'He associated himself with their goods and their progeniture and made them fine promises. But the promise of the devil is only an insane temptation!'

I also asked him to let me eat my fill of whatever has not been purified by lawful alms and also to eat all food with which usury and unlawfulness have been mingled and also all goods that have not been blessed by invoking the name of God to protect them against me.

Every man, too, who sleeps with his wife and who omits to protect himself against me, by invoking the name of God, well, I shall sleep with his wife at the same time as he and the child that shall be born to him will be submissive and obedient to me. Every man who mounts a beast and goes off to carry out some act that is not

lawful, I shall accompany him. God himself has revealed
it: 'Urge them to foot or to horse!'
I asked God to assign me a residence and he created the
hammam!
I asked him for a temple and he created souks!
I asked him for a Holy Scripture and he created poetry!
I asked him for a call to my prayer and he created the
bagpipes!
I asked him for bed companions and he created
drunkards![17]

An admirable speech! The men who live from usury are fellow trenchermen, fornicators his companions; drunkards share his bed; thieves are his guests, sorcerers his lieutenants; to swear by the repudiation of one's wife is to link one's fate with that of the devil; to miss one's Friday prayers is to sink to his level. . . . Iblis eats with his left hand. He likes to take refuge under men's fingernails; his house is the hammam, his temple the souk, his book poetry; and the bagpipes take the place of prayer.

What a magnificent constellation of symbols: the left and the fingernails, the hammam and the souk, poetry and wind music. The essence of Muslim Satanism is there. This is because Iblis is able to play with men, to whisper to them from the inside, furtively, an endless stream of evil wishes.[18]

The devil is a tempter, and without being strictly speaking the creator of evil within us, he is highly skilled at using our evil thoughts and desires and turning them against us. We have to admire the highly systematic, perfectly organized way in which Iblis operates, for his strength lies there. As a good 'manager' he has structured his strong army of nearly five thousand million little devils (70,000 of Iblis's own children, each having in turn 70,000 smaller devils). Despite demographic expansion, mankind is still surrounded by evil. There are more devils than men in the world! Indeed this makes possible a systematic 'partitioning' of mankind by a series of 'commandos' specialized in the art of tempting certain groups such as the learned, the young, the old, the ascetics. He even has at his disposal three highly qualified sons as generals: 'Atrā, the 'retarder', specialized in the art of putting people to sleep during prayers by pissing in their ears; Mutaqādhī, the 'denunciator', who drives servants to divulge the secrets of their masters and wives those of their husbands; Kuhyala, 'he who makes eyelids heavy', who puts men to sleep at Friday prayers or at learned conferences.[19] Only the *Ṣāliḥūn*, the holiest of saints, really escape the influence of the devil and his lieutenants.

Indeed the devil has the mysterious power of living in men's bodies, of wandering through them at will. He circulates in our forty veins and, by inserting himself in our living flesh, he can wear us out. Sometimes he even shares the sexual intercourse of the most lawful of husbands who has omitted to arm himself against Iblis's evil intentions by speaking the appropriate quranic words. All Iblis then has to do is to install one of his descendants on the wife's rear and another in her groin for her to become particularly attractive when she leaves her house. Made aware by these two devils of the charm that she can exert over men she has only to provoke them ever so slightly, by revealing just a fingernail, and she has taken the irremediable road to dishonour.

Indeed the myth of Satan ends in masterly fashion. For the devil recognizes that he has no hand in man's wandering astray, just as Muhammad has no hand in their good guidance. The Prophet is one of God's arguments against his creatures; the Evil One a means of carrying out an earlier condemnation. But the devil has been so sincere that his dialogue with the Prophet approaches the sublime. The devil's confession makes him so likeable in our eyes and in Muhammad's eyes that Muhammad suggests to the 'Father of Bitterness' that he return to God and thus regain Paradise. But Iblis, faithful to himself, still refuses: 'my fate is sealed and the pen is dry.' The devil is on deferment and the temptation symbolized is as perpetual as the race of the sons of man.

There is ultimately something splendid about the devil's rejection. He ends the myth with the veritable demystification of the devil. Indeed at the outset Muhammad has warned his companions to exercise intelligence and understanding. Indeed one has only to understand Satan's stratagems to avoid their dangers. In the end Satan is both rationalized and de-realized. There is no mystery of evil. There is a transparency of the devil, which is revealed in the course of the dialogue. The devil himself shows us how to arm ourselves against him: by the words of the Quran, by purity of intention, by faith and virtue.

The Islamic vision of the world, then, helps individuals to integrate their fantasies, not only because of the sexual lyricism that is essential to it, but because it is one of the few systems of thought to have given a social, juridical, legal place to sexual relations with spirits. Like the djinns, the devils have a status, a role and a function that Muslim theology has defined in the most precise, most positive way. Belief in Satan, in the devil, in the spirit of evil is, of course, universal. It might be thought that it is incompatible with the spirit of Islam which, rationalizing life and giving sex its legitimate place, might have been able to do without demonology. In Christian demonology one might see the effect of 'a concerted plan, a war machine, that aims at making the world ridiculous or vile, by assimilating it to the themes of a diabolical teratology. . . . In other words, the direct, immediate view of impurities is alone capable of curing the crowds of them.'[20]

Behind Satan what is in question is all the lechery imputed to the flesh. Satan is the medieval Christian archetype of all sexual excess. In the devil are embodied the obsession with the flesh and the depravities that stem from it. For in the Christian view the world is the geometrical locus of desires, sins, vices. Satan is excluded from the order of grace, condemned, expelled from Paradise. But although he has fallen, he remains an angel, endowed therefore with virtues, imagination, cunning. He is stronger than man and he is always victorious over men who cannot place between themselves and him the effective barrier of faith. Hence the meaning of the pact with the devil, black masses, witches' sabbath and sorcery.

The erotic significance of Christian demonology has often been pointed out.[21] But Michelet's theory that relations with the diabolical result from a profound lack of satisfaction in love has seldom been bettered. It was because they were disappointed in their flesh and in their spirit that the men of the Middle Ages turned to the witch and the devil.

> All that was once said to the confessor is said to the witch. Not only the sins that one has committed but those one wishes to commit. One confides to her both physical illnesses and those of the soul, the burning concupiscences of a bitter, inflamed blood, pressing, furious envies, sharp needles with which one is pricked and pricked again.
>
> Everyone visits her. One is not ashamed to talk to her. One speaks frankly, one asks for life and for death, for remedies and for poisons. A girl arrives, in tears, to ask for an abortion. . . . Then the stepmother arrives . . . to say that her husband's child by an earlier marriage still eats a lot and

shows no sign of dying. The sad wife arrives, burdened every year with children that are born only to die. She begs her compassion, learns to freeze the pleasure of the moment, to make it unfruitful. Then, on the other hand, comes a young man who would buy at any price a love potion that might move the heart of a lady in high estate, persuade her to ignore the distance that separates them and to look with favour on her young page.[22]

As we have seen, the devil had a very precise function in Christian society. At the official, orthodox level, he symbolizes all our temptations and everything that is evil in us. He is the attention that is continually attracted to the thousand and one weaknesses of the flesh. His myth is destructive, his image repugnant. Moreover he is both a source of anxiety and tension and the expression of continual conflicts. He is both repressed and represser. But, on the other hand, at the level of everyday life, of concrete experience, he liberates anxieties and sorrows and, as such, he does possess a certain curative value. The myth of the devil is therefore liberating and sometimes one of collective liberation.

The richness and importance of the concept of the devil derive from that ability to repress and liberate at the same time and to sustain contraries within himself. He is the beautiful and the ugly, cunning and stupidity, in short, the fallen angel. The biblical Satan is a devil, while at the same time Lucifer, the bearer of light.

The quranic Iblis is a creature of fire, he is *nār*, not *nūr*. In Islam, of course, as in Christianity, the diabolical subconscious is opposed by the celestial subconscious and the ambiguity of our double connection with the animal and the angel remains. But although Islam takes over the biblical content of demonology it does so by taking into account the sensual lyricism that is inherent in it. Thus Islamic demonology is, in a sense, a rationalization of our unlawful desires.

The devil may be an outcast, but he is not an unsympathetic one. He is an amiable enemy. He is not to be trusted. But after all did not the Prophet himself converse with him? Muslim theology was to make another step along this road with the djinns, with whom relations are so close that they even include sexual relations, since there are perfectly good canonical grounds for a possible *nikāḥ* between men and djinns. Here we are at the antipodes of Christianity and at the very heart of that commerce with the invisible that characterizes all Muslim oneirism.

Indeed the djinns[23] form one of the most fascinating areas of Islamic belief. The Quran accepts the possibility of union between women and djinns: 'Those elementary beings', to use Louis Massignon's term, have, as we have seen, a well-defined status in the fiqh. They are normally invisible to the naked eye, for they love to hide themselves from our gaze. Indeed etymologically the word *jān* means the hidden, the invisible.[24]

And belief in them constitutes an important credo of Islam itself, even if in the course of time its importance has changed. Ibn Majīm in his essay *al-ashbāḥ wal naḍhā-ir* supplies all the data of the problem; indeed he draws most of his documentation from al-Shibli, Suyūti and the fiqh treatises. He cites innumerable examples to show the perfect lawfulness, as far as the fiqh is concerned, of sexual relations with djinns. People from Yemen wrote to Malek to ask his opinion concerning *nikāḥ* with djinns. One djinn had asked for the hand of one of their slave girls and claimed to have honourable intentions. Malek replied that there was no religious objection to such a *nikāḥ*. His only fear was that every pregnant woman, when asked who the father of the child was, would reply that it was a djinn. 'It would become all the more difficult to uncover unlawful sexual relations.'[25]

A recent author maintains that it is lawful for a man to marry a djinnia, but not for a woman to be married to a djinn. The *nikāḥ*, he adds, must be carried out in the presence of two witnesses.[26] The same author advocates the use of this marvellous, but curious prayer: 'My God, procure for me a djinnia who will keep me company wherever I go.'[27]

The sexual relationships with djinns are regarded as very widespread. The *Tazyīn al-ashwāq* provides details of six 'true' cases.[28]

This is because we live in a silent world, peopled with invisible beings: everyone has his angels and devils and at least one *qarīn*. Indeed some *qarīns* became very famous, like the djinn of the beautiful Aysha, the Prophet's wife, who made her beautiful, desirable, entrancing, but also coquettish, feminine and jealous. Every inspired poet, musician and artist is supposed to owe the virtues of his creation to his *qarīn*.

By taking our fantasies seriously, the fiqh helps us to give them meaning and, by absorbing them, to purify ourselves. A brilliant essay by C. G. Jung has helped me a great deal to understand the logic of the fiqh, which connects the individual's dreams and fantasies to the great myths of Iblis and the djinns:

> To apply correctly the right archetype is not only the art of the primitive medicine-man, but also that of our directors of conscience; for the suffering of the symbolic hero on which the entire Christian religion rests is also an archetypal image of a kind that, while assuaging it, raises the suffering of each individual to the level of the suffering of all. In what does the assuaging power of these images lie? Great suffering, a great shock of some kind, removes us from the foundations of our lives and instincts, and the subject affected in this way then experiences an excessive sense of his particularity, a sense of isolation and disorientation. These salutary images show the suffering soul the state in which he finds himself, the kind of stage in his life that he is living through; if he is able to glimpse what they convey, he will benefit enormously from them. In everyday life, as we can see, we use a similar approach, without having at our disposal however the same resources of amplification.[29]

'To apply correctly the right archetype. . . :' this is just what the fiqh has done. To recover not only man himself, but also his instincts, his deepest tendencies, in a word, his shadow.

For the djinns of the Quran are merely our doubles, the underside of ourselves, the object of our desires. We must accept this shadow. And Islam urges us to do so. Better still, it helps us to integrate it by 'rationalizing' it, by finding for it an explanation that is capable both of dedramatizing situations and of freeing man from guilt. This is what the myth of Iblis means, this is the deep meaning of the djinns. Through that shadow of himself, accepted and assumed, man realizes himself and frees himself.

Muhammad's dialogue with Satan, the *ins-jānr* relations, are ways of rationalizing the irrational. If we were to take over Jung's terminology, we would say that the profound meaning of this Islamic commerce with the invisible is to help us to integrate the shadow and to pass from a 'fallow anima' to an actual anima. By offering him an image in which he recognizes himself, Islam makes man capable of having stimulating, even exalting relations with his own personality. Yes, each man has his *jinniyya*. Yes, each woman has her *qarīn* and everyone should follow the example of the Tunisian followers of Sidi Abdeslam Lasmar, who, facing the invisible, ended their initiatory dances with this very beautiful, deeply meaningful verse:

> If every man has a furtive inspirer who inspires his actions.
> By God, it is Thou alone who art my furtive inspirer.[30]

The fundamental law of Islam, then, is one of totalization, integration. Nevertheless whatever is not integrated into the personality runs the risk of being projected. This controlled, rationalized projection exists none the less. And this is the profound meaning of the myth of Paradise.

CHAPTER 7
The infinite orgasm

The preponderant role of sexuality is closely bound up with Muslim representations of Paradise (*Janna*) and of hell (*Nār*). The traditional eschatology is of interest here on two accounts. Firstly, paradise is a place of sexual pleasure. Secondly, the symbolism of the delights and torments of the afterlife is of such oneiric richness that it is necessary for our purpose to dwell on it for a time since it implies the dual integration of life with the hereafter and of the hereafter with life. More than three hundred verses of the Quran deal with this question, in terms that repeat, complement and qualify one another and are the point of departure for a whole dynamic mythology.[1]

Furthermore the Sunna has left us hundreds of hadiths that expand on the theme and orchestrate the way in which the good and bad actions of human beings are rewarded. Around these venerable texts an abundant literature has grown up.[2] As Louis Gardet remarks, 'tradition constantly embellishes and enriches with ever new details'[3] the eschatological vision of the afterlife.

Without wishing to ignore the importance of the evolution of traditions that have changed throughout the ages by undergoing the influence of extra-quranic, Christian, Judaic, but also Iranian and Hindu traditions, it is enough for my purpose to consider that those traditions more or less stabilized in the twelfth and thirteenth centuries. I would like to leave to one side any conjectures as to relations through historical connections and consider the dynamic configurations and images conveyed by popular tradition. Two compilations, generally published independently, seem to me to be highly representative in this respect of the way in which the people – and the elites – traditionally saw the afterlife. The epistle *Daqā-iq al-akhbār al-kabīr (sic) fi ahikr al-jannati wal nār*, by the imam

Abderrahman Ibn Ahmed al Qādhi, and the *Kitāb al-durar al ḥisān fil ba'thi wa ha'ā imil-jinān*, by the sheikh Jalal Addin al Suyūti,[4] are two exceptional documents in terms both of content and of popularity.

These two treatises present both a highly coloured, highly pictorial description of paradise and hell and a universal cosmogony of the afterlife. Everything begins with the creation of the supreme soul from the tree of certainty, with its four branches, reaches a high point with the creation of Muhammad's *Nūr*, placed under a veil in the form of a white pearl, and ends with the eternal torments of hell or the heavenly contemplation of the face of God. But let us concentrate our attention on paradise.

Indeed paradise is merely the splendid, reassuring counterpart of the infernal nightmare. It is vast, as big as hell, comprising a hundred degrees, each separated from the other by five hundred years. Its eight gates are in solid gold, encrusted with emeralds, diamonds, rubies, corals, enamel and other precious stones. The first bears the inscription: 'There is no God but Allah and Muhammad is his prophet.' Through this gate enter the prophets, the martyrs, the tender-hearted (*al-askhiā*).

Through the second gate enter those who purify themselves and say their daily prayers in a perfect, regular fashion. The third is reserved for those who give as alms what for them is dearest and most desirable. Through the fourth pass those who are able to order good and to dissuade others from carrying out evil. Through the fifth gate enter those who have been able to resist their desires and passions. The sixth is reserved to pilgrims; the seventh to those who fight for the faith, the last to pious men who abstain from casting indiscreet and concupiscent looks and who perform only good actions.

The eight gates lead to the eight paradises. The first, *bar al-ḥalāl*, (House of Lawfulness), is made of white pearls. The second, *Dar al-salām* (House of Peace), is made of red amethysts. The third, *Jannat al-ma-wā* (Garden of Retreat), is made of green emeralds. The fourth, *Jannat al-khuld* (Garden of Eternity), is made of red and yellow coral. The fifth, *Jannat al-na-'īm* (Garden of Delights), is made of white silver. The sixth, *Jannat al-firdaus* (Garden of Paradise), is made of red gold. The seventh, *Jannat 'adn* (Garden of Eternal Stability), is also made of red gold. As the pivot (*qaṣaba*) of eternity, it leads to all the other paradises. It is made of alternate gold and silver bricks. The ground is covered by a clay made of musk and a dust made of amber.

The grass that grows there is of saffron. There are abundant rivers. The river of Clemency runs through all the paradises. The river of Kawthar is Muhammad's private property. The Kāfūr, the Tasmīm, the Salsabīl and the Raḥīq have their source in a cupula and more precisely in the four words that make up the *basmālah*[5] written on this cupula, which is the centre of centres.

> God offers drink to the Elect. On Saturday he serves them the water of paradise, on Sunday he gives them his honey, on Monday his milk and on Tuesday his wine. When they drink, they become drunk; when they become drunk, they fly off for a thousand years, at the end of which they reach a huge mountain made of sweet-smelling pure musk. The Salsabīl has its source in this mountain. The Elect drink from it on Wednesdays. They fly off for a thousand years again and then reach a very high castle. In this castle there are raised beds and prepared goblets, as it is said in the verse. Each Chosen One sits on a bed. He is then given ginger wine, which he drinks. It is then Thursday. Then for a thousand years a white cloud of pearls falls on the Elect. To each pearl a houri is fastened. They then fly off for a thousand years and reach the seat of sincerity (*Maṣ'ad ṣidq*) on Friday. They sit at the table of Eternity, receive the *raḥīc al-makhtūm* sealed with a seal of musk. And that is the ultimate drunkenness.[6]

The trees of paradise have also inspired marvellous descriptions.[7] The branches of these trees never grow hard or dry and their leaves remain eternally green and laden with sap. The Tūbā tree is particularly described in detail. The trunk is a pearl; the middle of the tree is made up of hyacinths; the branches are topazes and the leaves silk. It has seventy thousand branches, but all tied to the sky of our visible world. Indeed in paradise every room, dome or tree is shaded by a branch of a Tūbā.

There are also many other different trees on the tops of which grow richly worked costumes and on the bottoms of which grow winged horses, already saddled and bridled, and encrusted with pearls and hyacinths. These horses have neither bile nor urine. The Elect of God mount them and fly off through paradise.

Paradise is a place where one eats as much as one likes without having to undergo the inconveniences of digestion and evacuation.

Suyūti tells us that 'the food of paradise is perpetual. When the Elect have eaten or drunk something, they have just a little sweat, which is as fresh and sweet-smelling as musk. The inhabitants of Paradise have no behinds. These behinds were created for defecation and in Paradise there is no defecation.'[8]

Pleasure there is also carnal. For paradise is peopled with houris. These creatures are as feminine as can be imagined, their faces white, green, yellow and red at once. Their bodies are made of saffron, musk, amber and camphor and their hair of raw silk. 'From the toes to the knees they are made of saffron, from the knees to the breasts of musk, from the breasts to the neck of amber, from the neck to the top of their heads of camphor. If a houri spits on the ground, the place on which she spits is turned at once into musk. On their breasts is written the name of their husband, linked with one of the beautiful names of God. They wear on each arm ten gold bracelets, on each finger ten rings and on each foot ten rings of precious stones and fine pearls. . . . All the houris are in love with their husbands. . . .'[9]

Every man who observes the fast during the whole month of ramadhan is married by God to a houri of paradise of a special type known as *Ḥūr al'ain* (black-eyed houri) and God sets them in a tent hollowed out of a white pearl. Each houri wears seventy veils. Each man has seventy alcoves, each carved out of a red hyacinth. In each alcove are arranged seventy beds; on each bed is a woman awaiting the Chosen One, surrounded by a thousand negresses, each holding a bowl and feeding the woman and the husband.[10]

In paradise men wear seventy costumes, which change colour seventy times an hour. Their faces are reflected in the faces of their wives and similarly the faces of the wives are reflected in those of their husbands. There are no beards and the only hair on the body is that of the eyelashes, eyelids and hair on the head.

One grows more beautiful with every day. One's appetite increases a hundredfold. One eats and drinks to one's heart's content. Man's sexual potency is also multiplied. One makes love as on earth but each climax is extended and extended and lasts for twenty-four years. . . .

According to Suyūti the houris are at the lawful disposal of the Elect, 'each Chosen One will marry seventy houris, besides the lawful wives that he married on earth, and each of them has an appetizing sex'.[11] Their bodies are so diaphanous, so transparent that 'one can see the bones through the flesh and the marrow through the bones, just as a drinker can see the ruby red of the wine through the clearness of crystal'.[12]

'Whenever one sleeps with a houri,' Suyūti adds, 'one finds her a virgin. Indeed the penis of the Chosen One never slackens. The erection is eternal. To each coitus corresponds a pleasure, a delicious sensation, so incredible in this vile world that if one experienced it one would faint.'[13]

This pleasure is experienced not only with the houris. Earthly couples will also know the pleasures of heavenly love when they sleep with one another. They will become young again and eternally beautiful and purified. There will be no urine, no wind, no defecation, no sperm, no menstrua and men will often hear their earthly wives say: 'By the power of God, I could find nothing in paradise as beautiful as you!'[14]

Of course the sensual delights are not exclusive, or the only ones to be found in Paradise. Other, more spiritual pleasures are reserved for those who will be capable of attaining them. Suyūti, with his decidedly fertile imagination, describes for us a discussion that takes place in paradise.[15] God presides over the Assembly of the Elect on a throne carved out of a red hyacinth, 'a thousand years high' and raised above the seat reserved for the prophets by one step. Each of these prophets takes up his place at the appropriate degree. Muhammad takes his place on the degree of mediation (*darajat al-wasīla*).

> Then come the pious men, the pure, the sincere, the friends of God, the martyrs of the faith, the saints, and all the nations and men who people paradise. All take their places on the mounds of musk and amber. A herald then calls out: 'Abraham! Come and preach to your people.' Abraham the Khali, the friend of God, rises and recites from beginning to end the sacred texts that were revealed to him. Then he returns to his place. A highly placed herald then calls upon Moses, who says: 'Here I am, ready, my God.' He is then told: 'Rise and preach to your people.' Moses rises and reads the Tora from the first to the last line. Then the call of God is addressed to Jesus, so that he may preach to his people. Jesus rises and reads the Gospels from the beginning to the end, then goes and sits down. The herald who speaks in the name of God cries out: 'O David, rise, go to the tribune and let my friends

hear the ten chapters of your psalms.' David rises and recites his psalms on ninety different tones. Everyone is entranced by David's voice. Delighted, they weep with emotion, so enchanting is David's voice. It is certainly worth ninety oboes! When the men recover and their ecstasy is calmed, God, may His glory be glorified, asks them: 'Have you ever heard so beautiful a voice?' 'No, our God, we have never heard a more beautiful voice than that call coming from God the Most High.' Then God in person says: 'My friend, Muhammad, go up to the tribune and recite the Suras "*Ta Ha*"[16] and "Ya Sin".'[17]

Muhammad reads the two Suras and his voice is seventy times more beautiful still than that of David, may Salvation be upon them. The people go into ecstasy and trance. But also the chairs on which they are sitting and the torches that decorate the throne go into ecstasy. And the angels, too, begin to sway with ecstasy. And also the houris and the ephebes of Paradise. Nothing that is animated is not moved to ecstasy by the voice of Muhammad, on whom may God spread His salvation and blessings.

God then says: 'You have heard the singing of my Prophets and My Messengers?' 'Yes, Lord.' 'Would you now like your God to read you something?' 'Great is our desire to hear.' Then God recites the Sura 'The All-Merciful' (*al-Raḥmān*)[18] . . . or, according to other traditions, the Sura 'Cattle' (*al-An'ām*).[19]

When the Elect hear the reading of the Truth, may His Glory be glorified, they lose consciousness. The angels are in ecstasy, as also are the veils, the palaces, the trees. The leaves of the trees applaud, the birds sing, the rivers become agitated. So strong is the ecstasy felt on hearing the Magnificent and All Powerful recite. The enchanted Throne shakes, the Seat sways in wonder. Nothing in paradise remains indifferent or is not transported with compassion, with desire for God the Most High. . . .

When the Elect and all other things recover from their ecstasy, God, may His glory be glorified, asks them: 'Servants, does any desire still remain within you?' 'Yes, we have still to see Your August Face.' God the Most High then orders Kurūb[20] to draw a little the veil that separates him from his servants. A breeze then spreads and clothes begin to stir,

> faces become radiant, hearts are purified, bodies become happiness, horses begin to frolic, birds to sing. . . .
>
> Then God asks Kurūb to remove completely the divine veil that separates Him from his servants. Once the Holy Face is revealed He asks: 'Who am I?' 'You are God.' 'Yes, I am God the Most High! I am Peace (*salām*) and you are the Muslims (*muslimīn*)! I am Faith (*ma-man*) and you are the believers (*mu-minūn*)! I am the Veil and you are the veiled! Here are My Words, listen to Them! Here is My Light, contemplate it! Here is My Face, look upon It!'
>
> The Elect then look upon the face of the Eternal Being, may His glory be glorified! They look upon it without hindrance. When the Light of Truth reaches them, their faces light up and remain for three hundred years transfixed before the Face of Truth, may His name be glorified, the only God, the Incomparable.[21]

Considerable historical scholarship has revealed the analogies between Islamic traditions and certain Christian traditions. Tor Andrae, Ahrens, Grimme and more recently still Gaudefroy-Demombynes[22] have shown the importance of a comparison between Muslim eschatology and the *Hymns* of Bishop Ephrem. Gaudefroy-Demombynes provides an admirable summary of the question in the following passage:

> The houris are of Iranian origin, but they were adopted by the legends of the peoples of the Near East, in particular by the Christians. I observe . . . a close similarity with the writings of Bishop Ephrem, which seem to have influenced Muhammad. 'And when a man has lived in virginity, they will welcome him in their immaculate womb, since as a monk he has not fallen into the bed and womb of an earthly love.' He will therefore also find eternal youth: 'Think, old men, of paradise. When once its odour has refreshed you, its perfume made you young again, your wrinkles disappear in the beauty that then surrounds you.' There is the example of Moses. No doubt, Ephrem adds, his pictures of paradise do not correspond in any way to reality; they hide joys quite different from those of this world and are not understood by the vulgar. . . . And Andrae shows, quite rightly, that these images were widespread in the popular beliefs of the East: the Jews reserved for the pious a stay on an earth of prodigious

fertility, where every pleasure awaited them, including those of sexual relations.[23]

For my part I am struck by the similarity between the quranic apocalypse and that of St John. One is inevitably reminded of the Quran when one reads:

> Then I saw a great white throne and him who sat upon it: from his presence earth and sky fled away, and no place was found for them. And I saw the dead, great and small, standing before the throne, and books were opened. Also another book was opened, which is the book of life. And the dead were judged by what was written in the books, by what they had done.[24]

Nevertheless, one must insist on the specificity of the Islamic view, which is of a psycho-sociological and, of course, theological order, and not a historical one. We owe it to ourselves, whatever admiration we may feel for historical scholarship, to observe that it is not after all the presence or absence of a theme in both writings, belonging to two divergent traditions, that will bring them together! It is at the very heart of these traditions, and of the world views that they imply and the values that they transmit that we must place ourselves.

Of course Christianity has worked out a cosmology of the after-life and a precise topography of the celestial world. Certain Fathers of the Church were even pleased to develop a vision of paradise for themselves in which it is difficult to know whether dream or imagination predominates. The *Hymns* of St Ephrem are a very fine example of this. In the Edenic-geography the various residences of the creatures are laid down on different levels from the depths of the valley to the top of the tree of life. The Elect occupy different levels according to their degree of guilt – or sanctity. But in spite of everything this is a mere 'system of representation', in Cardinal Daniélou's words.[25]

With remarkable continuity, Islam has given so total, so detailed a vision of the afterlife that it constitutes a veritable credo. St Matthew, on the other hand, gives us the very essence of the Gospel view of man's future life by reducing it to a mystery. The Sadducees, who did not believe in the resurrection, tried to embarrass Jesus by saying to him:

> 'Teacher, Moses said, "If a man dies, having no children, his

brother must marry the widow, and raise up children for his brother." Now there were seven brothers among us; the first married, and died, and having no children left his wife to his brother. So too the second and third, down to the seventh. After them all, the woman died. In the resurrection, therefore, to which of the seven will she be wife? For they all had her.' But Jesus answered them, 'You are wrong, because you know neither the scriptures nor the power of God. For the resurrection, they neither marry nor are given in marriage, but are like angels in heaven.'[26]

In other words, the Christian will be a-sexual in paradise, whereas the Muslim will experience infinite orgasm.

This is because for the Christian survival after death forms part of the mystery of Christ. It is essentially unknowable. The response of the Gospel is that the hereafter cannot be an object here of knowledge or imagination. Cardinal Daniélou provides an admirable and, it would seem, authoritative summary of the Catholic point of view when he declares:

> Christ took possession of that life beyond death. One of the most admirable phrases I know in the Gospels is when Christ, after the Last Supper, is talking to his Apostles, who are saddened at the thought of his death, and says: 'I go to prepare a place for you,' and elsewhere: 'I shall come so that where I shall be, you will be with me. . . .' All our response concerning the afterlife is here: Christ has taken possession of it and he asks us one thing: to deliver up to him everything that concerns that mysterious world, which is indeed no longer mysterious since it is no more than He himself.[27]

So there is nothing more to be said about the afterlife except that it will be the resurrection in Jesus Christ. The last word in Christianity, if one may put it in this way, is ultimately no more than a question mark.

I do not believe that this is ultimately a position radically different from that of Judaism. Of course Jewish exegesis also involves a set of eschatological notions such as the judgment of the soul (the Hebraic Kadish), which lasts for a year. Nevertheless the happiness in the afterlife described by the Bible applies only to Messianic times. And the future world remains ultimately unknowable. As an authority in the field, Rabbi Josy Eisenberg, puts it:

> All we may know of the future happiness of mankind or of the times of apocalypse refers to the messianic period, but in *this* world. As for the beatitudes, no one can describe them, and the most precise text, if I may so put it after saying that, is a text of the Talmud that is practically the only text we possess concerning the Jewish belief in survival, and which says: 'In the future world there is no eating, no drinking, no procreation, no commerce, no jealousy, no hate, no competition, but the just are seated, their diadems on their heads, and enjoy the brightness of the divine presence.' Something is promised, but that something is hidden from us.[28]

We see how far we are therefore from Islamic attitudes. Islam has certainly taken over old traditions. But the psychological content that it gives to the notions of resurrection, paradise and hell is radically different. Owing to a failure of understanding on their part, certain orientalists have indulged in fictitious speculations on these questions. A materialistic Islam is contrasted with a spiritual, de-realized Christianity. Gaudefroy-Demombynes himself does not avoid this danger. He writes: 'It is certainly a paradise for bedouins. No more burning sun, no cold, "shade and springs", "orchards and arbors", etc.; rich robes, jewels; boy servants. They will be in luxurious tents or palaces.'[29] And Gaudefroy-Demombynes, carried away by the enthusiasm of his 'demonstration', denies that the vision of God is possible in Islam: 'There is nothing to prove,' he writes, 'that the blessed will see the face of God.'[30] And a little later: 'The average orthodox doctrine admits that the blessed will enjoy the view of the face of Allah, but they give up trying to explain how that would be possible, *bila Kayfa*.'[31]

Louis Gardet writes: 'The definition of eternal beatitude, then, is not God himself.'[32] Certainly Louis Gardet is sufficiently well versed in Islamology to know that the vision of God is confirmed in a quranic text[33] that has been the object of innumerable exegeses. But that does not stop him declaring: 'Despite these lines of approach, one cannot see it however as the equivalent of the "beatific vision" in the Christian sense of the term. To begin with this paradisiacal "vision" is intermittent, linked to God's "appearances". Moreover it remains "spectacular", as Louis Massenet puts it, not transforming and beatific.'[34]

Once again it is Fakhruddin Razi who gives us the most condensed, most significant commentary:

> Earthly pleasure may be divided into three categories: to satisfy a desire, to appease anger or the illusory pleasure obtained by money or others' esteem. All this is derisory, for the animal, too, experiences one or other of these pleasures. The supreme good of which God speaks here is radically different from these low pleasures. It could only be the soul impregnated with holy spirituality, adorned by his glorious divine presence.[35]

In fact it is my impression that the vision of God constitutes the very essence of the delights of the Muslim paradise. But it is not exclusive. It is like an extension of the other, as it were physical, delights promised to the Elect. The difficulties encountered by non-Muslims in understanding are hardly surprising, for they amount in one way or another to the co-extensiveness of the sexual and the sacral. From the Christian point of view, for example, it is unthinkable that the working of the flesh, a source of original sin, could find its place in the hereafter. The redemption of man was obtained at the price of a renunciation of sensuality, whose mission is at most earthly. For Islam, on the other hand, there is something essential in Eros. The original couple disobeyed, of course, but their sin was paid for more than enough by the expulsion from Eden. Earthly existence, with all its trials and tribulations, is more than enough to reduce them. Hence that sense of responsibility felt by the man who has to account for his acts and who, having proved by a just, exemplary life that he is essentially a good man, finds himself in paradise.

To be in paradise, then, is the fulfillment of self. This fulfillment can be realized only in love conceived, as I have constantly pointed out, as a transfiguration, a transcendence of self in others. It is no accident that hell is solitude, non-presence of others, in a word, absence of love. Paradise, on the other hand, is total, full, infinite love. It is unity in harmony with the world, with oneself and with God.

Paradise is first of all a reconciliation of man with nature, that is to say, with matter. Hence that material profusion that characterizes *Janna*. It is a feast of all the senses. In an earlier chapter we saw the role attributed to the look in the Islamic view of sexuality. Now sight, which is at the very heart of existence, is also an integral part of the human essence. So everything begins with the look and everything ends with it. Is it not the look that gives the houris their very name. To see and to be seen, to contemplate, to look, that is a form of happiness. Pleasure is ocular. Hence that precious luminosity. Hyacinths and gold, diamonds and topazes, pearls and emeralds, sapphires and corals form a unique palate for the Chosen One. These precious stones that make up paradise act in a mystical way like the pearl in which Arab alchemy is fond of recognizing, as a substitute for the purest sperm, metaphysical and magical qualities. It has, according to Abshīhi, the rare virtues 'of rejoicing the heart, dilating the soul, embellishing the face, purifying the blood of the heart'.[36]

Smell, too, has its part to play in this feast of the senses. For the exhalations of paradise are of musk, ginger, amber and form the very ground of Eden and the bodies of the houris. With the gaze, and perhaps even more so, perfume is a quasi-immaterial pleasure of matter itself. Hence all that therapeutics through scent so dear to the Arab tradition.[37] And Abshīhi has Galen say: 'Musk fortifies the heart, amber the brain, camphor the lungs, aloes-wood the stomach, *ghāliya*[38] dissipates head colds, sandalwood tumours.'[39]

Hearing is not neglected, for there is music typical of paradise. The universal melody is the sonorous ground against which the voices of the Elect, angels, prophets and God himself stand out. It is significant that human speech is integrated into the paradisiacal world for the recital of the sacred texts forms part of the delights of the hereafter.

In this clutch of symbols it is striking to observe that little place is given to vegetative symbolism. From time to time of course there is a reference to vegetation. It rains sperm. There are trees, birds and flowers that decorate paradise. But even the trees are in a sense lithified, for they are made of precious stones. The vegetation of Eden is lithoid. The lithic symbolism dominates over any other form of symbolism. Sensuality dialecticizes matter. This is because the whole of life is placed on the side of love, which abolishes differences, unites contraries, and, dematerializing matter, gives a full, positive content to invisible immateriality. A full meaning is given to existence in the world of post-existence.

So the Muslim projects on to matter his own depth. Hence the need to multiply and accumulate metaphors, images, symbols. A profound, exuberant dream, the myth of paradise is merely an oneiric affirmation of self. Bachelard remarked: 'In dreaming of depth, we dream our depth. In dreaming of the secret virtue of substances, we dream of our secret being. But the greatest secrets of our being are hidden from us, they are in our most secret depths.'[40] What is typically Muslim is that this is achieved through the mediation of lithic symbolism. A hyacinth, *yāquta*, can arouse within us a symphony of images, fantasies and dreams, assuaging all pain, past, present and to come! The hyacinth is the Throne of the Lord. It is also the 'queen of stones', which, again according to al-Mostatraf, 'gives esteem and dignity to those who wear it. . . . It facilitates the solution of affairs . . . assuages thirst, neutralizes the effects of poisons and strengthens the heart'.[41]

It is as if the reconciliation of man with God were mediated through the reconciliation of man with nature. This is the meaning of the pleasure that is the fulfillment of the body and the end of frustration. Thus the individual texts show quite unmistakably that the pleasures of paradise, while sensual, are not material. It is not paradise that is materialized, it is the nature of man that is immaterialized in a sense, for it is reduced to pure pleasure and absolute sensation. Moreover, the pleasure is produced without any earthly counterpart. There is no excretion or pregnancy in paradise.

The meaning of paradisiacal pleasure is certainly that it takes the body seriously. Far from derealizing our desires, Islam teaches us to realize them more fully. The evocation of Paradise is a vigilant oneirism. It is not the theological that is at issue here, but the psychological. The image of the Muslim paradise is positive and affirmative of self. Islam does not repress the libido. In paradise our desires will be accommodated, taken seriously. This means that the peace of paradise is achieved through self-fulfillment. For paradise is first of all a meeting with others. Love is in a sense multiplied by the presence not only of wives, but also of houris. This pluralization of love implies its own transcendence in others. In paradise everyone will have at least one companion, for 'there is no celibacy in paradise' (*mā fil jannati min a'zab*).[42]

Paradise, then, is crowded. Without the *Ahl al-janna*, the 'people' of paradise, it would lose all meaning. An empty paradise is inconceivable. Moreover the myth shows us that the desire of the believer to meet the houris is not a one-way affair, for the houris, too, await impatiently the arrival of the blessed to whom they have been promised. Sometimes the houris ardently wish to see their earthly masters. They leave their palaces. The archangel Radhūan sometimes takes them to the summit of paradise from where they can contemplate their masters.[43]

Man, then, is expected. He is the object of desire, of attention, affection; even while still on earth he is already the object of paradisiacal love. Transcendence to others is certainly a fundamental element in the happiness of the afterlife. Hence that perpetual, eternal pleasure. Paradise is the time of suspended pleasure. It is also the place of perpetual erection and orgasm that lasts for twenty-four years. If earthly orgasm gives some foretaste of paradise, one must admit that life in paradise is an infinite, eternal orgasm.

In fact the very image of paradise activates the consciousness of the believer, who assumes through it the plenitude of his being and projects himself straight into this total vision.

Of course the erotic is not the ultimate pleasure. It is merely one stage in the reconciliation of man, a stage that comes after harmony with things and which prepares him for the dazzling vision of God. The final scene narrated by Suyūti describes the summum of life in paradise, which is communion and universal oecumenism, that is to say, the passage from the meeting with the other in the form of the eternal feminine to the meeting with others within the community of the Elect and lastly the meeting of the latter with their Supreme Creator.

What is striking is this unity of the theme of creative, purifying love. The true beatifying transubstantiation passes through love. What results is a veritable revalorization of Eros, which alone enables us to understand the first stages of the dialogue with God himself. It seems to me that a loop closes and begins with the creation of the original couple of the verge of paradise. From Eden to Eden, there is a remarkable continuity. The odyssey is only apparent and seen from this point of view the passage through earthly life is merely a stage, an essential one of course but a stage none the less. To realize himself man must undergo an apprenticeship in life and history. He must become earthly in order to become heavenly: this is man's great way. Now, if this continuity implies no tragedy it is because it passes through the love discovered before the fall, experienced with a greater or lesser degree of happiness on earth before being fully realized in paradise. If there is a break between the earthly and the celestial, between the now and the future, it will be overcome through love, which is tension, call, search for a plenitude that will be realized and fully attained in the heavenly life.

Islam, then, is an economy of pleasure. It is its over-conscious valorization. To integrate the sexual in the sacral is, I believe, ultimately the great lesson and the great merit of this Islamic vision of the afterlife. It is, I believe, in the final analysis, the import of what the Quran calls parable, *mathal*.

In fact orthodox Muslim thought will find in the writing of the Imam Rāghib the most powerful expression and certainly the one that opens up to analysis the most fruitful and most beautiful ways. For beyond the object of desire what matters is the dynamism of the desire, the dynamism of the man who experiences the pleasure rather than the nature of the pleasure itself.

For Rāghib the very definition of paradise is that faculty enjoyed by any individual to be able to satisfy his desire.[44] Paradise is the total and absolute satisfaction of desire. Now this could not be achieved only through reference to the imaginary. If the Quran can enable us 'to have all that our souls desire, all that we call out for',[45] it is because God has created us beings of desire, that is to say, capable of imagining in advance the very nature of expected pleasure. Desire implies imagination and volition; so paradise is first of all the reign of imagination. And Rāghib says: 'The souk designates here the divine word that is the source of all power to create images in terms of volition and the way in which the power to perceive is informed in a stable, permanent way that is as durable as volition itself, and not episodic and involuntary.'[46]

Paradise, then, is the reign of the imaginary. The object of desire may change of course. But the power of the imaginary will remain. And it is the accord between the real and the imaginary, whatever the object of this accord, that is the foundation of the belief in paradise.

> When desires change, gifts, pleasures, power, aptitudes also change. Divine goodness has granted through the mediation of prophetic revelation, to all creatures, the faculty of achieving what their faculty of understanding may conceive. We must trust, therefore, that those things that transcend the conceivable are also conceived and admitted.[47]

It is easy to understand how the images of paradise and of the life hereafter have been able to free the Islamic consciousness. Once again the sexual proves to be co-extensive with the sacral.

CHAPTER 8
The sexual and the sacral

In Islam, then, sexuality enjoys a privileged status. Whether in the texts that regulate the exercise of sexuality in social life or in those that allow the dream its full oneiric density, the right to the pleasures of sex is stated forcefully. Islam is a lyrical view of life.

Indeed from the outset the sensual dimension of sexuality was recognized. To the biological and ethical dimensions of love the Quran adds another that is essentially aesthetic. Love as a ludic activity is also part of God's benefits. The Quran declares: 'Decked out fair to men is the love of lusts.'[1] We should note the word *zuyyina*: sexual pleasure is apprehended as a *zīna*, a pleasant setting, an ornament. The same word is used by the Quran to describe the stars that decorate the sky, horses and jewels. *Zīna* is not, of course, the essential thing in life and the same verse declares that 'children, heaped-up heaps of gold and silver, horses of mark, cattle and tillage' are all, like women, objects of our 'lusts' and, on the other hand, that these are merely 'the enjoyment of the present life' and that only with God, 'with Him is the fairest resort'.[2]

It is the Quran itself that defines woman as 'one who is reared among ornaments and, in a quarrel, lacks clarity'.[3] One could hardly bring out better the 'ornamental', 'superfluous' character of the woman who is ornament and ambiguous speech.

Nevertheless, sexual pleasures are conceived by Islam as constitutive of the earthly conditions of life and, as such, they must be welcomed by Muslims. A hadith declares that 'the world is a possession and the best possession is a virtuous woman'.[4]

Profound, sincere love and the concupiscence that accompanies it are, therefore, a way of achieving cosmic harmony. 'When a man looks at his wife, said the Prophet, and she looks at him, God looks upon them both with mercy. When the husband takes his wife's hand and she takes his hand, their sins vanish between their fingers. When he cohabits with her, the angels surround them from the earth to the zenith. Pleasure and desire have the beauty of mountains. When the wife is with child, her reward is that of fasting, prayer, *jihād*.'[5]

Indeed, systematically, tradition lays it down that '*nikāḥ muraghghabun fīh*', that it is 'highly recommended to marry'. It is a pleasure, but it is also a duty.[6]

Hence that strict conception of the obligation of physical love between spouses. Indeed it is not permitted to one of the two partners to give himself or herself up, without the consent of the other, to surrogate religious practices that might obviate or postpone the working of the flesh.

The delay legally laid down for the fulfillment of one's marital duties, which is four months, cannot be extended for reasons of mystical chastity. An adage current among the kadis has it that devotion in no way exonerates the rights of the flesh, '*Al zuhdu lā yamma 'u min qadā al-murrād*'.

It is also forbidden to castrate oneself or to castrate anyone else. Any attack on the sexual faculties is as serious as an attack on life itself.[7] The corpuses of hadiths traditionally include a whole chapter 'Of the blameworthy character of castration and voluntary chastity'. Some of the Prophet's companions, finding the retreats on military campaigns long and difficult to bear, asked the Prophet permission to castrate themselves or to drug themselves. Muhammad always refused.[8]

Conversely women must not refuse their husbands. One hadith even lays it down that 'the woman who refuses her body and sleeps elsewhere than in her husband's bed is accursed by the angels until she returns to it'.[9] According to another tradition the Prophet cursed the *maswwifa* and *mughallisa* woman. The first is the woman who, when invited by her husband to make love, always replies *saufa* (not just yet). The second is the woman who falsely claims to be having her period.[10] One day a woman asked the Prophet what the rights of the husband consisted of: 'A woman must never refuse him, even on a camel's back.'[11] According to another version, 'a woman must never refuse her husband even on the topmost edge of a burning oven.'[12]

For the same reason, divorce is not favoured by Islam, which, like the Prophet, sees it as 'the lawful thing most hated of God'.[13]

A famous saying of the Prophet recommends: 'Always marry, never divorce. God certainly does not love tasters.'[14] Paradoxical as it may seem, 'Don Juanism' and Islam are not compatible.

According to the same reasoning, getting others to marry is a work of piety. The ethics of marriage are far-reaching. One must help others to get married. Parents must do all they can to assist the marriage of those placed in their charge. The Quran says explicitly: 'Marry the spouseless among you and your slaves and handmaidens that are righteous; if they are poor, God will enrich them of His bounty.'[15] A pious son must watch over the chastity of a father who has been made a widower by helping him to marry again. This duty of the *ta'fīf* is no less important than that of the *kafāla* (food pension).

In short, the working of the flesh is a benefit of God, whose pleasure must be put at the disposal of all, from puberty to the ripest old age, which every Muslim, like Jacob, hopes to be green and vigorous. Polygamy, the rotation of wives, the permutation of men, the quasi-obligatory character of the sexual act, from which there is no escape, not even through devotional practices, all this gives a special character to the sexual ethics of Islam.

It might be thought that this corresponds to a physiological need and is related to the demographic increase of mankind in general and of the Islamic community in particular. Certainly, when speaking to his community, the Prophet himself was fond of giving clear recommendations along these lines: 'Couple and procreate. I shall derive glory from your number at the Day of Judgment' ('*tanākahu, tanāsalū fa innī mubāḥin bikum yaum al qiyāmati*').[16]

It may also be said that Muslim ethics defined in this way correspond to economic and military conditions. Women are a biological capital that must not be allowed to remain unproductive. But considerations of prestige also come into play. 'The best of this community, declared Muhammad, are those who have the largest number of wives.'[17]

However, one cannot deny the fundamental 'hedonism' of the Quran, of tradition and of the fiqh. Love in its most carnal form is seen as forming the essence of being. Hence the extraordinary value placed on love. Hence, too, the absolute, total condemnation of celibacy: 'Those who live as celibates are the worst kind; those who die celibate are the lowest of the low.'[18]

This is understandable since marriage is a recovery of otherness. The profound meaning of the institution of *nikāḥ*, an institution so strong in Islam, lies in the recognition of the harmony of the human couple as an essential ideal of life. The complementarity of the sexes is at once the law of the world, a sign of human perfection, the will of God and the renewed miracle of creation. Man alone is an impotent being; woman alone is also an impotent being. Only their meeting, in the canonical framework of *nikāḥ*, is creative, because based on the complementarity of the sexes. Only this meeting, provided for by the Providence of God, allows pregnancy and the awakening of life. What we have here is a divine prerogative that enables man to go beyond nature and to achieve a veritable sexual mission, which, Islam teaches, should be carried out in the joy, exaltation and intoxication of creation. This is how we should understand Muhammad's words: 'To marry is to perform half of one's religion.'[19] Love, then, is half of faith. The personality of man finds fulfillment only in the intimacy of the sexes. The unity based on *nikāḥ* is a creative mission, because it is based on a freedom assumed within the framework of life with others. This essential intuition makes *nikāḥ* a sacred mission. Sexual pleasure brings us close to God. Woman is not a mere possession of man, nor an evil in herself, still less an object of pleasure for man. And man, in turn, is not the woman's possession, or even a lesser evil for her or a mere source of pleasure. What counts is the relation of affection that unites them. So, in Islam, love is actually prayer.

'It has been given to me to love three things in your base world: women, perfumes and prayer, but the apple of my eye is prayer.'[20] This hadith, which is one of the Prophet's most famous ones, has been the object of innumerable profound commentaries. That of Khafāgi is particularly illuminating. He rightly sees in it the affirmation and rootedness of God's Messenger and, therefore, of the Divine Word. Perfumes, women and prayer are merely mediations that make this rootedness possible.

Another, even more extraordinary text compares the working of the flesh with alms. Nawawi's twenty-fifth hadith tells us:

> Certain poor companions among those who accompanied the Prophet on his hegira from Mecca to Medina sought him out and said to him: 'What matters is money in the reward promised by God in the afterlife! The rich pray just as we pray. They fast just as we fast! But on top of that they are able

> with their excess of goods to give alms, while we have nothing with which to give alms!'
>
> And the Prophet replied to them: 'You think that God has given you nothing to give in alms? But each glorification of God is alms! Each exaltation of God is alms! Each praise of God is alms! Each command to do good is alms! And in each working of the flesh there is alms!'[21] The companions were astonished and asked: 'How, Messenger of God, are we to satisfy our desire and be rewarded for it?' 'Doing it unlawfully certainly deserves punishment! Just as to do it lawfully deserves reward!'[22]

This is understandable. Orgasm is certainly a pleasure. But a shared one. And it is in the pleasure derived from another at the same time as oneself that this work of piety resides, a work analogous to fasting, prayer and chastity. Eros and Agape, then, are both involved in sexuality. The sexuality encountered in others is also a projection in God.

Unconsummated marriage has no place, then, in Islam. Consummation constitutes an essential condition for the act of *nikāḥ* to have any validity where rights of succession are concerned. Unconsummated marriage is strictly prohibited in the case of a triple repudiation. Indeed a woman who has been rejected three times cannot return to her husband until a new marriage has been contracted, consummated and followed by divorce. A woman who calls on a pre-pubertal *muḥallil*,[23] with whom the marriage was merely a formality, is not regarded as having carried out the correct procedure. She must first 'taste the little honey' of her new husband, who in turn must first 'taste her little honey'.[24]

Another recommendation is intended to integrate fantasy in the sexual relations between spouses and to revive extinct desire by provoked desire: 'If one of you sees a woman who attracts him, let him run home quickly and make love with his wife. That will appease the ardour he feels in his heart.'[25]

One could not find a better example of the extreme tolerance of Islam with regard to eroticism, which is seen as the fulfillment and extension of sexuality. The Islamic view of sexuality involves assumption, not negation, joyous acceptance, not morose renunciation. This total view of love is based on the mutual possession of the couple by one another. Love is the law of life, of the world, of man, and should be accepted as such. Sexuality fulfilled, love realized in joy are a way of thanking God for the benefits that he showers upon us. To satisfy desire in joy and thanks is, according to the texts that I have just cited, the best way to follow, the way in any case that God recommends to us and which Muhammad, through example and words, laid before us. A thousand and one Muslim forms of pleasure are already subjacent in the essential sacred texts of Islam.

If that is possible it is because Muslim love is a love without sin, a love without guilt, in which pleasure and responsibility are coextensive. How, having reaching this stage in my analysis, can we fail to think of the Christian position, which seems to me to be the exact reverse? Compare the texts referred to above with the attitudes expressed in the New Testament. Take St Paul saying to the Corinthians: 'It is well for a man not to touch a woman. But because of the temptation to immorality, each man should have his own wife and each woman her own husband.'[26] Or take what he said to the Galatians:

> But I say, walk by the Spirit, and do not gratify the desires of the flesh. For the desires of the flesh are against the Spirit, and the desires of the Spirit are against the flesh; for these are opposed to each other, to prevent you from doing what you would. . . . Now the works of the flesh are plain: immorality, impurity, licentiousness, idolatry, sorcery, enmity, strife, jealousy, anger, selfishness, dissension, party spirit, envy, drunkenness, carousing, and the like. I warn you, as I warned you before, that those who do such things shall not inherit the kingdom of God. . . . Those who belong to Christ Jesus have crucified the flesh with its passions and its desires. If we live by the Spirit, let us also walk by the Spirit.[27]

There is something irreducible in these attitudes: a profound hostility towards sexuality, which must be tightly controlled, mortified, if not quite simply denied and which at best is sublimated.

Of course, over the past thirty years we have witnessed widespread questioning of this attitude within the Christian churches. Not only have Catholic and Protestant teachings been considerably relaxed on the subject, but research into Christianity and Judaism has revived interest in the question in a radical way.

Otto Piper suggests revising biblical exegesis in a direction that, in fact, brings it considerably closer to the quranic attitudes described above. For him, the unity of the work of God is manifested throughout the whole of nature. The sexual life inherent in human life can only be good, on condition, of course that it is directed towards ends that are in themselves in harmony with the divine intentions.[28]

Equally interesting is the renewal of biblical exegesis carried out by Seward Hiltner, for whom biblical sexuality is directed towards the realization of life in plenitude in conformity with the will of God.[29]

Christian sexuality cannot be a purely ludic activity. On the contrary, it is serious, for it is a matter of commitment and responsibility and it is this, far more than a sense of sensual joy, that characterizes it. Every form of reticence or possessiveness should be prohibited. This is because sexuality is self-revelatory. Through this revelation man transcends himself by discovering his own sexuality. Through it man is given ecstasy and proves capable of communicating it. He also becomes aware of his unsuspected power and the depths of his being. From the outset Christian sexuality is an apprenticeship of life in others. There is no valid solitary practice for sexuality. It is a discovery of others, fusion in them. And Hiltner recalls the biblical meaning of the word to know. Sexuality is a life open to one's neighbour. Lastly sexuality is a sacrament. Sexual union rests on a previous divine will, which is precisely that of the separation of the sexes. The sexual act, therefore, can be realized only in marriage, which is the joyful, unreserved acceptance of a precise type of human relationship and the recognition by society of that agreement between two persons, of which procreation is merely a consequence.

Nevertheless Islam remains more radical: Eros must be circumscribed within the limits of human nature as it has been fashioned by God. There can be no question of drowning the sexual in the miracle of creation as if it were merely an epiphenomenon.

But the concept of totality implies proposition, contradiction and ambiguity. And that is certainly why Islam conceives of sexuality in terms of tension. If it is true as Hiltner declares that Christian sexuality is serious, social and sacramental, Muslim sexuality, which is conceived in terms of the couple, is both serious and ludic, social and individual, sacramental and historical.

That the sexual act should be serious cannot be doubted. Inherent in the human condition it is a way of assuming oneself by becoming aware of one's own corporality. The Quran, as we have seen several times, lays it down that there is a true erotic understanding of the world and of self. The miracle of *zaujiyya* is often invoked as a marvellous symbol of divine glory. Through love, man becomes spellbound and at one with the cosmos and God himself. But this is not done in an abstract manner. And it is in the work of the flesh that this self-enrapture is realized. This erotic understanding of the world is not of an intellectual order. It is of the order of desire, for it is realized through the contact of one body with another, which is at once self-consciousness and projection outside self, self-centredness and otherness. Sexuality is 'an intentionality which follows the general flow of existence and yields to its movements'.[30] This observation by Merleau-Ponty seems to me to express an essential aspect of the Islamic view of sexuality.

Through sexuality the whole human being is taken seriously. This is why so much attention is paid to sexuality. Sexuality is to be taken seriously because it bears witness to the seriousness of existence. The whole of life, according to Islamic teaching, bathes in an atmosphere of sexuality. Sometimes this is carried to the point of obsession. One should marry. One should have sexual intercourse. Parents must marry off their children and among the duties of filial piety is that of getting a widowed parent to remarry. To make love is an overriding duty, from which there is no excuse, even devotion to God. Devotion itself is expressed in terms of the lawful satisfaction of desire. So, in its very practice, sexuality transcends earthly existence: the afterlife is again a sexual existence. Paradise implies orgasm and perpetual erection.

Though a serious matter, sexual activity is nevertheless ludic. Sexual games (*mulā'aba*) are warmly recommended by the Prophet, hence that specific erotological dimension. Love is not to be performed in sadness or gloom. It is not a painful duty. It is the most joyful gift of heaven. It is one of those 'good things' (*tayyibāt*) that God lavishes on existence. It is pleasure. Indeed it is the highest form of pleasure. It is the royal way to eudemony.

So, while being orientated towards something other than itself, sexuality may place that other thing in parentheses and be revealed as gratuity, adventure, fantasy, exuberance, freedom. Of course the sexual act normally culminates in procreation and rests on a realistic view of life. But it is permitted to depart from reality. The work of the flesh then becomes a free activity performed in joy and abandon. As a result all the contraceptive practices, whether *coitus interruptus* or the use of 'preservative clothing', are tolerated.[31]

As a fundamental structure of life, sexuality unfolds through existence, having no other faith than itself. Neither the useful, nor the effective, nor the 'cunning of reason' can alter in any way the fact that sexual pleasure is at once a condition and an end in itself. The game may be defined as a de-realizing operation. And it is the magic of love that de-realizes in realizing and realizes in de-realizing. Separated from its procreative function, as Islam accepts that it may be, sexuality is not deprived of its profound intentionality: its intrinsic content fills the void thus created and takes on an exemplary value. By becoming an entertainment sexuality changes direction and import. It departs from its procreative effectiveness only to be invested at once by an exemplary creative effectiveness, since it is an affirmation of spirituality and a witness to freedom. It is others *qua* partners, and no longer *qua* descendants, who then draw on the values of love.

In other words, the practice of sexuality is a dialectic of the ludic and the serious. That is why it has to be played seriously and why that game has to be taken seriously. Hence the grandeur of the Islamic intuition; hence, too, its essential ambiguity.

It was Merleau-Ponty who remarked: 'The intensity of sexual pleasure would not be sufficient to explain the place occupied by sexuality in human life or, for example, the phenomenon of eroticism if sexual experience were not, as it were, an opportunity, vouchsafed to all and always available, of acquainting oneself with the human lot in its most general aspect of autonomy and dependence.'[32]

It is as if the Islamic view were concerned to lose nothing of the richness of the sexual, to assume it, to live it intensely with all its tensions and conflicts.

And it is again the same conclusion that appears in the dialectic of the social and the personal. It is a truism to declare that sexuality is a transcendence of the individual and that even in its deviations there is never, in the strict sense, a solitary practice of the sexual life. Auto-eroticism is certainly accompanied by fantasies that are an imaginary form of the presence of others. One function of sexuality resides in its ability to unite individuals to the community. The *tanākaḥū, tanāsalū* lays it down quite explicitly that sexual life is unifying and that the Islamic Umma rests, in its grandeur and its misfortunes, on the genetic life. The total, social unity of men is a resultant of sexual dynamism. And, conversely, the community of the Umma also imposes its own requirements, its own tendencies on the individual's drives. Love, the universal principle of life, governs human development. Nevertheless love has a double 'entry', individualized and social. I noted above that God's purpose in creating the 'races and tribes'[33] under the rule of diversity was certainly to make possible mutual knowledge (the *li ta'ārafū*), in the biblical sense of the word. We have also seen that God created of each thing its double (*zaujaha*) so that it might cohabit with it (*li yaskuna ilaiha*).[34] Indeed, for Islamic tradition, cosmic becoming, organic life, personal development, social stratification and historical processes are closely bound up with one another and taken together are indissociable from God's purpose and from the wonders of his creation. Hence the polyvalence of sexuality, its ambiguity, its equivocity.

To love is to have intentions towards the beloved! Libidinal relations are mutual and form the basis of being-with-others. Moreover sexuality forms the basis, beyond the autonomy of the person of the lover, for the community of the lover and the beloved. It is certainly the awareness of the other that is aimed at through one's body, just as I sense that it is my awareness that is aimed at through my own awareness. Again let us quote Merleau-Ponty:

> If it [sexual desire] cannot accept the presence of a third party as witness, if it feels that too natural an attitude or over-casual remarks, on the part of the desired person, are signs of hostility, this is because it seeks to fascinate, and because the observing third party or the person desired, if he is too free in manner, escapes this fascination. What we try to possess, then, is not just a body, but a body brought to life by consciousness. As Alain says, one does not love a madwoman, except in so far as one has loved her before the onset of madness.[35]

The sexual act is made up of the reciprocity of the couple. I become aware of my own body through the reactions of my partner's body and my consciousness is freed in contact with the consciousness of the beloved. The genetic activity is the common act of the lover and the beloved or, to be more precise, there is no longer a lover and beloved, but a loving fusion of bodies and spirits. This is what Muhammad calls 'tasting each other's little honey'.

It is in the light of these considerations that the theory of the Muslim view of *nikāḥ* assumes its full meaning – a conception that, beyond the lawful practice of sexual activity, grounds the sexual in the social. *Nikāḥ* bears within itself a sociological definition of the couple that is expressed through statuses, roles and their respective hierarchies. The rejection of sexual anarchy rests on this specific unity that unites the couple not in an abstract, metaphysical unity, but within a real, concretely situated society. *Nikāḥ* situates the individual within the Umma. Hence that contempt for the bachelor. Hence, too, that moral condemnation of the celibate, *shirārukum 'uzzābukum*. Through *nikāḥ* the individual is integrated into the group and the group is integrated into the individual.

One must not forget the whole personal, even personalist dimension of Muslim sexuality, for it is based on the notion of responsibility: sexuality is certainly a 'deposit' entrusted to man. Each individual is responsible. Each Muslim man and woman is responsible in the first instance for himself or herself and for his or her body. Hence the importance of the chapters of the fiqh that lay down the responsibility of each of the two partners. Whether it is a question of capacity, potency, duration of widowhood, divorce, the status of the hermaphrodite or erotic relations with the invisible, the continuity is remarkable.

The equivocity of the sexual is again reflected at the level of the sacred and the historical. Sexuality is both sacramental and historical: to accept sexuality is an act of faith. Sexuality is in turn identified with prayer, alms, martyrdom, an act of piety, the renewed miracle of prophecy, a prefiguration of heavenly delights. . . . This is because it bears witness to a divine purpose. It expresses the will of God. To abandon oneself joyfully to it is truly to manifest one's gratitude to God around the continuous, overflowing miracle of the renewal of life.

So *nikāḥ* is a veritable sacrament. We have seen how consummated marriage transforms the creature who, *ipso facto*, falls under the rule of the taboo of *iḥsān*. We have seen how *zinā*, with all the gravity that accompanies it, is strictly and exclusively attached to the person of those who, men or women, having contracted a *nikāḥ* and having consummated it, violate the juridico-religious conditions for the practice of sexuality. *Nikāḥ* confers on the sexual act a psychological, social, affective and spiritual nobility so splendid that any departure from it is judged accordingly. Contrary to an all-too-widespread belief, Muslim marriage is quite as 'sacred' as a Christian marriage or a Jewish marriage. It is certainly not eternal or absolute. It is nevertheless an act of faith in oneself, in others, but first in God. And one may, paraphrasing Descartes, say that for a good Muslim 'an atheist could not be in love'. Moreover the Muslim has been created only for love. As the expressive Tunisian song has it: 'Our community was created for passionate love' ('*naḥnu qauwmum lil gharāmi khuliqnā*').

But the sexual life is not simply a reflection of God's will. It belongs to the order of existence and as such it is incarnated in historical bodies. Moreover sexuality is particularized in currents, in concrete, precise 'tendencies'. God's gift is not abstract, but situated. It is not anonymous, but personal. Indeed sexuality is a primordial means of acceding to the world and to life, but it is not the only one. It is a 'given' that grounds a precise relationship to the world and to men, just as appetite and thirst may ground a relationship of another kind.

To ground sexuality in freedom and in the autonomy of the person is necessarily to accept precariousness and relativity; in sexual matters, the will of God gives way to the will of man. Man's will is made up of successive choices and approximations, and not irrevocable decisions. Moreover Islam, while disapproving of divorce, that is to say, the breaking of the sacred link of *nikāḥ*, has in the final analysis to accept it.

Break and change are implied by the very nature of interpersonal relations based on love, a passion whose character is perfectly expressed in the idyll of the Prophet with Zaynab. The Prophet's short but moving prayer, 'My God who thus overturns hearts, strengthen mine' ('*ya muqallīb al qulūbi thabbitlī qalbī*'), signifies the force of love and of its hazards. In the last resort, there are no eternal marriages or absolute vows, and there are renewed choices and hopes, that is to say, a determination to be faithful to oneself and to the beloved. In addition to being a sacrament, sexuality is certainly a personal, historical commitment.

> Sexuality, it is said, is dramatic *because* we commit our whole personal life to it. But just why do we do this? Why is our body, for us, the mirror of our being, unless because it is a *natural self*, a current of given existence, with the result that we never know whether the forces which bear us on are its or ours – or with the result rather that they are never entirely either its or ours. There is no outstripping of sexuality any

> more than there is any sexuality enclosed within itself. No one is saved and no one is totally lost.[36]

This admirable passage from Merleau-Ponty really enables us to understand that if Islam posits sexuality in terms both of sacrament and personal commitment, it is because it wishes to apprehend it without either reducing it or mutilating it. Hence that sense of happiness sometimes bordering on the tragic that seems to me to constitute a fundamental aspect of the Islamic view of sexuality. Whereas Christianity reduces the sexual by sublimating or transcending it, Islam, while also wishing to transcend the sexual, sometimes by sublimating it, has always refused to reduce it and still less to destroy it. If sexuality is coextensive with faith, it is also coextensive with man. Hence both that sense of pleasure that springs out of the Quran and that hope that man, in spite of everything, will manage to save himself by accepting himself, that is to say, by loving.

PART II

Sexual practice in Islam

CHAPTER 9
Sexuality and sociality

The Islamic view of sexuality, then, is a total one. Its aim is to integrate the sexual as everyday experience. Islam is a recognition, not a misapprehension of sexuality. But this recognition, itself unequivocal, bears on a reality that is essentially ambiguous. The serious and the ludic, the social and the individual, the sacramental and the historical – these are the fundamental, but ambivalent dimensions of sexuality. To say that Islam wishes to integrate the sexual, without reducing it, means that it accepts it, with all its tensions, its conflicts, with the contradictions that are necessarily part of it.

But to refuse to reduce sexuality to one or the other of its elements amounts in fact to entrusting to the concrete social agencies the task of delimiting, selecting or at least stressing this or that dimension of the sexual. By admitting all sexuality, by rejecting no part of it, Islam lent itself to various incarnations of itself, which, while being more or less contradictory, could all claim allegiance to it. And it is at the level of concrete everyday life that the precise manners, the specific style that have made up the real embodiment of Islamic sexuality ought to be sought. For sexuality is experienced as much as it is conceived.

Thus the study of Islam and of sexuality brings us back to the most delicate, yet broadest approach of Muslims to their sexuality. Now that we are ready to pass from the theological, cosmogonic view to the social practice of sexuality, we must see how this Islamic vision has been expressed in specific behaviour. In other words we must grasp at the level of everyday practice the three-termed dialectic of the sexual, the sacral and the social. Within the limits of *nikaḥ*, Islam permits, tolerates the sexual life. It integrates it into the social, communal life of the Umma while warmly recommending believers to take their share (*nasīb*) of the sexual pleasures, which are an essential prefiguration of the pleasures of paradise. It thus posits the sacralizing character of *nikāḥ*, which is *iḥsan*, the strengthening or fortifying of being. But at the same time it accepts dissolution of marriage, that is to say, the temporary, relative character of matrimonial bonds. It also accepts polygamy, that is to say, the multivocity of the bonds created by *nikāḥ*. Now it is quite obvious that such prescriptions lead to diversity and difference according to the more or less moderate use that is made of them. Familial structures, processes of socialization and methods of upbringing are bound to be affected.

Paradoxically, Islam, a religion of theological unity, leads to social pluralization. The spiritual unity of the Umma in no way excludes difference. It is even the grandiose manifestation of God's will that has created for us 'races and tribes that you may know one another'.[1] This cannot be repeated often enough: there is no one Muslim society, but a multiplicity of social structures all claiming allegiance to Islam. Without going so far as to say that each has its own Islam, one can show that between black Islam, Arab Islam, Iranian Islam, Malaysian Islam, etc., there are differences of behaviour and attitude that are much more a matter of 'folklore'. I have already had occasion elsewhere to bring out this fundamental flexibility, this essential 'plasticity' of Islam, which in no way wishes to sacrifice the equivocity of being and the ambiguity of life.[2] Indeed is not any society a variation on variables and invariants and a temporary, precarious balance between the permanent and the changing? Only research carried out on this basis will be able to grasp the profound, dialectical dynamism of Muslim societies, whose permanent structures and historical development are irreducible, I believe, from one another.

Only a naive or dishonest mind could be surprised at the gaps that exist in any society between its ideals and its practices. The Arabo-Muslim societies are no exception. The fine egalitarian, democratic principles of original Islam have often remained at the level of pious intentions and Arabo-Muslim society has had its share of inequalities, aristocratism and feudalism. So it is perfectly conceivable *a priori* that the lyrical conception of life should exist in an Islamic society that is in fact prudish.

Hence the need to bring out certain sociological dominants. The dialecticization of sexuality and the development of the ethics of love in precise, concrete directions, in particular historical conditions and social structures, seems to me to be important. Three factors – concubinage, the cleavage between rural and urban social environments and the economic base of Arab kinship – seem to have lent their weight in giving the societies in question their own historical profile, but also in dialecticizing the Islamic view of sexuality and turning it in a direction compatible with properly sociological requirements.

Little analysis has been made of the role of concubinage in the development of Muslim societies and it is of the utmost importance to realize that the relations between masters and female slaves were also carnal relations. Polygamy was certainly limited by the fiqh to four wives, but the number of concubines remained unlimited.

The laws of *nikāḥ* could of course be applied to the female slave. But this implied that a proper marriage had been contracted with her. Outside *nikāḥ* the legal sexual relations of the master with his female slaves were governed only by the good will of the owner. The only prescriptions laid down were for the protection of the interests and rights of the third parties especially in the event of a birth. For then the female slave changed status and became *umm-walad.*[3] We read in Al Qudūri's *Mukhtaṣar*:

> When a slave gives her master a child, she becomes for him a concubine mother: *umm-walad*. He may neither sell her nor transfer her to the ownership of another. But he may have coitus with her, require that she serve him, praise her services to others, and marry her. . . .
>
> When a man has coitus in marriage with another's slave, if she gives him a child and he becomes her master, she will become his concubine-mother.
>
> When the father has coitus with his son's slave and she gives birth to a child whose paternity is claimed by the said father, the child's parentage is established in relation to him and this slave becomes the father's *umm-walad*, and it is the father who owes her estimated value. But he does not have to pay the indemnity for the usurpation of this slave's sex (*'uqr*), nor the estimated value of his child.
>
> If it is the father's father who has had this coitus during the lifetime of the father, the paternity is not established. . . .
>
> If the slave belongs jointly to two owners and she gives birth, and one of the two claims the child, the child is made his and she becomes his *umm-walad*. But he owes to the other

> half the indemnity for the usurpation of this slave's sex (*'uqr*) and half her estimated value. . . . If both the co-owners claim the child, its paternity is established with regard to both of them. The mother becomes the concubine-mother to both of them and each owes the other half the indemnity for the usurpation of the sex of that slave.
>
> If the master has coitus with the slave of his contractually emancipated male slave . . . and she gives birth and he claims paternity, paternity is attributed to the master if the contractually emancipated male slave accepts what the master says and the master will owe this emancipated slave the indemnity for the usurpation of this female slave's sex and estimated value of the child. But she will not become his concubine-mother. . . .[4]

This passage brings out the existence, which is confirmed by hundreds of other texts belonging to every school, of 'very free' morals in the matter of concubinage. The 'double' concubine in a sense marries her master and makes possible a greater satisfaction of desire. With her, pleasure is in a sense free of all constraints, since, in principle, she is not expected to give birth to children. The concubine changes status precisely when she does give birth. She becomes *umm-walad* and acquires by that very fact certain rights that, though not entirely freeing her, somewhat attenuate her servile condition. A concubine is expected to provide pleasure or work or both. But, as the *Fatāwa Hindiyya* puts it, one must 'respect the custom by which one gives better clothes to the concubine who provides pleasure alone'.[5]

The legitimate wife appears to benefit from a superior status. This is only an appearance, however. For in the end the concubine becomes a veritable 'anti-wife', by usurping femininity and taking it over entirely for herself. One is jealous of one's wife, not of one's concubine. The first must be serious, but the second must be ludic. The enclosing of women, the relative ignorance in which they were kept, almost never applied to the concubine. As a result there is a double status of woman in Islam, depending on whether she is orientated towards *nikāḥ* or towards concubinage. This distinction, we should point out, is not quranic. It derives from the economic, social, political and cultural conditions of life.

The *jawāri* became veritable anti-wives. They acquired a *de facto* situation that more than compensated for their servile condition.

A just revenge? Perhaps. But one should point out that the presence in a single household of beautiful female slaves must have created scenes of jealousy between co-wives, who were already often forced to share the same favours of the master among themselves and who saw themselves outwitted by concubines. The concubine was the intruder par excellence. Nor should we forget the innumerable rivalries that resulted from concubinage and which set brothers of different beds – and different condition – against one another.

But there was more to it than this. To differences of nature were added differences of culture. All these concubines were of different races, ethnic groups and 'styles': African, Sudanese, European, Iranian, Indian, Asiatic, Slav. . . . Educated in the manners of their own countries, they brought with them an exotic perfume of eroticism and contributed to the acculturation of Arabo-Muslim society – an acculturation at the base, so to speak.

Under the Ommayads and above all under the Abbasids, the value of a concubine increased with her beauty, but also with her 'skill', her good manners, her poetic gifts, her talent as a dancer or singer.[6]

The system of anti-wives organized on a large scale had an undeniable influence on the morals of classical Arab society, especially among the aristocrats and in the courts of the caliphs and other notables. Not all of them, of course, were of the quality of 'the girl with the beauty spot', who cost Harun al-Rashid 70,000 dirhems, or even of 'Tawaddūd', who, according to legend, cost only 10,000. But all strove to rival them and dreamed of one day having to submit like them to a lengthy examination before a jury made up of the greatest minds in the university world of the time. And it was with the greatest ease that Tawaddūd replied, it is said, to everything that was asked of her concerning medicine, astronomy, music, mathematics, philosophy, lexicography, rhetoric, fiqh and hadith.[7]

Parallel with his minions, El Amin, the son of Harun al-Rashid, organized a corps of 'pagesses', girls who wore their hair short, dressed as boys and wore silk turbans. This innovation was not slow in spreading throughout the rest of society. An eyewitness reports that one Palm Sunday, having presented himself to the caliph El Māmun, he found himself surrounded by twenty richly dressed Greek girls, dancing with gold crosses around their necks, palms and olive branches in their hands. . . . One author recounts how El Motawakkil had four thousand concubines, who all shared his bed. . . .[8] The competition must have been tough in that harem, but he was not exceptional.

The wife was defeated in advance by these 'anti-wives'. Arab feminism was a victory of these anti-wives. They alone, indeed, and almost to the exclusion of the legitimate wives, finally got their way over the men.[9]

The cultural heritage is such that the Arab feminine archetype still remains, even today, marked by these customs. It is as if all seriousness lay on the side of the wife and all pleasure on the side of the *jāriya*. The *jawāri*, writes Ahmad 'Amin,

> seem to me to have been more active than the 'free' women, from the point of view both of aesthetic creation and of the inspiration derived from the poets. This was due to the social organization of the period. Men, as we know from Jāḥiḍh, were more jealous of their free wives than of their *jawāri*. They veiled their free women strictly. If a man wanted to marry one of them a female marriage-broker was sent to inspect her and to come back with a description of her qualities and defects: but he himself did not see her until after the marriage. Things were quite different in the case of the slave women. To begin with any possible opprobrium caused by the *jāriya* did not reflect upon him as would have been the case if a relation of free condition had been involved. Besides, she was largely unveiled, because she could be bought and sold. It was also she who did the errands in the street. . . .
>
> From another point of view one was more preoccupied with the education of the concubine than with that of the free woman. . . . Indeed only a few members of a tiny privileged section of society concerned themselves with the education of free women. There was another factor: the *jawāri* were seen as a means of entertaining men. So those who exploited the *jawāri* took it upon themselves to refine these entertainments in accordance with the demands of the consumers. And since the *jāriya* was all the more able to conquer men's hearts in that she was skilled in letter writing (*adība*), music and poetry, no effort was spared to satisfy this demand. Of course we find many free women instructed in some of the sciences. But they were so almost always for religious purposes, specializing above all in the hadith and in Sufism.[10]

To sum up, wives enjoyed the austerity of knowledge, while

the anti-wives indulged in the delights of artistic creation and aesthetic inspiration! In the race towards infinite love was it not to be expected that it was the anti-wife who notched up the greater number of points? Certainly concubinage had no small part to play in the devaluation of the wife. What, in principle, should have been the harmony of the sexes often turned into a pretext for slavery. Femininity was smashed. What was intended as a complementarity of the ludic and the serious led to the establishment of two opposed, different types of woman: the serious wife and the ludic anti-wife. Hence that disaffection so frequent among Arabs for their own wives and their endless quest for something beyond the wife. . . .

Indeed concubinage was not the only preponderant social factor. Even more important was the cleavage between the town and the country. The system of concubinage, as indeed that of polygamy in general, affected only the towns, and even then only the better off classes. Consequently we must regard the countryside as having different norms of behaviour. Historians and chroniclers, it is true, have not been over-lavish in providing information about rural life.

One of the characteristics of the rural environment was that women worked in the same ways as men. Women picked the olives, harvested the alfa, gleaned, hoed the rice fields, tended the cattle, ploughed the fields; women concerned themselves with practically all the crafts. . . . It was they who carried water, ground the grain and brought in the firewood. The status of women, too, changed from town to country. Integrated through her work into active life, the peasant woman had a quite different status from her sister in the towns. Society continued, of course, to be divided sexually. But the division followed a quite different line from the town. Women were not confined; open air life did not allow it. There was no veil: it was not suited to work in the fields. There was no concubinage: the financial situation did not permit it.

One may wonder whether in the countryside polygamy played the role that it did in the town. Divorce, yes; that is to say, successive polygamy. But as far as we know from the few texts and documents that have come down to us the rural world was characterized by a greater stability of the family; the countryside was unaware of such refinements of civilization as the depreciation of the status of the wife, against whom the competition of the concubines played such a part. In sexual matters the Islamic view was to give birth to two divergent views, the 'bedouin' and the 'beldia'.[11] The first characterized by a greater attachment to the eternal feminine and an acute sense of fidelity, the second by a greater sensualism, refinement and sophistication. In one case one orientates oneself towards others and tries to lose oneself, in the other there is a hopeless quest for oneself that one wishes to realize through the multitude of experiences as varied and numerous as a rich and prosperous empire permitted. Introversion and extraversion, or, to put it another way, Don Quixote, the man who gives himself, and Don Juan, the man who seeks himself. . . . Majnūn and Ibn Abi Rabi'a.

It is certainly no accident if the two doctrines of love very soon polarized the individual and social psychical energies that have been referred to as bedouin love and urban love, *ḥubb al-badāwi* and *al-ḥubb al ḥaḍāri*.

Chastity and fidelity are in fact essential features of bedouin love. The erotic works of a bedouin poet are entirely devoted to one exclusive lady. Chastity is *de rigueur*, for sexual union is the worst enemy of love. One loves and one delights in moral suffering. The tribe of the Banni 'Udhra was made famous by its chaste, pure, but unhappy lovers. Thus, through the ages, couples were formed. They became legendary and went on firing the imagination of both the rural and the urban world: Qais and Leyla, Jamīl and Butayna, Kutayir and 'Azzā, etc.

It is as if, by this means, bedouin woman had sensed that she had at her disposal great power, which allowed her to make up for everything in the rising Arab civilization that was fatal for her. In this way, in a sense, the bedouin woman took revenge on her urban sister. Indeed the imperialism of love alone could bring the Arab woman revenge for confinement, the veil, in a word, derealization. The Islamic view of love as infinite and life as lyrical was to be transformed into sublime spiritual forces. The bedouin woman was to become a spiritual value *per se*, because she embodied beauty, freedom, justice, happiness, the absolute. To love was to attach oneself to that ideal. The bedouin erotic poets became the 'standard bearers of women'.[12] Thus, without knowing it, Arab poetry committed itself to a feminist enterprise that identified the ideal with femininity. Sexuality and the flesh remain silent and it is the spirit that speaks – in a sense a desensualized love.

Urban love, on the other hand, was licentious (*ibāḥi*) lightness, frivolity and carnal union. What mattered was the flesh and the most highly prized woman was the one who procured the biggest and longest orgasm.

It is perhaps al-Walid II who represents the very type of this tendency. Blachère sees in him 'a repressed man who liberates himself in the debauchery of an impossible love'. Gaston Wiet describes him as 'a poet, a composer and singer, who indulged in every form of debauchery, whose conduct was scandalous not only in Damascus, but in the Holy Places. . . .'[13]

This apposition of the *badāwi* and the *ḥaḍāri*[14] in erotic poetry was to lay down a fundamental alternation that was to last for centuries, right up to our own day. It is as if the totality conceived by Islam, *qua* doctrine, could not but fall apart in contact with the facts of life. Henri Pérès has also found it in Andalusian poetry.[15] After observing that for Ibn Sārā *'udhri* and *'afāf* are synonymous, he writes:

> The cult of woman, then, was carried very far by the Andalusians; it is legitimate to believe that the poets merely reflected the ideas of their time, or, if many of their contemporaries had different ideas, they were able . . . to modify their attitude towards woman, cultivate in themselves, in order to bring them out all the more, the natural qualities that led them to be discreet, courteous, exquisitely refined.[16]

And it is Ibn Dāwūd who, in that endlessly sensual Spain, posited that 'the ideal is not the union of bodies, but the mutual renunciation that is perpetuated desire!'[17]

So it is as if the harmony of the sensual and the spiritual were so difficult to assume that Islamic doctrine was ultimately transformed into a creative tension. This was because the conditions of practical life necessarily imposed gaps that dialecticized, while exploding, the quranic views of love and sexuality.

To be more precise, the reciprocity of the perspectives in the sexual act and in love is broken. Love ceases to be the common act of the lover or of the beloved and becomes a hopeless quest. In bedouin love we have the beloved, desired woman who is impossible to possess. In the urban view we have the vainglory and swagger of the lover, desired by the ladies, but himself haughty, insensitive and blasé.

Love is no longer a meeting and complementarity. The agreement of the participating persons is no longer anything more than a theoretical aim laid down by the Quran. The break in the equivocity of love culminates in fact in sublimating the beloved or in driving the lover into splendid, narcissistic pride. On the one hand, we have male egocentrism, a desire to possess that amounts to the enslavement, the demeaning and even the negation of the partner, and, on the other, a sincere, but gloomy, complaint, sometimes not untouched by sado-masochism. In any case, there is a loss of reciprocity in sexual relations. The quranic balance, has, in actual fact, rarely been attained!

Yet another sociological fact, and one likely to dialecticize the Islamic view of sexuality is the economic base of the familial group. Islam set up women's rights in paternal inheritance. But this breech in the traditional system of the circulation of wealth and capital was never accepted by the Arab societies.

Germaine Tillion[18] has shown in a book of penetrating insight the extent to which the question of inheritance was determinant in the pastoral societies in creating an endogamic system and impeding the circulation of women. Wealth circulated at the same time as women. The more rapid the one, the more rapid the other. And if one wished to impede one, one had to impede the other. The pastoral economy, above all, was expressed in the inferior status of women, whose lessened condition was still more emphasized by systematic exclusion from inheritance. Refusal to share the patrimony, lands and animals deprived woman of any claims to the inheritance. A woman was allowed to share in the inheritance only on the express condition that she did not marry outside the group. Now Islam had set up a rapid rotation of women: polygamy and repudiation ought to have been expressed in fact in relations of filiation, kinship, sororate, cousinship, in such a way as to fragment the patrimony of the groups.

Islam may have limited the share of the daughter's inheritance to half that of the son, but the risk was nevertheless enormous. One has only to see the extraordinary complexity of the Islamic rules of inheritance to realize the importance of the chapter. A whole science, the *'ilm al farā-iḍ*, governed inheritance law. By admitting a daughter to the inheritance of the father and by organizing the rotation of women, Islam threatened one of the most secure economic bases of the social structures of the Mediterranean groups that were converted to it.

Hence that wealth of ingenious reasons for dissociating the circulation of wealth from that of women through the system of the *waqf* or *habus*, or again, for impeding the rotation of women through endogamy. In either case the effect is the same: a veritable sexual discrimination. There was no shortage of rationalizations to justify this disinheritance: in any case, women were weak creatures and needed protection, didn't they?

This disinheritance usually took the form of the *habus* (*waqf* in the Middle East), which consisted in a deed of immobilization of property. The *habus* seemed to favour the woman, 'for in the absence of any contrary stipulation, the share of the heir of female sex would be equal to that of the heir of the male sex.'[19]

In fact it is nothing of the kind. To begin with, it only needed the man claiming ownership of the patrimony under *habus* to stipulate the contrary. But above all, although the daughters of the deceased were admitted on an equal footing to the enjoyment of the inheritance, the usufruct of which they shared with their brothers, they were not able to convey their rights to their children of both sexes. The right of daughters to the usufruct of a *habus* died with them. For the juridical *akeb* restricted the benefit of *habus* wealth to the children of both sexes of the founder, that is to say, to the first generation, but thereafter to the children of both sexes of their descendants of male sex to the exclusion of the daughters. Furthermore the founder had a perfect right to constitute the *habus* solely to the benefit of the males and to the exclusion of the girls, whatever their degree and relationship. It is true that one sometimes added, perhaps to give oneself a quiet conscience, the following minor clause: 'unless the girls are indigent or unmarried'.[20] How far we are from the feminism of the Quran! The intention is quite clear: to prevent the patrimony leaving the familial group at any cost. Women will circulate alone: wealth will not follow them. Indeed in innumerable contexts of customary law (*uorf*), the daughter was quite simply excluded from the succession. Usually the land, the house, the commercial property, jewellery, the library or arms went exclusively to the male children.

Popular Tunisian opinion, which was not lacking in humour or cynicism, called this operation of disinheritance of the daughter *ikrād* or 'elimination of ticks'. One could hardly express more clearly the notion that the rights of women to a patrimony constitute for a group a veritable scourge that must be rooted out as soon as possible! Woman was certainly a parasite and one had to limit the damage she wreaked.

Just as effective in the Arabo-Muslim societies was the practice of endogamy. We know that Islam accepted marriage between cousins even in the first degree. The systematization of marriage between consanguine cousins made it possible to reconcile the demands of the continuity of the group based on the permanence of the property with the *ḥudūd-Allah*. Marriage between consanguine first cousins, while remaining within the bonds of God's will, avoided the circulation of patrimony. As a result matrimonial alliance within the same fraction of the familial group had 'a certain stabilizing effect',[21] as Cuisenier points out. 'For what a man gains as a brother on the withdrawal of a sister, he loses as a husband on the withdrawal of his wife, so that at each inheritance the land is divided into as many parts only as there are male descendants of the deceased.'[22]

After a meticulous, patient study of Ansarine, in Tunisia, Cuisenier arrives at this conclusion, which forms an excellent basis for reflection: 'At the third generation all men who were able to do so effectively married their parallel cousins.'[23] I have myself made similar observations at Kairwan, where, in the large families, marriage with the parallel cousin has been the rule and the system right up to present-day generations and is always justified in the same way: 'It is pure madness to give one's wealth to others', or again, 'Why irrigate the jujube tree? Priority for water belongs to the olive tree.'

The same practice is to be observed further east. Jacques Berque, using his own observations and the researches of Abbas al-'Azzawi,[24] insists on 'the "preferential" marriage that qualifies the son of the paternal uncle, *Ibn al-amm*, to obtain, so to speak, his female cousin. This agnatic aspect is so marked in the *Ahwār* that a decreasing rate of the *mahr* sanctions the parental proximity of the claimant, that the uncle has a right to veto, *nahwa*, in his niece's marriage and that, if it is ignored, he can resort to punishment.'[25]

We can even speak of a veritable system of 'cousinage'. Preferential marriage with the consanguine cousin closes the agnatic group upon itself, impedes the rotation of women and leads to social exclusion of women from the group, further emphasizes sexual division and derealizes women. The man gets major status, the woman eternal minority. The woman is nothing more than man's shadow.

Three major facts, essentially social in nature, then, have worked against Arabo-Muslim women and led to a *de facto* status markedly inferior to the quranic ideal. Concubinage and the concurrent, permanent presence of educated, gifted, beautiful anti-wives, scrupulously selected from various parts of the empire; the gap between urban and rural life, with their different sharing out of work and leisure; the economic basis of endogamy systematizing the practice of cousinage and in doing so impeding the rotation of women, the expansion and expression of any love that does not conform to the interests of the group, all this could only lead inevitably to a scarcely disguised 'slavery' of Arab women. Despite a juridical status that was markedly favourable in principle, women were reduced to the role of housewife and mother, providing children and supervising the running of their husband's household. Femininity deserted the Arab wife, who was literally dispossessed of herself to the advantage of mistresses of every kind. Arab man is haunted by extra-matrimoniality. This is astonishing, given the laxity of *nikāḥ*, but perfectly logical when concrete socio-cultural structures are taken into account.

It is precisely in terms of specific social contexts that we must understand why quranic equivocity ceased to be a harmony and became a matter of tensions, conflicts and contradictions. What was unified in Revelation fell apart at the historical level. Here the social reduced neither the sexual, nor the sacral, but fully exploited them, if only to allow each to violate the other. So the libidinal as well as the sacral found itself integrated by the group in terms of vital social needs. It was this dialectical adjustment of the sacral, the sexual and the social, it seems to me, that gave Islamic civilization its specificity and accounts both for what is permanent in it and for what is a matter of history and circumstance. It is this 'interplay' that I now propose to analyse in certain of its most typical manifestations. Without claiming to exhaust the question, I shall content myself with locating a few characteristic moments in this formidable profusion of attitudes and expectations, aspirations and nostalgias.

CHAPTER 10

Variations on eroticism: misogyny, mysticism and 'mujūn'

One might be surprised at this variation on Islamic sexuality in the form of three Ms and find paradoxical that misogyny, mysticism and *mujūn* may be conceived together. The paradox is only apparent, for these three forms of behaviour are all ways of outwitting the spirit of Islam.

Islamic civilization is essentially feminist. One ought to be able to deduce from this that a Muslim cannot be a misogynist. Islam and 'hatred' of women appear to be incompatible *de jure*. And yet the devaluation of femininity in the Arabo-Muslim countries is such that the mildest of feminism is still widely regarded even today as an anti-quranic revolution!

This 'contradiction' between law and fact derives fundamentally from the socio-economic status and the socio-cultural situation of Arab women: one really cannot deprive women of their economic and civil rights or frustrate them of what the Quran grants them and at the same time magnify them! Hence that male bad faith that betrays women, sexuality and pleasure in a thousand and one ways.

Hence, too, the flight before woman. Fear of women, anxiety when confronted with the procreative forces that they bear within them, the strange unease that is aroused by that mysterious attraction for an unknown being who is often no more than the unknown of being. In many societies all this frequently turns into a rejection of women.

Arab culture abounds in misogynist features and moral austerity. But mysticism, Sufism and Marabutism also express, in their own ways, this flight from women that is reinvested in a state beyond love. And even sexuality is sometimes regarded as merely a preparatory technique for mystical ecstasy and refuge in the Supreme Being.

But sometimes, too, this flight from woman becomes a flight into woman, into lechery, in short, into *mujūn*. Make no mistake, misogyny, mysticism and *mujūn* are merely variations in three Ms on one and the same thing: sexuality. All these forms of behaviour conceal a veritable obsession, conscious or unconscious, assumed or refused, with woman, whom one devalues only in devaluing oneself. The negation of woman is always a negation of self. Misogyny encloses us in our own empire. Mysticism sublimates us. *Mujūn* releases our inhibitions. Three ways of dealing with a single problem.

In actual fact, many of the texts of the fiqh and sunna, but not a single text of the Quran, can be given a misogynist interpretation. Whatever the authenticity of the hadiths, one has only to remember that an apocryphal one is perhaps even more significant than a true one. It expresses a historical moment, a need felt by the community. Nevertheless tradition is hard on women and on sexuality. It was Muhammad, for example, who declared, on the occasion of his nocturnal ascension, that he had 'noticed that hell was populated above all by women'.[1] He went on to say, 'If it had been given to me to order someone to be submissive to someone other than Allah, I would certainly have ordered women to be submissive to their husbands, so great are a husband's rights over his wife.'[2]

Muhammad lived with his mother Amina for only two years. When orphaned, he transferred to his nurse, Halima, the vibrant, frustrated affection that was to make him say that 'paradise is to be found at the feet of mothers'.

Omar was quite the reverse. He congratulated himself that he was responsible for the introduction of the veil and for Muhammad's victory over his harem.[3] It was he who said: 'We Quraichites were masters of our wives: but we have come to live at Medina among people who are dominated by their wives. Just imagine!'[4]

The Imām Ali was fond of saying: 'Woman is wholly evil; and the worst thing about her is that she's a necessary evil!'[5]

The history of Arabo-Muslim culture swarms with resolutely anti-feminist declarations. The beginning of the celebrated poem, *Lamia*, by the Ibn el Wardi,[6] is illuminating from this point of view. It begins thus:

Do not trust songs! And flee from love poems!
Say only serious things and break with those who indulge
in facile pleasantry!
Beautiful women must be abandoned: there is no pleasure
in them.
Such is the way of glory, power, honour.
Flee musical instruments, and handsome youths.
Do not be misled by their plump, seductive behinds. . . .

Here is a significant commentary: 'Since women constitute the basis of all *fitna* (revolt against God), since they are the principal element in Satan's traps, the author of the poem begins, quite rightly, by putting us on our guard against them.'[7] *Fitna* and *Ḥabā-il al-shaiṭān*! There is a whole programme there. *Fitna* is both seduction and sedition, charm and revolt. For it is when they are under women's charms that men revolt against the will of God. Female beauty is a bait that leads to perdition, to damnation. From this point of view, woman is regarded as one of Satan's traps. And Mas'ud al-Qanāwi also explains that 'looks cast at women's finery are Satan's arrows'.[8] Then comes a quotation from the Imām Ali:

> Men, never obey your women in any way whatsoever. Never let them give their advice on any matter whatsoever, even those of everyday life. Indeed allow them freely to give advice on anything and they will fritter away one's wealth and disobey the wishes of the owner of this wealth.
>
> We see them without religion, when, alone, they are left to their own devices; they are lacking in both pity and virtue when their carnal desires are at stake. It is easy to enjoy them, but they cause great anxiety. The most virtuous among them are libertines. But the most corrupted among them are whores! Only those of them whom age has deprived of the shadow of any charm are untainted by vice! They have three qualities particular to miscreants: they complain of being oppressed, whereas it is they who oppress; they make oaths, whereas they are lying; they pretend to refuse men's solicitations, whereas they desire them most ardently. Let us beg the help of God to emerge victorious from their evil deeds. And preserve us in any case from their good ones.[9]

There is the same suspicious attitude towards the evil thoughts that the sight of beardless (*amrad*) boys can arouse. It is unlawful to look at a male face that is not covered by a beard, even if the look is not accompanied by concupiscence and even if one is protected from all *fitna*. 'The beardless boy is like a woman. He is even worse. It is even more criminal to look at him than to look at a strange woman.'[10] Of course a pious man will certainly refrain from touching a youth's hand or even touching him at all. His mistrust will be all the greater when the young men are particularly handsome, well dressed and coquettish. Rich men's sons are especially dangerous from this point of view, so their teachers must take particular care – the very nature of their task places them, alas, in contact with young men in whose welfare they must take a close interest. A good teacher, therefore, should turn his back to his pupils.[11]

Indeed the author gives us valuable information on the mores of the time. Homosexuality was widespread in the student communities and especially in the confraternities. In the sessions of mystical initiation, 'the accolade was frequently given by the adults to the young initiates behind and in front. . . . Some felt immense pleasure and relaxation in this. This is what is called the relaxation of the poor. And they dare to claim that this was the love of God, whereas it is a sin that arouses God's anger and punishment.'[12]

In time the progress of austerity came to reduce sexuality to an activity that was to be mistrusted and controlled. We have entered the cycle of repressive sexuality. Muslim society was differentiated at two heterogenous levels: that of male austerity, the only one to be taken seriously, and that of dangerous feminine facility. And youth was repressed together with femininity.

If misogyny constantly recurs as a leitmotif in Arab culture it is because it has a meaning. It is evidence for us of a break in the quranic harmony. Arab societies drew from Islam not the idea of the complementarity of the sexes, but, on the contrary, that of their hierarchy. Misogyny is really no more than a sociological conditioning. The debate about female emancipation thus takes on a striking significance. In any case, it cannot mask the fundamental position of the group that intends to maintain its own economic, patriarchal and male base. Misogyny is something other than an accident along the route of the structuration of Arabo-Muslim societies!

The negation of woman cannot be total. The most misogynist man is forced to recognize the depth of what he is so determined to oppose. Indeed, within Arabo-Muslim society other compensatory attitudes emerge that are a recovery of sexuality in a sublimated form. Mysticism, for example, takes us from the renunciation of woman to her sublimation. Without wishing in the least to reduce it to that, we might say that mystical spirituality was nourished in Islam from the sublimated cult of woman.

In an earlier work I had occasion to stress those things that, from a psycho-sociological point of view, separated Marabutism, which is concerned to fill the void left in Islam by the absence of an institutionalized Church with a series of mediations between the creature and the Creator, and Sufism, which is entirely orientated towards immediate fusion with God.[13] I should add that although Marabutism does not necessarily involve a displacement of the object of sexuality, this is certainly not the case with Sufism. Marabutism is a social organization of the religious. And the confraternities constitute collective orders that draw upon the sacred for values that will assist them in realizing their cohesion and upon the social for forces that may be placed at the service of the religious community. Hence that military, committed, militant aspect of Marabutism. If Marabutism can be accused of anything it is that, in a sense, it exacerbates rather than stifles sexuality. It is notorious that Marabutist festivals, the *ziyāra*, both in the Maghreb and in the Middle East, turn very easily into licentiousness.[14]

In concrete terms, we are speaking of a confraternity of men, or of women, who are bound together by the memory of a saint or eponymous ancestor and commune with one another in the course of collective mystical ceremonies. Promiscuity is the rule and it is but a step from ecstatic effusion to amorous effusion. Hence that licentiousness in the collective, seasonal practices and that scarcely disguised haemophilia at the name of God in the initiation ritual that so aroused the disapproval of the orthodox.[15]

Sometimes sexuality is exacerbated in the Marabutic ritual, as in extreme cases where the practices include ancient survivals of cults of Cybele, Venus and Bacchus.[16] Nevertheless Marabutism remains a technique of collective exaltation. Hence the importance of the ritual of the confraternity. For Sufism, on the other hand, this can in no sense be the case, since it is essentially a matter of isolating oneself before God. All the affectivity of the Sufi mystic is directed towards God and his Prophet. It involves a significant displacement upwards that implies a sublimation of sexuality.

One remembers the famous hadith, 'he who loves, observes chastity and dies of it, dies as a martyr'. Some versions add as a condition of martyrdom that the love be kept secret. These two conditions – chastity and secrecy (*'iffa* and *kitmān*) – are essential if one is to grasp the very essence of the passage into mysticism. Hence the role of women in the development of mysticism.

Take the Andalusian Mohieddin Ibn 'Arabi. He provides a perfect example of this idealization of woman and sublimation of love: 'I bind myself by the religion of love whatever direction its steeds take: love is my religion, love my faith.'[17] We know that Ibn 'Arabi married a pious woman who helped him to discover both profane love and mystical love. It was largely Mariam al-Bajiya who gave him a taste for meditation and contemplation. She certainly nourished his soul, thus enabling him, in experiences that were certainly very rare, to combine orgasm with ecstasy. An ardent soul in both senses of the word, she pointed him in a particular direction and persuaded him to learn Sufism from another pious woman, Nūna, the famous Fatma Bent Ibn El Mutanna of Cordoba. Mohieddin joined her as a servant and *mūrīd* for two years. Ibn 'Arabi then met, on his pilgrimage to Mecca, another girl, 'Nidhām', with whom he fell in love and to whom he dedicated a series of poems: *Turjamān al Ashwaq* (The Interpreter of Desires), as well as his masterpiece *The Revelations of Mecca.*[18] Ibn 'Arabi remains an example of the man who has lived at its most intense the fundamental unity of poetry and religion, love and faith. From sensuality to spirituality there is a path to be crossed that is the very essence of Sufism and which carries within it the sublimation of sexuality. Profane love is the starting point and spiritual love embraces everything. Sexuality is a mystery of procreation that has meaning only in projection into God.

Ibn 'Arabi's *Diwān*[19] would itself require a thorough analysis, for it is from beginning to end a variation on the theme of mystical and profane love.

In these thousands of verses, the poet conceives of God in terms of passion. As much in the style as in the images conjured up by the *Diwān*, the poet expends his love upon God. Union with God is the end to which the soul aspires. The amorous possession of God expresses a sublimation of Eros and the transubstantiation of the beloved object. And it is again the same form of supersession or transcending that dominates the work of perhaps the greatest of the Muslim mystical poets, Omar Ibn al-Faridh, a contemporary and eastern emulator of Ibn 'Arabi and whom tradition has called 'Sultān al 'āshīqīn', the lovers' sultan. His *Diwān* has been the subject of a masterly commentary by Hassan al-Būrinī and Abdelghani al-Nabulsi.[20] And the late lamented Emile Dermenghem did much to make his name better known in the west with his magnificent French translation of the *Khamriad* (*Eloge du vin*).

There one finds again the fundamental themes developed by Ibn 'Arabi of the unity of existence, of regenerating union through the knowledge and love of God. But it is shot through with the essential themes of 'Udhrite love, enslavement, fidelity, the oneness of love.

After the magnificent researches of Louis Massignon, Al Hallaj holds few secrets for us. And the excellent Qasida, *The Innovation of the Pilgrim on the Threshold of the Sacred Territory*, in which Massignon saw the symbol of union, is written in the same vein.

> Here I am, here I am! O my secret, O my confidence! Here I am, Here I am! O my purpose, O my meaning! I call thee, no, it is Thou who calleth me to Thee! How could I have said, 'It is Thou', if thou hadst not murmured, 'It is I'? O essence of the essence of my existence, O purpose of my plan, O Thou, my elocution and my utterances and my stammerings. . . . My love for my Lord has eaten into me and consumes me. How could I complain to my Lord of my Lord?[21]

This somewhat rapid summary makes no claim, of course, to exhaust Sufism, whose abundant literature would require an analysis that would go well beyond the bounds of this book. It is enough for my purposes here to bring out the sublimated character of Sufi passion.

Sufism borrowed everything from Bedouin love: its ideology, its themes, its motifs, its stereotypes, its images. In fact it is a substitute for it and there is a basic equivalence between the rejection of the flesh and the spiritualization of sexuality. Indeed 'Udhrite love led historically to nothing. It was the gratuitous, chivalric cult of the lady. And, quite naturally, Sufism brought it a finality that it lacked. It is as if the original dissociation of love could not lastingly ignore the carnal aspect of love without having to turn towards the starkest, most ardent faith, that inspired by the love of God. There is a passage from Eros to Agape, the meaning of which appears in each mystic, but, again, in the most admirable way in Ibn 'Arabi and Ibn al-Faridh.

I have purposely taken up here the terms used by the famous Lutheran theologian Anders Nygren.[22] His thesis, which has aroused reservations in Catholic circles, finds a justification in the passage from original Islam to the mystical tendencies. Muhammad unified Eros *qua* genetic force and carnal attraction with Agape, *qua* love of God. Hence for him the profound unity of the love of women and prayer, the work of the flesh and alms. The Sufi mystics 'Platonized' the Islamic Agape, just as the 'Udhrites 'Platonized' the Muslim Eros.

The relationship with God, then, is Love. But although from the Sufi point of view it is direct and requires annihilation in him, it nevertheless necessitates the mediation of the prophet Muhammad. It is precisely around the personal relationship established with him that Marabutism and Sufism are at one. For Muhammad, the friend of God (*H'abību Allah*), is also the friend of men or quite simply the Friend. His being is at the centre of a network of convergent relations conveying both amorous and mystical forces: those that unite believers and both sexes to his Holy person. It required the blindness of an orientalist to maintain with René Basset[23] that the greatest quality of Būsīrī's poem *La Burda* is that it is devoid of any mystical spirit! As if that magnificent, perfectly made *qasīda* did not begin with a classical *nasīb*, and that precisely because for Muhammad love was described as 'Udhrite.[24] Praise of the Prophet is mixed with evocations of the most ardent love. And the Kairwanese were not wrong when they collectively recited the poem as they followed their dead to their last resting place. Is not the love of Muhammad the best mediation when wishing to confront the Face of the Lord?

Despite the differences between levels and conceptions, carnal love and spiritual love prolong one another and imply one another. Hence that stress laid on the complementarity of the sexes, on their harmony and understanding. 'When husband and wife look at one another, God looks at them both with compassion' (*Madhara rahmatin*), as a famous hadith, already quoted, puts it. 'When the husband takes his wife's hand, their sins fall between their hands,' declares the same hadith. One could not express more succinctly the notion of purification through love or the association of God with human love. From the human to the divine there is unity, continuity and ascendance. And it is called Love, of which the various forms (physical, 'Udhrite, mystical) are merely stages of an irreducible totality.

In paradise the vision of God, which is the ultimate in happiness and perfection, is attained only after a series of sexual pleasures. The rain of paradise is a universal sperm. Allah is described in the Quran as *Wadūd*, full of love, all-loving.[25] It is God who promises 'so remember Me and I will remember you'.[26] It is he who promises reciprocity in love: 'If you love God . . . God will love you'.[27] Lastly the soul finds peace in its return to God: 'O soul at peace, return unto thy Lord, well-pleased, well-pleasing. Enter thou among My servants. Enter thou My paradise.'[28]

Love is reciprocal right up to and including the love that binds man to God. It is this reciprocity that constitutes the mystery and grandeur of the Islamic vision of love. Even in love for God there is an erotic element, which has been especially stressed by Sufi mysticism, just as in Christian mysticism Eros plays a crucial role. Hence the use of carnal images on which the imaginary reference confers an even stronger force than the most sensual earthly love. But unlike Christian mysticism we find, at least among the great mystics, no morbid delight in suffering, no sense of profound guilt, still less any attempt to achieve union with God through asceticism and renunciation.

In private life, many Arab mystics were quite simply pleasure-seekers. In the Persian domain people even came to doubt the mysticism of Omar Khayyan and Jalal Addin al-Rumi. In the specifically Arab domain the ambiguity was scarcely less great. And with good reason! Ibn 'Arabi himself certainly mixed carnal love with mystical love. This is because man's rootedness, even in the case of Muhammad himself, passed through the assumption of sexuality and through physical love. It was through sexuality that the fundamental unity of flesh and spirit was formed. It is sexuality that, realizing personal unity in others, makes possible the quest for God. If the unity of self passes through the two poles of sexuality and the love of God it is because they are ultimately one and the same thing. Moreover in both cases there is reciprocity and reaction. Neither with the human partner, nor with God, does Islam accept one-way love. And reciprocity in one case implies reciprocity in the other.

Contrary to appearances, mystical love cannot really be excluded from 'Udhrite love. The latter is a renunciation of the flesh, a sublimation turned back upon itself. Mystical love, on the other hand, is a continuity from the carnal to the spiritual. For it, liberation in the flesh and liberation of the flesh are inseparable.

So the paradox is only apparent and one should not be surprised if a 'systematic', 'strict' puritanism co-existed in the Arabo-Muslim societies with the art of carrying one's sexual pleasures to their highest summit. Arab eroticism is so refined, so elaborate, so all-inclusive, that, in the eyes of many scholars, it has almost eclipsed all the other aspects of Muslim civilization. There is nothing surprising in this for, if my analysis is correct, we must admit that the value of eroticism comes very largely from the certainty that faith alone can confer.

Arab sensuality has its roots in the most authentic or quranic traditions. I have stressed the importance of legitimated pleasure in the sexual act. The pleasure factor itself may sometimes have eliminated the others: *coïtus interruptus* was canonically accepted; a form of *nikāḥ* known as *nikāḥ al-mut'a* was tolerated; the satisfaction of sensuality was warmly recommended by the Prophet.

Coïtus interruptus was apparently widespread in the first Islamic community. The Prophet knew this and never regarded it as reprehensible.[29] He even once added: 'It certainly does not belong to you, if God has decided to create a soul that will live until the Last Judgment, to prevent its coming into the world.' This hadith distinguishes explicitly between the creative acts of God and contraceptive practices. And do not these practices in a sense form part of God's plan?

'Aini relates that the Prophet was questioned one day by one of his companions concerning a concubine with whom he liked to sleep on condition that there was no risk of pregnancy. Muhammad then recommended him to practise the 'restrictive embrace', adding: 'What God has decided for her will happen in any case.'[30] In other words there is no incompatibility between *coitus reservatus* and the mystery of creation. In short, the purpose of the sexual act is not confined to procreation alone.

The *Fatāwā Hindyya*, like so many other treatises, provides valuable information. *Coïtus reservatus* is seen there as subject to the agreement of the wife of free condition or the master of the concubine when she is not the property of the man who is practising the coitus. With the fully owned concubine, *coïtus reservatus* is subject to no other condition.[31] Abortion, too, may be canonically provoked, on condition that the differentiation of the forms of the foetus have not yet been achieved, which, according to Muslim theologians, occurs only after a hundred and twenty days. The 'human forms' are canonically differentiated with the appearance on the foetus of such body growth as hair and nails or clearly visible organs.[32]

Indeed there is a certain laxity in the matter of *coïtus reservatus*. 'In our unhappy times,' our disabused authors add, 'given the legitimate fears inspired by bad descendance, the husband must be authorized to practise *coïtus reservatus* even without seeking the opinion of his wife and even if certain opinions do not favour it.'[33] In these circumstances abortion may be provoked 'in any case', that is, after the canonical limit of four months.

These texts, apart from having the advantage of providing a very precise canonical reference, confirm the idea that in Islam procreation is not necessarily the purpose of the sexual act, which has a value in itself. The fiqh legitimizes both crude sexual desire and the rejection of the child, two of the principal axes of Arabo-Muslim erotology.

The autonomy of desire assumed such importance that primitive Islam hesitated for a long time. At one moment it even legitimated a very curious type of *nikāḥ*, *nikāḥ al-mut'a*, temporary marriage, whose purpose therefore was pleasure (*mut'a*). It was, therefore, a temporary, but legal union. Travellers and soldiers could take advantage of it. Pilgrims, too, for whom the ritual of desacralization is a reinsertion in sexual life. The sacralization of *ḥajj* involved among other things, as we know, total sexual abstinence. The end of the ritual is marked by a return to civil life, by the raising of all taboos, the sacrifice of the hair and a return to sexual life. It certainly derives from a survival of the sacred prostitution that took place in Greco-Roman antiquity.[34] At first Muhammad kept it. Then, at Khaybar, he forbade it. Then he authorized it again on the day of Awtas, then finally forbade it the day he returned to Mecca.[35]

'It is not *nikāḥ* in the ordinary sense of the word, or debauchery, *nikāḥ wa lā sifah*, but a sexual pleasure tolerated by God at a particular moment. It is the hiring for money of a woman with a view to sexual pleasure that must last for three days and three nights, after which the two parties separate and their situation is regularized by a deed of *nikāḥ*.'[36] And it is a quranic text that warranted this tolerance:

> Lawful for you,
> Beyond all that, is that you may seek,
> using your wealth, in wedlock and not
> in licence. Such wives as you enjoy thereby,
> give them their wages apportionate; it is no
> fault in you in agreeing together,
> after the due apportionate.[37]

In other words, there is a price and a gift, but at the centre there is pleasure, *tamattu'*, *mut'a*.

The Prophet himself was very attentive to the art of coupling, the art of sexual pleasure. For sexual bliss was a way of living in the hereafter by anticipation and I have already demonstrated the extent to which orgasm and paradise were co-extensive. Kissing, the right words, scent, fore- and afterplay are themes on which the Prophet laid particular stress, unhesitatingly setting an example, and thereby inaugurating a whole art of sexual pleasure that is regarded as one of the most complete and most systematic.

It was he who founded in law a veritable erotology, a full, positive science of pleasure in all its physical and psychical forms, to which the next chapter will be devoted. If eroticism invades literature, art, everyday life, it is because it is integrated in the Islamic view of the world and is situated at the heart, not at the periphery, of ethics.

A typically Arab notion sums up this fundamental feature: *mujūn*, the object both of disapproval in its inevitable excesses and of envious admiration on the part of those who are incapable of abandoning themselves to a happiness that can lead to a permanent, socially recognized commitment. Observe the ambiguous and equivocal richness of the root *ma ja na*, which signifies, according to the *Lisān al 'Arab*,[38] the density, the depth, the lack of shame, the frivolity, the gratuity, the art of mixing the serious and the lighthearted, pretended austerity, true banter. *Mujūn* is the art of referring to the most indecent things, speaking about them in such a lighthearted way that one approaches them with a sort of loose humour. In principle *mujūn* ought not to go beyond words. In fact it is fantasy present through words. It is oneirism, collective experience and liberation through speech.

One will understand the import of *mujūn* better if one considers the following two examples taken from two of the greatest *fuqaha* of the period. In the commentary by Sheikh Salaheddin Assafadī on Tughrā-y's *Lamiat al-'Ajam*, the venerable sheikh, wearied no doubt by the austerity of the poem and by the conventional thoughts that he was developing, makes a *mujūn* digression, no doubt to poke fun at his students and readers, but also to make his commentary less rebarbative! The theme of the flight of time provides him with an opportunity of evoking the theme of memory and of the pleasant moments of life. There follow five pages[39] of concentrated and agreeable writing that constitute a veritable anthology of salacious anecdotes, riddles, plays in verse, in short, everything that had been written by poets of former times on . . . the size of the holes of women and boys!

This is how a *qāḍi* filled a minister's evenings. The vizir Abu Abdallah al-'Aredh invited the famous faqih Abu Hayan al-Tuahīdī to give a series of learned talks on various subjects. We come, in due course, to the eighteenth evening.

> Once the minister said to me: 'Let us devote this evening to *mujūn*. Let us take a good measure of pleasant things. We are tired of serious matters. They have sapped our strength, made us constipated and weary. Go, deliver what you have to say on that point.' I replied: 'When the *mujjān* had gathered together at the house of Kufa to describe their earthly pleasures, Kufa's fool, Hassan said: "I shall describe what I myself have experienced." "Go on," they said to him. "Here are my pleasures: safety, health; feeling smooth, shiny, round forms; scratching myself when I itch; eating pomegranates in summer; drinking wine once every two months; sleeping with wild women and beardless boys; walking without trousers among people who have no shame; seeking a quarrel with sullen people; finding no resistance on the part of those I love; associating with idiots; frequenting faithful fellows like brothers and not seeking out the company of vile souls." '[40]

And the text of the eighteenth night is extended by ten pages of *mujūn* that made even the publishers blush. Take this note:

> It will not pass unperceived that the author presents in this night *mujūn* of the lowest kind and recounts unseemly anecdotes. Were it not for scientific honesty and a concern to serve history scrupulously we would have omitted most of this text and contented ourselves only with what conformed to good taste.[41]

All is relative! And in fact the western or westernized reader is often shocked by so many obscenities so apparently unworthy of a respectable faqih and a grave minister! Here is a sample.

At Bassorah there was an effeminate man who liked to organize orgies and with this end in view invited couples (of all kinds) to his house. Now he was madly in love with a young man who shaved himself (*mahlūb*). Our effeminate constantly pursued him with his assaults until he had completely seduced him.

> When the people moved closer,
> And the talk ripened
> And feet touched feet,
> And saliva had covered the inside,
> And the rods beat the eggs,
> And the spears began to gambol,
> Then the generous one was patient and, losing all fear,
> Became submissive, obedient, all rebellion gone,
> The guests then departed, at peace,
> Taking away with them the best catches,
> Breasts unburdened,
> Fiery hearts quenched,
> All desire stilled.
> All inclination to flee the lover was forever killed,
> The ropes were put end to end,
> And the union was tied with an indissoluble knot.[42]

It is difficult, in translation, not to soften the impact of the original. It cannot in any case convey the formal beauty of the Arabic text, which is all the more striking in that it is quite simply a pastiche of the Quran, of the Sura 'The Earthquake' itself![43]

Orientalists do not usually translate these texts . . . or they do so into Latin. They regard this kind of *mujūn* as worthless, vulgar obscenity. Yet it forms an essential part of *adab*, the teaching of which must have provided the students of the period with an enjoyable and relaxing break. One may, paraphrasing Mauss, speak of 'education through jokes'. Indeed Tauḥīdī himself stressed this, by way of self-justification, at the end of this celebrated eighteenth night – and the vizir did not fail to draw favourable conclusions from so much *mujūn*.

> Give priority to the art of *mujūn*, he advised him. I would never have thought that it could have furnished a whole session.

> One may have serious reproaches to make to this kind of discourse. Wrongly, for the soul needs gaiety (*bishr*). I have been told that 'Ibn Abbas was fond of saying, as he sat in the midst of his listeners, after long, thorough commentaries upon the Quran, the sunna and the fiqh: 'Now tell me something spicy' (*aḥmiḍu*). I think all he wanted to do by this was to give balance to the soul so that it might recover enough energy to resume the examination of serious things and to make it receptive and attentive to what would be addressed to it.[44]

The B'uyid minister al-Muhallabi had a salon in which he would receive the fuqaha one day, the *qāḍi* another and the philosophers (*mutakallimūn*) another. In these gatherings, wine, *mujūn* and erudition were all partaken of.[45] Yaqūt even relates how two nights a week were reserved to *mujūn*.

> One then threw off all shame, all restraint. One abandoned oneself to revelry, drunkenness and *hubris*. These *kadis* were the finest flower of the fiqh of the period! Ibn Ma'rūf, Tannūkhi Ibn Qāria . . . all had fine, white, long beards, like the vizir al-Muhallabi himself. When they were all beginning to enjoy themselves, when the company became pleasant and the ear enchanted, they were all so gay that they generously abandoned the last veils of their shame to the generous workings of wine. Golden goblets filled with glowing red wine were handed round. Everyone wet his beard in the forbidden beverage. When all the liquid had been drunk they sprinkled one another. They then danced, though not before taking off their clothes, though it is true that they kept thick garlands of flowers around their necks.[46]

Of course women were not absent from these 'orgies' any more than were pretty boys. 'Next day,' Yaqūt adds, not without a touch of malice, 'they returned to their usual puritanism, their self-conscious dignity, their scrupulous respect for the external marks expected of *qāḍi* and to the shame that befits great sheikhs.'[47]

If such was the feeling of men who were reputed to be pious, if that was their attitude, what must have been the behaviour of people less close to religion, of the young, of the ordinary people?

Each social category had its *mujūn*! And to judge by the innumerable descriptions in the *Book of Songs*, the *Golden Meadows* or *The*

Thousand and One Nights, Arab civilization integrated *mujūn* as much as faith. The cities had in their suburbs or in the surrounding countryside highly frequented pleasure gardens, with open-air cabarets and cafés set up on the farms attached to Byzantine, Roman, or Persian castles, or even Christian monasteries. In the best viticultural traditions, the monks provided plenty of wine and pretty girls for the 'joyous companions of sincerity', the *fityāna sidqin* of which Abu Nawas speaks.

These taverns were places where many kinds of pleasure were served up without shame and without exclusion. Singers, dancers, gamblers, but also pleasure-seeking young fellows, homosexuals of both sexes, taught the art of pleasure, without let or hindrance, to a youth whom Islam had freed from any sense of shame or guilt.

> These cabarets, which the poet Ibn al Mu'tazz called the 'ephemeral paradises', were generally set up in large gardens where the limpid water supplied by a canal gushed forth in artificial springs and cascades; large benches covered with matting were arranged under the trembling shade of sycamores, poplars, willows that stood beside cypresses, pomegranate trees, orange trees and palm trees.
>
> The pleasure of going out and breathing fresh air and partaking, in the shade, of roast kid and good wine or mead, while listening to music, was increased by a pleasant outing on a gondola and a return journey by the same means to the city; for these regions were marked by endless canals winding through the plains where barley and wheat stretched as far as the eye could see.[48]

This evocation of Baghdad at the time of its splendour provides an interesting glimpse into an atmosphere that was to be found equally at Kairwan or Cordoba.

Throughout the whole of the Muslim world, from the end of the Ommiads, a set of permanent characteristics appeared that bore the mark of a *mujūn* that we still find almost intact in our own time, despite the enormous upheavals to which that society has been subject for centuries. A desperate love of pleasure that spread beyond the courts and wealthier classes of the city, *mujūn* was an *ars vitae*, a permanent *carpe diem*. The Andalusian *muwashshaḥ's aghrim zamānak lā yafūt* had and still has its counterpart throughout every section of the population.[49]

The great monument of *mujūn* and of Arab eroticism remains incontestably *The Thousand and One Nights*. Apart from the Quran there are few books in Arabic that are so widely read, so well-known, so popular and so rich. One has to have attended a popular gathering at which extracts are read to grasp the importance and role played by these tales. The erotic vision that emerges from them is so total and so totalizing that it seems inseparable from the socio-cultural context in which it came to birth and in which life integrated Eros, in which everything sang of faith in God, love of life and absolute pleasure. The lyrical vision of life is mingled in it with the fantastic and the marvellous. It is a festival of the real and the imaginary. Dream becomes act and act is transfigured into overflowing oneirism.

The very project of *The Thousand and One Nights* brings us to the heart of eroticism. Indeed is it not a question of arousing the desire of king Shahryar? What Shahrazād is trying to do is to put off from night to night the execution of the terrible threat that hangs over her. The tales begin with a noble challenge and are presented as a strategic ruse, a response to the inhuman cruelty of a king determined to despise and punish women in general and virgins in particular. Had he not decided once and for all to put to death one virgin each night after satisfying his sexual appetite with her? Indeed the tales begin with a terrible declaration of misogyny. All men are cuckolds, for all women are whores. 'Trust not at all in women, smile at their promising, for they lower or they love at the caprice of their parts. Filled to the mouth with deceit. . . . Only a miracle brings a man safe from among them.'[50] The only solution is to marry, without leaving the wife time to become unfaithful. In order not to become cuckolds husbands have only to become cruel: the alternative of death and love. But by the end of the tales Shahrazād will have substituted an alternative of love and life.

For Shahrazād, then, it is not only a question of saving her own head and that of all the threatened virgins, but also of outwitting destiny, restoring the rights of femininity and demonstrating that nothing can conquer women. Bluebeard must not be allowed to conquer as in the west. *The Thousand and One Nights* is precisely an attempt to wear down Bluebeard through the power of the imagination, through the enchantment of renewed sexual pleasure. Shahryar, whose sexual appetite is renewed, after having been very well satisfied, was in no doubt that he was giving in against his will to a militant, frenetic, ardent, but effective feminism and . . . in every point in accordance with Islamic teaching.

The myth of Shahryar and Shahzamān, the two brother kings, takes us to the very heart of conversion through love and eroticism. Here are two apparently happy men. They have everything, power, intelligence, money, pleasure, love. Love? No – and that is the point. They thought they had it. But they know what anguish, what 'spleen' drove them towards one another. *Tawaḥ-ḥashā ba'ḍahumā ba'ḍan*, as the Arabic text puts it. The brothers want to meet. They both feel a lack of fraternal affection. Here fraternal love prefigures that of the two sisters Shahrazād and Dunyazād. It is as if the brotherly and sisterly relationship was the only pure, full, positive one. Throughout the tales it is this relationship alone that is not affected by crises of one kind or another. On the contrary it always provides a haven in time of danger.

Shahzamān, then, gets ready to go away. But, of course, it is a false departure and he is already cuckolded. He has not yet left when he discovers his misfortune. He takes his revenge there and then by killing the two guilty parties. But the evil is deep-seated: he realizes at last that he lacked love, that is to say, the essential thing, precisely when he thought he was at the peak of happiness.

When he arrives at his brother's, he soon discovers that they both share the same misfortune, which goes some way towards consoling him! The two go off on a journey and then discover that cuckoldom is universal, that what has happened to them is no fortuitous accident. They realize the reason for their anxiety: woman, whom man hopes to be pure, modest and faithful, is essentially a thieving, libidinous creature, devoid of feeling. 'They are all whores.' There is no such thing as love. When one realizes that, everything collapses. Men are left with only one course: female infidelity must be matched by cruelty. This is because unhappy experiences in love not only make men unhappy; they also make them unjust, bloody and terrifying.

We are here at the peak of misogyny. Then Shahrazād appears to reverse the tendency dialectically. For her, it is a question of curing the king. She sets in train a whole therapeutic process through the spicy tale, eroticism, words, fantasy, dream. Shahrazād is self-revelation through the mediation of woman. Woman, who brought man to perdition, can also save him. 'How beautiful and marvellous is your story!' Shahryar constantly repeats. This is because Shahrazād is 'educated'. She has studied the whole of human history, biographical treatises, poetry, the celebrated adab, the fiqh, astronomy. . . . Shahrazād is the Arab Diotima. Still more so perhaps, for she adds eroticism to femininity. To knowledge she adds accomplishments. She reinvents the secret that cures souls: eroticism, which alone soothes crises of conscience and restores trust in life. This conversion to life in a thousand and one sessions is an initiation into knowledge through love. We have to admire the triptych: eroticism, knowledge, imagination. Eroticism directed against misogyny allows us to rediscover the meaning of Allah's work and, in doing so, the vertigos of knowledge. We pass from extreme hallucination to extreme exaltation. Hence the curative virtue of Shahrazād's enterprise.

Gaston Bachelard was fond of speaking of rhythmanalysis. 'There is a place, in psychology, for rhythmanalysis, as one speaks of psychoanalysis. One must cure the suffering soul, in particular the soul that suffers from time, from spleen, by a rhythmic life, by rhythmic attention and repose.'[51] Shahrazād is simply doing that! She is an expert in rhythmanalysis. Through her tales she sets up a new relation of capture. She achieves a sort of mental homeopathy. By small doses she arouses dream and desire and always brings rest. This is because Eros does not like to be forced, rushed or constrained. Happy Shahryar who can say, with Bachelard: 'Our repose was lightened, spiritualized, poeticized, in experiencing those well regulated, temporal diversities.'[52] The eroticism of *The Thousand and One Nights* is a permanent creation that denounces and transcends anxiety and helps one to discover the pleasure of living.

But nothing is as 'moral' as the tales that Shahrazād tells, we must not forget, in order to save her young sister Dunyazād, hidden under the marriage bed, the scarcely embarrassing, or embarrassed witness of the frolics of her elder sister and her royal and choleric husband. Appearances are always saved. The dénouement of the tales is always such as to satisfy the most demanding puritans. Filial piety, justice, honour, fear of God and honesty are exalted. But above all the most carnal love is always allied with the most spiritual faith. For love is the work of God. It is therefore the divine symbol of perfection and of Allah's creation. God is blessed as the giver of pleasure and the arouser of joy. God is perceived as the support of love and as the permanent arousal of Eros. For the orgasm is a marvel that helps us to become aware of God's effectiveness. It helps us to read the book of creation. Love is a personal experience of the miracles that makes us aware of the work of God. Shahrazād exclaims:

> Glory to Allah who did not create
> A more enchanting spectacle than that of two happy lovers.
> Drunk with voluptuous delights
> They lie on their couch
> Their arms entwined
> Their hands clasped
> Their hearts beating in tune.[53]

In these tales everybody evokes the Quran, God and his Prophet to magnify the work of the flesh. Almond is described thus:

> Her slight body has the colour of silver, and stands like a box-tree; her waist is a hair's breadth, her station is the station of the sun, she has the walk of a partridge. Her hair is of hyacinth, her eyes are sabres of Isfahan; her cheeks resemble the verse of Beauty in the Book; the bows of her brows recall the chapter of the Pen. Her mouth, carved from a ruby, is an astonishment; a dimpled apple is her chin, its beauty spot avails against the evil-eye. Her very small ears were lovers' hearts instead of jewels, the ring of her nose is a slave ring about the moon. The soles of her little feet are altogether charming. Her heart is a sealed flask of perfume, her soul is wise. Her approach is the tumult of the Resurrection! She is the daughter of King Akbar, and her name is Princess Almond. Such names are blessed![54]

The body of a woman, therefore, is a microcosm of the masterly work of God. To lose oneself in it is to find oneself in God. To run over it is to continue the great book of Allah. For it is a reference to the Quran, the Calam and the Resurrection. To take possession of it and to travel with it towards orgasm is to live in anticipation the delights of *janna*. This is how Shahrazād, towards the end of the cyle, on the 998th night, sings this splendid hymn to divine love:

> Love was before the light began,
> When light is over, love shall be;
> O warm hand in the grave, O bridge of truth,
> O ivy's tooth.

> Eating the green heart of the tree
> Of man![55]

How can one resist Shahrazād, who knows so many good things about love and who knows how to evoke them in such a way as to move the most insensitive hearts. On innumerable occasions she describes the joys of the flesh with consummate art:

> Then the girl suddenly dropped her nonchalant pose, as if driven by some irresistible desire, and took me in her arms, and held me tight against her body, and, turning quite pale, swooned into my arms. And she was soon in movement, panting and bubbling over with so much pleasure that the child was soon in its cradle, with no cries, no pain, like a fish in water. And, no longer having to concern myself with my rivals, I could give full vent to my pleasure. And we spent all day and all night, without speaking, without eating and without drinking, in a contortion of limbs. And the horned ram did not spare this battling ewe, and his thrusts were those of a thick-necked father, and the jam he served was the jam of a big pizzle, and the father of whiteness was not inferior to the prodigious tool and the one-eyed assailant had his fill, and the stubborn mule was tamed by the dervish's stick, and the silent starling sang in tune with the trilling nightingale, and the earless rabbit marched in step with the voiceless cock, and the capricious muscle set the silent tongue in movement, and, in short, everything that could be ravished was ravished, and what could be repeated was repeated; and we ceased our labours only with the appearance of morning, to recite our prayers and to go to the baths![56]

One can see how Shahryar was seduced during a thousand and one nights! Who could have complained! In any case Shahrazād was able to interpose between her and her terrible companion the enchantments of love poetry and its poetic loves had an immediate effect since they created in the most admirable way a durable love, a peace of hearts. So much so that at the end of the cycle the king is cured. He emerges convinced that the love in which, when he was jealous and selfish, he did not believe is something marvellous and majestic. It is the king himself who draws these conclusions when he declares to Shahrazād's father: 'May God protect thee, since thou hast married to me thy generous daughter, who hath been the cause of my repenting of slaying the daughters of the people, and I have seen her to be ingenuous, pure, chaste, virtuous. Moreover, God hath blessed me by her with three male children; and praise be to God for this abundant favour!'[57] To be converted to love, therefore, is to be converted to God. The more one cultivates the flesh the better one worships the Lord and the worship of God is a continuous, heartrending call to savour again, to savour forever the constantly renewed joys of a pleasure that is divine in essence. The fervour of the flesh is a fervour of God.

What is even more astonishing is that Shahrazād does not invite us to this conversion by travestying sexuality, by concealing women's defects. On the contrary, the realism, the honour, the cruelty that unfortunately exist and that often exasperate love are not killed, but exposed and often elaborated quite crudely. One abandons everything, business, kingdom, wealth, parents, to find the love that is presented, as in the olden days, as total, embracing all its deviations. For *The Thousand and One Nights* is a sort of sexological encyclopaedia before its time. And nothing is missed out: prostitution, polygamy, homosexuality, male and female, impotence, frigidity, voyeurism, narcissism – and almost anything one can think of![58]

If *The Thousand and One Nights* was so popular it is because its tales do not in fact idealize and magnify woman as she was represented in courtly society. They also succeed in showing the back of the décor. They allow the humble to speak for themselves, but they show everything that women are capable of.

Indeed love is universal and everybody has a right to it, the street porter and the vagabond, as well as the prince and the rich merchant. But, alas, not everybody realizes his dream. And, in *The Thousand and One Nights*, not every love is satisfied. There is, for example, the unhappy tailor, who is tricked by a woman who promises to give herself to him, but in fact denounces him to her husband. He is forced to work free of charge for the suspicious husband: His fate is often that of the poor and humble. He loses everything. Five things combine to bring him low: love, lack of money, hunger, nakedness, tiredness. Tricked and ridiculed, he is thrown out naked into the street.

> He found himself falling headlong into the street of the leather-sellers of Baghdad. When these good fellows saw Haddar appear among them, shaven, naked, and with his face all

> ruddled like a harlot's, they hooted at him and began thrashing him with their skins, until he fell down in a faint. Laughing robustly, they set him on an ass and made a procession with him round all the markets. Finally they carried him to the wali who asked: 'Who is this?' 'He fell among us,' they answered, 'through a trap in the house of the grand wazir. He was like this when he did so.' The wali then ordered Haddar to receive a hundred lashes on the soles of his feet and to be driven from the city.[59]

The tales also convey the social values of love. They are imbued with sociality. They are like a social protest through the demand for love: brigands, *ayyarun*, are not always antipathetic and there are hunchbacks who know how to make love admirably. And why is it so surprising if a woman who has fallen into the hands of a grumpy or suspicious husband takes revenge on him in her own way by cuckolding him? She avenges her class in avenging her sex. Shahrazād wins our applause for adulteries that are merely good tricks played on old greybeards.

Take the lady who, having collected the rings of a hundred lovers who have slept with her, makes this confession:

> 'The givers of these seal-rings have all coupled with me on the unwitting horns of this Ifrīt. So now, O brothers, give me yours!' Then they gave her their seal-rings, taking them off their hands. Whereon she said: 'Know that this Ifrīt carried me off on the night of my marriage, prisoned me in a coffer and placed that coffer in a box and fastened about the box seven chains, yes, and then laid me at the bottom of the moaning sea that wars and dashes with its waves. But he did not know that whenever any one of us women desires a thing, nothing can prevent her from it.'[60]

This is pure *mujūn*, but assumed in the lucid mode of radical feminism. From misogyny to intransigent feminism, *The Thousand and One Nights* develops a remarkable logic.

It is the same continuity that I have tried to develop through the variations evoked in this chapter. These variations situate us in relation to eroticism at points and counterpoints that seem to be contradictory, but are in fact subtly connected to one another through the combined dynamics of love and faith. Misogyny is ultimately a homage to physical love in the sense in which hypocrisy is a homage to virtue, or, to put it another way, it is an anti-homage paid to *mujūn*.

Mujūn seems to me to be one of the summits of Arabo-Muslim culture and *The Thousand and One Nights* is erected as a monument to the glory of fundamental unity. But we can now see that at the level of everyday life and at every level of social life the sacral and the sexual support each other and are both engaged in the same process: that of the defence of the group. This ethics of marital affection based on a frenetically lyrical vision of life leads to a veritable technique of Eros that is itself indissociable from its religious base. Just as there is a religious ritual, there is an erotic ritual and each parallels the other. Arab eroticism, then, is a refined, learned technique whose mission is to realize God's purpose in us. It is therefore a pious, highly recommended work. Indeed it is a matter of helping nature, concretizing life in its most beautiful, most noble aspects and realizing the genetic mission of the body.

In this respect eroticism is a technique of the body and of the mind. Perhaps Arab misogyny is an illusion after all! Supposing it were merely a ruse of love? Or the starting point for any conversion? In every Arab man there may be a dormant Shahryar and in every Arab woman an unsuspected Shahrazād. And here the identification of the teller and the told is not a gratuitous device. It is not a tendency to be sublimated, but an example to follow and a fantasy to be realized. Hence, it seems to me, that unity in functionality of both the descriptions of paradise and the techniques of love. It is not a question of opposing the superior and the inferior. They are welded together as one. So a good orgasm culminates in morning prayers. It is as if prayer is also an expectation of pleasure. Our God, give us this day our daily orgasm!

Lyricism and sacralization of life, the art of assuming sexuality and satisfying it, on the one hand, glorification of God and of his works, on the other, combine in a single reaction: wonder. Wonder conceived by the imaginary and realized in orgasm gives, beyond appearances, the unity of the personality in Arabo-Muslim society. Hence, ultimately, that dialectic of the sacral and the sexual of which misogyny or blasphemy are merely negative moments, and therefore herald the full positivity of orgasm and the vision of God.

CHAPTER 11
Erotology

Arab eroticism, then, flourished in socio-cultural conditions that were exceptionally favourable to it. Over the centuries, an erotology of great scope and refinement (*bāh*) developed that is only now beginning to be studied. Pious souls, grave lawyers, eminent theologians, worthy *kadis* and venerable sheikhs devoted themselves without the slightest embarrassment to the study of eroticism: none of them could have conscientious scruples, for none of them was contravening either the letter or the spirit of the canonic teachings. Muhammad himself set the example, when he encouraged his disciples to venerate the flesh, to attend to the preliminaries of love-making, to sexual play and to fantasy. Beauty is a gift of heaven that one must know how to exploit and set off. For there is an art of making things beautiful, of releasing and refining pleasure. And it is a pious duty for a good Muslim to help all other members of the Umma to become aware of the art of pleasure, to use it consciously, to benefit from it, in a word, to assume their bodies. The techniques of sexual pleasure must be widely spread among the faithful so that the community of Allah does not suffer depression or sorrow. Being a Muslim means knowing how to be happy and cheerful and to know that God's purpose is achieved through the beautiful, not through the ugly, through pleasure, not through contrition. 'Your mouths', said the Prophet,[1] 'are a passageway for the Quran. So perfume them and place *suwāk*[2] in them.' An author who deals with questions of eroticism, perfumery, hygiene and beauty has no reason to blush, therefore, when approaching questions that are neither more nor less noble than grammar, prosody, canon law or history.

The development of Arab civilization, together with its contacts with other eastern cultures, Persian and Hindu in particular, was to create a still greater erotological demand. Concubinage and a more refined lifestyle aroused in everybody a thirst for the new, for change, for fashion and a concern to avoid satiety, monotony and disgust.

Even the norms and canons of the beautiful change from one place and time to another. The ideal woman, for instance, might be variously corpulent, plump, slim or obese. Sometimes large breasts were preferred, sometimes firm round ones. Pink flesh, chubby and curved (*samīna*, *malḥūma*), a wasp-like waist or bamboo-like figure (ghusn al bān, *quḍīb khaizurān* . . .) were fashionable in turn.

Salaheddin al-Munajjid, in a fine essay on 'The canons of female beauty among the Arabs',[3] lays down the various stages in the evolution of taste in this matter in the history of Islamic civilization. Over the centuries taste moved from fat women to well proportioned (majdūlat) women, to tall, slim ones. Bellies with folds of fat, which had been the delight of men in the pre-Islamic period, lost the hold that they had exerted over men, only to be rediscovered in the Ottoman Empire. The Ommayads and Abbasids preferred them taut and smooth. Huge breasts like goats' udders, which had been so highly prized right up to the first century of the Hegira, came to be despised. Increasingly men came to prefer well-proportioned or hemispherical breasts, just large enough to be held in the palm of a single hand. Sometimes even the eccentricity of a fine flat chest had its hour of glory.

The extremely slim waist and the upright bearing came to dislodge the heavy, 'duck-like' walk, only to lose out in turn to a calm, assured step and a more proportioned waist. Pre-Islamic woman was often compared to a cow, a gazelle, the moon or the sun. This reference to nature declined and woman came to be loved for herself alone and the canons of the beautiful became once again more human. 'Can one deny,' Jāḥiḍh wonders, 'that the human eye is in every respect more beautiful than the eye of the gazelle or the cow and that between them there is an irreducible difference?'[4] On the other hand one became more sensitive to the beauties of the mind and to the art of conversation.

Two features however remain permanent: a firm, well-rounded behind and a large, but well-proportioned and clearly visible vagina.

On this eternal evolution of taste as far as women were concerned a very marked homosexual element sometimes played a role. Faced with competition from boys, Arab women sometimes tried to resemble them. The Abbasids, for example, even preferred a tomboy type of woman, with hair cut very short and a manly stride. There is a whole area of Arab erotology – the shaving of the vagina, for instance – that cannot be understood except by reference to this homosexual element that played such a crucial role in the development both of pederasty and of lesbianism.

So there was a strong demand for erotology and the various specialized handbooks responded to that demand in a systematic way. The erotological literature known to us stretches at least from Jāḥiḍh to Hassan Khan, that is to say, a period lasting almost a thousand years. Unfortunately very little of it has survived. Ibn Nadīm's *Fihrist*, of the late tenth century, gives us the titles of about a hundred treatises, almost all of which are lost. Some have survived in manuscript form in public or private, eastern and western collections. There are also, as we might expect, a good many 'inventions', of which the *Jawāmi'al-ladhdha* (Encyclopaedia of Pleasure), at present in the hands of Salaheddin al-Munajjid, is a fine example. But at present fewer than ten or so of the treatises have been published.

The oldest treatise in our possession is certainly Jāḥiḍh's *Mufākharat al-jawārī wal ghilmān*[5] (Concubines and Youths in Competition), which dates from the ninth century. The *Kitāb al'urs wal'arāis* (Book of Marriage and Newly-weds) has also been attributed to Jāḥiḍh, but would seem to be of a later date.

To the same period belongs a book that is now lost, but whose contents we know: *Al alfiyya* (The Thousand). It consists of the 'Memoirs' of a Hindu woman who, having married a thousand men and thus acquired an unrivalled sexual experience, wishes to share with the reader the lessons that she has learnt. Moreover the book was illustrated, a rare thing for the period, with erotic nudes illustrating the various sexual positions. This learned, exhaustive, systematic anthology was highly successful. It was plagiarized and copied, but unfortunately has not survived.

Ibn Nasr's *Jawāmi'-al ladhdha* has not yet been published. We know it through the work of al-Munajjid, who seems at present to be the owner of the only copy.[6]

Then there is the *Nuzhat al ash'āb fi mu'āsharatal aḥbāb* by As Samaw-al Ibn al-Maghribī al-Israyly, who died in 1170/576. Chapter 10 of that book is of particular interest. It concerns the buying of concubines and provides judicious information on the mores of the time. It gives useful advice as to how to palpate and examine the merchandise so as not to be cheated by the slave merchants. Before concluding a deal over a new acquisition one should proceed to a detailed examination of the organs of the body one by one. Chapter 10 also refers to physiognomy (*'ilm al firāsa*), which, as we can imagine, had great importance at the time: how can one deduce from the body of a *jāriya* the spiritual and intellectual qualities that she may possess? The same chapter provides the 'tricks' to be used against the ploys of the *nakhkhāsūn* (concubine merchants), who set up their stalls in fairs or street corners and who all too often try to deceive the purchasers. This manuscript is still unpublished.[7]

Ahmad Ibn Yūssef at Tīfashī (died 1253/651) left a work entitled *Nuzhat al-albāb fī mā lā yūjadū fī kītāb.* This treatise is devoted almost entirely to forbidden loves. How is *zinā* to be performed undisturbed, how is one to recognize at a distance and beneath her canonical veil a woman who is ready to trade her charms, even if external appearances do not at first sight reveal this? Pederasty and its advantages are described at some length. There are also youths who are available and the chapter described how they are to be located and seduced. Hermaphrodites are not forgotten. There are even precise instructions as to how to make the best of their company. Lesbianism and nymphomania are the subjects of a well-documented and salacious chapter. Another chapter is devoted to masculine women, who behave like males with effeminate passive men. This book is also in manuscript.[8]

The *Kitāb al-bāhyya wal tarākīb alsulṭāniyya* by Nusayr al-dīn al-Fūsi (died 1273/672) is devoted above all to medicine and pharmacopoea. It includes a very interesting chapter devoted to a sort of erotology of clothes in relation to the different seasons. Clothes are seen as an oneiric value capable of concealing or improving the body and therefore of arousing desire. There is a whole art involved here that takes advantage of seasonal changes.[9]

Better known is the *Rujū' al shā-ib ilā ṣibāh.* (How an Old Man Rediscovers his Youth) by Ahmad Ibn Sulayman, also known as Ibn Kamal Basha (died 1573/940). This book, written at the request of the Sultan Selīm Khan, is an intelligent and exhaustive compilation, largely made up of borrowings from earlier works. The author stresses the purity of his intentions in coming to the aid of the sexually handicapped, who are 'incapable of realizing their wishes in a lawful manner'. The book gives an important place to medicine, to which the whole of the first part is devoted. The second, more varied part concerns the arousal of desire, perfumery, poetry, techniques and positions, narcotics, drugs, somnambulism and semi-conscious states.[10] The *Tuḥfat al 'arūs wa rau ḍhat al-nufūs* by Mohammed al-Maghraby al-Tījānī (died 1543/950), begins with a very classic evocation of chastity in marriage. The search for satisfaction of the sexual appetite is legitimate and to be recommended on condition that it is carried out in a lawful manner. There follow very detailed, very pictorial and highly eroticized descriptions of the female body. Chapter 12, which concerns 'coitus and dance', is highly original. Chapter 13, on 'coitus elsewhere than in the vagina', provides information concerning intimate and sometimes unexpected behaviour in Arab societies. This book, too, as far as I know, is as yet unpublished.[11]

Mention should be made of an anonymous poem of 2,400 verses, *Nuzhat al nufūs wa daftar al 'ilm wa rauḍat al 'arūs fi umūr al nikāh wa ghayrihi.*[12] This is a compendium of Arab eroticism in the form of *urjūza*, a strictly classical form. One chapter is devoted to physiognomy and a sort of characteral geography of penises and vaginas ('*mā yata'allaqu min 'ilmal-firāsa biljimā wal dhukūri wal furūj wa tibā'i ahl al-bilādi*').

It would have been surprising if the prolific Suyūti (died 1505) had not devoted some of his time to erotology. In fact he wrote several treatises, some of which have survived, including the *nawāṣir al-īk fi nawādir al-nīk, al-wāfī bil wafiyat, al-wishāh fi fawā-id al-nikāḥ,*[13] *al-yawāqīt al-thamīna fī ṣifāt al-samīn, mu'akkid al-maḥabba bayn al muhibb wa man aḥabb.*[14]

These five books are still in manuscript. On the other hand, *alidhāḥ' fi 'ilm al nikāḥ*[15] has been published many times: it is a very popular work. Special mention should also be made of another of Suyūti's books, *al-raḥma fil-ṭibb wal-ḥikma,*[16] which includes twenty-nine chapters devoted to therapeutics and sexual pharmacopoeia.

Certainly the book written by the sheikh Nefzāwi in the sixteenth century for a bey of Tunis, *al-Rauḍ al'āṭir fi nuzhat al khāṭir,*[17] more commonly known in the west as *The Perfumed Garden*, represents the most popular prototype of this erotic literature. After describing in turn what is praiseworthy and blameworthy in men and women, the sheikh analyses in masterly fashion the various stages in the work of the flesh, accompanying his descriptions with spicy details, indecent stories and judicious advice.

Chapters 7, 8, 9 and 10 are a review of the various names given to the male and female sexual organs in man and in the animals. Chapters 11 and 12 add to the pleasures of the act itself an evocation of female wiles. Then come the aphrodisiacs (Chapter 13), sterility (Chapters 14 and 15), abortion (Chapter 16), the untying of laces (Chapter 17), prescriptions for enlarging the male member (Chapter 18), perfumes (Chapter 19), pregnancy (Chapter 20) and, finally, a supplement devoted to the art of increasing one's virility. All this is intercut with erotic poetry, witticisms, riddles and spicy antecdotes.

Is it mere chance or is it because *The Perfumed Garden* is so perfect that erotological literature seems to have dried up? It was not until the nineteenth century that a revival of the genre began to take place, but then the influence of Europe was particularly marked. Only one handbook from this period seems to me to be worthy of its illustrious forebears. This is an essay by Mohammed Sādiq Hassan Khān published in Constantinople in 1878/1296, under the title *Nashawāt al-sakrān min sabbā tidkhār al-ghizlān*,[18] which may be translated as *Delights, Drunkenness, Wine, Memories and Gazelles*. It is in a sense the swansong of Arab erotology. After the first part, devoted to *'ishq* (passionate love), the author analyses the notion of the beautiful (*ḥusn*), distinguishing between the beautiful woman who reveals her beauty at once (*jamīla*) and the one who reveals it only gradually, as one explores her with one's eyes, gestures or any other way (*malīḥa*).[19]

Hence the pleasure of discovering and the acted-out inventory of the female body. Love is an aesthetic, explorative adventure of the other's body. All eroticism consists, then, of a woman beginning with *malāḥa* and with *jamāl*. The opposite betokens a lack of taste, an error of judgment and a crime against pleasure.

The author, who was well acquainted with the *Kāma Sūtra* and the *Atharvaveda*, sets out to explain the erotic differences between the Hindu and Muslim domains in terms of the difference in juridical status enjoyed by women in the two cultures.[20] In India a woman is always the woman of a single man. She follows her husband even to the funeral pyre. Furthermore, in India, it is the woman who takes the erotic initiative, whereas in Islam it is the man who does so, since the rotation of women gives him a measure of choice. The author also provides us with valuable historical clues as to the homosexuality of his time. At first, it was a matter of Greek acculturation; then it became Turco-Persian before being fully integrated into the Arabo-Muslim societies. However, homosexual eroticism was to remain unknown in India. The 'typology' of women, which the author draws up according to age, acquired experience[21] and natural gifts[22] is not without interest or insight. The end of the essay is an anthology of erotic poetry in which rhythm, metaphor and expression constitute a veritable festival of mind, heart, imagination and, of course, body.

I have mentioned only those works that I have been able to consult personally or those concerning which al-Munajjid has provided valuable information. But there are many others, scattered throughout various public and private collections. In the Bibliothèque Nationale in Paris there are other erotic manuscripts, but I have not been able to study them.[23]

I have given some idea of the quantity of this technical literature. It developed according to a number of axes, the most important of which I shall now analyse.

By a curious coincidence, the sheikh Nefzāwi, like Shahrazād, also had to save his head. And it was the promise made to the monarch who had just condemned him to death to write the *Rauḍ al-'Āṭir* that was to get him pardoned. According to a legend well known in the Maghreb, he was about to be put to death by the bey of Tunis when, in order to save himself, he promised the sovereign to write a book that would arouse his exhausted ardour. As in the project of *The Thousand and One Nights*, initiation into the secrets of eroticism is presented as the only thing worthy of bringing back to the joys and pleasure of life not only those whom one has initiated, but also the initiator himself. Eroticism saves love and maintains life in the master as well as in the disciple. The purpose of the erotological project is to provide a sufficient dose of *joie de vivre*, the renewed miracle of sexuality, both at the level of practice and at the level of knowledge, at the level of experience and at the level of the art of organizing experience.

When we look at the content of Arab eroticism more closely, we cannot fail to be struck by the role invariably played by language and by speech skilfully used to incantatory ends. It is as if the verbal evocation of sexual acts, gestures and organs were itself erotic. There is an erotology simply at the level of naming. The accumulation of words creates a veritable verbal hallucination.

The magic of erotic discourse explodes in the three chapters of *The Perfumed Garden* in which the sheikh gives the series of words that designate the organs of generation. 'The male organ is called the bellows, the dove, the piston, the untamable, the liberator, the rampant, the agitator, the witty gambler, the sleeper, the sledge-hammer, the hewer, the extinguisher, the turner, the striker, the master-swimmer, the enterer, the leaver, the one-eyed, the bald one, the battering-ram, the stubborn one, the necked one, the hairy one, the shameless one, the weeper, the raiser, the spitter, the lapper, the rammer, the seeker, the rubber, the rummager, the discoverer.' And the sheikh adds, not without explaining the reason and origin of each name, 'There are others and it is up to everyone to find other names for his own use!'[24]

When he comes to women, the list is hardly less exhaustive or suggestive for the vagina is also called: 'the crest, the asker, the hedgehog, the sprinkler, the taciturn, the starling, the crusher, the voracious one, the sweller, the glutton, the fortified, the broad, the dissimulator, the bottomless, the little hunchback, the doubly lipped, the restless one, the possessive one, the sieve, the complaisant one, the assistant, the moon, the cavernous one, the lengthened one, the stretched one, the one opposite, the fugitive, the patient, the purged one, the juicy one, the one that bites, the one that sucks, the delicately erect, the warm, the source of pleasure'.[25]

The sheikh is quite obviously amusing himself here, as he is throughout the book. Indeed he is merely continuing a tradition that was well established in Arabic erotic literature in which the word conjures up a whole state of mind or series of images. One literally gargles with words. And the oneiric charge is made all the stronger. Of course rhythm and rhyme lead to poetry that is sometimes obscene, but sometimes of excellent quality.

A fine example is the magnificent poem that ends the *Nashwat al-sakrān* by Hassan Khan, who attributes it to Ghulam Ali Azad al-Baljarāmy. This poem of a hundred and five lines describes the poet's lady from top to toe. The forty-five parts of the body and the seven colours are each given a distych, the last line constituting a sort of conclusion. In this model of the genre erotic evocations are carried to an extreme and the poem as a whole is written in the most classical *qasida* style.

The breasts inspire these lines:

Two friends!
A profusion of elegance,
Breast of my lady,
Understanding with the heavens,
On the prow of the perfect,
Erection of pride;
And that little red cap
Stuck on the head.[26]

The vagina is evoked thus:

Gift of Eden,
Once given to my lady,
Two bananas perhaps,
To shorten, to entwine.
No. Double bow for a single arrow.
Hope, yes, my arrow,
Hope, that I shall not feel pain.[27]

Sheikh Nefzāwi's lines are hardly less moving or less obsessive, though they already advocate the art of 'making love not war':

I, fight
Against Turks, Arabs and Persians?
Never!
Love is my preference,
Work of the flesh, my joy,
Without fear or favour.[28]

The beginning of the *Īḍhāḥ* by sheikh Suyūti is interesting in a number of ways; for its verbal play and also for its great impertinence. The tone is irreverent and the text begins with what is quite simply a pastiche in rhymed prose of the traditional Friday sermon. This is extraordinary on the part of a pious *faqīh*, reputedly a great commentator on the Quran. Here are a few significant – and relatively decent – passages:

Praise be to God, who created rods straight and hard as spears to wage war on vaginas and hardly anywhere else!

Praise be to him who made our preference go always to girls and never to boys!

Praise be to Him who gave us as a gift the pleasure of nibbling and sucking lips, of laying breast against breast, thigh against thigh and laying our purses on the threshold of the door of clemency!

You who believe, may God be clement to you, be attentive, use to the full so many delicate pleasures!

Eternal glory and salvation be to those among you who know how to embrace as one should a delicate cheek, to give the right accolade to a slender waist, mount the largest vaginas in the correct way and sprinkle them quickly with the sweetness of their honey. . . .

Give thanks to God in fitting manner, let us rub and plunge, drink wine and warm ourselves, batter and retreat, make our demands and knock on the door, know how to alternate the proudest with the most energetic acts.[29]

The erotic pleasure itself is duplicated by that of impertinence. Blasphemy is an erotic factor, for it adds to the intrinsic pleasure the real joy of contravening common morality and of adding to the frissons of the flesh the spice of the forbidden. In so far as Islam tolerated the work of the flesh recourse to blasphemy gives a touch of non-conformity without which eroticism would be lost in the well-trodden paths of canonical tradition. Did not Abu Nawās show the way when he declared that 'a *mujūn* without blasphemy is worthless'.[30]

So the stories, descriptions, anecdotes, poetry with which the Arabic erotological works are studded, are very often recounted in a mocking, libertine tone – and sometimes quite simply in one of unbelief, apostasy and *kufr*. The love of a Christian youth inspires one poet to the following somewhat unMuslim reflections:

Perhaps my wrong is to be a Muslim in his eyes? But the sins that I have piled up since I have loved him have certainly lessened my faith!

My praying and fasting have become irregular and because of my beloved the unlawful has become lawful for me.

I would be very disappointed if my beloved did not allow me a victory.

Can I be for him a cross [that he would always wear]? I would then always be present at his side. . . .[31]

The homosexual affections of the qāḍi often give rise to fine, somewhat indecent jokes at the expense of religion.[32] The impertinence becomes cruder when the youth who has made the qāḍi lose his head is himself a Jew or a Christian.[33]

The story of Mossaylama, the man who claimed to compete with Muhammad in prophecy and to whom one owes the famous pastiches of the Quran, inspires sheikh Nefzāwi to a truly Voltairean tone. He recounts how a woman, Shajāḥ'a al-Thamīnya, who also claimed to be a Prophetess, threw out a challenge to Mossaylama, who, perplexed and annoyed, decided to follow the erotic advice that he had received from a friend!

> Tomorrow morning, erect a tent of many coloured silk. Spread rich silken materials on the ground. Sprinkle it with perfume of rose petal, orange flower, eglantine, jasmine, carnation, violet and other essences. Then in golden containers burn incense. Take care to make the tent air-tight so that none of the scents may escape. When the smoke of the incense has mingled with the odours of the scented waters, take your place upon your throne and send for her.
>
> Then receive her in the tent alone. When she has smelled so many odours, everything within her will soften. She will become intoxicated. She will almost lose consciousness. Then make advances to her worthy of a man such as yourself. She will give herself entirely to you. Possess her. Once you have lain with her she will be delivered of the evil that she can do to you and to her men.

Of course things turn out exactly as planned, since even our enemies cannot resist the intoxicating powers of perfumes. On her return home the false prophetess describes her conversion to 'the religion of Mossaylama' in these terms: 'He recited the revelation of God to me. And he showed me the truth. I am therefore joining him.'[34]

Elsewhere the sheikh shows great powers of observation and in what he writes sensuality is allied to spirituality. Amber paste and sandalwood are used in the making of sweet-smelling rosaries that are highly prized by the Muslims. Now, with time, these rosaries take on a fine, velvety, shiny polish. Sheikh Nefzāwi observed that, to the delightful aroma given off by the beads when stroked by the fingers, is added a sort of highly erotic tactile pleasure. For him, to tell his beads is to caress a woman and conversely!

> For a woman is like basil: if one wishes to savour its perfume

> one must take its leaves between one's fingers and rub them; then the plant will give off its scent, otherwise one will get nothing, for it will jealously keep its delectable essence. Similarly, to bring a woman to sexual incandescence, treat her like basil. Use every means of giving her your mouth, your tongue, your hands and your member.[35]

The vision of *The Perfumed Garden*, then, combines tactile and olfactory sensations, eroticism of the body, imagination and religious spirituality. In this it belongs to the authentic Islamic tradition. Furthermore all the handbooks of erotology devote some section to corporal hygiene and the use of scent.[36] For hygiene is an element of eroticism, just as eroticism is a factor in hygiene. Here is a simple recipe given by Suyūti: 'Pound some spikes of dried lavender, knead with rose water and place in the vagina.'[37]

Pharmacopoeia has an essential place in erotology. Compounds and simples are abundantly prescribed as aphrodisiacs or abortifacients. To increase virile potency Kamal Pasah advocates taking every morning honey mixed with fenugreek; eating in the evening, before going to sleep, pistachio nuts, pine kernels, walnuts, almonds and coconuts. Poppyseed also increases virility as does cinnamon, safflower and bastard saffron.[38]

The woman's pleasure is increased if, before the work of the flesh, one has been prudent enough to proceed in the following manner: take pomegranate peel, finely pounded, stir in honey, form into small balls and, prior to coitus, take one of the balls and suck it. One may also dilute this product in saliva and smear it on the member.[39] Kamal Pasha recommends as an aphrodisiac onion,[40] scammony,[41] purpura,[42] linseed, raisins, lavender seed, radishes,[43] and cress. Cabbages, too, have wonderful virtues.[44]

Ejaculatio praecox may be retarded by treatment with honey and nutmeg. Impotence may be cured by eating honey, pyrethrum, nettle seed, spurge, green ginger and cardamom.[45]

A treatment to keep the member erect consists in steeping leeches in good oil and smearing it on to the penis. The efficacy of the recipe is increased if one leaves the mixture to steep in a bottle that is itself buried in warm manure: this produces a homogeneous liniment.[46] If one wishes to make the member longer, then the best recipe is the following:

> Five measures of nitrated borax, five measures of lavender seed dried or powdered, five measures of honey and five measures

of milk. Pound well. Smear the member with a little of the product. Massage the member well, sprinkle hot water on it from time to time. When the member is red, wash it and massage it again. This recipe is guaranteed, well tried and effective.[47]

Sometimes it is the woman who is to be treated. Frigidity is cured thus: 'Camomile and asphodel pounded and mixed with lubin oil in equal quantities. The woman who smears it on her vagina will burn with desire and will not rest until she is satisfied.'[48]

Here is another marvellous recipe, known as 'the matter of life' (*mādaat al ḥayāt*), especially intended for the use of philosophers. An ounce of each of the following ingredients: ground pimento, essence of pimento, ginger, tubipore, pine kernels, *amlaj* and *ahlaj*,[49] a little of the powder known as 'cold fire', which may be replaced by walnut shell. To this one adds half an ounce of herbane, a coconut, and three ounces of the plants known as 'fox's testicles' and 'skeleton of red wolf'. Work into an oily paste. Each time one must take of it an amount equal to five times the size of a hazelnut.[50] This 'philosopher's jam is effective in eliminating phlegm, fortifying the spirits, aiding digestion, giving a youthful glow to the face, putting on weight, sharpening the wits, improving elocution, curing colds, cleaning the urethral tract, calming aerophagia, increasing and thickening sperm, lengthening the penis, keeping the teeth in place, eliminating aches in the back, the joints, the waist and the sides.'[51]

Sheikh Suyūti provides a marvellous recipe that was given him by a sultan of Tlemcen, who had tried it out himself and succeeded in deflowering fifty virgins in a single night. One takes the testicles of three (or eight or fourteen) male chickens. One adds green ginger, nutmeg, walnut essence, pimento essence, tubipore, cloves, cinnamon, dried earth from India, palm seeds known as the seeds of intelligence, an ounce of salt from Hyderabad and a quarter of an ounce of saffron. Grind, work together and pound with a good skimmed honey. Put the mixture into a glass container. Seal hermetically with a stopper made of a little clay of wisdom. Leave the mixture to simmer near a fire for three nights and three days until it thickens. Leave it to cool. Form into small balls the size of chick peas and take the equivalent of a lentil grain whenever one wishes to make love. The member then becomes erect and nothing will be able to soften it unless one drinks a little vinegar.[52]

Sheikh Nefzāwi recommends a diet of thick honey, almonds, pine kernels or a mixture of onion seeds pounded with honey. One may also 'rub the member with ass's milk or camel fat, which is a very effective lubricant. The man thus acquires a virile firmness that will win the congratulations of his partner.'[53]

Among the hundreds of recipes to be found in this prolific literature I have found ones claiming to cure love, others that inflict it, others that sharpen the appetites of old women, or suppress those of the young, others that treat dysmenorrhoea and amenorrhoea, others that recreate an artificial virginity in girls who for one reason or another have lost it. One curious treatment is suggested for jealous husbands who wish to protect themselves from being cuckolded: such a man has merely to smear wolf's bile on his penis and have intercourse with his wife. Any other man than he who tries to approach his wife will find himself impotent.[54] The birth control section is rich and varied: it includes camphor, which the woman is supposed to eat, the urine of a castrated ram, which she must drink, and a rabbit's heart embalmed in mint, which she must wear as an amulet. Another method of guaranteed efficacy is to place some alum powder in the vagina.[55]

Nor should we forget all the recipes available for curing sterility[56] and for 'waking the sleeping child',[57] or aborting an unwanted foetus.

The list, as we can see, is extremely rich, stretching from love philtres to abortifacients. Most of the recipes, whose effectiveness is praised and guaranteed, seem to be based on a good knowledge of the pharmaceutical virtues of a few simples such as lavender, fenugreek, scammony, ginger, saffron, etc. It certainly suggests a trade that must have been extremely active, survivals of which are still to be observed in the Sidi Mehrez souk at Tunis and at the Khan Khalili in Cairo or in Medina, where one can still find on sale dragon's teeth and ogre's milk or that celebrated clay of wisdom. . . .

The psychical factors, especially in the case of Sheikh Nefzāwi, are far from being ignored and are indeed approached in a most interesting and thorough way. 'There are subversive minds,' he writes, 'who attribute a woman's inaptitude in love to the intervention of evil djinns. This is an aberration. To make love well one has only to be healthy in body and mind – and above all not to be over fat, which forces men and women to exhausting and somewhat grotesque gymnastic exercise.'[58] He attributes impotence to psychological causes. 'It often comes from ill-observed causes. First a general coldness of temperament, which may be altered by various means. . . . Treatment by suggestion . . . is sometimes very effective if the patient is emotional.'[59] In fact the true remedy for impotence is – again – eroticism.

For nothing can beat a good kiss as a prelude to love: 'The kiss is a savoursome thing, like those delicacies intended to stimulate the appetite, but which must be followed by more substantial fare that nourishes a man's body.'[60] There is an art of kissing and even an entire gamut in that art:

> First on the cheeks, then on the lips, finally on the breasts, which one thus arouses into turgescence, then one descends lower to the belly, to the sweet convexity; the tongue is skilfully inserted in the crater of the navel, then into another more intimate one. . . . There is an art in bringing women's sensuality to the point of effervescence that leads to perfect bliss. One must not be hasty, but carry out all the formalities, which are so many necessary stages to complete pleasure. Pleasure must be reciprocal if it is really to be the great festival of the senses: the man who is concerned only with coming himself, without at the same time getting the woman to come, is a poor wretch who wastes his virile strength. . . .[61]

Of course there is nothing blameworthy in this art and the sheikh does not forget to remind us:

> Such are the recommendations of the Most High to bring to its height an act so essential that it should never be a chore, but always a means of achieving happiness by making a woman happy. This is the secret of human happiness, permitted by God and even encouraged by Him, to whom we owe life and everything that embellishes it.[62]

Lastly mention should be made of a sort of 'geo-erotology', the purpose of which is to distinguish the love practised by different peoples and to learn by varying the choice of partners to vary one's own experiences.

> Byzantine women are supposed to have very healthy vaginas, but they are reproached with having them wide, and lacking

> in depth. Spanish women are the most beautiful and most perfumed. Indian, Chinese and Slav women are the most hateful, least good looking, dirtiest, most stupid. Negresses are delectable and obedient. Distinctions must be made among Arab women. Iraqi women are the most exciting, Syrian women the most affectionate, but the best, of course, are the Arab and Persian women. They are the most fruitful, the most loving and the most faithful. Nubian women have very warm vaginas, better furnished posteriors, more harmonious bodies and repeatedly arouse desire. Turkish women have cold vaginas. They get pregnant at once, are ill-tempered and rancorous, but are highly intelligent. . . . Egyptian women are clever at saying the right things. They are warm in temperament and easily abandon themselves to the joys of love. The most agreeable Egyptian women for coitus are those of the upper Nile region. Those of the lower Nile have larger vaginas and the peasant women are the most insatiable.[63]

Such references belong of course to an erotic perspective historically conditioned by the political, economic and cultural factors of the period. The role of concubinage is obvious here, since it was this practice that made possible the co-existence in Muslim towns of *jawāri* from every part of the empire. Rotation of women, frequent changes of partner, contacts with civilizations geographically close to Islam provided something for all tastes and a desire to 'collect' a variety of pleasures. Hence that extraordinary erotic vision of the world open to every kind of amorous experience. Cultural exchanges and the processes of acculturation necessarily included an erotological dimension.

Unfortunately we cannot at present explore this area further, for little is still known about it. The history of Arab eroticism is still to be written. There is still not a single scholarly edition of any of the innumerable treatises referred to above – and I have had to confine myself to a few references that, moving away from the obscene, give us a splendid, refined view of love. But in doing so I have had to set aside innumerable other works.[64]

Indeed eroticism is so inextricably bound up with the cultural life of the Arabo-Muslim societies that annotations, passages, even whole chapters are to be found interpolated in any work of literature, law, history, etc. Eroticism is not exclusive.

Thus Ibn 'Abd Rabbih's *'Aqd al-farīd* includes a fine chapter on women[65] and an entire book on love. Muhammad Nāzli's *khazīnat al-asrār* is a book of mysticism that treats of the spiritual values to be found in innumerable verses of the Quran and the hadiths. Nevertheless it includes a chapter devoted to *zinā* and how to protect oneself from it by, among other things, reciting certain quranic verses.[66]

There is a treatise on physiognomy, the *kitāb al-siyāsa fi 'ilm al-firāsa* by the imam Shamsal-dīn al Ansāri. The descriptive analysis of the anatomy of the soft parts of the body provides an opportunity, which the author does not miss, of innumerable erotic digressions.[67]

The *Mustafraf*, which is presented as a sort of encyclopaedia, could not fail to pay a good deal of attention to the question. So chapters devoted to singing, musicians, love, women, poetry and affection find their place in the most natural way imaginable in the most specialized erotic treatises.[68] And of course Ibn El Qayyam al-Jawzia's *akhbār al-nisā* also contains a good measure of erotic material.[69]

Without going into greater detail, I think I have now given a sufficiently clear account of the scope, nature and function of Arabo-Muslim eroticism. Eroticism is the art of arousing, sustaining, satisfying and renewing desire. Hence so much refinement, constantly imbued with love poetry, unbounded fantasy and powerful oneirism. The erotic science of the Arab allows him to spend a whole night in an orgy of perfumes, feasting, drinking and marvellous women, in turn maintaining, satisfying and renewing desire. The time of love is a magnificent arabesque in which failure is approached, but always avoided and achievement, once attained, turns out to be a starting-point for a new beginning. Only dawn prayers can put an end to this skilful use of the night. The sublimation of women is ultimately an art of spiritualizing the flesh, of going in a sense beyond sensuality and grasping through the enchantments of orgasm and the magic of love the splendid mystery of the work and love of God. One may really speak of an Islamic art of sexual ecstasy. By accepting and recommending the joys of love Islam made possible that integration of all forms of sensuality in a lyrical vision of life.

This lyrical vision of life is also a sensualization in time. Nothing is so alien to our domain than the brief act. It is not a question of getting through the work of flesh as it were some chore that one has to carry out. One must lose oneself in pleasure and extend the time of its performance. Hence the importance of 'foreplay'. The woman who goes to the hammam and spends long hours preparing the most varied, the most studied, the most skilfully composed delicacies and the man who goes to the market looking for food, drink, silks and perfumes are merely preparing themselves for long nights of love. Sometimes the whole of daily life is structured with a view to the supreme end of sexual bliss.

Hence the importance of so many practices that seem, at first sight, far removed from Eros, but which are in reality merely a prefiguration of it.

Arab cooking is an erotic alchemy. Sport, hunting and dancing are also eroticized. The hammam is an eroticized place. In short, everything that concerns the body has a sexual dimension.

Eroticism is also an attempt to attain the absolute through the body. The techniques of the body play a role here similar to those of gestures in prayer. Hence that positional eroticism that I have already referred to and which, implying a permanent adjustment of the partners to one another, is a gift of love through the mediation of gesture.

So the bodies must be maintained in a fit condition so that they are able to carry out this mediating role. Hence the extraordinary place occupied by pharmacopoeia and perfumes. It is a question of nourishing the body, of arousing desire in it, of increasing its strength with a view to the splendid role that it has to play. Revelation is not a gratuitous gift, but is conveyed through the flesh. Mossaylama's *The Perfumed Garden* is particularly revealing in this respect.

Erogenous perfumes and aphrodisiacs throw us at once into the oneiric world in which matter serves as a support and contributes its immense power of suggestion. Erotic unctions, the use of smells, pleasant or strong, heavy or intoxicating, form part of the preparation for love. The erotic atmosphere is certainly enhanced by the odours, whose role in the treatment of anxiety and impotence are described at length in the Arabic treatises.

'The associative power of olfactory sensations is immense. The habit of practising coitus in a fragrant atmosphere, of linking the possession of a partner with a particular scent, is regarded as a very strong conditioned reflex.'[70] Here Gérard Zwang is merely taking up where Nafzāwi and Siyūti left off, but without knowing it.

Perfume is such an airy form of matter that it penetrates the body and gives the illusion of a marriage between the spirit and the senses. It is no accident if it is an attribute common to amorous and religious practices. Here again we find the intimate union of the most aroused sensuality and the most spiritual faith.

Eroticism is total. It goes well beyond the simple domain of coitus. As a quest for the absolute, it tends to reconstitute on the basis of the religious and the profane a sacred that embraces them both within a spiritual and carnal sacrality.

Canalizing the spirit and spiritualizing the flesh is, in my opinion, the essential feature of the Islamic undertaking. The sublimation of the flesh is the work at once of speech, the body and the material imagination. Arab erotology – and Muhammad himself set the example – insists that words should accompany coitus. Silent, furtive coitus is worthless. Love cannot be silent. This is because language conveys tenderness and makes the feelings reciprocal. It makes the desire shared. By giving expression to desire language makes it a possession shared jointly by the speaker and the listener. So speech becomes song, music, even pure music. If Eros and Logos go together it is because they are both carnal and spiritual reciprocity. And it is speech, in its true forms of poetry and song, that makes this reciprocity possible.

Hence the idea of a total, absolute Eros that is its own end. Procreation may occur, but it is neither necessary nor sufficient. One may try to integrate it or to eliminate it entirely. That is not the problem. For sensuality still preserves a value *per se*. It is a reunion with the absolute and even with a fourfold absolute: the absolute of my body, the absolute of the other, the absolute of love, the absolute of creation. Love, then, is so rich and so enriching that it is worth the trouble to bring everything possible into its service. Arab eroticism is ultimately a service of the absolute.

CHAPTER 12
Certain practices

In posing the radical legitimacy of the practice of sexuality, Islam helped in the formation of a specific form of culture. The continuous outpouring of oneirism, combined with the exuberance of the most delicate and most elaborate eroticism, gave birth to a particularly original and attractive mode of life. In various ways, conscious and unconscious, social and individual, enigmatic and clear, this mode of life reveals the many, sometimes contradictory implications of the fundamentally lyrical way in which Islam confronts life. To be attentive to one's own body, to assume it in its totality, to take one's own fantasies seriously, to make the quest for orgasm an essential aim of earthly life and even of the life to come, are some of the aims of Islam. This was expressed on the concrete plane by a number of 'features', which I have already described. A highly elaborate doctrine of *nikāḥ* and *ḥisān*; a vision of ritual purity; an obsession, mixed with a very serious hope, of having relations with the world of the spirits; a structure of domestic life based on the rotation of women and the complementary co-existence of wives and anti-wives; the promotion of eroticism to the rank of a science, on a level with grammar, the fiqh or quranic exegesis. . . . It also became apparent that social structures left their mark on a history of which I have been able to provide no more than a few glimpses. We have seen how concubinage finally affected Arab femininity and expressed in Manichean terms what in principle ought to be complementarity and harmony. If Arab woman *qua* wife came to embody seriousness, motherhood and the survival of the group, it was left to the *jawāri* to make their own the ludic, the poetic and aesthetic. Similarly it became apparent that economic, even ecological, considerations finally separated the rotation of women and the circulation of goods so that, excluded from inheritance and from any claim to a share of the patrimony, Arab woman saw her *de facto* condition fall well below that of the most solemn quranic statements. Hence the need to construct, on the basis of other sacred texts, which, though just as authentic as the first, were divorced from their context and interpreted from a misogynist point of view, a justification for the intrinsic inferiority of woman. Of course the development of eroticism and *mujūn* also involved, in view of this context, the terrible risk of reducing women to the rank of playthings whose sole purpose was the satisfaction of the sexual selfishness of more or less blasé males. Hence, too, that obsession with 'sexual renewal', sometimes impossible to achieve, except at the expense of enormous sacrifices imposed on women who, married too young and to old, impotent men, had no sooner reached womanhood than they were widowed.

In order to grasp the most radical implications of this dialectic of the sacral, the sexual and the social, perhaps one should go back to an even more basic level and try to understand the organization of sexual experience as it has existed in everyday life. Without in any way claiming to exhaust a subject that is as vast as life itself, I propose to examine a few particularly significant aspects of everyday life: the hammam, circumcision, prostitution and obscene folklore, all areas in which scientific exploration certainly makes possible a more detailed, more judicious approach.

1 The hammam

'Cleanliness is part of the faith,' a hadith declares. As we have seen, ritual purification is required after performing physiological activities. Washing oneself, cleaning oneself, purifying oneself, scenting oneself, in short, taking care of one's own body has always been the quranic obligation that has been most widely observed in all countries and at every period affected by Islam. So it is hardly surprising if the institution of the public bath (hammam) spread so widely and so rapidly during the period of Islamic expansion.

In the tenth century Baghdad boasted twenty-seven thousand hammams or even, according to some obviously exaggerated claims, sixty thousand. Cordoba had between five and six thousand. Whereas the Roman *thermae* were concentrated only in the larger cities, the hammams were everywhere. Every small township or village had its hammam. In the towns there was at least one hammam in each district, if not in each street. I have calculated that there was one hammam per fifty inhabitants in Baghdad and per eighty inhabitants in Aghlabite Kairwan.[1]

Certainly pre-Islamic Arabia does not appear to have benefited, as did the Middle East and especially Egypt, the Maghreb and Andalusia, from the Roman inheritance. But, in the civilization that it built up on the ruins of the Roman empire, Islam was to integrate the imperial *thermae*, taking over its structures and organizations, but putting it to new uses. A systematic comparison from the cultural point of view of the Roman *balneae* and the Muslim hammam would be fascinating and instructive. This is not the place to make such a comparison, but it is worth pointing out that the ludic, athletic aspect declined in favour of the performance of a ritual that is essentially religious. Moreover entry to the *balneae* was mixed: under Trajan, for instance, women bathed quite freely with the men. 'Those women who disliked this promiscuity were not obliged to frequent the *thermae*, but could go to *balneae* that catered exclusively for women. But there were now many women who had come to enjoy the sports that preceded bathing in the *thermae* and who, rather than give up their pleasure, preferred to compromise their reputation by bathing with the men.'[2] And it was not until Hadrian that the sexes were officially separated in the *balneae*: '*lavacra pro sexibus separavit*'.[3] Islam, on the other hand, appears to have had a very strict attitude on the separation of the sexes from the very beginning.

The vogue for the hammams was to rival the popularity of the Roman *thermae*. Both were an important aspect of a civilization and give us some insight into how men and women saw their bodies, their concern for hygiene and their cult of physical beauty. In both cases what we are dealing with is a form of culture. It was never simply a matter of having a dip and leaving, of having a quick wash, or hastily carrying out some necessary ritual. On the contrary, the bath was a place where one spent a great deal of one's time. There was a time scale proper to the hammam as there had been to the *balneae*.

The different rooms were placed in a special order. They began with the *sqīfa*, the mythological and functional equivalent of the apodyterium: a cloakroom situated near the entrance, where the bathers undressed and rested. There were broad, deep seats covered with rush mats or silk rugs, depending on the class of hammam. Next to this was the *bait al-bārid*, the successor to the frigidarium, which contained one or two pools filled with cold water, in which one immersed oneself. Then came the *wistya*, a large central room that, like the tepidarium, contained tepid water and served as an intermediary between the *bait al-bārid* and the *bait al-sākhin*, which, like the Roman caldarium, was the hottest part of the bath, where the high temperature caused one to sweat. Off the *bait al-sākhin* were small rooms to which one could withdraw for private, individual ablutions.[4]

So the *thermae* and hammams depended on an ingenious arrangement in which the most varied and refined forms of bathing were combined together: a hot, dry room for sweating, a steam bath, hot baths, cold baths, swimming pools, hot and cold showers.

The Romans had gone further: they had annexed to the *balneae* innumerable shops, gymnasiums, rest rooms, massage rooms, and even libraries and museums. The hammam, too, was a complex and very soon developed in the direction of a very specialized beauty centre. Firstly there were the masseurs, called *ṭayyāb* in the Maghreb and *mukayyir* in Egypt, experts in the art of cracking bones and relaxing muscles. Then there was the hairdresser, *ḥajjām*. The art of shaving heads held no secrets for him. With very sharp knives he would polish them, scent them and make them extremely shiny. But the attentions paid to the beard were much more delicate. It had to be washed, trimmed, dyed and scented. The hairdresser also practised medicine. He carried out bleedings, using lancets and cupping glasses, or quite simply by applying leeches to the appropriate place, where an incision had previously been made. And there were few hammams that did not have their quacks, magicians, herbalists, etc. So a multiplicity of functions, hygienic, therapeutic, aesthetic, were added to the initial ritual function of purification – so much so indeed that the original function often came to be regarded as secondary and incidental.

Of course the ladies went one better. For them going to the hammam was a real 'outing', a spectacle, an entertainment, a change of scene, in every sense. They would spend all afternoon, even all day there. We have been able to reconstitute from contemporary documents[5] a day spent in the hammam by a Baghdad lady of the thirteenth to fourteenth century. She arrives in the morning, by coach, accompanied by a maid and a eunuch carrying lacquered coffers or brass boxes containing all her toiletries: gloves, brushes, combs, creams and unguents, perfumes, towels, clothes, oranges, hard-boiled eggs, orange blossom water, orgeats and, of course, the eternal Arabo-Mediterranean gazuz or lemonade.

After undressing in the *sqīfa* or, if possible, in an adjoining *maqsūra*, or private room, she passes into the sweat room. After an hour or so an attendant comes and rubs her with an extremely fine, hard woollen glove: massage and cleansing of the skin combined. After a rinsing the head is smeared with Nile mud, or, failing that, Armenian mud or fuller's earth. This is followed by rinsing and a rub-down. Then comes pumicing of the feet with special stones that are usually to be found lying about in various parts of the hammam. The hair is then henna-ed, meticulously, lock by lock, making quite sure that none of the colouring touches the skin, and one then waits for it to take.

Usually at this point the morning comes to an end and food is taken. This is followed by a well-deserved rest, interrupted only by gossip. Then comes the shaving of the arms, the neck, the armpits, the legs and lastly the vagina. For this a strong ointment is used made of yellow arsenic (*dhaehab maqsūr*), iron arsenate *ḥadīda*) or a mixture of wax or caramel thickened with lemon.

The end of the afternoon was devoted to the face: a slow, continuous massage, followed by delicate plucking of hairs. Unwanted hair was plucked hair by hair with tweezers (*mulqāṭ*) or sometimes, if the *ḥannāna* or beauty specialist was sufficiently expert, with two threads of silk wound around one another, in which the hairs were patiently extracted one by one. Indeed depilatory creams were never used for the face.

Then came the make up. One started with the teeth, which were whitened either with pounded eggshells, or with powdered vegetable carbon; after this the lady slowly chewed betel nuts or the outer layer of walnut root (*suwāk*), which, apart from the tonic, astringent effect that it had on the lips and jaw, gave the gums and lips a fine carmine colour and a highly sought-after brilliance. A foundation cream was spread over the face or a cream composed of a mixture of rice powder, white of egg and whiting. A little red cochineal powder and the cheeks acquired a fine pink sheen. The eyebrows were smeared with *dabgha* (*wasma* in the Middle East), a product of incense, tar, gallnut, yellow arsenic or copper sulphate. Antimony powder, *kohol* of Isfahan or *ithmīq* placed on the eyelids helped to enlarge the eyes. *Ḥarqūs*, a lighter, more perfumed variant of *dabgha*, served to decorate the face with delicate beauty spots and fine designs between the eyelashes, on the sides or on the middle of the nose or sometimes, as in Morocco, on the cheeks, suggesting two symmetrical lines of tears.

The list of strong, heavy perfumes is endless. Particularly highly prized were amber, saffron, extracts of camomile or violets, *ghalya*, which was a mixture of equal quantities of musk, camphor, civet and sandalwood (*qumāry*) or myrtle. Nor should we forget the list of lighter waters distilled from rose petals, orange blossom, or the flowers of jasmine, geranium, laurel or eglantine. Ylang-ylang was known, but was used more in funerary rites.

A dab of perfume, a little jewellery, clean clothes and a veil and the women, rejuvenated and regenerated, painted and embellished, tired but satisfied, made tracks for home, ready for a fine night of love, amply deserved and prepared for at enormous length.[6]

It had always been a short step from hygiene to eroticism. But unlike a modern beauty salon or the Roman *balneae*, the hammam went well beyond this functional level. We saw above what was involved in the religious obligation of *ṭahāra*, which embraces all the ritual techniques of purification. Whatever leaves the body bears impurity with it, whether it be blood, urine, gas, vomit or excrement. But whereas the waste matter of the digestive activities are the cause only of minor impurities, the products of sexual activity, sperm, menstrua, or lochia, produce major impurity, which can be cleansed by a general washing of the body, whereas minor purity may be obtained through local, limited washing.

When impure, man is moving dangerously towards evil. The protecting angels desert him. He is no longer permitted to pray, to recite the Quran, to touch the sacred Book, even to enter a mosque. He is no longer safe. Purification is a security technique. One should resort to it as soon as possible in order to reestablish the disturbed order and to chase away the shaytans (devils), which, as we have seen, lie in wait for the slightest show of weakness. The hammam is a place of safety or rather a transitional zone, a centre of alternation between purity and impurity.

Of course, according to Islam, there are three purificatory elements, which, in order of importance, are fire, water and earth. It is not possible to handle fire in a way that is safe for our bodies. Fire burns, destroys, violates. Earth has virtues that are limited from a practical point of view. It is dust and derision. It is a heavy, ambiguous material. If one is to use it, one does so in the form of lustrative stones (*ḥajarat al-tayammum*), in exceptional circumstances, when water is not available. But water reigns over all purification. It is identified with life, with growth, with wealth. Water provides a pleasure that is readily identified with revitalization. So the ritual of the hammam is quite clear. One must purify oneself with water, wash oneself according to a precise ritual: three times the mouth, three times the forearms, twice the head, etc.

So, as a place of major purification, the hammam is itself subject to a number of taboos. One enters it with the left foot; one leaves it with the right.

Certain phrases have to be used, such as 'In God's name' (*Bismillāh*). But once inside one must not recite the Quran. One must not greet people with the traditional *assalāmu 'alaikum*. One must stick to profane expressions. Indeed one must not forget that in the hammam everything is impure to start with and that it is a haunt of the djinns, who hold sovereign sway there.

But from another point of view, as a place of purification, the hammam is the ante-chamber of the mosque, for which it is a preparation. On leaving the hammam, the Muslim recovers his canonical purity and is reconciled with his faith and the absolute. He can then rediscover the rhythm of religious practice that he has abandoned only temporarily in giving himself up to the healthy joys of Eros.

So the hammam is a great deal more than mere hygiene or ritual. It is a highly eroticized place – so much so indeed that the name has come to signify for the masses the sexual act itself. In many Arab countries, 'going to the hammam' quite simply means 'making love', since going to the hammam is part of the process of removing the impurity consequent on the sexual act; and since the hammam, by virtue of the various forms of cleansing practised there, is also a preparation for the sexual act, it can be said that the hammam is both conclusion and preparation for the work of the flesh. The hammam is the epilogue of the flesh and the prologue of prayer. The practices of the hammam are pre- and post-sexual practices. Purification and sexuality are linked. The hammam appears as the necessary mediation between sexual pleasure, from which the Muslim becomes impure and loses his *ṭahāra*, and the moment when he prays, reads the Quran and returns to the security obtained by rediscovered purity. The practices of the hammam are a set of adaptations to the spiritual and appeasements of the physical and psychical tensions caused by sexual intercourse.

So the everyday life of the Muslim is subject to a rhythm in which sacrality leads to sexuality and sexuality to sacrality. Thus love and faith emerge as two poles of everyday existence. One must know how to pass as rapidly as possible from one to the other and this is precisely the role of the purificatory techniques available in the hammam. The rhythm of the practices of the hammam follow the rhythm of virility. There are those who go to the hammam every day in the early morning, there are those who go every two or three days. There are also those who go once a week, or every month. How much the manager of the hammam must know about the married life of the couples in his district! Of course, there may be financial reasons that force a man to go to the hammam only on Friday mornings to prepare himself for communal prayer, but a man who only goes to the hammam once a week certainly runs the risk of having his potency questioned by his friends and neighbours!

Indeed at the hammam one finds an extreme degree of intimacy: the North African adage puts it well when it says that a naked man meets another naked man only in the hammam. The hammam is the social meeting place *par excellence*. So *ḥisba*, *fiqh* and ethics in general have paid considerable attention to regulating its functioning. Paradoxically, this typically Islamic institution is at the same time the one that has perhaps aroused most disapproval. The Prophet, such a strong advocate of cleanliness and hygiene, was somewhat reserved as to the practices of the hammam. For al-Ghazāli entrance to the hammam was unlawful for women unless they were ill or in childbed.[7] And he insisted that they cover themselves with a pagne, or loincloth. For ʻUqbani the hammam was lawful in itself, but a husband was perfectly within his rights to forbid his wife to go to it. Even today, at Madhya in Tunisia, for instance, women go to the hammam only on exceptional occasions: a wedding or childbirth.

The problem of nudity in the hammam is at the centre of the question. All justification or prohibition of the hammam comes down to notions of *ʻaura*, of the lawful look, of decency. The separation of the sexes must be absolutely observed and one must expose to the gaze of others of the same sex only what is strictly permitted: for men, it is unlawful to expose the part of the body between the navel and the knees, but for women, the whole body 'except the face and the palms of the hands, and, if necessary, the arms and legs'[8] must not be exposed. A similar scruple arises in the case of massage. It is lawful to have one's leg or back massaged.

But what of the thighs? The buttocks? The belly? The breasts? This is why there were so many precise and restrictive rules, often regarded as casuistical and meaningless, whereas, on the contrary, they concern the obviously erotic signification of practices in the hammam. It is in this context that one must understand the *adab al ḥammām*, 'good manners for the hammam', to which al-Ghazāli[9] devotes a chapter in the *Iḥyā*. He lays it down that a man should wear a double pagne, one for the lower part of the body, to protect it from the indiscreet looks of others, and the other for the head in order to cover the eyes, lest some immodest bather expose some non-canonical part of his body to others' eyes.

Indeed 'Uqbani is scandalized by the shameless lack of modesty displayed by the men and women of his day. We learn that, despite the frequent warnings and closings of the hammam by the *muḥtasab*, men and women continued to frequent it in a state of undress. 'Uqbani concludes that the hammam is unlawful for women unless it has been completely emptied of men.[10] 'Uqbani gives us clear indications concerning the lesbianism that was widespread in his day and which obviously blossomed in the atmosphere of ostentatious nudity that reigned in the women's hammam. 'Especially when encounters with shameless women are an invitation to expose attractions likely to excite a desire that some find more agreeable to satisfy in contact with other women than in copulation with men.'[11]

The homosexual element in the practices of the hammam did not escape the attentions of the *fuqahā* and the censors. And indeed the poets have often sung of their love of boys, aroused by the constant spectacle of so many beautiful naked bodies exhibited to view.[12]

In fact an astonishing promiscuity reigns in the hammam that seems to have survived all the censors and prohibitions. In some Arabo-Muslim countries the total nudity of men is common, that of women almost everywhere the rule. The manager of the hammam always keeps pagnes available for men, who wear them in order to hide the small *'aura*, that is to say, the genitals themselves. But it is quite common to see men not bothering to hide themselves or even apparently turned towards a wall quietly shaving their pubic hair. As for the women there is little doubt that at least half of them are quite happy to wander about stark naked. The others wear a sheet, or some vague *cache-sexe*.

More important still, when the hammam is open to men, no

woman is admitted. Things are quite different when the hammam is open to women. No adult man is admitted, it is true, but boys are. Indeed it is customary for children to go to the hammam with the women and this continues up to the age of puberty. Since the age of puberty is not the same for everyone, the threshold at which one has 'grown up' is highly flexible; since a mother always tends to see her son as an eternal child and since the other women are in no way inconvenienced by the presence of a boy, young or not, and since taking a boy to the hammam is a chore that the father would prefer to leave, for as long as possible, to the mother, the spectacle of fairly old children, more or less adolescent, consorting side by side in their nakedness with women of all ages, is by no means rare. It would be enough for the young man to make some thoughtless gesture or say something out of place for the manageress to come up to the boy's mother and say: 'Your son has grown up, don't bring him with you any more.' What Arabo-Muslim has not been excluded from the world of naked women in this way? What Arabo-Muslim does not remember so much naked flesh and so many ambiguous sensations? Who does not remember the incident by which this world of nakedness suddenly became forbidden? We have been given more than a memory. One could not stop himself pinching that big, hanging breast that had obsessed him. Another was banned for being too hairy, for having too large a penis, buttocks that protruded too much, a displaced organ. . . . For a boy the hammam is the place where one discovers the anatomy of others and from which one is expelled once the discovery takes place. Here is quite an unexceptional childhood memory. 'I also remember,' says a Tunisian girl, 'all those hideous old women, with folds of fat and drooping breasts, who wandered shamelessly about among young children.'[13]

More detailed and more significant is the delicate, precise evocation to be found in a book by the Moroccan writer Ahmad Sefrioui,[14] which admirably describes the 'atmosphere' of the hammam through the eyes of a child who finds himself thrown into a strange and wonderful world. As the author makes quite clear, the hammam is a great deal more than merely a place for washing. An unexpected world, mingled memories, modesty and immodesty, lassitude and relaxation, everything is mixed together and melts together in the damp, steamy atmosphere of the warm rooms, but also in our minds. We are born, as children, in the hammam. And when we become adults we people it with our childhood memories, our fantasies, our dreams, and every Muslim can relive his childhood in terms of his experience of the hammam. Yes, one can speak of a 'hammam complex'. Indeed a whole area of sexual life is organized around the hammam: the real and the refusal of the real, childhood and puberty, transition and initiation, are integrated in a kind of constellation of meanings crystallized in the hammam.

For a Muslim to reach puberty is to enter the age of responsibilities. *Bulūgh* is the end of childhood, but it transforms the child into a *mukallaf*, a responsible being. The world known up to that point was that of the gynaeceum and the world of women. One waited impatiently to enter the male world and what that implied at every level of existence. Puberty is the moment when sexuality comes to the forefront, when one takes one's leave of the female world, where having become a man, one is expected to behave as a man. From now on one has to fast and pray. One is held fully responsible for one's actions and words. To enter the world of adults also means, perhaps, above all, to frequent only men, to see only men, to speak only to men. Female cousins and even nieces are all too often suddenly hidden from view. At home one's sisters and even one's own mother become semi-strangers. The gap between the sexes in Arabo-Muslim society is now consummated.

Indeed one must now enter another social sphere, that of monosexual promiscuity. Spiritual actions, but also political, economic, aesthetic and even biological actions are performed in common. The body is now literally snatched up by the male world. Purification is performed collectively in the *midhas* or hammams and prayer in the mosques. Everywhere, in the souk, in the medersa and in the café, the youth belongs to an all-male community. More seriously still, this is accompanied by the derealization of the female world. The world of women is a 'sub-world', devoid of seriousness and all too easily treated with the contempt that boosts the male's confidence in himself, in his knowledge, in his wishes and in his power.

The oath *bi-sa qawmin wallaw umūrahum imra-a* (woe betide those who trust a woman) applies not only to the political domain. Not only is it not necessary to speak to a woman about money or one's plans, it is even thought to be prudent not to do so. We have been taught that we should 'ask their opinion, but do the opposite', *shāwirhinna wa khālifhinna*. Woman herself, like her world, is derealized. At puberty the child becomes aware of this too. From that moment on, he is trained to direct all his energies towards the cult of a life shared with other males and towards the systematic depreciation of femininity.

This appears even in language. There are street words that one never says at home, at least in the presence of women. Women are supposed not to know them. They never say them, in any case in front of men. These words belong to what might be called obscene folklore. They create a sort of complicity between people of the same sex and transform the community of sex into a community of promiscuity, and even sometimes into a community of systematic infantilization. These blasphemies, these rude words, these indecent forms of behaviour are merely the expression of a sexual division based on misogyny and a collective derealization of woman.

Now this is, as we have seen, precisely the moment when the male child, excluded from the women's hammam, sets out on the road to the men's hammam. It is like an initiation rite into the hitherto alien world of the males. The practices of the hammam are structured in a new way from the moment one is taken from one's mother, so that the first hammam taken with men is like a consecration, a confirmation, a compensation. It is a confirmation of belonging to the world of males. Has one not been rejected by the women's hammam? Did one not hear the manageress declare: 'He's too old'? Did one not receive the congratulations of one's father's friends, whom one now meets for the first time scantily dressed and some of whom will not fail to make indecent propositions. . . .

The hammam becomes an imaginary return to the ancient world – a lost world of earlier times, rediscovered with each visit. Each plunge into the hammam bath plunges one back into childhood. Childhood fantasies, evocations of the past, aspirations, desires, all become confused in this hot and cold steam that calms the body and excites the spirit. The hammam is a place of infinite variety, haunted by so many memories, so many themes, so many visions, all jumbled together, in which one's mother, sisters and cousins and enigmatic neighbours' wives make up this oneiric bouquet of femininity that each man bears within himself.

One must know how to read the practices of the hammam in order to understand the extent to which it is a regression to the prepubertal stage. Frustrated in his sexual tendencies by the society of males, the young man necessarily finds himself back in the hammam at a more rudimentary level of behaviour. He has little control over his emotions, his discriminations are less subtle, his reactions less complex. Hence that sense of unease described by Sefrioui. So it is hardly surprising, as we have already seen, if the hammam is notoriously a place of homosexuality, male and female.

Indeed there is a whole tradition of popular beliefs concerning copulation at a distance through the hammam. Certain 'virgin' pregnancies were explained by sperm left on the marble slabs by males and absorbed a few moments later by women carelessly sitting down on it. So a prudent woman is careful to wash the place where she sits down in the hammam. More generally a man is advised against sitting in a place left vacant by a woman until it has cooled down, '*idhā qāmat al-mar-atu falā tajlis fī mauḍi-'ihā ḥaṭṭā yabruda*' – and conversely. A place warmed by the sex of the person that has just left is supposed to give a certain unlawful pleasure. Among many of our virgins there is even a sort of obsessional anxiety about getting pregnant in this way. Various forms of 'hammamophobia' arise from the nudity, promiscuity and psychical traumata that derive from it.

The hammam is a place where the sense of observation, especially of the female anatomy, is refined. There the child has all the time in the world to contemplate, examine and compare sexual organs. Sometimes they are young, without a single fold, close-shaven, polished and shining, but sometimes they are limp, soft things, flabby and drooping. The vulva appears as a beautiful thing to be ravished, or, on the contrary, as something disgusting and dangerous: a repulsive abyss with teeth. Hence the ambivalence of men's memories of the hammam in which the beauty and ugliness of female sexual organs are inextricably mixed.

Indeed many love affairs began in the hammam. I analyse one example in my *Dix contes tunisiens pour enfants.*[15] There are many others to be found in *The Thousand and One Nights*. There is Tuḥfa, the beautiful maid of Princess Zubeida, who stayed late in the hammam. There she saw a young lady. 'It was the moon. No one has ever seen or will ever see a more adorable creature. The whole universe has not known a more beautiful woman. . . .'[16] Cursed be the women who goes off and describes to her husband a beautiful creature seen in the hammam. It would not be long before this same beauty became her rival and co-wife!

The hammam is a sexually overestimated place. It may be seen as a uterine environment. It is so psychically and oneirically – as I think I have shown – but it is so also physically and topographically. Its labyrinthine form is highly significant. Unlike the Roman *balneae*, the hammams are below ground level in order to assist the water pressure and to preserve heat. The already complex and highly elaborate form of the Roman *thermae* is here complicated still further. Reaching the hottest centre, the *maghtas*, requires between seven and ten detours. One descends into the hammam as one descends into hell. One slides into it before finding onself in the *mathāra* or *khilwa*, the most intimate place, but also the most diabolical.

The myth of the hammam is marked not only by the S-shaped topography, but also by a whole dimension of fantasy. For no sooner has one plunged into the hammam than the corridor alone, with its series of ever deeper, ever warmer rooms raises up a whole world of dreams. To plunge into the hammam is to plunge into increasing heat and to isolate oneself increasingly from the outside world. It is also a place in which hot or cooling streams flow. They come from the furnace and they flow back into the depths of the earth. A mystery accompanies this 'stream', which comes from a hole, traverses a hole and plunges into a hole. Entering the hammam is to plunge into a mystery. It is to return in dream to the mother's breast.

That is not all, for there is also the use of the 'earthly' substance: fuller's earth or Nile mud (*tfal*) and 'broken gold' (orpiment, or yellow arsenic, known as *dhahab maksūr*), with which one depilates the genitals and armpits. There is the hard glove with which the masseur or masseuse rubs the skin. And there are all those magico-pharmaceutical medicines: cataplasms, unguents, facial paints, cloves, henna, incense, thyme, rosemary and other plants and still more aphrodisiacs. All these elements serve as symbols with a strong sexual charge. There is a whole dialectic of the elements in the hammam: hot and cold, hard and soft, feminine and masculine, clean and dirty, pure and impure, inside and outside, self and others, angel and devil. It is understandable, especially in the case of women, why its users are content to spend their hours there. What is one looking for and what does one find if not a warm uterine environment? In the hammam one rediscovers oneself and becomes reconciled with one's own childhood.

Yes, the hammam is a place of great activation, both physical and psychical. The heat activates the circulation of the blood; but the darkness, the shape, the various elements activate regression, the reanimation of old associations and repressed infantile tendencies. The sexual 'prohibitions' bound up with the separation of the sexes make the hammam both the accomplice of social regulation and also a model of more or less stereotyped behaviour. In so far as the hammam maintains the presence of parental images and their imperatives it remains bound up with the memory of the mother and identification with the father. It also extends and surpasses the moral constraints that weigh on the parents themselves. It seeps into the infantile personality at the very point where primitive drives meet the conscious functions of control.

The hammam plays a part, therefore, in the fixation on the mother, but it also tends to transcend that fixation. Indeed the practices of the hammam have the effect of preventing the regressing libido from stopping at the physical body of the mother. The regression so often remarked on only seems to be reducible to the evocation of the mother. In reality the hammam is the great gate opening on to the 'kingdom of the mothers'. What a beautiful and potent derivative! And what a magnificent invention of the Arabo-Muslim collective genius!

It enables one to grasp in living detail how the social uses both the sexual and the sacral to integrate them into one another. It is as if the hammam, the social place *par excellence*, were for society only a means of absorbing, of rationalizing sexuality by admitting the individual to the totality. If it is true that every Muslim is fixated on his mother, this complex, normally repressed, may reappear at any moment. The institution of the hammams dams up this continuous effervescence, allowing it full rein. But then the plunge into this 'semi-morbid' state will be of short duration.

Above all it will be normalized and therefore exorcized. Furthermore, Muslim society exploits this unconscious drive to its own advantage by integrating it into an institution that conforms much more to the interests of the group than the *fuqahā* have admitted. For what would have been an anarchic drive, ruinous for society, is transformed into rituals and myths, becoming crystallized and losing all its morbid characteristics. The hammam has been the way that has enabled Muslim society sufficient leeway. If Muslim society has been able to preserve itself for so many centuries, it may be because of the hammam, which has been able to function as a powerful release of all the tensions to which the Muslim is necessarily subject. In using the hammam Muslim society has forged a valuable instrument for itself to channel the sexual drives liberated by religion, but repressed by the misogynist puritanism that grew up over the centuries and by a strict, universal separation of the sexes that might have proved fatal to it.

Yes, life is pleasant in the hammam. But if, in spite of everything, life is pleasant in the Arabo-Muslim societies, it is also thanks to the hammam. As a Latin poet put it, with a touch of irony: '*balnea, vina, Venus corrumpunt corpora nostra sed vitam faciunt.*'[17] This is even more valid and may be said without irony of the Arabo-Muslim societies. Ibn Khaldūn[18] already noted that the euphoria sensed in the hammam impels people to sing. He was wrong to attribute this euphoria simply to the effect of heat, believed to disturb the physiological equilibrium. The euphoria is that of unlimited psychical happiness rediscovered in a total oneirism that blossoms in the hammam, a place where everything can be reconciled.

2 *Circumcision*

Ahmed Amin relates how, in the interwar period, a tribe in southern Sudan wanted to be converted *en bloc* to Islam. It contacted the Islamic University of El Azhar for information concerning the doctrine, practices and laws of Islam and the procedure to be followed to complete the conversion. It was given a list of what had to be done: at the top of the list was circumcision. When the adult members of the tribe refused to have themselves mutilated the whole idea was dropped.[19] This gives some idea of the importance accorded by El Azhar as indeed by almost all the Muslim populations to circumcision, which is regarded preeminently as the mark of inclusion in Muslim society. Indeed this practice is more or less unanimously observed at every social level and at whatever degree of development and acculturation. No one – not even free thinkers, communists, atheists, or even partners of mixed marriages – ignores the rule. Even in Tunisia under Bourguiba, which in so many respects has demonstrated its openness to innovation in matters of custom and religion, the number of the uncircumcised cannot exceed a hundred. In the last few years Tunisia has begun to accept that a Muslim Tunisian woman may marry a non-Muslim. This is a very brave measure, indeed one that is unique in the Muslim world and constantly being brought up in the Tunisian parliament. But what people find most shocking about the idea is that a Muslim woman can sleep with an uncircumcized man, even in a lawful marriage! Circumcision is a great deal more than a matter of hygiene, or of mere custom. It is deeply rooted in Islamic mores and certainly corresponds to something fundamental.

Like Turkey or Iran, the Maghreb does not practise female excision but everywhere else in the Muslim world it seems to be universally observed. Together with circumcision, it defines, where it is practised, membership of the Islamic community, expressed in such phrases as 'We the circumcised. . . .' 'We the excised. . . .'

And yet circumcision is an act that, according to the fiqh, is in no way compulsory. It is a *sunna* act,[20] that is to say, one that is strongly recommended. The excision of girls is even less obligatory. It is a *makruma*: a pious practice, like removing a stone from the road, clearing a public drain or maintaining a collective watertap. The question is so secondary that even the longest books of fiqh devote very little space to it. The *fatāwa hindiyya*, which stretches to almost three thousand pages, devotes only a third of a page to it. Al-Ghazali deals with the question in exactly seven lines in that summa of over two thousand pages known as the *Iḥya*. As for the great commentary of Aini on the Bokhari tradition, it is, in spite of its nine thousand pages, absolutely silent on this matter. The Quran says nothing about it. And Sidi Khalil, the great Malekite jurist, admits that collective prayer may quite validly be conducted by an uncircumcised man.

Indeed we do not know in what conditions the Prophet himself was circumcised. He must have been so since the act is a *sunna*, that is to say, an imitation of the Prophet, yet biographers attentive to the slightest details of the life of the Messenger of God have little to say about his circumcision. It is said that he was circumcised by his grandfather when he was forty days old. According to other traditions he was born already circumcised – by angels in his mother's womb. On the other hand tradition does tell us how his heart was purified (*taṭhīr*). Since we know that circumcision is also commonly called *ṭahāra* (purification), it may be possible to establish a correlation between the two notions. When Muhammad was being fostered by the Beni Saāds and was not yet four years old two angels took him and weighed him in order to determine his metaphysical value. They split open his chest, took out the heart, opened it, and removed the 'speck of black blood', which is the sign of the *shaiṭān*. They washed the heart with water from the sacred zemzem well contained in a golden bowl. They placed *sakīna*, 'peaceful quietude', which was like the face of a beautiful white cat, in the heart. They then put everything back in place. Lastly they placed between his shoulders the seal of prophecy (*khātam al-nubwa*).[21] The surgical operation had, of course, a very precise metaphysical meaning. It was intended to protect Muhammad's heart from any tendency to evil.

'Circumcision', says Ghazali, 'is practised by the Jews on the seventeenth day. We must differentiate ourselves from them and wait until the child's hair has begun to grow.'[22] The *fatāwa hindiyya* advocate the period between seven and twelve years. There was much concern about the circumcision of the adult who had become converted to Islam. Canonically an old man in weak health could be dispensed from it, but not others. Preferably he would circumcise himself; otherwise he would pay a concubine who was specialized in this sort of operation to perform it. Indeed she alone was permitted to see and touch her master's penis. Any other person ran the risk of breaking the rules concerning *'aura*. In extreme circumstances the manager of the hammam would be allowed to perform the operation.[23]

It should be noticed that Islam distinguishes carefully between *khitān*, circumcision in the strict sense, which consists in the circular section of the foreskin, and *khaṣi*, which is castration obtained by the total or partial removal of one or both testicles. The latter is strictly prohibited by the *fatāwa hindiyya*,[24] whereas Qādhi-Khan[25] merely declares it to be blameworthy.

Excision of girls, as we have said, was a widely tolerated practice. In principle, it ought to concern only the removal of the lower part of the cap. In fact, as we know, what is involved, except in abnormal cases, is only the semi-prepuce, which covers only the lower part of the clitoris. The excision of girls (*khifāḍ*) must not therefore be confused with clitoridectomy. The former is tolerated, the latter strictly prohibited. Indeed it is the only indication provided by tradition. One day the Prophet, seeing Um 'Attya operate on a girl, said to her: 'Circumcision is a *sunna* for men and only a *makruma* for girls. Just touch the surface lightly and don't cut deep (*ashmī wa ḷa tanhikī*). Her face will grow beautiful and her husband will rejoice.'[26] One certainly senses through these texts that the Prophet felt a certain reticence towards excision, which he wished to give a character more symbolic than mutilating.

Is it, as has sometimes been said, simply a survival from an earlier period? This is the opinion of Mazaheri, who writes: 'Christianity rejected this semitic custom and replaced it by baptism, which is of Zoroastrian origin; but Islam, believing that it is following in the supposed footsteps of the "prophet" Abraham, preserved the semitic practice of circumcision for both sexes.'[27] The explanation of survival is very convenient, but not very satisfactory, for in the Maghreb, the Berbers appear not to have known it and even the Phoenicians gave it up, it seems, when they settled in Africa.[28] It was introduced in the seventh and eighth centuries by the Arab conquerors. Indeed it is difficult to speak of survival for a practice so profoundly rooted in the collective life of the Arabo-Muslim societies. Circumcision provides an opportunity for familial ceremonies that are exceeded in scope only by wedding festivities. It is a solemn festival. It is not surprising if no prayer accompanies it, since it has no canonical character. But the child is dressed in his finest clothes, always new, almost always embroidered. Everyone goes off to the marabout, or shrine, of the holy protector of the town or family, Sidi Mehraz in Tunis or Imam Shafi'ī in Cairo. There is always a procession through the town.

When the moment has come, the uncle or grandfather takes the child in his arms and a barber (*ṭahhār*) performs the operation, which lasts only a second or two with a razor or sharp scissors. Then the wound is sealed with a little wood ash, spider's web, alum or other haemostatic. Just at the moment of the operation, a large red or black cockerel must be killed and the *ṭahhār* takes it away as payment. Just as the cut is being made, new pitchers must be broken by throwing them violently on the ground. Meanwhile, in front of the door, the child's friends from the *kuttāb*, or traditional quranic primary school, bellow out litanies, accompanied by a deafening din of drums, bagpipes and fanfares. The important thing is to make a noise, a lot of noise.

Then everyone comes in to congratulate the newly circumcised boy and give him sweetmeats, toys or coins. Then there are celebrations. Rich people, of course, make more of a show, spinning the festivities out to a week or more. There are concerts, known as *ḥafalāt ṭarab* in the Middle East or *'auāda* in the Maghreb. Some of these celebrations have gone down in history: there were those of Jahya, the grandson of al-Ma'mūn of Toledo, for example, or those of the son of al-Moizz Ibn Badīs of Kairwan.

As for the mutilated child, he could do nothing but cry out in pain and weep in shock at the violence done to his body. This wound in his flesh, these men and women torturing him, that gleaming razor, the strident oohs and ahs of inquisitive, indiscreet old women, the jugs smashing on the floor, the cry of the cockerel, struggling and losing its blood, the din outside and finally the endless stream of people coming to congratulate the patient on 'his happy accession to Islam', that is what circumcision means to a child.

One should mention too the obsessional anxiety of the *ṭahhār*, kept up before, during and after the event, and the painful wound, so often slow to heal; sometimes long, painful weeks were necessary, sometimes, too, accidents caused more serious complications; infections, haemorrhages, cutting through the artery or even right through the penis, removing part of the glans.

Circumcision, secondary from a religious point of view, would not seem to be explicable from a physiological point of view either. Though sometimes necessary in treating phimosis, nothing can justify its systematic use, especially without anaesthetic. It involves enormous dangers, on both the physiological and psychical plane. It is hardly surprising if some commentators see it as a barbarous, traumatizing practice.[29] A French dictionary of sexology speaks uninhibitedly of 'bloody sacrifice' and goes on to say:

> By exposing the glans permanently, circumcision often allows it to be covered by a skin that makes it lose much of its sensitivity. The merits of this semi-anaesthetic are often praised: the man needs a larger number of coital movements to reach orgasm, thus giving the woman the advantage of prolonged excitement. One must indeed have very little self-control to require such a surface anaesthetic.[30]

In view of all this, one may well pose the problem of the significance of circumcision in Islam. In Judaism this meaning is more or less clear. Indeed Genesis says quite explicitly:

> And God said to Abraham, 'As for you, you shall keep my covenant, you and your descendants after you throughout their generations. This is my covenant, which you shall keep, between me and you and your descendants after you: Every male among you shall be circumcised. . . . So shall my covenant be in your flesh an everlasting covenant. Any

> uncircumcised male who is not circumcised in the flesh of his foreskin shall be cut off from his people; he has broken my covenant.'[31]

The meaning of Jewish circumcision is perfectly obvious. It is a sacrificial rite. It seals the covenant with the Eternal, by offering him a bloody part of one's own body. It may be seen as a substitute for a more radical human sacrifice, a purification of the pleasures of the flesh, an initiation trial through endurance, courage and mortification, a subtle way of increasing sexual pleasure, or on the contrary, as Philo maintained, a way of directing oneself away from lechery.[32]

In a more general way, ethnologists and sociologists, comparing Jewish and archaic societies, have given vent to their theories. There is a good discussion, followed by an excellent summing up by Marcel Mauss that concludes: 'For me circumcision is essentially a tattoo. It is a tribal, even national sign.'[33]

Without embarking further on a theoretical discussion of such a widespread practice, we ought perhaps to say that the initiatory meaning of the rite is undeniable.

This is evident in the extraordinary passage in Exodus that describes Moses' circumcision. After living among the Midianites, Moses, who, in the meantime, has married Zippo'rah and had a son by her, returns to Egypt. There then follows an episode that has embarrassed Jewish and Christian commentators for centuries:

> At a lodging place on the way the Lord met him and sought to kill him. Then Zippo'rah took a flint and cut off her son's foreskin, and touched Moses' feet with it, and said, 'Surely you are a bridegroom of blood to me!' So he let him alone. Then it was that she said, 'You are a bridegroom of blood,' because of the circumcision.[34]

Not having been circumcised Moses had been excluded from Abraham's sacrificial ritual. Returning among his people and consummating his marriage, he had to regularize his situation, that is to say, seal his covenant with God. So he did this by substitution. Zippo'rah cut off the foreskin of their common son and touched Moses' parts with it. Moses then becomes for her 'a bridegroom of blood'. Their son's blood may be regarded as Moses' own blood. In his fine book, *L'initiation sexuelle et l'évolution religieuse*, Pierre Gordon rightly concludes that circumcision is 'a communion with the divine universe. . . . On the road from Egypt, the operation is carried out by a sacrosanct man, a man bearing the title of Yahweh, and who collaborates with God to bring the Prophet to his mission so that he may be better prepared to carry it out.'[35] The initiatory character of Mosaic circumcision would appear to be established beyond doubt.

Approaching the question from the Jewish tradition, Maryse Choisy eventually reaches a similar conclusion, while emphasizing the archetypal symbolism of the ritual of circumcision as exemplified in the incident concerning Moses. Having reached the Nile delta, Moses is almost swallowed whole by a python. Only his legs are left visible in the dragon's mouth. Zippo'rah guesses at once what God requires. Quick as a flash, picking up the first stone to hand, she circumcises her second son. With the blood from the foreskin, she anoints his legs.

> 'You are for me a *chathan dammin*,' she says.
> A voice rises from the Nile:
> 'Spit him out! Spit him out!'
> Then the serpent spits out Moses.[36]

Stressing the idea that 'the sacrifice of Abraham is the archetype of all evolution',[37] Maryse Choisy brings out the two fundamental characteristics of the ritual of Moses' circumcision; that it is performed by a woman and in a bloody manner. 'When the Bible translates *chathan dammin* by "bridegroom of blood", it loses the richness of meaning in the ritual. It stresses blood and female initiation.'[38] And Maryse Choisy concludes: 'In Genesis . . . the initiatory value [of circumcision] is not in doubt. A circumcised child is to the children of Israel what a baptized child is to Christians. A personal soul has been awakened in that spark of life. Through this sign he will survive the destruction of the flesh. By this sign he distinguishes himself from the pre-Adamites, from wholly mortal animals, which lack the divine light.'[39]

It can certainly be said that Jewish circumcision is a covenant with the Lord in the sense that it is a rite and a sacrifice intended to raise consciousness in the group and community. It is an initiation rite effecting a double passage from adolescence to the community of mature men and from the state of nature to the state of man, fertilized by the divine light and belonging to a chosen people privileged enough to maintain a dialogue with the divinity.

It is impossible not to be attentive to this Jewish constellation of the symbolism of circumcision. For Christianity was to deprive circumcision of this meaning. Apart from the Church of Ethiopia, which still practises circumcision, all the sects and Christian churches keep to the terms of St Paul's epistle to the Galatians:

> It is those who want to make a good showing in the flesh that would compel you to be circumcised, and only in order that they may not be persecuted for the cross of Christ. For even those who receive circumcision do not themselves keep the law, but they desire to have you circumcised that they may glory in your flesh. But far be it from me to glory except in the cross of our Lord Jesus Christ, by which the world has been crucified to me, and I to the world. For neither circumcision counts for anything, nor uncircumcision, but a new creation.[40]

So the symbolism of circumcision is explicitly rejected by the Gospels. Baptism came to replace circumcision. Communion with Christ took the place of the bloody covenant with the Lord.

So where does that leave Islam? Are we to believe that in restoring what Christianity had abolished, Islam was quite simply returning to a Semitic tradition? I do not really think so. Canonically and theologically, circumcision has no privileged status. It is not one of the five pillars of Islam (profession of faith, prayer, alms, fasting, pilgrimage to Mecca). It is merely a *sunna*. The ritual surrounding it is loose, imprecise, and more spontaneous than organic. It is accompanied by no prayer. The age at which the operation is performed is not fixed in any strict way and may take place at any time between one and twelve years. The fiqh is hardly concerned with it and the Quran not at all. Furthermore there is a systematic concern on the part of Muslims to distinguish themselves from the Jews on this matter, whereas in other cases the imitation of Jewish practices is hardly stressed in so systematic a way. For instance, a Muslim may eat meat killed according to the Jewish ritual; whereas, among the few recommendations given by Ghazāli is that not to practise circumcision at the age of seven days, 'in order to distinguish ourselves from them by postponing it'.[41] In Islam the seventh day of birth is marked only by a simple ceremony of presentation to the family and to the 'people' of the household, by which is meant the djinns. At Damascus, as at Cairo or Marrakesh, the child, bathed, scented, oiled, dressed in a thousand and one propitiatory amulets, is wrapped in a sheet. The midwife (*qābila ū dāya*) presents him at all the doors of the house by knocking on each one three times. She throws grilled chick peas, raisins and sweets on the ground, crying: 'The house is ours, the children are ours, here is the Prophet come to visit us.'

Circumcision, like excision indeed, is more a practice of Muslims than a practice of Islam. By that I mean that its sociological aspect, its social significance, is quite obviously more important than the clearly secondary sacral aspect. It is a question of marking membership of the group. The words 'We the circumcised' define a relationship of inclusion within the community. It is this that explains, it seems to me, the tenacity with which 'Muslims' and the less 'Muslim' cling to this practice. The festivities surrounding it are in fact ceremonies by which young children are admitted to the group. Hence the relatively advanced age at which it is practised. Circumcision is a passage to the world of adults and a preparation, carried out in blood and pain, and therefore unforgettable, into an age of responsibilities. In terms of Muslim society and religion, it exists at the same level as the practices of the hammam.

Looked at more closely, from a different point of view, in terms of the celebrations around it, it is difficult not to regard it as a sort of repetition of the wedding ceremony.[42] The two ceremonies are structured in the same way and some of the days bear the same name. The day before the eve of the day of circumcision is called in Tunisia, like the wedding night, *wuṭya*, from *waṭa-a*, to coit. The ceremonies of laying on henna, of washing in the hammam, of the visit to the hairdresser and even the day of rest (*rāḥa*), which separate them from the act itself, have much in common in each case. It is as if circumcision were only a mimicry of marriage and the sacrifice of the foreskin an anticipation of that of the hymen, the importance of which we shall examine in a later chapter. It is as if circumcision were a preparation for deflowering and indeed is it not a question of preparing oneself for coitus, of sensitizing oneself to the genetic activity, of valorizing in a sense the phallus, which is thus in turn purified and placed in reserve? The sexual significance of circumcision cannot be in doubt. And if anyone is still in any doubt on the matter, let him remember the traditional song sung in Tunisia on this occasion:

You begin with circumcision and you end in marriage, and still your horse neighs in the forest.
You begin with circumcision and you end in youth, and still your horse neighs among the bachelors.
Let us call quickly for his mother, let us call quickly for his aunt, let them come quickly and throw money on the procreative rod.[43]

The symbolism is perfectly obvious. Circumcision and marriage are marked here as the two steps, initial and final, in the single process of living. Circumcision is the open way to marriage, it is the promise of a permanent youth, in the sense that it will spare man the disappointments of old age. For in this business there is a horse that will always neigh and will always be standing, present and master of all, of the cohort of bachelors. What is this horse if not the 'procreative rod' (*'ammāra*) on which one asks the female relations to come and throw propitiatory money. The money must match this *'ammāra*, which must be strengthened, prepared, maintained, glorified and protected from the evil eye. Circumcision is both a promise and a guarantee of a future genetic life that one hopes will be as full, as great and as durable as love.

Everything is carried out in such a way, therefore, that circumcision is seen as quite different from castration. Does it succeed? The question really should be asked. For circumcision is carried out at an age when the boy has long since been made aware of the difference between the sexes. Very often a state of anxiety is induced in the boy by his family and friends. He is soon made aware of the exorbitant privileges that go with being a male. He has been made well aware of the importance of that 'little thing that hangs down', as little Muslim girls invariably refer to it. Hence the fear that it will be cut off if it is not circumcised or, even, that what remains will be cut off after circumcision. Such a fear is part and parcel of the paradox and contradiction of childhood experience. There is a symbolic valorization of the phallus and an obsessional fear of losing it. This situation is likely to last for a long time, especially in an authoritarian society and one in which the terrifying father holds all kinds of goods, pleasures, wealth – and women – in 'trust' for him. If, in the end, everything seems to settle down without too much difficulty and heartache it is certainly because of all the forms of socialization set in train, but also because of the early age of marriage, which follows soon after circumcision.

But for the young Arab girl in the Middle East excision is hardly less traumatic. Excision, which, despite the canonical regulations, is very often quite simply a clitoridectomy, is merely the first step in 'a veritable plot intended to frustrate the woman of her share of fulfillment', in Youssef al-Masry's words.[44] This 'blinding' of women is not dissimilar to the fear of mutilation felt by men. In both cases one can speak of a castration complex inherent in all Muslim child rearing and which, of course, has a quite different significance in a Christian, Jewish or animistic setting.

Commentators have often observed the correlation in Arab society between the use of narcotics, homosexuality, circumcision and excision.[45] The operation carried out on the genital organs cannot be considered in isolation from a set of social, sometimes a-religious, even frankly anti-Islamic practices. From the cradle to the grave, or rather 'from the uterus to the cumulus', and at every moment of life, the Arab female personality is ruthlessly, systematically, irremediably denied. The 'drama' of Arab frigidity that has all too often been observed clinically is to be inferred from a sexual life, physiological and psychological, that is a series of traumata that bring with them insurmountable fears and anxieties. Sometimes excised to begin with, but always brought up in the cult of necessary virginity, deflowered almost publicly on her wedding night, transformed into a child-producing machine, the Arab girl comes in the end to lose even what is biological in the act of loving. The evidence presented by Youssef al-Masry can leave us in no doubt. Having become resistant to orgasm, an Arab woman needs, if she is to be satisfied, a husband who is prepared to make ever increasing proof of his prowess and to try to acquire marvels of virility by resorting to artificial means. Indeed I have already pointed out the importance in Arab erotology of love philtres and herbal aphrodisiacs.

One should also draw attention to the relation, often observed in Arab culture, between violence and love, which is merely another variant of the castration dialectic. The mutilated man rapes. The raped woman is mutilating. Enver F. Dehoï[46] has already pointed out the extent to which the fear of castration is to be found in *The Thousand and One Nights*, which are in a sense a variation on the endless theme of sexual mutilation. In these tales the woman is all too often a castrator, the guaranteed prototype of so many strange, dangerous, anxiety-inducing Arab women. But let us hear the handsome Aziz recounting his own misfortune:

> The slaves did as they were bid, while their mistress put a red copper pot upon the fire, containing oil and soft cheese. When the cheese was well mixed into the boiling oil she came back to me and pulled down my drawers; alternate waves of terror and shame shook me, and I knew what was to happen. Having bared my belly, she took hold of my eggs and bound them at the root with the noose of a waxed cord; the ends of this cord she gave to two of her slaves, who bore strongly upon it, while she herself took up a razor and, with a single stroke, cut off my manhood.[47]

A just revenge by an Arab woman? Revolt, compensation? Violence against violence in the continuous war of the sexes? It is all of these things, as the story goes on to show only too clearly:

> When I came to myself, I saw that my front was like a woman's and that the slaves were even then applying the boiled oil and cheese to the wound. My blood soon stopped flowing, and my mistress came to me . . . saying scornfully: 'Return whence you came! You are no use to me. I keep all that was ever valuable to me.'[48]

Certainly from circumcision to excision, deflowering and the *vagina dentata*, there is a guiding thread. All the feminist demands, all the stereotypical beliefs about women's wiles (the celebrated *kaid al-nisā*) appear quite clearly here through a battery of symbols. The vulgar, obscene image of the merguez served up on a dish between two eggs is raised here to a higher literary level. The soft cheese, the boiling oil, the eggs, the cord, the copper pan, culinary magic, the chemistry of elements, satisfied desire. The beautiful girl is a penis eater: a fantastic displacement of virility in a society determined to refuse free expression to feminine affectivity.

We now understand why sexual mutilation (circumcision and excision) hold such an exceptional place in our Arabo-Muslim societies, whereas there is nothing in the law that would lead one to expect it. It amounts to an initiation into love, not in its more hedonistic aspects, but in its most negative ones. It is a warning that life is anxiety and danger, but it also teaches how this danger may be overcome and resolved. Circumcision and excision are like a vaccination against the dangers of sexuality.

In any case the deflowering of the virgin on her wedding night is much more an equivalent of the circumcision of the boy than is excision. Through festivities, violence, blood, pain and exhibitionism, too, we have in each case different types of traumata wittingly inflicted by the group in order to maintain its own cohesion: the sacrifice of the hymen is a rite having the same nature and the same meaning as that of the foreskin. As we have seen, there is a clear correspondence for the boy between circumcision and marriage. The wedding night is the time when the man experiences and proves his virility and when the girl proves her honesty. As Rachid Boujedra writes of his father's remarriage:

> A fully-fledged wedding. The bride was fifteen, my father fifty. A tense wedding. Plenty of blood. The old women were amazed when they washed the sheets, next morning. Tambourines, all night, had drowned the tortures of the flesh torn by the patriarch's monstrous orgasm. . . . The father was ridiculous and tried to show that he was still up to it: the young men of the tribe had to be silenced. Since he had made up his mind to remarry, he had taken to eating honey with a view to regaining the hormonal vigour of his youth.[49]

Virginity is an essential element of Arabo-Muslim erotic life. The Prophet himself advised Zayd to marry a virgin for preference. And indeed is not the houri of paradise an eternal virgin? Virginity is the object of a veritable cult. Of course in ancient societies virginity proceeded from the religious ritual. Pierre Gordon has shown in a striking and definitive way the essential role played by the sacred deflowerer disguised as a beast. 'Towards the end of the tribal initiation ceremonies, the young virgin was admitted to sexual life and offered to the divinity, who was represented by a sacred personage, filled with *supernatural mana*, the first fruits of her new existence; the divine world finally penetrated her and sanctified her in the shape of a sacrosanct deflowerer.'[50] In a later period it was the husband himself who became the deflowerer of his own wife: he could no longer leave the task to another. 'The idea that a girl could present herself as a virgin to her husband has long seemed repugnant and unseemly', the *Dictionnaire de sexologie* observes.[51] This certainly does not apply to the Arab girl: her virginity has to be the preserve of her first husband. She is reared to preserve 'that precious property, that *bakāra*, that would be the object, at the right moment, of a public examination and the secret loss of which would brand her forever with a redhibitory defect. The first steps in love are marked by a cruel wound, a narcissistic experience of oneself. Fear of castration is not confined to boys. If it is true, as Marie Bonaparte once wrote, that defloration engenders 'the lasting female rancour of pain', one has to admit that Arabo-Muslim society does everything it can to aggravate it still further. Is it a male strategy to devalue women? Perhaps that is what it amounts to.

3 Prostitution

Prostitution (*bighā, khanā*) has always flourished throughout history and throughout the Arabo-Muslim countries. And yet it might be thought that Islam's extreme tolerance in sexual morals would have protected our societies from the commercial exploitation of sex. I have shown how sexual relations in Islam rested on a total and totalizing view of the flesh, how the rotation of women and therefore of men was organized, how the structures of the polygamous family, the very simple procedure of divorce and remarriage made possible an adequate, permanent, varied, renewed and constantly lawful satisfaction of carnal desire.

That is no doubt why, considering his tolerance to be quite broad enough, Muhammad must have decided, very early on, and after much hesitation, to reject the temporary marriage of pleasure, known as *nikāḥ mut'a*, which is merely prostitution under another name. Having organized sexual relations within the framework of *nikāḥ* and concubinage, Islam regarded as sinful anything that lay outside the consensual contracts of sexuality.[52] As a result any distorted form of prostitution was vehemently condemned. Thus the female slave enjoyed a special status. She was required to render sexual services to her owner(s), but exclusively. The owner could not hand her over to a third party and force her into prostitution. Indeed the Quran recommends:

> And constrain not
> your slavegirls to prostitution, if they
> desire to live in chastity, that you may
> seek the chance goods of the present life.
> Whosoever constrains them, surely God,
> after their being constrained, is All-forgiving,
> All-compassionate.[53]

Tradition[54] adds some interesting details to this revelation. A rich man, Abdullah Ibn Ubayy, owned six female slaves, whom he put out to prostitution. Living from their income, he was eventually able to set up a system of contractual payments whereby they had to pay him a certain sum every day and it was up to them to find this minimum. In the end two of these concubines complained to the Prophet, who then received the revelation. According to another tradition the rich man himself took the initiative of going to the Prophet, accompanied by one of his beautiful slave girls, and made the following request: 'This is a *jāriya* who has been inherited by the children of such and such a man. If she goes into prostitution she will bring the orphans a great deal of money. Let me guide her in these activities.' The Prophet refused, but when the man insisted, the quranic verses were finally revealed.

Indeed, the request was neither impudent nor imprudent. In relation to the pre-Islamic mores it was perfectly 'lawful'. What it did betray, however, was that Ibn Ubayy, usually classed among the hypocrites (munāfiqūn), had failed to understand the new spirit established with the theory of *nikāḥ* and concubinage. In spite of his conversion he continued to think and behave as before.

Apart from lawful marriage the pre-Islamic Arab knew at least three other institutionalized forms of intersexual relations. *Istibdhā* certainly expressed a eugenic concern that seems very interesting today. A husband might order his wife to go and live for a time with another man, preferably a good-looking fellow, a poet, a sage, or some other intelligent, lucky man. . . . Indeed the husband himself abstained from any relations with his wife until he was assured that she was pregnant. In this way, the husband was assured of having a 'first-class' child. Thus in the pre-Islamic tribes there was a category of men to whom recourse was had to improve the Arab race. This distribution of sexual labour was fairly rare and original, especially in the institutionalized forms just described.

There was also collective marriage, known as *nikāḥ rahṭ*. A group of men, who must not number more than ten (hence the name *rahṭ*), collectively married a woman, with whom they lived in turn for a period laid down in advance. If the woman became pregnant she waited until her confinement, then summoned all her husbands to her house. None of them was allowed to absent himself. She then named the one whom she wished to appoint as father of the newborn child. This appointment was irrevocable.

The last institutionalized form of marriage was prostitution pure and simple (*bighā*). Specialized women were available to the public. They could be recognized by the flags that they hung over the doors of their houses. Anyone who was interested could go in quite freely. The woman did not have the right to refuse any client. If she became pregnant and gave birth to a child all the men who had visited her came to her house and skilled physiognomists (*al-qafāta*) were summoned to guess, on the basis of various external signs (colour of eyes, hair, shape of the nose, facial features, special marks, etc.), who the father was. The man decided upon was declared the father. He did not have the right to refuse and he took the child with him.[55]

It may be inferred that pre-Islamic prostitution was very widespread, took many forms and was legitimated by society. Islam was to tolerate only *nikāḥ* and concubinage and regard as *zinā* all other forms of sexual relation. And we have seen how *zinā* was classified among the most serious sins.

The surprising thing is that this did not in any way prevent prostitution from prospering. Aysha, the Prophet's wife, was complaining, only a few years after the death of her holy husband, of the shameful conduct of women. And 'Ainī added the following disillusioned comment: 'If Aysha had seen the blameworthy innovations (*bidā'*), the depravities, the crimes committed by the women of our time, her disapproval would have been even greater. As for the women of Egypt, they have invented indescribable acts and crimes, and no one knows how to stop them.'[56] And 'Ainī, who lived in the thirteenth century, provides details of every kind of depravity practised by his contemporaries. Among others he quotes the example of 'women who sell depravity to men in broad daylight', 'bawds (*qawādāt*) who corrupt women as well as men', 'prostitutes who seek out debauchery'. 'Some walk the streets looking for men', others 'set up their traps in specialized houses and in the hammam'; some 'present on behalf of men requests for coitus to married women, to whom they know how to present matters in an agreeable manner'.[57]

Thus we have ample evidence that brothels and red-light districts finally became accepted after long having been more or less secret. Indeed, in the end, the state came to accept them. It saw in them a considerable source of income. In Andalusia prostitutes were called *kharā jiyyāt*, those who pay the *kharāj*, or property tax! I do not know by what juridical subterfuge the tax on brothels came to be regarded as a property tax. We know, for example, that in the tenth century, under Sayf-al-dawla and under the Fatimids in Egypt prostitution was offically taxed.[58]

A. Mazahéri sums up the situation very well when he writes: 'At Latakia, a port in Syria, it was the *muḥtasib* himself who taxed and set the charges for each of his public women, according to age, attractiveness and beauty. Thus everyone knew where he was. At Suza the brothels were situated next to the mosque, and every town had its *harābat* bazaar, or brothel.'[59]

Again according to Mazahéri:

> In the medieval East there were three kinds of places of ill repute. The *harābat* bazaar was a string of taverns in which procurers received the clients and led them to an adjoining courtyard on to which opened the rooms of their resident girls. In this bazaar one found rather mean-looking houses in which low-quality prostitutes, covered with make-up and dressed in gaudy colours, sitting on sofas, gossiping among themselves and munching grilled pistachio nuts, awaited the clients. . . . The clientèle of such houses consisted of working men, soldiers and sailors.[60]

The gilded youth of the time and rich strangers had more elegant houses where the women were less vulgar. At a still higher level there were better known villas in which lived 'extremely expensive courtesans reserved for the use of noble lords, important functionaries and superior officers. In an atmosphere scented with amber, nard and incense, in a setting of refined luxury, these beauties of pearly complexion, langorous eyes made to look much longer with kohal, cheeks like tulips and pomegranate flowers, poured intoxication into men's hearts.'[61]

At Kairwan, or Tunis, there were, and still are '*quartiers réservés*', or red-light districts, situated near Zauias. At Kairwan over half the houses used for prostitution had been set up as church property (*waqf, habus*). The pious constituents had not hesitated to devote the income derived from these places of debauchery to the maintenance of the holy places. There is not a single Muslim town of any importance that does not have its brothels. The more important towns even had one per quarter. The situation could not have been very different from what one could still observe during the colonial period when 'every town', as J. Berque tells us, 'has its red-light district, which attracts peasant girls who have been sent away from home. . . . At Casablanca . . . tourists, artists, writers, including Gide himself, visited the Rue des Ouled Nayl at Bou Saāda.'[62]

First the Ottoman Empire, then the colonial administration were to organize prostitution as a legal and sometimes official and even military institution. In addition to the special military brothels, the French colonial authorities encouraged the Algerian *nailya*, the Moroccan *hajjala* and the Tunisian *azriya*. The obvious requirements of public order, writes J. Berque, 'have forced the police to confine one day to the legionnaires, another to the infantry, etc. For the slightest dispute soon turns into a brawl.'[63]

In Tunis, in the 1930s, prostitution would appear to have been organized along just such lines. At that time, Tunis, with a population of some 300,000 had five *quartiers réservés* (Rue Sidi-Abdallah-Quèche, Rue du Persan, Rue Sidi-Baïane, Rue Ben Osman, Rue Mahjoub), in which close on three hundred '*filles soumises*', or registered prostitutes, worked in six '*maisons de tolérance*', or licensed brothels ('La Mossa', 'Le Chabanais', 'La Féria', 'Les Palmiers', 'L'Athéria', 'La Grande Maison'). Furthermore ten '*maisons de rendez-vous*', or hotels of assignation, each run by a French 'Madame', were distributed throughout the new 'European' quarters. Lastly, there was a *maison de rendez-vous* for male prostitution, 'Le Mayol', in the *ḥāra* (former Jewish quarter), also known as the Étage des Waqui. In this apartment some fifteen resident prostitutes, all male (thirteen Jews, a Frenchman and an Italian, in 1937), wearing women's clothes and heavily made up, were at the disposal of clients. The official price of a visit varied from five to ten francs, according to the age, looks and skill of the prostitute and the duration of the visit. Of course the distribution between *quartiers réservés*, *maisons de tolérance* and *maisons de rendez-vous* depended on the clientèle, which was popular and noisy in the first case, discreet and better-off in the second and very well-off in the third.

The *filles soumises* over the age of twenty were authorized, after having requested and obtained their registration, to agree for money to have sexual relations with the first man to request it in a place planned for the purpose. Medical supervision was obligatory and they could not leave their place of work at night or during the day, except on Mondays, their day off. They could only be freed from their obligations after a series of steps had been taken and for certain reasons: the advanced age of the girl or her 'return to God'.

There was always a marked tendency to ageing in legalized prostitution. The distribution according to age could not have been very different from what it is today. In Tunis in 1967 prostitutes were distributed according to the following age groups: 2% between 20 and 25, 8% between 25 and 30, 40% between 30 and 40, 35% between 40 and 50, 7% between 50 and 60, and 7% over 60. Of course the youngest ones practised in *maisons de rendez-vous*, the older ones in the *quartier réservé*, and because everything has its price the cost of a visit varied from one place to another, though there was no fixed price system.

In the *maisons de tolérance*, the outer door led to an enclosed courtyard, which led in turn to the various rooms. The girls themselves waited for their clients in the bar. But in the *quartiers réservés* things are much less discreet. The registered prostitutes, very scantily dressed (bathing suit or bikini), wait in the shops, which give straight on to the street. Sometimes, especially when it is hot, they stay in the street itself, sitting on the threshold of their shop. The success of a girl, especially a new or young one, is to be measured by the length of the queue that forms in front of her shop. And it is not unusual to see men outside getting impatient, when a particularly favoured client takes too long.[64]

There is, then, a certain permanence in the particular, unlawful model of sexual relations represented by prostitution.[65] The gaps in our historical knowledge and the difficulties in filling those gaps are easy to understand. However we have enough information to state that Islam, despite its extreme tolerance with regard to sexuality, which it sees as self-fulfillment and happiness, despite the great ease with which it organized lawful sexuality – has utterly failed in preventing Arab societies from having recourse to prostitution. Though anti-Islamic *par excellence*, prostitution was nevertheless profoundly rooted in Arabo-Muslim mores. From the bazaar of the *harābats* to Bousbir and Abdallah-Quèche, there is a remarkable continuity.

Of course, from time to time, in a reaction of indignation, a particularly pious – or elderly – sovereign decided to close the 'houses of vice'. In 934 the Hanbalites organized raids in the houses of ill-repute in Baghdad and occupied the premises. In 1014 the Caliph al Hakin[66] went so far as to forbid women to go out into the streets. At Kairwan, in 895, Ibrahim Ibn Aghlab, in a public act of repentance, smashed his own wine jars, dismissed the prostitutes and cleaned up the city.[67] Not so long ago, even King Farouk had his moments of austerity. A law of 1949 decided to close the houses of prostitution throughout the kingdom of Egypt. But in such matters the most Draconian measures seldom last and their promulgators are driven to writing pamphlets or preaching sermons against prostitution, always to no avail.[68]

Such persistent ability to withstand all attacks upon it cannot be fortuitous and shows quite clearly that prostitution fulfills an essential need in the Arabo-Muslim societies, even when one might have believed that those societies had no need of such sexual services.

Despite a good deal of Phariseeism, the ostensible attitudes of official morality do not accurately reflect the realities that may be uncovered by objective research. In fact we can certainly say that the juridical framework of *nikāḥ* is insufficient to satisfy the sexual needs of the members of the group as a whole. To begin with, *nikāḥ* involves a dowry, which, though limited in principle, is all too often very high as a result of the pretensions of the family, or a sense of competition. And, in spite of everything, not everyone can afford to get married. Every society has its *déclassés*, its outcasts or, quite simply, those who live on the fringe of society. Whatever ability a society has to integrate the individuals who compose it, there will always be deviants and non-conformists. By institutionalizing prostitution society kills two birds with one stone: it controls the deviants as well as giving a status to deviance. In the last resort institutional prostitution forms part of the secret equilibrium of the Arabo-Muslim societies.

Indeed the prostitute is an 'outlaw', she is a-typical. But precisely as such she corresponds to a particular social type. In the traditional social organization, she is the safety-valve. She is still more or less institutionalized, very often legitimated, sometimes legalized. The prostitute has a precise role, a well-defined function in Muslim society. She canalizes vice and by giving it a status tries to circumscribe it. *De facto* tolerance with regard to prostitution is an instance of the dialectic of the normal and the pathological.

But, beyond the ethical and canonical problems posed by prostitution, what matters for us is to detect the psycho-sociological impact of the institution. Prostitution is a *de facto* institution by which boys are initiated into sexual life. Indeed the clientèle is largely made up of adolescents who, already pubertal but not yet married, have recourse to it to satisfy normal biological needs.

In the Arabo-Muslim town the red-light district is part of the familiar landscape of the town; sometimes, of course, as in Beirut or Kairwan, it is at some distance from the centre. But sometimes, as in Tunis, it is at the very heart of the city and even forms a link between the old and new quarters. 'For this reason the red-light district is in direct communication with the streets and quarters where honest, law-abiding families live and work. Similarly it serves as a short-cut for everybody to pass from the old town to the new town and vice versa. For these two reasons, one sees there every day children between twelve and eighteen, often clutching their school satchels.'[69] Indeed even when the red-light district is more or less concealed topographically from the town centre, this merely serves to point it out all the more clearly to the young, who always discover it anyway. In either case, prostitutes, especially in small towns, are known by name and they are not necessarily spurned. Sometimes they are even regarded as practising a profession like any other, until such time as they change their job and get married. They are sometimes invited to family celebrations to amuse the women and children with their indecent talk. Once married, despite some prejudice on the part of a few puritans, they invariably become re-integrated into ordinary life. This is certainly 'tolerance'. For her part, the prostitute does not seem to see herself, any more than does the maternal bawd, as really on the edge of society. 'Tonight, my son, I have a new delivery of girls, whose prices, per evening, vary according to their deserts.'[70] These words, spoken by one of the innumerable bawds in *The Thousand and One Nights*, are not exceptional. Well regulated prostitution of this kind suggests an atmosphere that has little in common with the austerity of the ḥisba and fiqh and the *sitt al-sutūt*, the 'ladies' lady', is not always an object of derision.

All this explains why the sexual life of the young Arabo-Muslim is very often, if not almost entirely, taken over by organized prostitution, whether public or not. Other experiences, with cousins, neighbours or maids, are in no sense a viable alternative.

I spoke above of maternalism. It is more than an empty phrase. For, in this initiation, the only one left in a society in which women are confined and the sexes strictly separated, we must take into account the gap in age between most prostitutes and their clients – the average age for prostitutes in Tunisia is at present forty-two. There is no reason to suppose that it was any different in the past.

Furthermore the bawd, the 'ladies' old woman' (*ajūzat al-sutūt*) helped to give prostitution a very strong touch of maternalism.

'Your father was my lover', said one 'Madame' to a young client. 'I'll give you a good bargain tonight.'[71]

I should now like to advance a hypothesis that does not seem to me to be in any sense absurd: in this initiation into love the prostitute is merely the substitute for the mother. In a society that exalts desire and, at the same time, impedes it, only the prostitute can transcend taboos, violate prohibitions and satisfy it. In a society in which a look is often sinful, in which the veil conceals shapes from view while deforming them, the prostitute offers total nudity. She represents a double promise of freedom: freedom from social constraint and freedom from the constraints of desire. The role of prostitution is to appease tensions, to transcend anxieties and to integrate, in an ambiguous form, the margins of sexuality.

What is disturbing is the systematic infantilization and regression that accompanies sex with prostitutes. It emerges quite clearly from research carried out in Cairo by Sami Ali and 'Abdelmonem al-Melīgī that '*qua* psycho-social behaviour, prostitution rests on a disturbed image of one's own body'.[72] Indeed there is a remarkable concordance in the clinical analyses carried out by the Cairo team, which insists on the disturbance of the vision of the biological human being. Prostitutes display an 'unhealthy interest' about their own bodies, and al-Melīgī adds: 'The results obtained have convinced us that prostitutes feel an intense aggression, which they direct in turn towards their own bodies and towards the outside world.'[73]

This research was carried out, of course, in a modern, underdeveloped context and we would be wrong to extrapolate general conclusions from it. The results of this research, which are extremely interesting in themselves, concur sufficiently with research that I have myself carried out to lead to the conclusion that prostitution represents not a positive initiation into sexuality, but, as much by the maternalism that it involves as by the promiscuity that is inherent in it, a systematic infantilization. Sharing as it does a context with the hammam-complex and the traumata aroused by circumcision and excision, prostitution cannot but be regarded as regressive.

4 Folklore: puritanical and obscene

Nothing is more curious than the organization of a society based on strict sexual division – and nothing could be more fascinating to study. The strict hierarchy of the sexes of Arabo-Muslim society gives rise to a strict sociological dualism: two worlds, two empires, two antagonistic views of things. Life in the harem, the enclosure for women, the veil, the notion of *'aura*, etc., institutionalize the separation of the sexes and tend to reinforce still further the divisions. In many social strata, encounters between the sexes are limited to the strict minimum indispensable to life and survival. From birth to death a woman sees only those males whom she is supposed to see canonically: the men of her own family and, of course, her husband. The *ḥazzār*, the 'jealous puritan', obsessed with keeping his wife and daughters protected from any temptation, is a stereotype still widespread today. 'He's so jealous,' a Tunisian saying has it, 'that he won't tolerate the presence in his home of any male, even a cockerel or a fly!'

The treatises of *ḥisba* meticulously regulate the hours, places and manner in which women may go out of the house. A woman who is not at home is *a priori* suspect. This is the impression that clearly emerges from 'Uqbāni's *ḥisba* treatise.[74] This strict authoritarian prohibits even visits to the hammam or to cemeteries.

> We ought to forbid . . . meeetings of women in the cemetery and public places where they find themselves side by side with young men, for a large number of libertines might also meet them and be attracted to them, on account of the intentions attributed to them and of the motives that are theirs. Some women set up tents between the graves and stay there a long time, pretending to avoid indiscreet looks. But this merely encourages desire and evil all the more. . . .[75]

One must also mistrust women who frequent the souks to buy or sell wool, for example. This is only a pretext, 'Uqbāni declares, to stop on the way in front of the shops, to exchange a few flirtatious words, abominable looks and who knows what?[76]

The prudent man, who cares about his reputation (*'arḍ*), should be just as suspicious of expeditions to fetch water or bread. For there 'women stand around for any other reason than the purpose of their expedition. On the contrary they stand and converse freely with debauched slaves and with a few libertines of free condition', which, 'Uqbāni adds, 'has resulted in innumerable little mulattos'.[77]

Women's festivities are even more suspect. How dreadful are such meetings, which are so frequent nowadays, 'Uqbāni goes on: 'Women, dressed up in their finest attire, meet one another, unveiled, around some singer, who is of course unmarried, who enchants and entertains them'.[78]

The most one can tolerate is a schoolmaster, preferably blind, who will confine his teaching to a few verses of the Quran and prayers. There must be no poetry, no correspondence. 'Indeed it would be better not to teach women to write.'[79]

'Uqbāni's suspicions are highly significant: they are evidence of the inanity of 'those useless precautions'. The social history of the traditional Arabo-Muslim world is a constant search for compensations, flights, subterfuges, to circumvent, to bypass the Manicheism of the sexes. Practices in the hammam and prostitutional maternalism are only two types of compensatory behaviour. If folklore is merely a tradition that has lost its meaning, if there is no practice that does not have a very precise function, then we should pay some attention to the sexual, artistic or obscene 'folklore'. This folklore contains an immense wealth of meaning. It is a veritable battery of safety valves in a rather enclosed social system, a permanent determination to correct sclerosis and to circumvent prohibitions in one way or another.

Indeed can a social system function in a vacuum?

Are not the two categories 'closed' and 'social' antithetical? Hence those innumerable 'flights' by which female and male energies each tried to escape, to free themselves, not without some measure of success. And even the feeling of liberation and the pleasure thus felt were merely increased by so many attempts that were doomed to failure. Indeed not all husbands paid as much attention to protecting their women as 'Uqbāni recommends. And the adjacent terraces of Arab houses made many escapades possible, when the doors of the streets were heavily guarded. The terrace was a convenient and discreet means of penetration into an Arab house. Even the veil was a two-edged weapon and men were quite capable of donning it by way of disguise. It provided an excellent mode of anonymity both for men and women. Indeed the veil was more of an aid to intrigue than a protection against it!

The promiscuity of the large family had a similar effect. A haven for so many unsatisfied aunts and repressed youths, a paradise for lonely cousins burning with desire, the large Arab household was a hotbed of unsatisfied desire. Supervision was relaxed and was difficult to implement in those houses where, as the eternal puritans put it, 'the rams are all mixed up with the ewes'.

Marriages between cousins were not only tolerated, but were, as we have seen, the only thing to hope for. What could be more natural than that the young would fall in love very early and have pre-marital sex long before the official consummation of the marriage? Were they not, so to speak, facilitated, encouraged by their environment? Was it not a common practice to match future couples as soon as a boy was born? Throughout childhood and adolescence, a boy and a girl were brought up with the idea that they were promised to one another. They saw each other in anticipation as future husband and wife. One can speak of a veritable 'cousinage' encouraged by the large household and the ancestral mode of life. Behind so much austerity there was so much laxity, and behind so much intransigence, so much facility and self-inflicted blindness! Even if it is very difficult to produce an objective account of facts of this kind, we do know that flirtation with cousins, neighbours, a friend's daughter or sister was far from exceptional.

Very precise information is provided by Ibn Hazm, who poses the problem of relations with very close relations. He expresses surprise that Abraham was able to marry his half-sister or that the Kharigites should have allowed marriage between grandparents and grandchildren or between uncles and nieces.[80] Indeed he tells us that Zāwi Ibn Zīrī the Berber had over a thousand wives, all of whom were descendants of his brothers.[81] Again he notes that a good Muslim will never covet his sisters and nieces, 'even if they be more beautiful than the sun and he the most debauched of men and the most prone to love. And if, most unusually, such a thing does occur, it is only in the households of impure persons on whom religion no longer has any hold and to whom therefore all lewdness is permitted and who are forever ready for love.'[82] And he adds this fine 'rationalization':

> One could not be sure that a Muslim's affection for his female cousin would not turn into passionate love and exceed the affection that he had for his own daughter and niece, even if they were both more beautiful than the first. Indeed he might

wish to obtain favours from his uncle's daughter that he would never expect from his own or his father's daughter.[83]

The very fact that the question is so explicitly posed and above all that love of the female cousin is placed on the same footing as love for one's own daughter or niece suggests a whole range of possibilities.

The three cases of incest recounted in *The Thousand and One Nights* reflect a certain climate, to say the least. Although it is true that Sharkān marries Nuzhat and has a child by her without knowing that she is his sister, Budūr falls in love with As'ad, son of Hayyāt-al-Nufūs, who in turn falls in love with Amjad, son of Budūr, knowing full well what they are doing.[84] The two young men are half-brothers.[85] It is also knowing full well what they are doing that two young brothers and sisters withdraw to live together. Indeed, walled up in a grave, they are burnt to death.[86]

The theme of flirtation with a female cousin has been taken up in innumerable novels and tales. There are the curious Tunisian confessions in which Shemseddin recounts his amorous adventures with his cousins Hanifa and Mahbūba.[87]

More recently, there is the fine evocation of the theme in Rachid Boujedra's *La Répudiation*, a rich mine of social observation.

'During the wedding, the women were separated from the men; but the boys of the house took advantage of a certain confusion to join the women who, in any case, were only too ready to dispense their favours.'[88] Of course, 'some women went home to content their excited husbands and came back in haste to have their breasts caressed by insatiable cousins in search of something to do that would not only pass the time, but that would also satisfy them.'[89]

A highly coloured, realistic passage describes how the 'hero' slips into his cousin's bedroom. 'She watched me come in, but all I could make out was my own shadow in front of me. . . . She saw me approaching her and she must have been afraid of that large, grotesque shadow. At first she said that she did not understand, then that she did not want to, on religious grounds. . . .'[90] Obviously the seduction had its effect and everything was consummated in sorry disenchantment. 'Suddenly, I went back to my room, leaving my cousin panting, stupidly female. . . . Grotesque, lazy and above all unhappy at the idea of a sin so sordidly consummated.'[91]

Rachid's ungovernable desire was to lead him to sleep with his beautiful stepmother, the young Zūbia.[92] 'We had no other recourse than rapine, incest and wine.' And there is this terrible observation: 'My parricidal pleasure gaped. To kill the cat, all cats. Rather swallow the sea! she said. . . . Did she often make love with my father? ("Why, would you be jealous?" she would ask, surprised. . . .) In order to make her husband hateful in her eyes, I recounted, with great bitterness, the story of my younger brother, who had been brought up in Arab traditions.'[93]

But there was more. In this tangle of sisterly relations with half-sisters, quarter-sisters, blood sisters and milk sisters, young Rachid was lost. Then there was a newcomer to the large house of Si Zūbir, Leila, who was like a new sister. 'I chased her from my bedroom when the buzzing of my senses warned me of the ineluctable squandering derived from the genetic father, for Leila did everything to excite me and became my accomplice. . . . Had I violated my half-sister?'[94]

To what extremities did the system of sexual division not drive one? How could one not speak of deviance and inversion? The meeting of the sexes was so enveloped in prohibition, so meticulously regulated, so jealously reduced to the strict minimum that there was a constant temptation to violate them.

Thus homosexual relations were relatively encouraged by the Arabo-Muslim societies, to the detriment of intersexual relations. In the end segregation exalted promiscuity. It is difficult for those who have not experienced it to imagine what life under a strict separation of the sexes is like. But it is understandable that homosexuality, so violently condemned by Islam, could be so widely practised among both men and women. *Mujūn* more or less included pederasty and lesbianism, despite the remonstrances and sermons of the 'Uqbāni. The fact that homosexuality was always being condemned proves only one thing: neither the religious nor the social conscience could put an end to practices that were disapproved of by Islamic ethics, but to which in the last resort society closed its eyes. Cousinage, prostitution, amorous intrigues of all kinds were inadequate to cope with the expression of desires that turned quite 'naturally' to homosexuality.

Pederasty and lesbianism were merely consequences, derivatives and compensatory forms created by sexual division and explicitly perceived as second best. Rachid Boujedra provides this fictional sample.

> In winter, he confessed, I'm fond of dozing off and the master can do nothing about it because I'm blackmailing him: last year he made immoral propositions to me and I agreed to them so that he would leave me alone. . . . Everyone accepts the quranic master's propositions! He furtively strokes our thighs and something hard burns us at the base of the spine. That's all there is to it! I know it isn't serious. . . . Parents, who generally know what's going on, shut their eyes to it, so as not to have to accuse a man who bears the word of God in his heart. . . . My sister says it's a consequence of the Arab golden age. Later, I understood that it was poverty that incites the *ṭālib* to homosexuality. For in our town one has to have a lot of money to get married. Women sell themselves in the public square . . . and the brothels are too expensive for small pockets.[95]

The victim expresses his bitterness thus: 'Yet again childhood had been pillaged, betrayed, attacked point-blank by some monstrous adult.'[96]

We should note, too, the hypocrisy of the schoolmaster: 'How could one denounce the wretch whom everybody had seen that very morning, saying his rosary and sacrificing his sheep.'[97] With its promiscuity of the sexes, its imprisonment of children, the cynicism of some adults and the sordid calculation of others, the whole system has failed, the young Rachid concludes. How many other Rachids, sickened and rebellious, has Arabo-Muslim society produced!

One may even wonder whether homosexuality did not constitute the exposed, conscious level of a deeper reality. The inversion of the male brought up in such an atmosphere cannot but find release in such a crude way as that described by Rachid Boujedra. It may seek other disguises, other justifications, in the same hypocritical way. For one will find with significant constancy and frequency certain features proper to male homosexual eroticism in female eroticism. The prototype of the masculine woman (the *ghulāmiyya*) refers back by antithesis so that of the effeminate boy and beardless ephebe. Such sexual equivocation and ambiguity tells us a great deal about the ambivalence of amorous feelings in a sexually divided society. One loved women, of course, but one sought to find them through boys and, in the end, one liked only women who looked like boys. Abu Nawās expresses well this ideal of *ghulāmi* love:

> Sufferings and love of boyish women.
> Kiss-curls on be-ribboned temples.
> Tall and slim-waisted.
> Striding off in buttoned shirts.
> Promises made and hopes of two loves.[98]

Does this account for the special affection given to the buttocks? Much debate in the fiqh has been devoted to *waṭ fi duburin* (anal intercourse). Such a polemic combined with judicial records, poetry and what we know of personal accounts show that the sodomization of women even in the framework of the most regular union is fairly widespread. There can be no doubt of the frequency of anal intercourse in both sexes. Plump, shapely buttocks have won the praise of more than one lyric poet.

Salaheddin al-Munajjid does not hesitate to write:

> The canons of female beauty require a protruding behind and voluminous buttocks. . . . The behind has to be tender and supple. It has been compared with a sand dune on account of its height and softness and also to a sandy hill. The two buttocks have been compared to two bags. Reddish and pink buttocks are preferable. Arabs have always had a passionate love of buttocks, boys' as well as women's, and poets, from the pre-Islamic period to our own time, have striven to sing of the praises of their suppleness, their fullness and their roundness.[99]

There is a whole social psychology of buttocks, which are often a prestige object. Full volumes give an idea of pleasure to the eye that is an anticipation of the possession of the object coveted in the course of the sexual act. Indeed Arab erotology tells us that they are an essential element in sexual pleasure. This is why women in the Maghreb, Egypt, Arabia and Iraq, etc., have resorted to systematic overeating (*tasmīna*). At Djerba, in Tunisia, the future bride was shut up for months on end in a cellar with a view to fattening her up. She emerged only when the family considered that she had reached an honourable weight and there would be no doubt in the public mind that the future bride did not come from a poor family. I completely agree with Gérard Zwang when he speaks of 'exclusive mythification'.[100] Indeed one can speak of a whole symbolism of the buttocks: 'Full, smooth, hairless and rounded, the buttocks are for many the mythical image of the female body.'[101]

What passion must have been aroused at the sight of bodies prostrating themselves in prayer (*ṣalāt*), thrusting the behind outwards and upwards. Indeed the language of the vulgar identifies prayer with coitus precisely because of this prostrated position.[102] And legend has it that Joseph, once the young, handsome man, indifferent to the charms of Zuleikha, the wife of Putiphar, became at last aflame with desire at the sight of her prostrated on the ground, her buttocks raised in the air, protected only by a veil of tantalizing thinness.[103]

In Arabo-Muslim culture there is a systematic passage from the values of the buttocks to the values of the woman's body as a whole. J.-P. Sartre has an admirable passage in which he elucidates the almost magical attraction of the buttocks. After observing that 'to know is to devour with the eyes',[104] which is strongly reminiscent of the *zinā* of the eye analysed in the fiqh, he writes:

> The idea of 'carnal possession' offers us the irritating but seductive figure of a body perpetually possessed and perpetually new, on which possession leaves no trace. This is deeply symbolized in the quality of 'smooth' or 'polished'. What is smooth can be taken and felt but remains no less impenetrable, does not give way in the least beneath the appropriative caress – it is like water. This is the reason why erotic descriptions insist on the smooth whiteness of a woman's body. Smooth – it is what re-forms itself in its passage over the stone which has pierced it.[105]

The smooth is an unfinished dream. The rough, on the contrary, prevents dreaming. Hence the rejection of hairs and the excitement aroused by hairlessness (*amrad*).

So the female sex is particularly loved when it is hairless. Indeed the fact is that depilation is an important element in the practices of the hammam, of hygiene, of the art of making oneself beautiful and ready for sexual activity. An unshaven woman is supposed to be repugnant, dirty, careless of her person. So-called superfluous hair is supposed to make a woman look unpleasantly manly (*mirjila*). Hairiness is anti-erotic and indeed only young girls and women in mourning are released from the obligation to shave pubic hair and depilate the body. An unshaven vagina is readily compared with an evil eye.

Hygienic considerations have certainly come into play: there is nothing more effective than shaving to eliminate parasites in the pubic hair. Indeed the custom is not confined to the Arabo-Muslim societies: it is equally Mediterranean, even African. It was practised by Greek women, among whom it corresponds, if Gérard Zwang is to be believed, to a desire 'to rob their sexual organ of part of its mystery, part of its complexity; if men's pubic hair rests on safe ground, femininity will always suggest, to the timorous, treacherous vegetation covering a swamp. It is in a sense in order to inspire less fear in the male that Greek women showed their vagina naked.'[106]

In my opinion, the explanation is to be found elsewhere: what depilation suggests is not so much a fear of the damp, hairy hole, as a homosexual element. It is a means of rediscovering the boyish girl in the very temple of femininity. An ultimate consequence of the sexual division of society, it is really no more than a compensatory practice that finds the best outlet in the psychology of the smooth, so admirably described by Sartre.

Of course there are other outlets in Arabo-Muslim societies. In addition to these erotic compensations there are others that are frankly obscene. For it is almost a miracle that Arab poetry and art succeeded in celebrating without bad taste a part of the body almost unanimously regarded as shameful, ridiculous and disgusting – in short, obscene. There is a flight into obscenity that, as a compensatory practice, deserves all our attention. It concerns neither nakedness nor eroticism. Sartre, to whom we owe an excellent analysis of obscenity, remarks:

> The most graceful body is the naked body whose acts enclose it with an invisible garment while entirely disrobing its flesh, while the flesh is totally present to the eyes of the spectators. The ungraceful, on the contrary, appears when one of the elements of grace is thwarted in its realization. . . . The *obscene* appears when the body adopts postures which reveal the inertia of its flesh. The sight of a naked body from behind is not obscene. But certain involuntary waddlings of the rump are obscene. . . . This revealed flesh is specifically obscene when it is revealed to someone who is not in a state of desire or without exciting his desire.[107]

An unshaven vagina is regarded as obscene because it is deprived in the partner's eyes of all erotic value – so much so indeed that a woman who exhibits her vagina unshaven to a man commits a serious injury, and is regarded as having turned a particularly dangerous evil eye upon him. Hence the power of so many of the gestures to be found in the Maghreb. In the streets, in the souk, in the market one still sees people scratching their behinds or proudly exhibiting their virile members. Quite obviously such gestures are crude affirmations of power and are the negation of desire and the death of pleasure.

Gestures are symbolic, spoken words still more so: the mother's – and secondarily, the sister's – vagina shares with the mother's – and, secondarily, the father's – religion, the sad privilege of being insulted and cursed all day and every day. A whole verbal flow, from spoonerisms (*ghashsh*) to double meanings, perpetually maintain an equivocal attitude that is indeed very Mediterranean. This compensation by gesture and word is merely a means of freeing oneself from sexuality by ridiculizing it, by emptying it of any meaning. It is a 'forward flight' whose infantile, regressive character is quite evident.

Sometimes it is a veritable ritual, in which women themselves take part, that takes place in public. Take the Egyptian *baṣbaṣa*.[108] Neither men nor women are shocked by this. A woman passes by in the street. She may be veiled, of course, but the way she walks, swings her hips and wears her veil, the tinkling of her jewellery and the heavy perfume she leaves in her wake serve to exhibit her to the public. Men then began to stare at her and to give vent to their delight with various more or less obscene exclamations. The woman must then slow down her walk, drag her feet, judging by the words addressed to her the measure of her own attractiveness. It is after all only a veiled form of 'counter-striptease'.

A woman who passes unnoticed in the street is much more often disappointed than one might believe. Sometimes the women perform a *baṣbaṣa* among themselves and even the men among themselves. . . .

Genuine pleasure is to be found at the physiological level of the look and language. One can understand the place of voyeurism in a society that regulates and codifies the look in its slightest details.[109] And this pleasure of the look rebounds upon the pleasure of speaking. Since Freud we know how profound are the links that bind language with the sexual drive. And we have innumerable examples of this in Arab erotology.

The multiplicity of names given to the sexual organs and to coitus belong to the magic of words. Words replace gestures and gestures refer back to words. The word in the physical way in which it is pronounced is a substitute. It is compensatory, but the pleasure that it procures is certainly real.

In another book[110] I have tried to show that tales are an opportunity to indulge in an oneirism whose links with the sexual are undeniable. The relationship between the teller and the listener, especially in the case of children, creates imaginary bonds that play a crucial role in the socialization of individuals. Myths, dreams and symbols refer back to one another in a psycho-social arabesque the most obvious effect of which is to maintain by speech and orality the compensatory models without which life would become unbearable.

Everyday life abounds with instances in which obscene words, spoken and repeated obsessively, end up as a substitute. The theme of *mujūn* discussed above is only the noble register of a veritable institutionalization of the obscene. It is as if obscenity concealed within itself a cathartic virtue. After all why should not obscenity also have the mytho-therapeutic or logotherapeutic effect that we have tried to examine in the case of tales? In pronouncing obscene words, one provokes, catalyses, drains the libidinous. One expresses it, tames it, diffuses it. One also provokes others; with it one creates a veritable relationship or complicity; by conjuring up obscene situations, one frees oneself and frees it. By gargling obscene words one finally masters, in a symbolic and temporary way, all one's anxiety-inducing fantasies – and there is no shortage of them in the Arabo-Muslim societies! Curiously, but understandably enough, it is perhaps the most puritanical societies that produce the most verbal – and obsessional – obscenity.

In fact the obscene word acts almost at the level of the breath, the wind that it frees. It is the mystery of the *flatus vocis*. But the other liberations of wind operate on the same principle. The fart, the belch, the yawn, the sneeze[111] have no other significations and one can hardly be surprised at the important place they hold in popular obscene folklore. Claude Gaignebet rightly remarks:

> The problem is clearly posed by Aristotle: 'Why do such other winds as the fart and the belch have nothing sacred about

them, while the sneeze is regarded as being so? . . . The fart is the wind that emerges from the end of the intestines and the belch comes from the upper belly, while the sneeze comes from the head. It is because this last region is the most sacred that we venerate as sacred the wind that comes from it.'[112]

This is certainly the case, for the sneeze is always received in Islam by ritual formulas, which is not the case with the other winds. At the opposite extreme the yawn is regarded as an act of the devil, who causes it in order to distract people from prayer or thoughts of God.

The fart has an undeniably liberating function. In our tales we have tried to show how it plays the role of that which symbolically resolves all problems.[113] There is even a certain musical value in the fart, especially when it is imitated by a series of obscene movements of the right hand against the left armpit. Not very long ago I even knew of a company of amateurs for whom the fart took the place of music. And the people of Kairwan are regarded as so expert in the art of farting that in Tunisia a fart is quite simply called 'the Kairwanese'. Lastly the fiqh gives some idea of the canonical importance attached to the fart by making it a break in minor purity.

The belch (*jushā*) – and this has not failed to shock westerners – forms part of a veritable *ars vitae.* A good belch is regarded as the sign that one is full and that a good digestion is likely to follow. It indicates well-being and health – God should be thanked warmly for so many benefits! Psychoanalysis, of course, has tended to see it as the symptom of an anal erotic fixation accompanied in certain pathological cases by an aggressive sadistic signification.[114] In Arabo-Muslim societies it certainly has a signification of well-being, but, of course, the two interpretations are not necessarily exclusive of one another.

Indeed systematically, consciously, one provokes belching by drinking all sorts of gassy drinks containing magnesium citrate or carbonic gas. The secret charms of *gazūza* (lemonade) are sung in the Egyptian counting rhyme: 'Away with tea, I prefer *gazūza*' (*ma shrabshi shay na ashrab azūza*).

The froth that bubbles out of a bottle of *gazūza*, the bubbles that twinkle in the glass, symbolize spermatic fecundity. A good *gazūza* sets one dreaming and prepares one for liberation upwards.

One cannot but admire the symbolic displacement of the low to the high and from dense liquid into airy gas.

Gazūza is the Islamic equivalent of wine. In its own way it is a water of youth. Refreshing, pleasant, it is valued above all for causing belching. There are civilizations based on wine and civilizations based on lemonade. Tell me what you drink and I will tell you what you are! The prohibition of alchoholic beverages may merely be a trick! Undeniably liberation through belching belongs, though in what seems to be a more innocent mode, to the same continuous line of compensatory practices as obscenity. Sonorous exhibitionism, autistic indifference and promiscuity belong in each case to the same networks of signification.

Sometimes these significations themselves are travestied by the subterfuges of art and religion. For a long time at Tunis, one could visit a living saint, Sidi Amor el Fayyash, now dead. The peculiarity of the saint was to be stark naked when he received his female visitors and, in his fits of dementia, he would give them 'sublime words', which were then interpreted by the *naqība*, or female attendant, who was permanently beside him. Travellers who over the centuries have visited and explored the Arabo-Muslim world have left innumerable testimonies of saints of this kind who use nakedness and obscenity as essential elements.[115] *Ziyara* and obscenity refer back to one another and it is well known that the cult of a saint was, and is still, a pretext for the unburdening of passionate and libidinous feelings.[116]

Obscenity is often institutionalized in a more 'public' way, so to speak. The village idiot, for example, played this role. Not long ago, at Kairwan, there was a holy man, curiously, but significantly, called 'El 'Aura' – that is to say, both 'one-eyed' and 'the indecent one'. A cohort of boys continually followed him, clapping their hands and calling on him to exhibit his 'watch'. And the holy man – for he was regarded as such – would lift his tunic and exhibit his nakedness to the great joy of the men and women passing by.

In Egypt there was Sidi Ali Kākā. This is how Ahmed Amīn describes him:

> He was a strange character and one who demonstrated the extent to which Egyptians are obsessed by their sexuality. He wore sandals and a belt, from which hung an object in the shape of an enormous penis. When women and children saw him pass by, he invariably brought on attacks of the giggles.

> On the occasion of a birth, sweets are made that have that [phallic] shape. They are made of caramelized sugar, transformed into sorbet. They are also called sharbet [sorbet]. And the vendors used to cry their wares in the street: '*Sharbet* dolls, *sharbet* husbands, *sharbet* mothers-in-law, *sharbet* Ali Kākās'.[117]

Sidi Amor el Fayyash, El 'Aura or Ali Kākā are pale figures compared with Karakūz, a character believed to be of Turkish origin.[118] The French 'Karagheuze' derives from the Turkish word *qaraqush*, which means 'black bird'. It is a marionette some eight to twenty inches high. But there are bigger Karakuz still. Karakuz is the hero of short plays performed throughout the Arabo-Muslim world especially during the month of Ramadhan to enliven the long nocturnal vigils. The words and situations are left to the inspiration of the marionette master. But obscenity is the rule, for Karakuz has the speciality of being endowed with an enormous, Rabelaisian *membrum virile*. He is the epitome of virile, triumphant pride arriving to conquer the world, thanks to his well-tried member. No one escapes his virility: the manageress of the Moorish baths, the *zaptie* (a policeman under the Ottoman Empire), the *meddeb*, the prostitute, the general, the local shopkeeper, the bedouin, the virgin sitting at home, the policeman and the Frenchman, too, all are subjected to the victorious effects of his sexual frenzy. Nature itself is not spared: the palm trees and olive trees are undermined at their roots and the *wadis* are diverted or stopped. Nothing can resist the furious blows of Karakuz's rod. Each feat was accompanied by obscene verses, indecent repartee, vulgar proverbs and the mixed audience, men, women and children, would laugh uproariously.

In Tunisia political protest was slipped in behind the character who in memorable performances attacked the bust of the beautiful Marianne and a stylized map representing France. René Millet, French resident general in Tunisia at the time, forbade the performances. But Karakuz is still alive and well and flourishing in the East.

Such a systematic use of obscenity cannot be fortuitous. One may speak of a ludic, but collective use of obscenity that seems to correspond to a very precise function. Collective obsessions are thus institutionalized and in a sense appeased. A sexually divided society limits to the minimum opportunities of meetings between the sexes. Sexual relations are limited to those permitted by the nature of *nikāḥ*. Essentially authoritarian, Arabo-Muslim society is castrating not only from the sexual point of view, but also from the point of view of individual autonomy in the political, economic, ethical and cultural spheres. Despite the intolerably stifling atmosphere that reigns in these societies, they have had sufficient genius to place enough safety valves at the right moments and the right places.

Hence that mechanism of compensation by which every possible opportunity is used: cousinage, homosexuality, voyeurism, verbal outpourings, obscene gestures and words. Indeed, very often, poetry and even the casuistics of the fiqh itself are little more than magical processes substituting a gesture charged with meaning for the complete sexual act and often a mere word for the gesture. Obscenity, of course, is only a game, but a most revealing one. It compensates through fiction. It liberates by symbolic realization. It releases passions and is the most potent, most effective safety-valve. Unfortunately, it is not effective enough.

As such the various manifestations of obscene folklore examined in this chapter represent an important and not ineffective defence mechanism. At the risk of repetition, I will say that it is of the utmost importance to understand the institutionalized character of these various mechanisms. Obscenity is not marginal; on the contrary, it is profoundly rooted in the collective life and sometimes manifests itself in an excessive way. It is, I believe, like prostitution and pederasty, a cause of psychological immaturity. Being essentially externalizing, formal and exhibitionistic, it soon loses all freshness, all spontaneity. Nothing is more frozen, so heavy and difficult to manipulate than the stereotypes of obscenity, which, by their nature, do not lend themselves to renewal. Obscenity is mere lack, a fragile persona, an external façade that ill conceals the true ego. The most obscene people are perhaps the most impotent. In this overcompensation, the personality runs the risk of losing its plasticity, its overflowing naivety, in short, its force. Obscenity is not always authentic liberation of the libidinous. On the contrary it is perhaps a supreme ruse on the part of society, which tolerates it precisely because it is castrating, because it lures the individual into the way of facility and because it drives him to adopt collective forms of behaviour. Nothing is so destructive of the creative spontaneity of the loving self than obscenity.

In the final analysis, nothing is so orthodox. From puritanism to obscenity there is continuity and unity.

Ultimately if obscenity were merely a temporary fantasy it would be of little consequence. On the contrary, as we have just shown, it is integrated in the system. From the outset it is an element of conformism, of systematic infantilization, of collective cretinization. In this 'anti-conformist conformism' the meaning of sexuality is lost. Love itself sinks into the ridiculous: love without joy, sexuality without pleasure. The tension of the sacral and the sexual is to be found at the very heart of a contradiction that we find over and over again: as a religion Islam makes possible a lyrical vision of life, but the Arabo-Muslim societies have almost succeeded in denying this lyricism by refusing it all foundation and by refusing it even to the point of denying self-determination.

CHAPTER 13
In the kingdom of the mothers

What aporias, then, and what contradictions! As a religion and as a view of the world Islam strives to be and presents itself as an exaltation of life. It sings of the fulfillment of being, of *gharīza* (innate tendency). Unity is attained by the affirmation of Eros, not by its negation. In various ways all the instruments of social control – art, literature, folklore – take up these ideals, which inform them in the sense that they are bound to obey the rigorous, but agreeable, requirements of the unity of life through love. A veritable 'pansexualism' runs through the Islamic ethic. Love is one, from bestiality to the vision of God. It does not even begin with the animals: even the trees are in love. The very stones sing of love. God himself is a being in love with his own creatures. From the thing to the Supreme Being love exists as a guarantee of unity. It weaves tight, indissociable links within earthly creation and beyond. Being is one, because love is one. And in order not to be unworthy of being, only one thing is required: love. So love is a prayer, an ever-renewed miracle by which one gives oneself in order to receive the better, that is to say, to assimilate oneself the better. To give oneself up to be seen and to see in order to give.

But one must probably be a prophet oneself, animated by the Revelation and the breath of the hereafter, if one is to grasp, conceive of and above all achieve this essential unity! To live carnal love, to live it to the limit, to assume its plenitude is to forge a safe way for oneself to the Absolute. Mysticism and eroticism complement one another.

Orgasm, that 'little death', is continuous rebirth. True enough, but unfortunately such an intuition does not seem to be very widespread. Nor does the valorization of love in the mode of unity seem to have found a practical means of becoming concrete at the level of everyday life. The organization of collective life is ultimately no more than the fragmentation of what Islam originally conceived as unified. Does this represent a failure on the part of Muslim societies to unify themselves and to conform to the spirit of Islam? Perhaps, but it is certainly also a nostalgia for unity when faced with the contradiction of the diverse.

The unitary ideal, rarely realized in fact, permits us to see ethics and the fiqh as an antinomy. In sexual matters it can be said that the fiqh opposes ethics, since it organizes communal life not in terms of the profound complementarity of the sexes, but in terms of their dissociation. The passage from the Quran and the sunna to the fiqh is a passage from the harmonious unity of the sexes to their duality. The fiqh organizes Muslim society in terms of sexual division. It is at the level of the fiqh, much more than at the level of ethics, that social bimorphism was to be structured, organized, institutionalized.

But the spontaneous structures were to go even beyond the structures organized by the fiqh. And although the fiqh speaks of bimorphism, the spontaneous structures were to set up a *de facto* sexual bimorphism even more rigid and even more serious for the evolution of the Arabo-Muslim societies. The Quran speaks of a gap 'of a single degree between the sexes, in favour of men'. The fiqh speaks of a natural disparity. The *de facto* groupings institutionalize the repression, derealization and negation of women. Of course everything is expressed in subtle terms and the status of women is certainly ambiguous, even in the Quran itself. Nevertheless there is a progressive decline of the Muhammadan ethic of marital tenderness. It is as if the continuous training and domestication of love led to a negation of love; that is to say, in a male-worshipping society, to the negation of women. It is as if the redistribution of the male and female roles to which Muhammadan ethics addressed itself had remained a dead letter – or almost. Hence so many subterfuges, so many safety-valves, so many more or less illusory compensations. At best infatuation, anti-love, ended up as no more than substitutes, which, robbed of their mythical halo, often turned out to be disappointing. In the socialization of love one can imagine what a terrible price is paid by society as a whole. The burden borne by women continues to be an exorbitant one. For it is nothing less than the sacralization of the masculine and the trivialization of the feminine.

The study of sexuality in the Arabo-Muslim societies reveals that, in practice, the derealization of the status of women has invariably led to the enclosure of women in a double role as objects of pleasure and as producers of children. In either case we are dealing with women-as-objects. A cruel contradiction! On the one hand there is a persistent tendency to sing the praises of sexuality, to celebrate love, to encourage a lyrical view of life. The libidinous forces are exalted, liberated, even unleashed. 'Couple' (*tanākaḥu*), the Prophet ordered. But, on the other hand, sexual dimorphism tends ultimately to place all positivity on the side of masculinity and to empty femininity of all value. To be more precise, femininity is reduced to being no more than the obverse of masculinity. Woman is the shadow of man, in the literal as well as the figurative sense. Everywhere denied, femininity hides itself and seeks refuge: woman becomes a creature of the home and of night. So it is hidden deep within the individual and collective personality that woman must be found. And it is in the depths of inferiority that essential femininity is hidden.

By confining woman to pleasure, one turns her into a plaything, a doll. By doing so one limits love to the ludic and one reduces the wife to the rank of woman-object, whose sole function is the satisfaction of her husband's sexual pleasure. Marital affection is reduced to mere pleasure, whereas in principle pleasure is only one element of it among others. Thus the wife is devalued. But by stressing the child-bearing role of women, one valorizes the mother. In fact misogyny represses woman into her maternal role and by that very fact sets up a veritable 'kingdom of the mothers'. For *nikāḥ*, in itself, is merely a consensual act that juridically regulates the relations between public and private. In fact social life actually goes well beyond the fiqh. Love may be seen only as an erotic manipulation. Nevertheless one cannot deprive the woman of her formidable power of producing life. And she alone holds the key to procreation. This represents an incontrovertible fact that imposes, at the biological level, the irreducible, undeniable complementarity of the sexes. However possessive love may be, it cannot but be oblative and the possessive instinct cannot be completely dissociated from the nest-building instinct.

Hence the cult of the mother that seems to me to constitute one of the keys to an understanding of the basic personality of the Arabo-Muslim societies. The physical mother/child relationship is transformed into an extended psycho-sociological unity. Let us say that privileged relationships are grounded in 'the psychic umbilical cord',[1] to use Helene Deutsch's felicitous expression. In fact the mother-child relationship has precedence over the mother-wife and the mother-father relationships. An exemplary virtue of the umbilical cord that links the adult to his *uṣūl*, his authentic roots, the 'vaginal bond' (*ṣilat al-raḥim*) is an exemplary bond, or, in the Prophet's phrase, 'an extension of existence'.[2]

Of course it is quite understandable that, frustrated of so many joys, enduring such a painful condition, burdened by so much misery, a woman should transfer all her affections to her children. If so many Muslim mothers are possessive, even to an abusive degree, the reason is not to be sought elsewhere than in a system that denies them their most elementary rights. We should not forget that in a society in which repudiation is so widespread and so easy, husbands change, but children stay. Children very often constitute therefore the only factor of stability. They alone give the *ṣilat al-raḥim* its true meaning and value – especially as custody of the children is almost always given to the mother.[3] Indeed the fiqh admits that in the interest of the child the relationships that bind him to his mother are stronger than those that bind him to the father. And one is quite right to stress that 'motherhood confers more solicitude for the child'.[4] When the mother dies custody passes to the mother's mother before passing to the father's mother, then to her before the sisters. In the absence of grandmothers, sisters have precedence over aunts, but maternal aunts have precedence over paternal ones.[5]

The equipollence of the affective and uterine is even accepted by the fiqh itself. Of course it expresses the permanence of a universal, widely observed human fact. Nevertheless the projection on to the child of all maternal affectivity conceals in the male-worshipping Arabo-Muslim environment a crucial significance if only in the economic, social and cultural consequences that it brings with it.

Children are loved for other than practical and immediate reasons. For the mother they constitute a veritable system of insurance for old age and illness, a guarantee against destiny that is all the more effective in the case of repudiation. What could the fate of a woman be who did not have the good fortune to become a mother? A sterile woman has scarcely any other prospects than that of being an unwanted, inopportune burden on her father or brothers. Married without children, she can hardly aspire to be anything but the servant of her younger, more beautiful or more fruitful co-wives. On the other hand, a mother is guaranteed that at least her children will not 'drop' her and that everywhere she will be protected from poverty and need. Not to mention the prestige, honour and 'presence' conferred on a woman by children, especially male children. Besides every mother hopes to become in turn a venerated, 'protective' (*ḥamā*) mother-in-law. By reigning over her daughters-in-law she will reach the summit of glory before dying, respected and surrounded by her grandchildren. Having children in the traditional Arabo-Muslim society is the fundamental element of security for a woman. Woe betide the sterile woman! On her weighs the threat of repudiation. The best she can hope for will be to be lucky enough to have a rich and 'charitable' husband and to share his bed with other co-wives. But if one of these wives gives birth to a son, she will be forgotten and sent home!

There are problems, too, concerning inheritance. Sons inherit most of the patrimony. Mothers are given a mere eighth. In view of this the son's mother will prepare a better 'retirement' for herself. But the situation can be worse still: Muslim inheritance law lays it down that in the absence of male descendants the collaterals of the first or second degree have a right to the inheritance. So it is understandable how fear of the *ghāṣib* (intruder) could be the source of so much conflict and transform the situation of a sterile wife into tragedy. For her brothers-in-law will scarcely entertain such tender feelings towards her as she might expect from her own male children.

Motherhood, then, was a protection. It was the only security for a woman – there was practically no other. The Quran may affirm that 'wealth and children are not essential to earthly life', but children are certainly the way to material happiness and a sense of security. So, given the 'system' and the structures of the environment, the Arab woman tries to increase her chances by having as many pregnancies as possible. Hence that obsession with children – have children, more children and still more children!

And, after all, did Princess Shahrazād in *The Thousand and One Nights* really owe her 'success' to anything other than the fact that she had wasted no time in giving her master three male children in thirty-three months? 'One of them walked, and one crawled, and one was at the breast.'[6] Every traditional Arab woman dreams of just that. And, in the popular expression, 'the month must not be broken', by the arrival of menstrua, always tantamount to disaster. Fear of an empty womb, terror at a miscarriage, obsession with repeated female births and the misfortunes of infantile mortality – this is the fourfold fear that haunts the Arab mother. The social status of the Arabo-Muslim wife owes much more in fact to her performance as a mother than to her physical charms. In the final analysis the anti-wife, the concubine or the temporary mistress count for little. Faded roses, illusions of freshness, the indelible marks of time. No, for our parents, unfortunately, beauty was not always the most important thing. One accepts beauty, but one seeks motherhood. Beauty will pass, but the child will remain. The fruitful mother (*al-walūd*) is well aware that the future belongs to her. The rivalry between our mothers was settled by the number of male children they had; even if deceived, even if abandoned, a fruitful mother has infinitely more prestige and social presence than a beautiful, unfruitful woman. Motherhood is equivalent to usefulness, sterility to uselessness. This is because motherhood is equivalent to function and sterility to marginality. There is practically no other institutionalized social role accorded to women than that of mother.

Hence the search of motherhood at all costs and the importance given to magico-religious practices and traditional pharmacopoeia, a good part of which is directed against sterility and towards increased fertility. In one of his ephemeral literary reviews, Mouloud Feraoun has an admirable account of the dramatic consequences of sterility in Maghreb society.

> They dreamt of having many children, especially boys. When, at the beginning of their marriage, someone expressed the wish that they would have seven sons, the wish was received with a beatific smile: that was the intention. They began to worry by the end of the first year. Was it a matter of fate or had a curse been put on them? They would have to take precautions: they would have to obtain the forgiveness of those they had wronged, even those they had forgotten until then, visit the dead, distribute sweetmeats on their graves to solicit their good will, go to reputable *kubas*, leaving offerings and promising still greater ones. Each of these rites was carried out with the greatest humility. All month Sliman said his prayers, Shabba purified herself night and morning, their love-making, in the dark, of course, was as vigorous and as hopeful as ever. On the morning of the twenty-ninth day, the young woman could no longer be in any doubt when she felt a warm trickle

between her thighs. She ran to the back of the house, to the small reed hut and lifted her *gandura* to examine her shame: her mortification was given vent to in a flood of insults addressed to anyone or anything: the chicken scratching around in the ditch, the chipped pot that she had carelessly knocked, a door that wouldn't stay open. Sliman guessed at once. He got up without a word and took himself off to the café.[7]

This cult of motherhood has its roots deep in the mists of time. Nevertheless it is an essential feature of the Arabo-Muslim societies. 'Paradise,' says one hadith, 'is under the heels of the mothers' (*al-jannat taḥta aqdāmal ummahāt*).[8] Women who die in childbirth are regarded as witnesses to the faith (*shahīdāt*), in the same way as men who fall in a Holy War.

This attitude to motherhood is ultimately the basis of the relationship between spouses. When, speaking of his wife, a husband says *umm aulādī*, he is showing infinite respect, boundless esteem, eternal gratitude. And, conversely, the wife accepts whatever treatment her husband chooses to mete out to her because 'he is the father of my children', *abu aulādī*. The interpersonal bond created between spouses through the mediation of children is so strong that the mother-child relationship has far greater importance than the direct mother-father relationship. The latter is based on the former, and not the other way around.

But this is done only at the cost of a double decline, physical and psychological, that has always threatened our mothers. In a profound and well-argued analysis, a Tunisian psychiatrist, Sleim Ammar, noted as long ago as 1962:

> Abundant procreation, itself deriving from continual promiscuity, from the scarcity of leisure activities, from ignorance of contraception and often from men's indifference to and unawareness of the matter, creates not only an extremely heavy burden for the family and for society, but also helps to undermine and weaken the very organism of the woman, who is the pillar of the home and family cell.[9]

It is at the price of her physical and psychological health, and often to the extent of actually shortening her life, that the Arab woman pays for a security that turns out in the end to be illusory.

The traumata of imposed marriage and semi-public deflowering, and the fear of sterility, the phariseeism of the patriarchate have long combined to bring about the systematic cretinization and alienation of women. Arab woman pays dearly for her dominion over the unconscious.

From the children's point of view, one can equally well declare that the relationship with the mother is, paradoxically perhaps, far more important than the relationship with the father.

Precisely because of its excessive masculinity the social world is inevitably perceived by the child as castrating. Paternal authoritarianism cannot fail to devalue childhood in the same way that it devalues femininity. The child is a miniature adult, capable at most of childishness. His value lies in what he will be, not in what he is. The same type of barriers that separate male from female separate the adult from the 'little ones' (*ṣighār*). Childhood is derealized to such an extent that it is deliberately ignored by the fathers, who willingly hand over to the mothers responsibility for their sons for a large part of their childhood. The only valid models of experience are those of the adult. It is up to children to conform to them, to approach them. Just as one can in no sense speak of the autonomy of women, so the autonomy of children is unthinkable.

Indeed, in terms of socio-economic status it can be said that children have quite simply been exploited by the patriarchal socio-economic structures to a relatively advanced age. In agriculture, in the crafts, in commerce, the child joins the family firm in which he works without being able to claim a wage. The firm belongs to the parents, the working relationship is virtually indistinguishable from the father-son relationship. In the strict sense, such relationships cannot really be distinguished from relationships of 'proletarianization'. Hence that stereotype of the son who waits endlessly for his father's death in order to inherit, that is to say, in order to reach economic autonomy – which he then establishes on the exploitation of his own children. One can hardly turn on Radio Tunis, Radio Algiers or Radio Cairo without finding one of the innumerable radio plays dealing with the theme of inheritance!

There is a terrible image of the father: *Ab*. This all-powerful, all-serious colossus cannot but represent an impenetrable wall between the child and his father. Jacques Lacan, in one of those densely written texts that he has made his own, has a passage that seems to me to sum up a permanent feature of the collective Arabo-Muslim personality:

A function at once of power and temperament, an imperative

> that is not blind, but 'categorical', an individual who dominates and arbitrates the greedy laceration and jealous ambivalence that forms the basis of the child's first relationships with his mother and with the fraternal rival, that is what the father represents and, it seems, all the more so in that he is at some remove from the first affective apprehensions. The effects of this appearance are expressed in various ways by psycho-analytic theory: but quite obviously they appear in it warped by the traumatizing effects in which experience first allows them to be perceived. They do not seem able to find expression in their most general form: the new image 'floculates' in the subject a world of individuals who, in so far as they represent nucleii of autonomy, alter completely the structure of reality for him.[10]

A Muslim upbringing was, of course, authoritarian. As such it was no different from many other things. The authority relationship has deep roots in our traditional society. It binds not only man to woman and parents to children but also teacher to pupil, master to disciple, employer to employee, ruler to ruled, the dead to the living and God to man. It is not only the father who is castrating; society as a whole emasculates.

However, in the midst of this universal emasculation there is one haven: the mother. By a subtle, but very natural strategy, mothers and children have decided since time immemorial to combine their efforts to hold in check if possible, in any case to circumvent and to compensate for, whatever is abusive in patriarchal power. We have seen how a mother expects that her children will provide for her future. In addition to that they also act as valuable 'antennae' for her. Our children are certainly expert at 'keeping their ears open' in male circles, lying in wait in the street, keeping an eye on the father or the family-in-law, serving as messengers, carrying secret presents, buying forbidden articles, selling tiny objects that 'disappear' from patriarchal view. In short everyday life leaves innumerable bonds of complicity between mother and child. The child is aware that he is performing a service for his mother. He is not unwilling to do this, for he knows that his work will be rewarded with gratitude. But above all what pleasure there is in outwitting the father, or taking revenge, with such delicious and relatively safe complicity! Our children are certainly skilled at making themselves agreeable to their mothers and proving that the rule of the male adults is all a sham. A fine revenge for so much humiliation! A just compensation in a life in which chastisement is an everyday occurrence!

What mother has not had, one day or another, to establish with her own children a complicity such that the uterine relation is extended, fortified and consecrated by the sweet bonds forged during a common victory against the heavy threats of derealization? Here complicity is tantamount to positivity and, in the dialectic of intra-familial relations, it proves an effective negation of the negation. So in an Arabo-Muslim setting the mother appears even more as a font of affection, all the more precious in that it is a restful oasis in the arid social desert. How pleasant her water is to drink under the hot midday sun! And these private bonds between mother and child are reinforced by the fact that the fathers hand out so parsimoniously the external marks of their own affection. 'Where is my mother?' clamoured the Iraqi poet Zahāwi. 'Give me back my mother. I don't want anything to replace her. . . . I need my mother's love.'[11]

Indeed the mother often plays the role of buffer between the father and his children. She comes between them whenever a threat appears. She knows how to mediate. And often she manages to make the father give in. There is a whole comic dimension, in the form of shared jokes, between mothers and sons. It is quite normal for licentious, indecent words and phrases, which more or less run counter to the sexual taboos, to pass between them. A very important, very subtle relationship is established between them which I have tried to analyse in terms of the storyteller-listener relationship.[12] It is not unusual to see the mother pushing understanding 'a little too far' in view of current customs and accepted morality. She would encourage a secret meeting or arrange to be absent from a certain place. She would defend some misdemeanour and encourage uncanonical practices. In any case it was she who would choose the 'daughter-in-law' and then take charge of her.

We have seen how, in the case of the hammam and in the case of prostitution, the uterine relationship, extended into the mother-child relationship, tended to reappear at the slightest opportunity. Men brought up in this way would miss no opportunity to create, to re-create, to rediscover the uterine environment through memory, imitation, dream or fantasy. Side by side with the real world one forges for oneself an exquisite private world of compensations. One establishes the kingdom of the mothers. The Arab woman is the queen of the unconscious even more than she is queen of the home or of night.

Rachid Boujedra's novel, *La Répudiation*, exhibitionistic as it sometimes is, gives us the most telling examples of this truth.

> Solitude, my mother! Under the shadow of a heart cooled by the ultimate announcement [of repudiation], she continued to busy herself with us. A hodge-podge of wrinkled bruises! Scowling sex. Yet, gentleness. The deep furrows made by her tears became deeper. Dumbfounded, we witnessed a final attack. In fact we understood nothing. My mother could neither read nor write, but she sensed the existence of something that was breaking down the framework of her own unhappiness and splashing all other women who had been or could be repudiated, women eternally dismissed, running backwards and forwards between a capricious husband and a hostile father who saw his peace disturbed and did not know what to do with such an encumbrance.[13]

Over and above its intrinsically literary value as a novel, *La Répudiation* is invaluable as a document. It supports the views that I have been trying to develop: on the foundations of a castrating, patriarchal society is built the kingdom of the mothers. What Boujedra recently said about Algeria is still broadly valid for the Arabo-Muslim world as a whole: 'A castrating society with regard to the sons, but at the same time one doomed to incest. The revolt of the sons against the father takes the form of debauchery. When sexuality is repressed it is a political act to claim, to declare sexual freedom. Patriarchy holds economic power.'[14]

In a more serene tone, President Bourguiba once made the following confession:

> When I was little, men always used to say to me: 'Don't sit next to women; one must fear their evil fate.' But what they meant by that was that women were an instrument of humiliation and, because of their sex, vile creatures. . . .
>
> It was thanks to my contacts with the female element, in the family atmosphere sustained by my mother and grandmother, that my mind was awakened, my eyes opened and I realized the evil fate that was theirs, despite their gifts, their abilities, their struggles and the services that they gave in bringing up and educating their children. At the same time they were

> dominated by a feeling of inferiority. Words were used about them that I dare not repeat, so gaping is the wound that they left in me. . . . Deep down inside I suffered for them and I told myself: but they are human beings. Furthermore they are necessary to society! They do their duty! . . .
>
> Such a childhood, with the strong relationships that I established with women and particularly with my mother, have made me regard the feeble creature that woman is with immense affection.[15]

More than one Arab identified with the Tunisian president when he admitted in public what most men preferred to keep to themselves. By the pity that she inspires and by the love that she unstintingly gives, the mother appears as an effective, unconscious recourse against the castrating intentions of the environment. In such circumstances it is hardly surprising if the relationship with the mother is preferred to the relationship with the father and that every patriarchal society is doomed to be marginally maternalistic. Marginally! No, rather at the very heart of the private, personal life.

A woman's relationship with her husband will be of the same type and nature as her relationship with the feared father. For the Arabo-Muslim girl marriage is merely the passage from one type of submission to another. The form will change but the authoritarianism will remain. However, it will be mitigated to some degree, for a certain freedom achieved through the exercise of her charms and through the advantages brought with pregnancy will bring her some compensation. Though far from being the free fulfillment of being and the full affirmation of the body dear to the quranic ethic, marriage will certainly represent an improvement on life under the paternal roof.

For the boy, marriage is quite likely to be a prolongation of his relationship with his mother. All too often the wife is merely a substitute mother. Of course, this tendency is universal, but it is particularly striking in the Arabo-Muslim societies. In any case C. G. Jung's fine description of the imago of the mother is evidently valid in the socio-cultural context that concerns us here: 'The first bearer of the soul-image is always the mother; later it is borne by those women who arouse the man's feelings, whether in a positive or negative sense.'[16] In Arabo-Muslim societies, the negative certainly dominates the positive, given the distribution of male and female roles, the status of children, the different types of child rearing and the rigidity of the relations between the sexes and age groups.

The emancipation of the son from the dominant influence of his mother represents a crucial stage in his life that circumcision and the expulsion from the women's hammam, for instance, have prepared him for, but only in what may seem a terribly inadequate way. The child is literally snatched up by the adult male world, the only world that society teaches one to take seriously and which indeed immediately exerts its power. To live with the world of the fathers is to assume one's social responsibilities, to be accepted by the group, legitimated, integrated. One rejects the kingdom of the mothers or one remains marginal. In the world of the fathers, the Arabo-Muslim boy has no other choice. Indeed he has no choice at all for he is thrown into it almost without knowing it.

Jung goes on: 'The consequence is that the anima, in the form of the mother-imago, is transferred to the wife; and the man, as soon as he marries, becomes childish, sentimental, dependent, and subservient, or else trenchant, tyrannical, hypersensitive, and always thinking about the prestige of his superior masculinity.'[17] Of course it is this second attitude that will dominate him like a mythical halo, with which the husband clothes his wife, who all too frequently plays the magical role of mother. Hence that excessive idealization of woman inevitably followed by disappointment. The instability of marriage expresses, it seems to me, that profound inability to detach oneself entirely from the mother and to perceive the woman-wife as an equal partner in the work of building up a family together.

I have already noted that Islam inaugurated a system based on the rotation of woman. In fact the system turned all too often into a scarcely disguised Don Juanism. The Prophet may condemn 'those who are merely tasters in love' (*al-dhawāqūn wal dhawāqāt*), but the Arab is a born Don Juan who has found his best ally in the fiqh. It has been observed that 'in Egypt there are many men who have married twenty or thirty women in the space of ten years. Similarly, women who are by no means old have successively married a dozen or more men. I have heard of men who are in the habit of changing wives every month.'[18] Again this is a reality of everyday observation. This instability is such that in present-day Tunisia, the government seriously considered for a time forbidding any remarriage during the year following a divorce! The Arab loves to marry. He is a born *mizwāj*. This tendency is so deeply rooted in every section of society that one begins to wonder whether there is not something fundamental here that frequently prevents the male in our societies from being a man with a single wife. It is as if there were for him only one ideal model of purity and perfection and that he is therefore doomed to a hopeless, perpetual, ever-renewed quest for a woman who can measure up to that ideal.

My own research and observation have convinced me that there is a profound erotic anxiety here. Each new wife arouses such expectations that reality, in the shape of a wife herself conditioned by the same society, cannot but fall short of it. In his magnificent trilogy, Najib Maḥfūdh[19] describes one admirable example: Yā Sīn, the eternally unsatisfied man. His inadequacies as a lover, defects of character, attachment to a frivolous mother, all these factors combine to turn into failures a series of marriages, which always begin well, but which the most refined erotological techniques are unable to save. Behind the ideal woman, the jealousy of the male, the search for a perfect marriage, what one is ultimately looking for is a mother-substitute. 'His fear of the dark incalculable power of the unconscious,' Jung writes, 'gives his wife an illegitimate authority over him, and forges such a dangerously close union that the marriage is permanently on the brink of explosion from internal tension – or else, out of protest, he flies to the other extreme, with the same results.'[20] This fine analysis seems to me to sum up the problem under discussion and to account both for the prestige of the mothers and the ambivalence of the roles that Arabo-Muslim society accords women.

One cannot stress too much, then, the privileged relationship of mother and son, which dominates all other types of interpersonal relationships within the group. In a sense the mother constitutes the pivot and epicentre of life.

Again it is *The Thousand and One Nights* that provides an exemplary image of this in the tale of Judār.[21] The hero, Judār the fisherman, guided by a Moorish magician, has set out in search of treasure buried in the depths of the earth. The magician Abdessamad, after burning incense and reciting secret formulas, manages to dry up a river beneath which entry to the treasure is to be found. Judār had to open the first six doors by reciting the appropriate formula in each case. But he must be courageous enough not to blench when he is given a mortal blow, from which he will miraculously recover.

> You will then knock at the seventh door, and it will be opened by your mother. She will say: 'Be welcome, my son. Come near, that I may wish you peace.' You must answer: 'Stay where you are and undress!' 'My child, I am your mother,' she will say. 'You owe me respect, because I suckled and educated you. How can you think of setting me naked?' You must cry out on her, saying: 'If you do not take off your clothes I will kill you!' When you take down a sword, which you will find on the right wall, and bid her begin, she will try to move your pity. Be on your guard against her wheedling and, each time she takes off one of her garments, cry: 'The rest, the rest!' and menace her with death until she is quite naked. As soon as she has no more clothes, she will vanish. Then, O Judār, you will have broken all the charms and loosened all the enchantments without hurt to yourself.[22]

And the Moor adds: 'Have no fear for that, O Judār, the guardians of the door are but phantoms.'

But when Judār finds himself confronted by his mother he dares not ask her to remove her final garments. He is troubled by his mother, who goes on berating him: 'O my son,' she says in a shamed voice, 'It was indeed lost labour when I reared you! Is your heart of stone that you make me show my middle nakedness? Do you not know that this is forbidden and a sacrilege?' When he hears the word *ḥarām* (unlawful, a sacrilege), he gives up his plan and says to his mother: 'I allow you to keep on your drawers.' The exultant mother then cries: 'Beat him, beat him, for he has drawn back!' And Judār is given a sound thrashing and thrown out of the treasure hall, the doors of which immediately shut behind him.

However the Moor and Judār refuse to acknowledge defeat. A year later Judār begins his magical operations again, but this time with more success. His mother undresses until only her drawers remain. 'Remove them, O hag!' he orders, and 'as they dropped about her feet she vanished.' And Judār is able to seize the treasure.

We cannot fail to admire how the fable, whose richness is unsuspected by those who still refuse to take the tales of *The Thousand and One Nights* seriously, expresses faithfully the preferential relationship that is established between the child and his mother.

Life is a treasure that can be acquired only if one is first able to kill the inanimate shades (*shabaḥ bilā rūḥ*). Psychological maturity is an attack on the mother. One must kill in oneself the image of the mother, profane it, demythify it. To kill in oneself the false image of the mother is to find security (*aminta*). It is our hesitations, our scruples, our childhood memories that prevent us from realizing our desire for happiness. Respect for our mothers prevents us from flying with our own wings. We have to see the mother, that is to say, the truth, in her complete nakedness, face to face, without blenching, without accepting the slightest veil. When we have stripped her of all her garments we will then see that she was merely a creation of fantasy (*ashbāḥ*) and that the soul (*rūḥ*) was elsewhere. We are prisoners of the shades of our mothers, that is to say, ultimately doubly prisoners. We are suffering from what Jung calls 'the anima in the form of the mother-imago'.[23] He who does not free himself from the mother-imago is beaten and defeated in advance. On the other hand, everything is possible to him who has the courage to hold fast to the end and tear away the false bonds that bind him to his mother. This tale of Judār is a good lesson in demystification and teaches us, in the profound words attributed to the Imam Ali, that 'one must kill the soul in ourselves in order to be born again'.

What the myth of Judār tells us is that it is only the image of the mother that holds us back. In order to release consciousness (*'irfa' al-awsād, ibṭal al-awsād*', as the Arabic text puts it), we must free ourselves from the abusive presence of the false image, the fantasy of the mother.

But the tale goes on to tell us that Judār has to behave in this way not only in his own interest, but in that of his real mother. As long as Judār hesitated to cross the Rubicon, in this instance the final garment that concealed her sex, their life together would be a poor one. The real mother had sunk into dire poverty, a dirty, wandering beggarwoman, sitting at the city gates, holding her hand out to passers-by. But as soon as her son is able to realize in himself the necessary conversion she is saved. For Judār's first concern when he has possession of the treasure is to give her the same security that he had obtained for himself.

This is what the decipherment of the *rumūz* (symbols) consists of. The mother is a riddle that one must follow to the end. She must know how to distinguish between true respect for one's mother, the true filial piety that takes the form of giving help and security, the struggle against hunger, poverty, uncleanliness, humiliation and the false marks of uterine fetishism. Only then will the 'locks' (*al-awsād*) be broken. One could not have a better demonstration of how the uterine relationship may be a source of repression and how psychological maturity depends on the liquidation of the survivals of maternal desire.

Do we not have here all the elements, psychological and social, individual and unconscious, pathological and normal, rational and oneiric that enable us to speak of a 'Judār complex' in the sense in which one speaks of an Oedipus complex? Certainly there is, it seems to me, a fundamental unity of the universal Oedipus complex, which we find at the heart of Arabo-Muslim culture. But in so far as, according to Roger Bastide's profound words, 'there are as many types of unconscious as there are . . . types of society',[24] it may be said that Judār brings an archetypal but specific response to the great questions of life, love, hate, violence, insecurity and need. It defines a type of behaviour stripped of all guilt. The true Oedipus is guilty. He has after all committed parricide and incest. So he pierces his eyes. But Judār deals only with false appearances, and it turns out that his act is an authentic liberation of himself and of his own mother. It seems quite legitimate to me to see the Judār complex as the form of the Oedipus complex that is specific to Arabo-Muslim culture, an Oedipus, that is, unburdened of all guilt.

Oedipus' guilt is, of course, eventually removed, but at what cost? And could sexual dimorphism lead to anything other than a heavy tribute paid by women to ensure the socialization of Eros?

And the mother does not play her role in an exclusively male society with impunity. Men derive a certain freedom from the multiplicity of roles that they play. Women on the other hand can only suffer when they see themselves reduced to a role that is mutilation and lack. Arab women can find security only by playing to the utmost of their awareness and ability the cards of pregnancy, weaning and childbearing. These very rights are the ones evoked by Judār's false mother when she begs him to abandon his sacrilegious intentions. But the true mother is a poor woman, the victim of an iniquitous fate, brought about by her son's absence.

If Judār is an archetypal image of the Arabo-Muslim adolescent, Judār's true mother represents the Arab mother at her best. She is the faithful prototype who has lost neither the symbolic value, nor the economic, social and cultural characteristics that are still attached to the role of mother in our societies today.

This, too, is what the myth of Judār is telling us. In the common interest of the man and his mother one must tear away the veil of the mother and demystify motherhood. I think I have shown that the divorce between the quranic ethic and the requirements of society have imprisoned women in a *de facto* 'status', rationalized in law after the event, that is essentially ambiguous and ultimately has the effect of reducing the mother's role. If Islam has developed historically a logic different from that laid down in its theology, it is only by advocating the lyrical vision of life, by giving back to the flesh all its value, by removing guilt from love that it has opened up the way to the acceptance of nature. The mother is everywhere the reference and the vessel of concrete existence and everyday experience. The social finds its ultimate realization only in reference to nature. Hence that 'pan-sexualism' that is the golden rule of Islamic poetry, art and theology. As one of Ibn Rumi's poems has it:

> Today nature is a pleasure to the sight,
> Spectacle, unveiling, vision.
> Praise be to God, creator of the rain.
> The earth is in flower.
> Its clothes are all new.
> Luminous with light,
> Flourishing with flowers.
> Gone all modesty.
> The female burns with desire for the male.[25]

Indeed the Arab feminine is the conductor of nature. It is what makes it possible to unveil mysteries, decipher signs and also to countermand the prohibitions that are imposed upon it. Yet man refuses this essential role, thus blocking off so to speak the femininity in himself. Woman, who is all, is regarded as no more than a shadow. The eternal feminine is then relegated to a bygone age. At best woman is a complement, an adjunct, an ornament, a figurehead perhaps. She who is the essence is denied.

Is not that too what the myth of Judār means? One accedes to the truth of femininity only after drying up a river, crossing seven doors, experiencing death seven times and taking advantage of a propitious astrological conjunction. One has to plunge into a pit deep down in the earth. In short, motherhood and naturality are accomplices of one another. The *rumūz* (symbols) of nature are fully deciphered only in so far as one is able to distinguish in the maternal woman what is shadow (*shabaḥ*) and what is truth (*ḥaqīqa*). The *awsād* (locks) have secrets that only the penetration of the deepest truth of the mothers can help one to decipher. Everything begins and ends in the mother! Hence that double struggle of Arabo-Muslim woman in relation to man and in relation to nature. It is hardly surprising if she is exhausted in this double effort and pays very dear for the maintenance of the Arabo-Muslim personality. But if in each Arab there is a dormant Judār, where are the magicians who will initiate us into the art of forcing the locks, deciphering the riddles and rediscovering peace of mind?

CONCLUSION

The crisis of sexuality and the crisis of faith in the Arabo-Muslim world today

These various historical adjustments, then, have meant that the sexual ethic experienced by Muslims and the vision of the world that underlies it have less and less to do with the generous declarations of the Quran and of Muhammad himself. One can even speak of a degradation, which began at a very early date, of an ideal model. The open sexuality, practised in joy with a view to the fulfillment of being, gradually gave way to a closed, morose, repressed sexuality. The discovery of one's own body and that of another, the apprehension of self through the mediation of otherness, turned in the end into male selfishness. Furtive, secretive, hypocritical behaviour assumed an ever more exorbitant place. Sexual division turned into an inhuman, untenable social dimorphism and a source of untold suffering. All freshness, all spontaneity were eventually crushed as if by some steamroller. The price paid by women and by the young in the maintenance of this social *status quo* was a terrible one. This reification of being deprived it of all autonomy, freedom and value. Youth and femininity were finally robbed of all seriousness and even denied any real existence.

This picture, already dark enough and itself the result of a slow political, economic, social and cultural decline, was further complicated by the arrival of colonization. This violation of the collective personality, this seizure of the environment, of institutions and even of language, were to reinforce still more the tendency to closedness and sclerosis. Arab society was to set up structures of passive defence around zones rightly regarded as essential: the family, women, the home. The strategy invented by Arabo-Muslim collective experience was to limit the extent of the alienations of modern times, to limit the colonial impact to externals, while fiercely defending the essential values of private life.

The response to colonization was to be significantly double: sexual and religious; indeed with each supporting the other. Colonization was to stop at the threshold of the Arab family, which it respected, with good or ill grace. By depreciating Arab morality, ethics, women and love, colonization did not realize that it was helping to maintain the collective personality. In a sense, it ceded almost involuntarily to a fierce wish on the part of the native community to limit foreign penetration to a merely geographical occupation of the territory and a merely economic exploitation of the country's wealth. This was already enough in all conscience, but not enough to destroy the essentials. Whether or not it was 'fanatical' or 'intolerant', the Islamic faith was able to raise an effective barrier between itself and the new masters and to undermine any attempt at assimilation.

This meant that Arab women were now promoted to the historical and unexpected role of guardians of tradition and of the collective identity; women had thus found a new function. Outside, men could compromise themselves with the new order of things as much as they wished. But, once he was at home, the Arab man rediscovered an atmosphere steeped in the past, one in which yesterday was an eternal beginning. In these circumstances it was inevitable that the procreative role of Muslim women should be stressed still further. Speaking of the Arab, J. Berque remarks that 'the fecundity of his women, his sexual and familial morality have assisted in his emancipation: both through the pressure of the ever-increasing population and through youth which, constantly lowering the average age, gives added force to the desire for change and for a break with the past.'[1] J. Berque is right when he speaks of the 'contribution of the wife to national freedom'.[2]

Occupied, denied and humiliated, the Arabo-Muslim societies were to discover, perhaps without always being sufficiently aware of it, that sexual divisions and the reduction of femininity to motherhood were weapons unrivalled in their effectiveness. Thus in indirect and unexpected ways Arab women rediscovered a strange redoubtable power. Recourse to the mother turned out to be the best defence against loss of identity. The sexual ethic of Islam and the role that it accords women have given the mother a very special function as refuge and shelter of the collective identity. The social has been able to use both the sacral and the sexual to ensure its own survival So the conjunction of the sexual and the religious has spilled over from their own domains into matters of concern to society as a whole. Erecting themselves into total social phenomena, they have, depending on the social, cultural and political context, served as an alibi or as a refuge in the maintenance of social structures.

This has become all the more apparent in that modernization takes the form of a formidable irruption of technology, which comes between self and nature and even between self and self. Of course the use of a machine extends my body, but, by the same token, it interrupts direct contact between my body and the world. In innumerable instances of everyday experience, change creates, often in quite imperceptible ways, a new apperception of the body.

Sitting on the ground is not sitting on a bench or a seat. To drive in a car or to ride a bicycle is not the same thing as to walk. To eat with a fork also implies a quite different relationship with food, which one handles at a distance, than the direct relationship of a man who, face to face with his food, picks it up in his hand and takes possession of it through a very precise magico-religious ritual.

Take a simple example: modernization is also the transition from the hammam to the bathroom. The functionalism of the latter involves a desacralization and trivialization of the rich oneiric experience of purity. One passes indeed from the ritual of *ṭahāra* to a technological view of physical hygiene.

Let there be no mistake, entry into modernity means a radical change in the way in which one attends to one's own person. How indeed could it be otherwise from the point of view that concerns us here when the technology of family planning becomes part of the thinking both of the elites and of the masses. It does not matter how it is done: the elite may act on individual initiative and the masses may follow official campaigns. For the 200,000 Tunisian women using official contraceptives or for the 100,000 others who use private medicine the effect is the same: physical love is no longer a direct, spontaneous thing, but a hormonal self-discipline, a conscious, organized modification of one's own corporality.

Indeed contraception is in itself merely one part of a wider, more complex programme for the trivialization of sex and the de-eroticization of sexuality. The abolition of the veil, the movements towards ever-increasing nakedness, promiscuity, the mixing of the sexes, dancing, the cinema, erotic advertising, prostitution on view at the street corner, all this feeds our fantasies in a quite different way and in any case changes the nature and signification of intersexual relations. Between sexual partners comes more and more the artifice of technology, which, considerably aided by the enchantments of the mass media, breaks that essential harmony without which love becomes degraded into physical manipulation and eroticism into pornography.

So it is hardly surprising if the old dialectic of eroticism and sacrality is replaced by other processes that lead to the desacralization of Eros and to the de-eroticization of the sacred – and to a morose, joyless religiosity combined with a sad, trivial sexuality.

The distortions of the unhappy history of the Arabo-Muslim countries are not confined, then, to the political level. They are also to be found in a self-perception profoundly disturbed, in the body's relations with nature and with others, by a terribly indiscreet technology.

Of course we are just emerging from the colonial Middle Ages. But what effect can one, two, three or even four decades of independence have? And yet how much change has taken place in such a short time! Of course where modernity is concerned, sudden, brutal change cannot but prevail over the unchanging and the permanent. So for Arab women and for the young, modernity takes the form of a brutal, peremptory rejection. Modernization is felt not so much as the adoption of a new way of living and thinking as the rejection of the old. And what is still a problem, as far as the common consciousness is concerned, is the rejection of tradition much more than the acceptance of progress. The most conservative forces in our societies claim to be in favour of progress – but only of a progress that will not turn its back on the past. And it is around this distinction that for a century or more the battle has been waging between various forces. Tradition and progress are the two greatest enemies of our society. But what is striking is that in matters of sexual ethics, modernity can only be a matter of rejection: rejection of the negation of women, rejection of the various prohibitions that surround sexuality. It is no accident if modernity has, from the beginning, been synonymous with the emancipation of women and that today it has become synonymous with sexual emancipation. If women and sexuality have been the last refuge of a certain private, personal permanence, it was only to be expected that the work of renewal should begin there. But let us make no mistake, the 'sexual crisis' is merely the obverse of the religious crisis.

This is not the place to recount the history of the emancipation of Arab women.[3] It is as if Arab woman now refused to be the eternal sacrifical victim, as if she wanted at last to *live*, to take up Layla Ba'alabakki's cry of protest and affirmation in the *anā aḥyā*.[4] A single cry of 'live!' marks the Arab woman's rejection of her past condition. To a far greater degree than men, Arab women are discovering the will to live. Curiously enough, in the Muslim context, where the lyrical vision of life is a fundamental presupposition, it is only quite recently that women seem to be rediscovering the attractions of life – a life assumed, demanded with all the energy generated by centuries of despair and frustration. So, by an apparent, but logical and rigorous paradox, the lyrical vision of life has become a lust to live. One should almost speak of sexual frenzy. In the Middle East and the Maghreb emancipation has come to mean enjoyment – enjoyment to the full. Following the latest fashion in clothes, extra-marital 'affairs', 'pure romances' or outrageous scandals are merely the setting against which the lust to live is expressed, whether through violence and tumult or gentleness and enchantment. Modern eroticism, imported from the west, is not merely an extension of traditional eroticism, created by men for men. Arab women no longer wish to live in perfumed gardens. What they are demanding is the right to take the initiative in love and fulfillment through the gift of oneself. Female emancipation is also a recovering of sexual initiative. The Arab male can put away his erotology.

Hence the great problem of confronting public opinion, which has remained too often, too conveniently, too piously conservative. For the Arab woman emancipation has always come up against social censure. The words *'ār* (opprobrium) and *'aib* (shame) recur like a leitmotif through Arab feminine and feminist literature. 'It is *'ār*,' cries Līna, the heroine of *anā aḥyā*, 'if I weep; if I rebel, it is *'ār*, if I defend my ideas and my rights, it is *'ār*; *'aib*, *'aib*, *'aib* . . . because I'm a female and dare to sit at a café terrace!'[5] The 'agony columns' of various Arab women's magazines provide valuable information. Here is one case taken at random from dozens of others that have appeared in the Tunisian magazine *Faiza*. A nineteen-year-old girl dares to write in public that she has lost her virginity. 'I stayed a virgin too long, but last January, we lost our heads and – catastrophe! – I lost my virginity. In short I am this man's mistress. Though I regret my present situation, I cannot do without this forbidden love. He says my [future] husband won't notice. . . .' And the 'innocent' girl asks 'whether the loss of virginity can destroy a girl's life'! One can hardly believe it. But the magazine's answer is even more remarkable: '*Faiza* neither approves nor condemns your conduct. Every day life shows that a girl with character succeeds better than one who gives in all the time. . . . I think that once one has transgressed the norms of society, one should have the courage to go further – beyond "right-minded" society. There are eternal values.'[6] There is no shortage of 'provocations' of this kind in the Tunisian press. A 'pretty, sensitive girl, with a good body' advertises through the press for a husband. To make quite sure that the answers will not go astray, she gives her own complete address.[7] Another girl, more demanding, but clearly in revolt against Tunisian males, specifies in her advertisement that 'the husband must be of French or American nationality'.[8] Tunisians in particular and Arabs and Muslims in general are thus being told through the press that they need not apply.

The question of mixing the sexes has given rise to enormous discussion in the press. One local newspaper[9] even organized a referendum, from which it emerged that 41% of the girls consulted were in favour of 'flirtation' and 71% for co-education and free mixing in public places. Some time later in the same newspaper[10] there were demands that one should stop exalting 'the primacy of virginity'. 'A Tunisian woman,' one reader wrote, 'runs the risk of remaining an eternal minor. She enjoys the privilege of minors: protection in sexual matters. But in our cultural context, as in other conservative contexts, the sexual subordination of women is the basis for all forms of subordination.'

'The right to flirtation' is demanded by another reader of *Faiza*,[11] who declares, also in the 'agony column', that it is the only way of freeing 'those girls . . . tied, chained, frightened, practically incapable of doing anything at all without looking before and behind them. A single silent question occurs to them: what will people think?'

How outmoded, timorous and lukewarm now seem the feminist campaign and the 'sexual' demands of thirty years ago! Let us compare the Tunisian women's magazines of yesterday and today: how far away, how 'archeological' seem the preoccupations of even twenty years ago! A comparison of *Faiza* at the time of independence (1956) and *Leila* published between the wars is highly instructive. The struggle in Tunisia was then not about flirting, but about sending girls to school and the wearing of the veil![12] An article, revolutionary at the time, would make the young girls of today smile:

> The veil strikes a race at its most vulnerable, most vital point. It strikes its youth, depriving it of the essential means of all human activity, of all desire for progress, glory, conquest. Throughout the world young people know the freshness and purity of love at twenty. Only Muslim youth remains shrivelled up, sterile, frozen at the stage to which the evil veil has reduced it, for there is no love in present-day Islam.[13]

Emancipation has changed its level and its meaning. Despite considerable differences between the various Arab countries demands have become more radical – and more activist too. And this takes place first of all on the biological level.

Emancipation takes the form of active participation at the level of sexuality. The refusal expressed by Arab women is a refusal of sexual passivity. In Arab woman, a sexist subject is taking the place of a sexual object.

The psycho-social approach is confirmed by valuable medical information. In a relatively recent clinical study of 'hysteria among Tunisian girls and young women',[14] two Tunisian psychiatrists conclude that nearly 30% are suffering from conflictual themes predominantly if not exclusively of a sexual order (forced engagements, indefinite waiting for a husband, the departure of a husband on military service immediately after the wedding, etc.). In the same population '20% of the cases of sterility are associated with hysteria.' The two doctors observed that 'the cases of sterility appear predominantly among young married women'. But if compared with the situation prevailing in Tunisia before independence there has been a decline in hysteria:

> The more liberal attitude of families and a less strict upbringing of girls means that young women are less subject to coercive, 'infantilizing' structures. The very fact that there have been fewer orphans between 1957 and 1960 [the date of the investigation] might lead one to think that adolescents of the new generation are even more resistant on this matter.

We should pay particular attention to the doctors' conclusion:

> Where breakdowns and crises of an obviously sexual order are concerned they no longer have anything to do with the long-

term immaturity once so common in an educational and familial context that today has become more and more a thing of the past.

Yes, Arab women are certainly losing their morbid maternalism described in earlier chapters. Today they are discovering life at the full. This has brought us a women's literature of great depth and expressiveness.

A Jordanian woman, Fadoi Touquan, gives us a poetic account of what the hard apprenticeship of a Muslim woman's determination to live meant for her. For it was in mental torment and physical imprisonment that she paid the pricc of life and freedom.[15]

But Fadoi Touquan's controlled rebellion explodes into a protest against injustice and waste, against *ḍayā'*, as Ghālī Shukrī puts it so well.[16] Her revolt takes the form of a dialectic of giving and receiving. 'Ayda, the heroine of Layla Ba'alabakki's *Metamorphosed Gods*, brings this out in a highly significant way: 'I admit that I have given to excess. But men always receive much more than they give. . . . Yes, man is a god. But I am only a servant girl enslaved by his two magic hands.'[17] This is the central theme of the *Metamorphosed Gods*: Arab woman, eternally giving, demands at last reciprocity. She, too, wants to receive. Layla Ba'alabakki certainly puts her finger on an essential fact: female emancipation is the refusal to see herself reduced to a hollow sex.

'No,' protests Līna, the heroine of *Anā Aḥyā*, 'you will never be able to convince me that I am nothing, the mere form of a woman that you desire, that I'm just a cigarette-end between your fingers that you can throw away whenever you want, an insect on a chair. Dead. Am I dead?'[18]

On the contrary, Līna puts herself at the very heart of the dialectic of life. 'Do I love? No! I have a sense of what I am losing (*aḥinnu ilā-l-ḍayā'*). I receive and I give. Life in all its splendour offers me a wealth of untold experience. I am she who possesses an immense, hidden gift.'[19]

Arab woman erects herself, then, into an ability to give and Layla Ba'alabakki is right when she declares: 'That is the great experience: I give, therefore I live.'[20] It is this admirable dialectic of giving and receiving that Arab woman wants to take part in today. She intends to be no longer a hollow object.

For the passively defined female condition reduces woman to a receptacle into which man strives to pour himself. Gérard Zwang, who writes some penetrating pages on this theme, concludes:

> The Greeks created a word that is difficult to excel to describe this mortal hole: they called it *Barathra*. It was among the Greeks that the aberrant, pernicious coupling of Eros and Thanatos was born. So the most essential part of feminine values, that which implies hollowness, the cavity that complements the male convexity, is rejected with horror. . . . A devaluation of woman inevitably follows.[21]

One is reminded of Ferenczi's penetrating analysis of the notion of the sea in his celebrated essay *Thalassa*. Woman, like the sea, is a gulf that swallows everything up. To be swallowed up by one's wife is in one way or another to return to the mother's womb and the profound meaning of the male libidinal drive is the desire to return to the mother.

Today Arab woman is striving to renounce the illusory kingdom of the mothers and is aspiring to an affirmative, positive rule, rather than a mythopoeic one. She no longer wishes to be that derided, 'broken pisspot' that the males of the Maghreb have so often called her. She is determined to affirm her ability to give. Live! That is the rallying cry of Arab women today. The emancipation of Arab women is now situated on the only valid terrain, that of sexuality. I give love, therefore I am. *Coeo ergo sum*. Thus the Arab woman is rediscovering, but to her own advantage, that ethics of experienced pleasure, that sensation of existing through love that the Arabic language admirably terms *wijdān*.

And yet there is a curious ambiguity inherent in the concept of female emancipation, as if the partners could be dissociated from the question, as if one could emancipate oneself alone! As if Arab man were not alienated by his own masculinity! Authentic female emancipation requires male emancipation.

The sexual liberation of woman requires the liberation of man. That is the price to be paid if the harmony of the couple – and indeed that of society – is to be achieved. On this very precise point attitudes and motivations are very divergent, stretching from a very strict conservatism to a futuristic, avant-garde modernism. For Arabo-Muslim society is still largely male-worshipping, in essence and in its appearances, in its deep structures and in its superficial manifestations. At best women are still perceived as subsidiary creatures. How could it be otherwise, when the traditional models and the models imported for Europe co-operate in maintaining the primacy of the male and when the deep causes that have produced the largely anti-Islamic status 'accorded' women continue to be felt, perhaps even more so than in the past?

Women's true emancipation cannot be total, any more than men's can. And it is at every level that the battle of modernity must be fought. A modernity that confines itself to one level of everyday experience is no more than a pseudo-modernity, that is to say, a mystification, an alibi, a diversion to avoid true modernization. Indeed since Marx and Freud we know that, from a certain point of view, productive labour is the result of the transformation of the pleasure principle into the reality principle. One may even go further and admit that the more repression there is, the more necessary it is to transform the vicissitudes of instinct into socially productive reserves and, ultimately, the more labour there is. In the end the organization of social life and the civilization that springs from it take over our instincts and canalize our vital energies. In these circumstances, it is to be feared that a liberation that is only sexual may be to the detriment of economic and social liberation. Sexuality would then be merely subterfuge, a flight from the responsibilities that face the Arab conscience at grips with the redoubtable problems of poverty, ignorance, disease, underdevelopment, that is to say, independence and survival.

By demanding a new sexual ethics, Arab women want quite simply to change their function. By demanding a different function in society they are changing by the same token the group's view of the world. Their determination to emerge into social life brings with it a radical restructuring of it. So the work of liberation is the effective way followed by tens of thousands of Arab women who find in it a means of living positively and to the full. Other transformations are following the same course: the nuclear family, family planning, free choice of spouse, monogamy, divorce at the instigation of the woman. . . . All this is a serious threat to the status of men, without however resulting in the necessary radical rearrangements. This is because the privileges attached to the male condition are not only sexual or matters of prestige. They are political, economic, financial. The sexual exploitation of women forms part, as we have seen, of a more general, wider system of exploitation. How can a revolution be only sexual and avoid the problems of a Revolution that must embrace the sexual and the economic, the political and the cultural? When confronted by universal opposition, a single response is valid: total, permanent Revolution. If this is forgotten, one eventually confuses true and false revolution.

Najib Maḥfūdh shows in his magnificent trilogy that the relation between the sexes in a monopolistic society (*mujtama' iqtā'ī*) can only be a relation of consumption (*'alāqa istihlākiyya*). Bain al-qaṣrain's principal hero, Aḥmad Abdeljawād, envisages the relationship between the sexes only as a pure relation of pleasure. As Ghālī Shukrī, who has appreciated how correct and penetrating these analyses are, says:

> Man has deprived woman of her will, and therefore of her being and of her existence, when the social order deprives her of the means of realizing herself and proving her existence. . . . In a monopolistic society the relationship between Aḥmad Abdeljawād and his wife can be no more than a relationship of consumption, since she is no more than a woman, an appetizing sweetmeat. Even the norms of the beautiful derive from this principle. When the woman is reified, she can no longer be valued except in terms of weight. . . . Weight is not a measure of being, but of the body. So, in a monopolistic society, the beauty of a woman is measured in terms of fat. . . . The most beautiful woman is the fattest, the one who has most flesh on her. Ultimately she is something one eats, sucks, consumes.[22]

We find here a fundamental feature of oral eroticism. It is no accident if it re-emerges here in the midst of our modernity. Rather it has the permanence of a model. In fact, women wish to change their function. Without radical changes in social structures, a woman still cannot do so: in the eyes of her male partner she has not yet ceased to be what she has always been. The image that others have of us is not without importance!

Najib Maḥfūdh's hero, Aḥmad Abdeljawād, says as much. Of course, he is only giving voice to a very widespread opinion.

> 'If you love so many women,' an old sheikh told him, 'why don't you do as your father did and marry twenty times and never take the path of disobedience to God?' Abdeljawād replied with a giggle: 'My father was almost sterile, though he married again and again. He only produced me, but the patrimony was dispersed between myself and the four wives

who were in his possession when he died – not to mention the innumerable food pensions he had to hand out to left and right during his lifetime. But I'm a father of three sons and two daughters. I can't allow myself to have more wives and dissipate what little God has given me. Let's not forget, O sheikh, that the beauties of today are the concubines of yesterday whose buying and selling God tolerated. And after all God is clement and pardons our sins.'[23]

Abdeljawād certainly stresses the economic basis of sexual life. Modern financial difficulties mean that one must keep to one wife so as not to reduce still further an already small patrimony. But a single wife does not mean a single sexual partner!

The obsession with the anti-wife has survived until modern times and the sexual pseudo-liberation of man is dependent on her. How far we are from the 'authentic' revolution of true sexual emancipation! What a divorce there is between the sexes on this point! If there is a rupture between the generations of women, the continuity between the generations of men is only too real.

Najib Maḥfūdh saw this very clearly in his fine trilogy. One day, Abdeljawād's son, Yāsīn, is in an hotel of assignation when he recognizes the voice of his own father. Yāsīn, who sees women in exactly the same way as his father, is delighted to hear him singing and dancing in female company in the room next door. The son discovers the truth about his father. He is overcome by a feeling of great joy. He forgets everything except his own joy – as if he had just made the best discovery in his life. He is overcome by enormous love and admiration for his father. And he tells himself: 'Congratulations, father! Today I have really discovered you! Today is the day of your rebirth within me. What a wonderful day! What a wonderful father! Before now I was an orphan. . . . I am proud of you.'[24] It is no accident if the son communicates with the father precisely in an hotel of assignation, since it is the anti-wife, much more than the mother, who creates strong, deep links between the generations of men.

And Yāsīn makes the same discovery when, twenty years later, he is to find himself, once again, cheek by jowl with his youngest brother in another brothel. And there, too, beyond the generation gap, there is the same type of communion, around the anti-wife.[25]

Najib Maḥfūdh's fiction is a wonderful illustration of a fact too often ignored, namely, that the failure of women's liberation derives from the quasi-morbid inability of the male partner to throw off the mirage of the anti-wife and to rediscover the fundamental unity of the eternal feminine. This is unavoidable since sexual liberation cannot have the same significance for both sexes. What for the woman is a refusal becomes for the man all too easily a fight. Arab man is still obsessed by the anti-wife whom he seeks in every possible form: dancer, film star, singer, prostitute, passing tourist, neighbour, etc. The dissociation of the ludic and the serious examined above still continues, then, and acts as a stumbling block to the sexual emancipation not only of women but also of men. The Arab male, apart from a few exceptions, of course, is still not ready to give up his will to power. Despite appearances to the contrary, male imperialism still continues to maintain almost intact the essential element that is the cause of women's problems: sexual dimorphism.

As a consequence the Arab woman who adopts modern ways all too often merely changes her role and emancipation too frequently consists in exchanging the role of wife for that of anti-wife. After all, what does everyone dream of, if not money, pleasure and joy? Does the ultimate in emancipation and sexual liberation amount to being free to have relations of pleasure with men?

The ethical reference to the framework of *nikāḥ* implied respect for a number of values including purity, sensuality, justice and marital affection. That reference and those values are being lost. Sexuality is today less and less part of an overall system whose coherence and limits I have tried to examine. It used to belong to a totalizing, lyrical vision of life, to an ethic of marital affection. However limited the practical import of the Islamic ethic may have been, it did at least exist!

Today sexuality runs the risk of finding itself increasingly deprived of any reference. Furthermore it often takes the form of a protest against the system of traditional values regarded as archaic, antiquated, inflexibile, worm-eaten and dead. Among our students and young people generally, it would seem that the seriousness of sexuality is increasingly denied and that more and more an 'ethic' of amusement is taking its place. Sexual inhibitions are less and less operant, it is true, but the plenitude of a meaning to be found behind an act for which one assumes responsibility is being more and more lost. The sexual act is becoming facile, brief, straightforward and joyless.

For many, western eroticism, endlessly turned out by the

powerful media of mass communication, is becoming an exclusive end in itself. Striptease, advertising, nudity, 'sexy' clothes, pop music, drugs . . . this is the new imported 'ideal' offered by modern 'civilization' which, far from affirming sexuality, is desacralizing it and killing it. We should ponder the words of Vladimir Jankélévitch:

> Be in no doubt, the overwhelming, suffocating eroticism into which we are being plunged and which serves, like the motorcar, holidays, bars, to stupefy mankind, that eroticism is neither a cause nor a consequence of the aridity of modern life, it is that aridity itself. . . . Where there is no joy, no sincerity, no passionate conviction, no spontaneity, there is room for the industrialists of eroticism. Eroticism and violence are the two alibis of a time profoundly deprived of love that finds in sexual excitement some pitiful compensation for its incurable aridity.[26]

A new danger lies in wait for the Arabo-Muslim societies: the ethical void, cretinization through sex, systematic infantilization. The negation of traditional references is certainly a necessary stage in our history, but the negation of those references is still a reference. The great risk is precisely non-reference. The easy models of sexual behaviour, imported from North America or Europe, relentlessly diffused through all the mass media, do not help us to find much meaning in sexuality. And our young should reflect on the remarkable words of Henry Winthrop:

> True freedom and personal authenticity require intellectual and moral depth. . . . An authentic morality, sexual as well as non-sexual is always an obligation that one imposes upon oneself. One must regard others as subjects and not as objects. The new sexual freedom and the cult of nudity are a way of escaping from our responsibilities towards our fellow human beings and of avoiding I-Thou relationships in human affairs. The new sexuality is above all egocentric. . . . The sexual partners are often, strictly speaking, strangers in the night, and very often in broad daylight too. But, above all, in this new sexuality, the partner is regarded as an object, not as a subject.[27]

Of course the sexual crisis in the Arabo-Muslim countries is part of a world-wide sexual crisis. For many Arab men and women this is a factor for liberation. But it is to be feared that for many others it is rather a flight into sexuality.

In so far as the integration of Eros in the social is no longer occurring either according to traditional norms thought to be out of date or in terms of adjustments internal to the social structures, themselves in crisis and transition, in so far as imitation and acculturation are defeating any serious reference to the meaning of sexuality, one may well speak of a veritable 'counter-socialization' of Eros. By that I mean that the exercise of the flesh is no longer a prayer, a quest for harmony, a desire for affirmation. It is an alibi, a distraction, a soporific, in short a flight. Traditional society exalted love in mythifying it. In the delicate phase that our society is at present going through, it is to be feared that 'modern love' and 'liberated sexuality' may turn out to be no more than pure mystification. Studying the question objectively and without prejudice we must admit that the vision of the world that accorded such a place to eroticism can do so only by ceasing to give political, economic, social and cultural problems the importance that they deserve. This is already largely the case in industrial societies, where mass eroticism has lost its attractions. It is also to be feared that sexual pseudo-liberation is all too often for Arab men and women merely a way of avoiding their other responsibilities in public life. An authentic liberation must not be exclusive or lose sight of the intense effort that must be made with a view to restoring the true values of labour. Sexuality is certainly an important aspect in any revolutionary enterprise. In no way has one the right to reduce them to one another.

Authentically understood, the sexual revolution to which our young people legitimately aspire has the merit of drawing attention to the need to produce new cultural, ethical and religious values. But a flight into Islam is no more salutary than a flight into sexuality. The Muslim world is also undergoing a religious crisis: a crisis of faith in the first instance. To a youth disillusioned, confused, humiliated, poor, hungry and sick, present-day Islam does not seem to bring the right message. This is because, unlike Christianity and Judaism, Islam has made little use of the enriching, innovating contribution of the human sciences, linguistics, history, psychoanalysis, sociology, etc. Islamology is proving incapable of providing adequate spiritual nourishment. Islamic pastoral care has remained practically unchanged for centuries. It is still content, at best, to condemn 'disorders', 'anarchy' and 'atheism', or to anathematize heretics. The renewal of Islamic theology is today a prime requirement. It is the objective study of the Arabo-Muslim societies that brings out this need for elucidation of the religious. For, on the contrary, there is a flight into religion, just as there is a correlative flight into sexuality.

There is a total crisis in the relations of the Arab with himself, with nature and God. The Arabo-Muslim societies caught up in processes of more or less rapid social change, just emerging from colonial domination, still in the grip of imperialism and Zionism, still waging an inadequate and uncertain battle against underdevelopment, constitute a model of what Georges Gurvitch called 'effervescent' societies. They are subject to centrifugal and centripetal movements of destructuration and restructuration at every level of life, political, economic, or socio-cultural.

It is in this precise context that we must situate the sexual crisis and the religious crisis; both merely reflect an anomic situation. Everything is measured in terms of explosion: the demographic and the urban, the educational and the liberalization of morals. After being for so long the world of moderation, the Arabo-Muslim world has become the world of excess; excess of need, excess of life, excess of the social, excess of being. There is a crisis, a total crisis of the Arabo-Muslim consciousness. And it is this crisis that is indicated by the difficulties experienced by sexuality in defining itself in a context in which modernism is apprehended both as a refusal of an unabolishable yesterday and as a determination to live a tomorrow that is rather too slow in coming. J. Berque has already analysed this 'rupture of traditional man'[28] and that opposition, not unfortunately always dialectical, of an ancient, organic *qadīm* and a historical, new *jadīd*.

In that search for lost norms there is a quest for the authentic on the basis of the potentialities offered by a modernity that conceals within itself a thousand and one new resources. The exploitation of nature, rational modes of production, aesthetic creation, the apprehension of others, the understanding of the world, of life and of existence, all this is transformed by contemporary science and philosophy. . . . And certainly for many the future is already emerging on the horizon, the light at the end of the tunnel is already visible.

However, in spite of appearances to the contrary, never has sexuality been such a problem. Indeed the sexual liberation of women creates, as if by way of reaction, a sort of sexual nostalgia on the part of men that sharpens and revives uterine memories. Backward looking, even in matters of the faith, expresses an undeniable desire to return to the womb. The fiqh, the *sunna*, the golden age are ultimately so many substitutes for what Ferenczi calls *thalassa*. Traditional religious knowledge is an 'ocean' in which we still like to submerge ourselves. Is this again an instance of flight into religion? It is, in any case, certainly a flight into a sacralized past.

For the flight into sexuality cannot be other than a fear of oneself and of the world. Ostensibly the search for the 'harem', 'orgies' and provocatively overt homosexuality express a desire to stay where one is. There is something infantile in the desire to create a scandal. Certainly sexual maturity and therefore psychological maturity are today two of our most serious preoccupations. Anxiety and fear are merely signs of our inability to adapt to one another. The sexual crisis in interpersonal relations, like the crisis in faith, is a rupture in the dialogue with God.

On these two very precise points I must admit the limitations of my knowledge. In the absence of precise empirical and theoretical research, which would avail itself of the resources of psychoanalysis and sociology, I am unable to formulate any hypotheses. In the light of the brief analyses to be found in this chapter it would seem that sexuality and religion, after providing for centuries a sort of happiness, peace and integration, are today being transformed into types of alienation. Reduced to itself, deprived of the ethic of marital affection, of the lyrical vision of life that the Muhammadan view of the world was able to give it, sexuality today is no more than a 'commerce' of the body without the participation of the spirit. Deprived of its myths, its taboos, it has also become dehumanized and alienating. The notions of *iḥsān*, *zinā*, and *nikāḥ* enveloped sexuality in a halo that both veiled and revealed others. By organizing the sexual game on an institutional basis, by introducing into it a delicate dialectic of public and private, lawful and unlawful, Islam gave a positive meaning to sexuality, and therefore, ultimately, to oneself and to others. By depriving sexuality of its mystery I rob myself of my own meanings. Hence that joyless, savourless, colourless eroticism that is no more than bestiality.

Conversely, the Islamic faith, founded on the meaning of the dialogue with God and orientated towards the vision of God, was able to integrate the orgasm into the transcending self. The exercise of sexuality was a prayer, a gift of oneself, an act of charity. Preoccupied with defending a doctrine challenged on every side and increasingly at odds with life, Muslims gradually came to attach themselves to the external forms of sexual activity, rather than to the soul that ought to animate it. Hence that aberrant hostility to sex. Preoccupied with saying what has in any case been lost one has not tried sufficiently to understand and to think. Those anathemata and excommunications certainly express in their own way the same anxiety, the same fear that can be detected in so many apprentice Don Juans. It is not a paradox if religious conservatism and sexual pseudo-revolutionism express one and the same malaise. They are merely a flight from a world that has become enigmatic, difficult to understand, in which political, technological, economic, scientific and artistic success appears all too often as beyond our grasp. In a world in which frustration, aggression and anxiety have become everyday conditions, hypersexuality and religious puritanism are certainly convenient ways of escaping our responsibilities and masking our failures.

To emerge from this malaise we must at all costs rediscover the sense of sexuality, that is to say, the sense of the dialogue with the other partner, and the sense of the faith, that is to say, the sense of the dialogue with God. The authentic encounter with the other sex, the search for the secret life of the other enable me to rediscover the sense of my own existence. It has often been said that it is not sexuality that invents love, but love that reveals sexuality. It is not so much the flesh that is liberated as the spirit that is revealed through the flesh. For sexuality properly performed is tantamount to freedom assumed.

But this respect of the other is a revelation of meaning. The meaning of God cannot be revealed outside love. The transcending of self is also an act of faith. If the flesh involves charity it is because faith implies love. To rediscover the meaning of sexuality is to rediscover the meaning of God, and conversely. Hence the value that we attach to so many of the lessons provided by the Islamic tradition. The rereading that I have proposed in this book is intended to nourish a reflection orientated towards action and towards life. And, of course, we know very well, where faith is concerned, as also where love is concerned, everything is always to be reinvented and rediscovered. Man can find himself only in a tomorrow that is still largely unknown. No one is born by spontaneous generation and in cultural matters the legacy may be alienated, but the most authentic revolutions are always those that are able to rediscover the profound continuities of tomorrow with today and with yesterday.

Now the meaning of Islam cannot be dissociated from that of sexuality. That is why I gave myself the double task of disengaging the context inherent in the perception of sexuality by Islam and in the concrete reality of sexuality within the Arabo-Muslim societies. This is because Islam is neither a philosophical system, nor a doctrine, nor a sect, nor even an 'ideology'. It is, for us, a living, concrete reality. It is a vision of the absolute inscribed in the historical. Islam in general is a junction of the eternal and the historical. From the point of view that concerns us here it is a symbol of love and faith. It would be seriously misleading to see it simply as a technique to be used in the relations between God and man. Islam is a deepening awareness of self in order to unveil the divine majesty inseparable both from others and from oneself. For man is the only creature capable of apprehending the majesty of God and of giving a meaning to being-sexually-with-others. Throughout my work I was made aware that Islam posited unity of meaning: the meaning of God, the meaning of others, the meaning of man spring from the same intuition. That is why the message of Muhammad is not to be confined to a particular religious experience, or to a single experience of love. It is a message: the continuous renewal at all times of the vision of man concomitant with a vision of the world in which sexuality plays a leading role. But Islam aims to place the humanity above the animality within us. Hence the meaning given to sexuality that is constitutive of the humanity within us. If it is true, as Gaston Bachelard has said, that 'man is half-open being',[29] it is because that opening is at one and the same time faith and love.

To pose the question of the meaning of sexuality is ultimately to pose the question of the meaning of creation – and therefore that of the meaning of God and that of the meaning of man. For man is the only being for whom such a question can have any meaning. Ultimately, everything in Islam revolves around the question of meaning, perceived both as an urge towards the erotic and as spiritual inspiration. This meaning, to be found in the lyrical vision of life and the search for a transcending of self through marital affection, seems to be on the decline today. It is precisely that meaning that we must rediscover.

Notes

Note: All references to the Quran are to the Oxford University Press, 1983 edition.

Part I The Islamic view of sexuality

1 J. Berque, *Les Arabes d'hier à demain*, p. 14ff.
2 Quran, 'Thunder', XIII, 35, p. 244.

Chapter 1 The Quran and the question of sexuality

1 Quran, 'The Greeks', XXX, 16–26, pp. 411–17. The Quran expounds in many passages this conception of the duality of creation and becoming involving all creatures. Cf. 'The Cow', II, 187; 'Women', IV, 1; 'The Battlements', VII, 189; 'Thunder', XIII, 38; 'The Bee', XVI, 72; 'Abraham', XIV, 44–5; 'The Believers', XXIII, 13ff; 'The Poets', XXVI, 36; 'The Companies', XXXIX, 8ff; 'The Scatterers', LI, 49; 'The Star', LIII, 45ff; 'Noah', LXXI, 12ff; 'The Resurrection', LXXV, 37; 'The Tiding', LXVIII, 20ff.
2 Cf. the commentaries of Razi, vol. VI, p. 545ff; commentaries of Qortobi, vol. XIV, p. 14ff.
3 Ibn Mandhūr, Lisān al-Arab, vol. III, p. 115ff.
4 *Ibid.*, p. 115ff; Quran, LI, 49.
5 *Ibid.*, p. 115ff; Quran, XXVI, 36.
6 Quran, 'Women', IV, 1, p. 72. Cf., also 'The Battlements', VII, 186; 'The Companies', XXXIX, 8; 'The Star', LIII, 45ff; 'Noah', LXXI, 13–14; 'The Tidings', LXXVIII, 20–1; 'The Resurrection', LXXV, 37–8.
7 Quran, 'The Cow', II, 183–7, pp. 24–5.
8 Quran, 'The Companies', XXXIX, 8, p. 471.
9 Quran, 'The Believers', XXXIII, 12–17, p. 343.

10 Raghib, *Safinat*, ed. Bulaq, Cairo, 1286h., p. 15ff.
11 Quran, 'The Battlements', VII, 189, p. 166.
12 Cf. Quran, 'The Cow', II, 28–39; 'The Battlements', VII, 18–30. Cf., also, al-Qortobi, vol. VII, p. 179.
13 Quran, 'Women', IV, pp. 77–8.
14 Quran, 'The Cow', II, 228, p. 32. Cf. Abu Ḥayān, II, 190.
15 Quran, 'Light', XXIV, 32, p. 356.
16 Quran, 'The Forbidding', LXVI, 1, p. 593.
17 Quran, 'The Table', V, 89, pp. 113–14.

Chapter 2 Sexual prohibitions in Islam

1 Quoted in al-Bahy al-Khūly, al-mar-atu baynal-l-bayt wal-mujtama', p. 34: 'faslu mā bayna-phalāl wal ḥarām aldaffu wal-sawtu fil nikāḥi'.
2 Quran, 'The Cow', II, 164: 'Women', IV, 19, 29, 30; 'The Table', V, 7; 'The Bee', XVI, 92; 'The Night Journey', XVII, 34; 'The Believers', XXIII, 7; 'Light', XXIV, 3–11, 18, 23, 33, 34; 'Salvation', XXV, 68–70; 'The Spider', XXIX, 43; 'Counsel', XLII, 35; 'The Woman Tested', LX, 12; 'The Stairways', LXX, 31–2.
3 Cf. Quran, 'Women', IV, 22, 26–7.
4 Razi, III, p. 189.
5 *Ibid.*
6 Cf. Havelock Ellis, *Studies in the Psychology of Sex*, vol. 1, New York, Random House, 1936 ed., p. 189ff.
7 Illegitimate children must be accepted by the community. They are always presumed to be free and of the confession of the majority of members of the social group that takes them in.
8 Quoted by Ahmed El Banā, *Aḥkām al-walad*, p. 12.
9 Quran, 'The Disputer', LVIII, 2, p. 569.
10 Kaffāra: a pious action, taking the form of freeing a slave, fasting, alms giving, extra prayers, carried out in order to expiate some crime.
11 'Ḥattā tadhūqua uṣailatahu wa yadhūqua uṣailataha', cf. Abu Ḥayān, II, p. 200.

Chapter 3 The eternal and Islamic feminine

1 Emel Esin, *La Mecque, ville bénie; Médine, ville radieuse*, p. 97.
2 Quran, 'The Battlements', VII, 18ff.
3 Quran, 'The Ant', XXVII, 22–44.
4 Quran, 'The House of Imran', III; 'Mary', XIX. Cf. also 'The Prophets', XXI, 31; 'The Believers', XXIII, 52; 'The Forbidding', LXVI, 12.
5 Quran, 'The Battlements', VII, 81ff; 'Hood', XI, 83; 'El-Ḥijr', XV,

59; 'The Ant', XXVII, 58; 'The Spider', XXIX, 33; 'The Rangers', XXXVII, 135; 'The Forbidding', LXVI, 10.

6 Quran, 'El-Ḥijr', XV, 61.

7 Quran, 'The Forbidding', LXVI, 10.

8 Quran, 'The Prophets', XXI, 89ff., p. 330.

9 Quran, 'The Story', XXVIII, 8, p. 392; 'The Forbidding', LXVI.

10 Quran, 'Joseph', XXI, 23ff, p. 228.

11 Gaudefroy-Demombynes, *Mahomet*, p. 67. Cf. Bokhari, the chapter devoted to Khadija, vol. V, p. 41ff. Cf. also Bent al-Shāty, *Nisā al-Nabi*, Beirut, undated, 'Khadija', pp. 27–50.

12 Quran, 'Joseph', XII.

13 Genesis, 39.

14 Quran, 'Joseph', XII, 22–34, pp. 228–9.

15 Razi, vol. V, p. 119. Cf. also Abu Ḥayān, vol. V, pp. 293–301.

16 Quran, 'Joseph', XII, 24, p. 228.

17 Razi, vol. V, p. 120.

18 Razi, vol. V, p. 120.

19 Razi, vol. V, p. 124.

20 Quran, 'Joseph', XII, 28, p. 229.

21 Razi, vol. V, p. 127.

22 Razi, vol. V, p. 126.

23 Abu Nasr al-Hamadhāni, *al-Sab'iyāt*, included in the *Kitab al majālis al sunniiya fil kalām 'an al arba'īn al nawawiyya*, by the sheikh Ahmad al-Fashni, Cairo, 1299h., pp. 123–7.

Chapter 4 The frontier of the sexes

1 Alūsi Zādeh, *Ghāliyyat al-mawā'idh*, vol. II, p. 6.

2 *Ibid.*, p. 5. Cf. 'Ainī, vol. X, p. 279.

3 *Liwāṭ* sodomy. Cf. Alūssi Zādeh, vol. II, p. 4. Cf. also al-Jassas, *Akkām al-qurān*, vol. III, p. 263; Razi, vol. VI, p. 245ff. Cf. also Quran, VII, 78ff; XI, 79–84; XXI, 74; XXII, 43; XXVI, 165–75; XXVII, 56–9; XXIV, 27–33.

4 Razi, vol. VI, p. 247, vol. III, p. 182; Alussi, vol. II, p. 5; Jassas, vol. III, p. 263.

5 Cf. Genesis, 19, 1–23.

6 Genesis, 19, 30–40.

7 Cf. Quran, 'The Battlements', VII, p. 143ff.

8 *Dictionnaire de sexologie*, p. 273.

9 Alūssi, *Ghāliat al-mawā'idhi*, vol. II, p. 7.

10 Bokhāri, vol. VII, pp. 158–78.

11 *Ibid.*, p. 166.

12 *Ibid.*, p. 170.

13 *Ibid.*, p. 177.

14 *Ibid.*, p. 177.

15 *Ibid.*, p. 179.

16 'Ainī, vol. X, p. 228.

17 *Ibid.*, p. 186. Cf. also 'Ainī, vol. X, p. 306.
18 Bokhāri, vol. VII, p. 182.
19 *Ibid.*, vol. VII, p. 183.
20 Cf. Souques, *Mahomet et l'hygiène*; *Mahomet et les parfums*; H. Zayat, *Le port de la barbe en islam.*
21 Bokhāri, vol. VII, p. 182.
22 After *Nawādir al-ishrāq fi makārim al akhḷāq*, quoted by H. Zayat, *loc. cit.*, p. 735.
23 *Shams al-dīn al-Ansāri, Kitāb al-syāsa fi'ilm al firāsa*, lithographed, Cairo edition, 1882, p. 29.
24 A. Mazahéri, *La Vie quotidienne des musulmans au Moyen Age*, p. 70.
25 *The Thousand and One Nights*, II, pp. 374–5.
26 I shall return later to the theme of depilation of the pubis as a prelude to the sexual act and as a factor in eroticism.
27 'Ainī, vol. II, p. 320.
28 Quran, 'Light', XXIV, 30–1, pp. 355–6. Cf. Razi's commentary, vol. VI, p. 295ff. Cf. 'Ainī, vol. IX, p. 100 and vol. X, p. 480.
29 Ibn Ḥazm, *Le Çollier du pigeon*, trans. Bercher, p. 325.
30 J.-P. Sartre, *L'Être et le néant*, p. 327; *Being and Nothingness*, trans. Hazel. E. Barnes, London, Methuen, 1958, p. 268.
31 *Ibid.*
32 Razi, vol. VI, p. 296. Cf. also Alūssi, p. 13.
33 Zayla'i, vol. VI, p. 18: 'yakūnu ablaghu fī taḥṣīli ma'nā allaqhdhāti'.
34 *Ibid.*
35 Razi, vol. VI, pp. 297–8.
36 Ibn Manḍhūr, *Lisan al'Arab*, vol. VI, p. 293ff.
37 Zayla'i, vol. VI, p. 17.
38 *Ibid.*
39 *Ibid.*, p. 18.
40 *Ibid.*
41 Alūsi Zādeh, vol. II, p. 13.
42 Cf. *Fatāwā Hindiyya*, vol. V, p. 327.
43 Alūsi Zādeh, vol. II, 7.
44 *Ibid.*
45 Quoted by Ibn Ḥazm, *Le Collier du pigeon*, p. 323.
46 *Fatawa Hindiyya*, vol. V, 351.
47 Ibn Ḥazm, *Le Collier du pigeon*, p. 323.
48 Bokhāri, vol. VII, pp. 52 and 58. Cf. 'Ainī, vol. X, p. 279ff. Moslem, vol. V, p. 444ff.
49 Ḥabīb Zayyat, *La Femme garçonne en islam*, p. 156.
50 Al-Washtāni, commentary by Moslem, vol. V. p. 444ff.
51 Moslem, vol. V, p. 445ff.
52 Ibrāhīm Ḥalbi, *Multaqa al-abḥur*, pp. 224–5.
53 For their prayer, said in the company of a woman, may be regarded as null and void. It is more prudent for them to begin it again.
54 It is his prayer that runs the risk of being null and void, if he later proves to be of the male sex.
55 For one would not know of which sex the person who would wash

him should be. Since one cannot buy a slave woman from a dead man she would not belong to him and therefore be allowed to touch him.
56 As would be done in the case of a woman – just in case.
57 That is to say the same order as during his lifetime in the mosque.

Chapter 5 Purity lost, purity regained

1 For all these analyses I have followed a number of authors chosen by way of example from an inexhaustible literature: Bokhāri, *Ṣaḥīḥ*, vol. I, pp. 40–85; Zayla'i, Sharḥ Kanz al daqā-iq, vol. I, p. 2ff and p. 328ff; Ḥalbi, *Multaqa al-Abḥur*, p. 3ff; Safti-Hāshia, *'Ala sharḥ Ibn Turki*, pp. 26–112; *Al-Fatāwā al-Hindiyya*, vol. I, pp. 3–50 and 202–8; but above all, for its clarity and depth, Ghazali, *Iḥyā 'ulūm al-dīn*, vol. I, pp. 117–34.
2 Cf. G. Bataille, *L'Érotisme*, p. 64; *Eroticism*, trans. Mary Dalwood, London, John Calder, 1962, pp. 45–6.
3 Ibn Manḍhūr *Lisan al-Arab*, vol. I, p. 189ff.
4 *Ibid.*, vol. XIV, p. 6ff.
5 *Ibid.*, vol. XX, p. 176. Cf. *Qāmus al muḥīṭ*, vol. IV, p. 385.
6 *Ibid.*, vol. I, p. 25.
7 *Ibid.*, vol. 14, p. 288.
8 *Al-Fatāwā al-Hindiyya*, vol. I, p. 47.
9 *Ibid.*, vol. I, pp. 47–8.
10 Ghazali, *op. cit.*, vol. I, p. 22: 'allamanā rasūlu llāhi kulla shay-in ḥatta lkharā-ata'.
11 The fiqh distinguishes systematically between:

– the male *mani*: 'The seminal fluid, which is thick, viscous, white. Its smell is like that of the spathe of a palm tree. When it flows the penis grows soft.' In other words, sperm;
– female *mani*: 'A fine, yellowish, seminal fluid, of strong smell.' This is the vaginal fluid;
– *maḍhi*: 'A light, whitish fluid. It appears on a man during the erotic games prior to coitus.' This is the prostatic fluid;
– *qaḍhi*: the female equivalent of maḍhi;
– *wadi*: 'Very thick urine. It flows after post-coital washing or after urine itself.'

Cf. *Fatāwā*, vol. I, p. 10 and 'Ainī, vol. I, pp. 626 and 630.
12 *Fatāwā Hindiyya*, vol. I, p. 10ff.
13 Indeed sleep systematically breaks minor purification, for it is possible that wind may have escaped without one being aware of it.
14 There was a widespread belief in women's ability to ejaculate.
15 *Fatāwā*, vol. I, pp. 14, 15 and 16.
16 Cf. *Fatāwā*, vol. I, pp. 204–5; Ghazali, *Iḥyā*, vol. I, p. 209ff.
17 *Fatāwā*, vol. I, pp. 36–7.
18 For all this passage, cf. *Fatāwā*, vol. I, pp. 36–40; *Zayla'i*, vol. I, pp. 54–69.

19 Ghazali, *Iḥyā*, vol. I, p. 117ff.
20 Quran, V, 'The Table', p. 101.
21 Ghazali, *Iḥyā*, p. 117.
22 *Ibid.*, p. 118.
23 *Ibid.*, pp. 118–19.
24 Cf. for example Muhammad Arkoun, 'Lexique de l'éthique musulmane', in *Bulletin d'Etudes Orientales*, vol. XXII, 1969.
25 A. Souques, 'Mahomet, les parfums et les cosmétiques colorants', *Presse médicale*, 1940, no. 25–6, pp. 301–2. Cf. also A. Souques, 'Mahomet et l'hygiène', *Presse médicale*, 1940, no. 47–8, pp. 545–7. Cf. El-Akrout, *Les Pratiques de la Prière et de l'hygiène chez les musulmans*, thèse doct. méd., Paris, 1936. Cf. A. Bouseen, *Contribution à l'étude du jeune dans l'islam*, thèse doct. méd., Paris, 1942.
26 Cf. *Iḥyā*, pp. 122–9, where the word *waswās* occurs twelve times.
27 G. Bataille, *L'Érotisme*, p. 96; *Eroticism*, p. 96.

Chapter 6 Commerce with the invisible

1 Cf. Quran, 'The Believers', XXIII, 72, p. 348 and Qortobi, vol. XIV, p. 254ff.
2 Razi, II, p. 304, 'al-makhlūqātu al-mukallafatu afḍalu min ghayril mukallafati; wahya al malā-ikatu wal insu wal jannu wal shayāṭīnu'. 'Responsible creatures are better than non-responsible ones, and these are the angels, men, djinns and devils.'
3 'Idha inṭafati al unūthatu, inṭafa al-tawāludu', Razi, vol. I, p. 298.
4 Razi, vol. II, p. 302: 'lā shahwata lahum ilā alakli wa ilā-mubāsharati'.
5 Cf. 'Abbās Maḥmūd al-aqqad, *Iblis*, pp. 138 and 146.
6 Qortobi, vol. X, p. 23.
7 Qortobi, vol. XIV, p. 254: (awwalu mā khalaq-allāhu ta 'ālā minal insāni farjahū; wa ālā hādhihi amānatun astawda'tukaha . . . fal farju amānatun.)
8 Gaudefroy-Demombynes, *Mahomet*, p. 317.
9 Maryse Choisy, 'L'archétype des trois S: Satan, serpent, scorpion', in *Etudes carmélitaines*, 'Satan', 1948.
10 Cf. Aqqad's good comment in *Iblis*, p. 214ff.
11 L. Massignon, *La Passion d'al-Hallaj*, p. 869ff.
12 I have translated the texts quoted above from the edition given at Cairo by Muhammad Efendi Mustapha in 1310h., pp. 27–32.
13 Cf. in particular Bokhāri, vol. I, p. 105; vol. IV, p. 110; vol. VI, p. 209; vol. VII, p. 129; Moslem, vol. I, p. 234ff; vol. II, p. 243ff; vol. VI, p. 6ff; vol. VII, p. 301ff; Qastallāni, vol. V, p. 290ff; Abu Ḥayān, vol. IV, p. 206ff; vol. V, p. 418ff. Cf. also 'Ainī, vol. III, pp. 614–18 and vol. V, pp. 270–95; Razi, vol. II, p. 80ff; Qortobi, vol. X, p. 23ff.
14 *Ibid.*, p. 27.
15 Ibn Manḍhūr, *Lisan al-'Arab*, vol. III, p. 176.

16 *Ibid.*, p. 27.
17 *Ibid.*, pp. 30–1.
18 Razi, vol. II, p. 80ff.
19 *Ibid.*, p. 31.
20 Roland Villeneuve, *Le Diable, érotologie de Satan*, p. 16.
21 Cf. Rosette Dubal, *La Psychoanalyse du diable*, Paris, 1962. And, of course, Roland Villeneuve, *op. cit.*
22 Jules Michelet, *La Sorcière*, ed. Viallaneix, Paris, 1966, pp. 116–17.
23 Cf. Razi, *Mafātīḥ al ghaib*, chap. LXXII; Al-Absh-hi, *al-mustaṭraf*, vol. II, p. 159ff., trans. Rat, vol. II, p. 325; 'Ainī, vol. VII, p. 285ff; Qastallāni, vol. VI, p. 303ff; Abu Ḥayān, vol. II, p. 206ff and vol. V, p. 418ff; Rāghib, *Safina*, pp. 266–75; Al-Shiblī, *Akām al-marjān fi an'kām al jān*.
24 Razi, vol. I, p. 297.
25 Ibn Najīm, *Kitāb, al ashbāḥ wal anādhdhur*, p. 131. Cf. also the commentary *Ghamr 'uyūn al baṣa-ir* by al-Hamwi, vol. II, pp. 183–7, Istanbul 1257 h.
26 Muhammad Yussef al-Kāfi, *Al Masā-il al-Kāfiyya*, Cairo, 1934, p. 7ff.
27 *Ibid.*, p. 8.
28 Dāud al Antāqi, *Tazyīn*, p. 181.
29 C. G. Jung, 'Introduction à la psychologie analytique', sixth lecture, delivered at Basle to the Société de psychologie, 1934. This passage is to be found in a collection of Jung's writings published in French under the title *L'homme à la découverte de son âme*, p. 327. These lectures do not appear in the English version of Jung's *Collected Works*, presumably because much of the material was reworked and delivered in another form.
30 (In kāna li-nnāsi waswāsun yuwasisuhum, fa anta, wallāhi, waswāsī khannāsī.)

Chapter 7 The infinite orgasm

1 Cf. in particular Quran, 'The Pilgrimage', XXII, 20ff., p. 335ff.; 'Prostration', XXII, 12–22, pp. 424–5; 'Muhammad', XLVII, 13–18, p. 527; 'The All-Meaningful', 33ff., pp. 558ff.; 'The Terror', LVI, the entire Sura, pp. 560–3; 'The Resurrection', LXXV, 22ff., pp. 619–20; 'Man', LXXVI, 12ff., pp. 621–2; 'The Tiding', LXVIII, 17ff., pp. 262–7; 'The Stinters', LXXXIII, 18ff., p. 635ff.; 'The Enveloper', LXXVIII, 1–16, p. 642. Cf. also Razi, vol. IV, p. 139; vol. VII, p. 44ff; vol. VIII; 'Ainī, vol. IV, p. 220ff.
2 Cf. in particular Bokhāri, vol. II, 105ff.; vol. IV, 110ff.; vol. X, 96ff. and 133ff.; Qastallāni, vol. V, p. 279ff.; Moslem, vol. VII, p. 209ff.; 'Ainī, vol. IX, 165ff.; vol. X, 676ff.; vol. XI, 522ff.
3 Louis Gardet, *L'islam, religion et communauté*, p. 95; Cf. also the excellent article by the same author in *L'Encyclopédie de l'Islam*, vol. II, p. 459ff.

4 Published at Tunis, undated. Cf. also al-Ghazali, *'Al durrat al-fākhira fi kashfi'ulūm al-ākhira*, trans. L. Gauthier, Geneva, 1878.
5 *Basmālah*: inscription, 'In the Name of God, the Merciful, the Compassionate.'
6 Daqa-iq, p. 42.
7 *Ibid.*, pp. 42 and 43.
8 Suyūti, *ibid.*, p. 26: 'lā ghā-ita fil jannati'.
9 *Ibid.*, p. 43.
10 *Ibid.*, p. 43.
11 *Ibid.*, p. 31.
12 *Ibid.*, p. 27; cf; Qastallāni, vol. V, pp. 281–2; Moslem, vol. VII, p. 213.
13 *Ibid.*, p. 28.
14 *Ibid.*, p. 29. Cf. also Bokhāri, vol. V, p. 279.
15 *Ibid.*, p. 36.
16 Quran, 'Ta Ha', XX, p. 311.
17 Quran, 'Ya Sin', XXXVI, p. 450. This Sura is very highly regarded. It is considered to be the pivot of the Revelation. Its reading constitutes an essential stage in the Muslim funeral service.
18 Quran, 'The All-Merciful', LV, p. 557.
19 Quran, 'Cattle', VI, p. 121.
20 *Kurūb*: an angel entrusted with protocol in paradise.
21 Suyūti, pp. 36–8.
22 Tor Andrae, *Mahomet, sa vie et sa doctrine*, trans. Gaudefroy-Demombynes, Paris, 1945, p. 160. Tor Andrae, *Les Origines de l'islam et le christianisme*, trans. p. 62ff; H. Grimme, *Mohammed Munster*, 1892–5; Gaudefroy-Demombynes, *Mahomet*, p. 434ff.
23 Gaudefroy-Demombynes, *ibid.*, pp. 435–6.
24 Revelation, 20, 11 and 12.
25 In Maryse Choisy, *La Survie après la mort*, prefaced by R. P. Daniélou, p. 20ff.
26 Matthew, 22.23–30.
27 R. P. Daniélou, 'La survie dans la perspective catholique', intervention au colloque de l'Alliance mondiale des Religions des 7 et 8 juin 1967, in Maryse Choisy, *La Survie après la mort*, pp. 33–4.
28 Rabbi J. Eisenberg, *La Survie selon le judaïsme*, in Maryse Choisy, *loc. cit.*, pp. 149–50.
29 *Loc. cit.*, p. 434.
30 *Loc. cit.*, p. 438.
31 *Loc. cit.*, p. 439.
32 L. Gardet, *L'Islam, religion et communauté*, p. 106.
33 Quran, 'The Resurrection', LXXV, 22, p. 619. 'Upon that day faces shall be radiant, gazing upon their Lord.' ('Wujūhun yowma idhin nādhiratun ilā rabbihā nādhirat.') Cf. Razi, vol. VIII, p. 266. For Muslim orthodoxy the vision of God is proved by this verse.
34 *Loc. cit.*, p. 107.
35 Razi, vol. VIII, p. 281.
36 Al-Abshīhi, al-Mostatraf, trans. Rat, vol. II, p. 315.
37 Cf. Souque, *Mahomet et les parfums*, *op. cit.*

38 Ghāliya: mixture in equal parts of musk, amber, camphor and myrtle wood.
39 Al-Mostatraf, vol. II, p. 78.
40 G. Bachelard, *La Terre et les rêveries du repos*, p. 51.
41 Al Mostatraf, trans. Rat, vol. II, p. 366.
42 Moslem, vol. VII, p. 212.
43 Ṣuyūti, *loc. cit.*, pp. 39–40.
44 'idh ḥadd al jannati anna fīha li kullī insānin mā yashtahī', *Raghib Safina*, p. 115.
45 Quran, XLI, 31, p. 494 ('wa lakum fīha mā tashtahi anfusukum wa lakum fīha mā tad'ūn'.
46 *Raghib Safina*, p. 114.
47 *Ibid.*, p. 115.

Chapter 8 The sexual and the sacral

1 Quran, 'The House of Imrān', III, 14, p. 46.
2 Cf. the fine commentary by Razi, vol. II, p. 430ff. One should note the first place occupied by women 'whose pleasure is the greatest and whose company is the most complete': ('li anna al iltidhādha bihinna akthara, wal isti-nāssu bihinna atammu'). Woman is a completion of man – and conversely.
3 Quran, 'Ornaments', XLIII, 17, p. 506 ('man unashsha-u fil ḥilyati wahwa fil khiṣām ghayru mubīn'). (I have amended Arberry's version of the second part of this quotation – 'and, when the time of altercation comes, is not to be seen' – in line with the author's own version and argument – tr.)
4 Moslem, vol. IV, p. 99.
5 Quoted by Qanāwi, *Sharḥ lāmiyyat ibn al-wardī*, p. 14.
6 Moslem, IV, p. 98; Bokhāri, VII, p. 2; 'Ainī, IX, p. 354; Nawawī, p. 96.
7 Bokhāri, vol. V, II, p. 4; Moslem, vol. IV, p. 9; 'Ainī, vol. IV, p. 361; *Fatāwā*, vol. V, p. 356.
8 'Ainī, IX, 362.
9 *Ibid.*, IX, 484.
10 *Ibid.*, IX, 483.
11 'Wa in kānat 'alā ḍhahri qaṭabin': 'Ainī, IX, p. 484.
12 'Wa in kānat 'ala ra-si tannūrin'; 'Ainī, IX, p. 484.
13 'Inna abghaḍha al ḥalāli 'inda allāhi al ṭalāqu'.
14 Jassas, vol. II, p. 110.
15 Quran, 'Light', XXIV, 32, p. 356. Cf. also 'Ainī, IX, p. 414.
16 Qastallāni, vol. VIII, p. 8.
17 *Ibid.*
18 Qastallāni, vol. VII, p. 3.
19 Cf. Ahmed al-Fashnī, *Al-mājalis al-sanya'*, p. 95.
20 I have taken this very well known hadith from Shihabaldīn al-

Khafāgi's *Turāz al majālis*, p. 50, which gives the most profound commentary, p. 157ff.

21 'Wa fi buḍ'i aḥādīkum ṣadāqa'. Literally: 'and in your sexes, too, there is alms.'

22 Cf. Sā'adaldīn Taftazāni, *Sharḥ al-arb'īn alnawāwiyya*, Tunis, 1295h., p. 115ff. Cf. Ahmed al-Fashnī, *Al-majālis al sānya fi lkalām 'ala al araba'īn al-nawawiyya*, Cairo, 1299 h., p. 929ff. Ibrahim al-Shibrikhā-iy, *al futūḥāt al wahbiyya*, Cairo, 1318, p. 214ff.

23 Muḥallil: that which makes lawful what was not so previously.

24 Bokhāri, vol. III, pp. 178 and 184; Moslem, vol. IV, pp. 56 and 58; 'Ainī, vol. IX, pp. 539 and 546.

25 Moslem, vol. IV, p. 12. On Muhammad's erotic behaviour, cf. Ibn al-Quayyim al-Jawzia, *al ṭibb al-nabawi*, pp. 98 and 116.

26 I Corinthians, 7, 1ff.

27 Galatians, 5, 16–26.

28 Otto Piper, *L'Evangile et la vie sexuelle*, Delachaux and Niestlé, 1955, p. 25.

29 Seward Hiltner, *Sexuality and the Christian Life*, New York, 1959.

30 M. Merleau-Ponty, *Phénoménologie de la perception*, p. 183; *Phenomenology of Perception*, tr. Colin Smith, London, Routledge & Kegan Paul, 1962, p. 157.

31 Cf. 'Ainī, vol. V, p. 597 and vol. IX, p. 494.

32 *Phénoménologie de la perception*, p. 195; *Phenomenology of Perception*, p. 167.

33 Quran, 'Apartments', XLIX, 13, p. 538.

34 Quran, 'The Greeks', XXX, 21, pp. 412–13.

35 *Phénoménologie de la perception*, p. 195; *Phenomenology of Perception*, p. 167.

36 *Phénoménologie de la perception*, p. 199; *Phenomenology of Perception*, p. 171.

Part II Sexual practice in Islam

Chapter 9 Sexuality and sociality

1 Quran, 'Apartments', XLIX, 13, p. 538.

2 A. Bouhdiba, *A la recherche des normes perdues*, p. 93.

3 In becoming *umm-walad*, a co-owned female slave becomes *ipso facto* the property of the father who has claimed paternity. The other co-owners lose their share in the enjoyment of their concubine. The father of the *walad* must therefore pay them an indemnity on account of *'uqr* (sterility) or sexual usurpation. The same applies when a non-co-owner claims paternity of a child born to a concubine of a third party. The estimated value is that of the concubine *qua* slave with a market value. The *'uqr* is an indemnity affecting loss of sexual

enjoyment with a particular concubine to whom one must have been emotionally and sensually attached.

4 Al-Qudūri, *Le Statut personnel en droit musulman*, trans. G.-H. Bousquet and L. Bercher, p. 180ff.

5 *Fatāwā Hindiyya*, vol. I, p. 568: 'wa yazīdu al jāriyata allatī lil istimtā'i fil kiswati lil'urfi.'

6 Aboul Faraj al-Açfahni, *Le Livre des chansons*, Beirut 1962 ed. in 24 vols. Cf. the fine chapter by Aḥmad Amīn in *Dhuḥ āl-Islam*, vol. I, p. 79ff.

7 P. Hitti, *Précis d'histoire des Arabes*, p. 109.

8 *Ibid.*

9 I subscribe entirely to Sharāra's declaration: 'The victory of woman was won only thanks to the *jawāri* and *qiyan*' (in *Falsafa al ḥubbi 'indal Arab*, p. 112).

10 Aḥmad Amin, *D'huḥ'al-Islam*, vol. I, pp. 98–9.

11 Bedouin: rural. Beldi: urban. I have devoted an article to this theme, 'Bedouinisme et beldisme dans la Tunisie actuelle', in *A la recherche des normes perdues*, p. 20.

12 Abdellatif Sharāra, *Falsafat al-ḥubbi 'inda al 'Arab*, p. 105.

13 Gaston Wiet, *Introduction à la littérature arabe*, p. 50.

14 Cf. Régis Blachère's comments in the article 'Ghazal', in *Encyclopédie de l'Islam*, vol. II, pp. 1051–7.

15 H. Pérès, *La Poésie andalouse en arabe classique au XIe siècle*, p. 423ff.

16 *Ibid.*, p. 425.

17 Dāwūd al-Antāki, *Tazyīn al-aswāq*, p. 3.

18 Germaine Tillion, *Le Harem et les cousins*, Paris, 1966. Cf. in particular pp. 81–7 and 168–79.

19 Cf. *Recueil de notions de droit musulman* by Ettouati, trans. Abribat, Tunis, 1896, p. 63.

20 Cf. Ettouati, p. 70. Cf., on this question, *Fatāwā Hindiyya*, vol. II, pp. 350–491, which contains a clear and exhaustive discussion of the question.

21 Jean Cuisenier, *L'Ansarine*, p. 127.

22 *Ibid.* I have benefited here by observations by R. Radcliffe-Brown, *African Systems of Kinship and Marriage*, London, 1950; J. Berque, *Structures sociales du Haut-Atlas*; T. Azhkenazi, La tribu arabe, ses éléments, *Anthropos*, vol. XLI–XLIV, 1946–49; K. Daghestani, *La Famille musulmane contemporaine*, Syria, 1931; J. Cuisenier, 'Endogamie et exogamie dans le mariage arabe', *L'Homme*, mai-avril 1962, p. 80.

23 Jean Cuisenier, *L'Ansarine*, p. 130.

24 Cf. Abbas Al-'Azzawi, *'Ashā-ir al-'Irāq*, vol. I, p. 414ff.

25 J. Berque, *Les Arabes d'hier à demain*, p. 156.

Chapter 10 Variations on eroticism: misogyny, mysticism and 'mujūn'

1 Bokhāri, vol. IV, p. 91.

2 Razi, vol. I, p. 297. Cf. also Qastallāni, vol. I, pp. 339–40.

3 Razi, vol. VI, p. 218.

4 'Ainī, vol. X, p. 478. Cf. Gaudefroy-Demombynes, p. 231.
5 Quoted by Sharāra, *Falsafi al ḥ'ubbi 'indal Arab*, p. 59.
6 A poem rhyming in l by Ibn el Wardi, who lived in the fourteenth century. My translation is taken from the Arabic text, published in Tunis, 1342h. Cf. also Commentary of El Qanāwi, Cairo, 1310h.
7 Mas'ud al-Qanawi, *Kitāb fatḥ al-raḥmān*, p. 4.
8 *Ibid.*
9 *Ibid.*, p. 14.
10 *Ibid.*, p. 16.
11 *Ibid.*, pp. 18–20.
12 *Ibid.*, p. 20.
13 Cf. my 'Essai d'une typologie de l'islam maghrébin', in *A la Recherche des normes perdues*, p. 96.
14 Cf. the fine book by Emile Dermenghem, *Au Pays d'Abel.*
15 Mas'ud al-Qanāwi, *Kitāb fatḥ al-raḥmān*, p. 21.
16 H. Renault, *Les Survivances du culte de Cybèle, Vénus, Bacchus.* Cf. C. Lecoeur, *Le Rite et l'outil*, p. 121ff.
17 Quoted by Sharāra, *ibid.*, p. 180.
18 *Al-futūḥāt al-makkiyya*, Bulāq, 1270h (1854), in 2 vols.
19 *Diwān Ibn 'Arabi*, Bulāq, 1271h (1855).
20 Sharh, *Diwān, Ibn El Fāridh* by Hassan al-Būrini and Abdelghani al-Nābulssi, Cairo, 1269h, in 2 vols.
21 *Le Diwān d'Al Hallaj*, ed. Massignon, p. 14.
22 Anders Nygren, *Agapé and Eros*, 3 vols, trans. A. G. Herbert, London, 1932–9.
23 Article 'Burda', *Encyclopédie de l'Islam*, vol. I, pp. 815–16. Note that the phrase 'one can see no trace of Sufism in it and that is not the least of its merits' has disappeared in the new edition.
24 Verse no. 10: 'You who reproach me for my *'udhrite* love, I excuse you. If you knew what it is, you would not reproach me.' Cf. Ed. Zāwaq, Tunis, 1959.
25 Quran, 'The Constellations', LXXXV, 14, p. 638.
26 Quran, 'The Cow', II, 147, p. 19.
27 Quran, 'Imran's House', III, 29, p. 49. Cf. also 'The Table', 59, p. 109, where God speaks of the people whom he loves and who love him.
28 Quran, 'The Dawn', LXXXIX, 27–30, p. 644. For the exegesis of these verses I refer to: Razi, vol. II, p. 751ff and Abu Hayān, vol. I, p. 470.
29 Qastallāni, vol. VIII, pp. 103–4; Moslem, vol. V, p. 64; 'Ainī, vol. IV, p. 496.
30 'Ainī, vol. IX, p. 494ff; vol. V, p. 597.
31 *Fatāwā*, vol. I, p. 335.
32 *Fatāwā*, vol. V, p. 356. Cf. also 'Ainī, vol. II, p. 123.
33 *Fatāwā*, vol. V, p. 356. We must remember that these texts date from the seventeenth century.
34 Cf. Gaudefroy-Demombynes, *Mahomet*, p. 563.
35 Moslem, vol. IV, p. 13.
36 'Ainī, IX, p. 404ff.

37 Quran, 'Women', IV, 28, p. 76.
38 Ibn Mandhūr, *Lisan al 'Arab*, vol. XVII, p. 286.
39 Salaheddin Asfadī, *Kitāb al ghayth fi sharḥ 'Lāmiyyaat al-'Ajam'*, 1st ed. in 2 vols. Cairo, 1305, vol. II, pp. 138–43.
40 My translation is based on the editions by Ah'mad Amīn and Ahmed Azzīn, *Kitāb al-imtā' wal mu-ānasa* by Abu Hayan al-Tawhīdī, Beirut, Dar al-Hayat, undated, in 2 vols. Vol. II, p. 50.
41 Note on p. 50 of vol. II.
42 *Ibid.*, pp. 52–3.
43 Quran, 'The Earthquake', XCIX, p. 654.
44 Tawḥīdī, *op. cit.*, p. 60.
45 Yāqūt, *Mu'jam al-udabā*, vol. III, p. 190; cf. also vol. V, p. 343.
46 *Ibid.*, vol. III, p. 186.
47 *Ibid.*
48 Aly Mazahéri, *La Vie quotidienne des musulmans au Moyen Age*, pp. 177–8.
49 The bibliography of this aspect of Muslim civilization is very rich. The greatest source is the collection of the *Kitāb al-Aghānī*, a good analysis of which has been done in Arabic by Muhammad Abdaljawād al-Asma'i, *Abul faraj al-aṣfahāni wa kitābuhu al-Aghānī*, Cairo, 1951. I would also refer to the following works: Aḥmad Amīn, *Fajrul-Islam*, 10th ed., Cairo, 1969, p. 122ff; Aḥmad Amīn, *Dhuh'ā al-Islam*, vol. II, 2nd ed., 1934, p. 88ff; P. Hitti, *Précis d'histoire des Arabes*, and in particular p. 103ff; G. Marçais *La Berbérie musulmane*, p. 184ff; H. Jenhani, *al-Qayrawān*, p. 150. For the Andalusian region I would refer to: Lévy-Provençal, *Histoire de l'Espagne musulmane*, especially to the second volume: *Le Siècle du califat de Cordoue*; and to Henri Pérès, *La Poésie andalouse en arabe classique au XIe siècle*.
50 *The Thousand and One Nights*, tr. Powys Mathers, London, 1958, vol. I, p. 5.
51 G. Bachelard, *La Dialectique de la durée*, p. x.
52 *Ibid.*, p. x.
53 *The Thousand and One Nights*, 'The Tale of Young Nur and the Warrior Girl', vol. III, pp. 155–6.
54 *The Thousand and One Nights*, 'The Tender Tale of Prince Jasmine', vol. IV, p. 522.
55 *The Thousand and One Nights*, vol. IV, p. 522.
56 Enver Dehoï, *L'Érotisme des Mille et une Nuits*, pp. 48–9.
57 *Arabian Nights*, vol. IV, p. 299, trans. E. W. Lane. I have used the Lane translation here because that of Mardrus and Mathers does not make the author's point. (Cf. *The Thousand and One Nights*, vol. IV, p. 532.)
58 Cf. Nikita Ellisseef, *Thèmes et motifs des 'Mille et une Nuits'*, pp. 86–183. Enver Dehoï, 'Petit dictionnaire de l'érotisme', in *L'Érotisme des Mille et une Nuits*.
59 *The Thousand and One Nights*, vol. I, p. 242.
60 *Ibid.*, I, pp. 4–5.

Chapter 11 Erotology

1 Quoted by Ghazali, *Iḥyā*, vol. I, p. 124.
2 Walnut bark, which gives the gums a carmine colour.
3 Salaheddin al-Munajjid, *Jamāl al-mar-ati 'ind al-'arab*, Beirut, 1957, especially, pp. 36–7.
4 Jāḥidh, *Mufākharat al-jawārī wal-ghilmān*, quoted by Munajjid, p. 37.
5 Published by C. Pellat, Paris, 1953.
6 Salaheddin al-Munajjid, *Jamāl al-mar-ati 'ind al-'arab*, Beirut, 1957; al-Munajjid, *Al-hayāt al-jinsiyya ind al-'arab*, Beirut, 1958; al-Munajjid, *Bayn al-Khulafā wal khula-'ā fil'asr al 'abbāsi*, Beirut, 1958.
7 A copy is to be found in the Bibliothèque nationale, Paris, no. 3054–Ir-643 (1) I–982.
8 A copy is to be found in the Bibliothèque nationale, Paris, under the no. 3054–Ir–532 (1) I–892.
9 A copy of the manuscript is said to be at Damascus by al-Munajjid, *op. cit.*, p. 121.
10 This book has often been published. I have worked on an edition published in Cairo, 1317h.
11 A copy is to be found in the Bibliothèque nationale, Paris, under the number 3061–3063–3064–58–87–58 99 IIr 334 (I) II–368. Another copy is in Tunis, the Abdellya Collection, no. 10–269.
12 Manuscript mentioned by al-Munajjid, *op. cit.*, p. 124.
13 Copy in the Bibliothèque nationale, no. 3066–7.
14 Copy in the Bibliothèque nationale, no. 3039, fol. 146–51.
15 Two copies in the Bibliothèque nationale, 4643, fol. 201–36, and 5320, fol. 54–97, fol. 24–55.
16 Several manuscripts in the Bibliothèque nationale, Paris, no. 3060, fol. 138 v-145. Edition in Tunis, notably Mhamedi edition, undated, and the Cairo edition, undated.
17 Many editions. I have worked on the one published in Tunis (Mhamedi, undated). There are three manuscript copies in the Bibliothèque nationale, Paris (nos. 6669, 6677 and 6693). A copy in Tunis, Abdellya Collection, no. 4200. Numerous French translations. The best and oldest is that published in 1886 by Isidore Liseux (new edition 1906, Paris). A recent edition was published by Leopold Blondeau, Paris, in 1960 under the title *Le Jardin enchanté*. A fine illustrated copy may be consulted in the Bibliothèque nationale, Paris, no. 974. Cf. also nos. 1147 and 1327.
18 Al-Jawāib, Constantinople. Many scholars regard this as a plagiarism of an Indian text. But the authenticity is of secondary importance here. Even if it is 'false', its evidence is authentic.
19 *Ibid.*, p. 18.
20 *Ibid.*, p. 30.
21 *Ibid.*, p. 41.
22 *Ibid.*, p. 54.
23 Alā Addīn As Shāfi'ī, *Nikāḥ*, no. 3039, fol. III, v°–127 v°; Abderrahman Alshayzārī, *Īḍāḥ fi asrār an nikāḥ*, no. 2776, vol. 1–72;

Muhammad Triqi al-Falātī, *Mu'āwanat al ikhwān fi mu'āsharat al-niswān*, no. 5622, fol. 8, 9 a; Ahmad Ibn Qulayta, *Rushd al-labīb ila mu'āsharati al-ḥabīb*, no. 3051–2; Muhammad al-Tijānī, *Tuḥfat al-'arūs wa nuzhat al-nufūs*, no. 3061–3; Khalil Aybaq As Safadī, *Lau'at al-sāqī wa dam-'at al bāki*, no. 3074–3048, fol. 72–107; Muhammad Ibn 'Umal al-Ghazlāwī, *Yāsamīn al rawḍ al-'āṭir fī nuzhat al-khāṭir*, no. 3069–70, fol. 1–38.

There are other anonymous manuscripts also: *Irtiyāḥ al-ārwāḥ fi'ādat an nikāḥ*, no. 3039, fol. 109 v° 110; *Misbāh fī asrār al-nikāḥ*, no. 3039, fol. 36 v° – 61; *Qiṣṣat lūt*, no. 1932, 105 v°–115; *Risāla fil jimā'*, no. 3039, fol. 30. *Tuḥfat al-ash'āb fi mu-'āsharat al-aḥbāb*, no. 3039, vol. 51–259–267–268.

24 Arabic text, pp. 32–7; Cf. French text, ed. Blondeau, pp. 106–68.
25 Arabic text, p. 37–44; French trans., ed. Blondeau, pp. 169–82.
26 *Loc. cit.*, p. 100.
27 *Loc. cit.*, p. 102.
28 *Jardin parfumé*, p. 11.
29 *Iḍāḥ*, p. 1.
30 Abu Nawās, *Diwān*, p. 242.
31 Antaki, *Tazyīn*, p. 164.
32 *Ibid.*, pp. 161–4.
33 *Ibid.*, p. 170.
34 The Arabic text of *The Perfumed Garden*, p. 78; cf. the translations by Isidore Liseux, p. 16ff. and Bonneau, pp. 36 and 45. My own translation is more faithful. It follows the text closely without unnecessary editions.
35 *Ibid.*, ed. Bonneau, p. 99.
36 *Ibid.*, chap. XIX, ed. Bonneau, p. 247ff.
37 Suyūtī, *al Rahma*, chap. XXXIV, p. 135.
38 *Rujū' al-shaikh ilā ṣibāh*, p. 21.
39 *Ibid.*, p. 54.
40 *Ibid.*, p. 59.
41 *Ibid.*, p. 54.
42 *Ibid.*, p. 59.
43 *Ibid.*, p. 50.
44 *Ibid.*, p. 65.
45 *Le Jardin parfumé*, ed. Bonneau, p. 248.
46 *Ibid.*, p. 249.
47 *Rujū' al-shaikh*, p. 51.
48 *al-Raḥma*, p. 124.
49 Two desert plants whose French or Latin names I have been unable to find.
50 *Al Raḥma*, p. 125.
51 *Ibid.*, p. 124.
52 *Ibid.*, pp. 127–8.
53 *Le Jardin parfumé*, ed. Bonneau, pp. 242–3.
54 *Ibid.*, p. 131.
55 *Ibid.*, p. 148.
56 *Ibid.*, p. 150.

57 *Ibid.*, p. 152. Indeed, according to Arab tradition, the foetus may cease to develop for an indeterminate time, often for several years, before resuming its normal development.
58 *Ibid.*, pp. 244–5.
59 *Ibid.*, p. 248.
60 *Ibid.*, p. 135.
61 *Ibid.*, pp. 96–9.
62 *Ibid.*, p. 101. Of course the positional eroticism is very important. But it does not seem to me to have been treated with sufficient originality. Nefzāwi particularly recommends ten or twenty-four positions, depending on the text. Some of these are recommended in cases of anatomical deformation (the infirm, the hunchbacked). Indeed there is a passage suggesting the uses to which an amputee's stump might be put, for example.
63 Suyūtī, *Idhāh*, p. 78; cf. also *Nashwat al-sakrān*, pp. 28, 31, 32; Salaheddin al-Munajjid, *Jamāl al mar-at*, p. 47.
64 For example, *The Book of Pleasure, Bah Nameh*, was translated from the Turkish into Arabic several times (cf. the French translation by Abdel Haq Efendi Erze-roumi, undated, 'Enfer' of the Bibliothèque nationale, Paris, no. 20). We tend to fall too often into the vulgar and obscene, though Europeans have often exaggerated this aspect.
65 Ibn 'Abd Rabbih, *Al 'aqd al-farīd*, vol. III, pp. 209–30, ed. Cairo, 1300h.
66 Muhammad Haqqui al-Nāzli, *Khazinat al asrār*, ed. Cairo, 1307h., 'Chapter of the virtues of verses and hadiths for the amendment of the *Zāni and zānia*', p. 77ff.
67 Shams al-dīn al-Anṣāri, *Kitāb al-siyāsa fi'ilm al-firāsa*, Cairo, 1299h., lithograph, cf. pp. 19, 26, 37.
68 Al-Abshīhi, *Al-Mostatraf*, trans. Rat, vol. II, chaps. LXVIII–LXXIII.
69 Ibn Al-Qayyam al-Jawzia, *Akhbār al nisā*, Beirut, 1960; cf. in particular Chaps. VII devoted to *zinā*.
70 Gérard Zwang, article 'Odorat', in *Dictionnaire de sexologie*, p. 274.

Chapter 12 Certain practices

1 A. Bouhdiba, 'Le Hammam', *A la Recherche des normes perdues*, p. 121.
2 J. Carcopino, *La Vie quotidienne à Rome*, p. 298.
3 *Ibid.*
4 Cf. W. and G. Marçais, *Les Monuments arabes de Tlemcen*, pp. 162–9. Cf. also H. Terrasse, 'Trois bains mérinides du Maroc', in *Mélange W. Marcais*, p. 311ff.
5 Cf. Ali Mazahéri, *La Vie quotidienne des musulmans*, pp. 68–70. *The Thousand and One Nights* provides innumerable references of great value; cf. in particular the tale of Abusir and Abu Qīr (931th–940th Nights).
6 For this passage I have used, in addition to my personal knowledge

of the question and various readings, the following sources: A. Mazahéri, *op. cit.*, pp. 67–8; Ah'mad Amīn, *Qamus*, pp. 95–7 and pp. 362–74; H. Pérès, *La Poésie andalouse*, pp. 311–18; E.-G. Gobert, pamphlet *Tunis et les parfums*, extracts from which were published in *Les Nouvelles esthétiques*, mai-juin 1963, under the title of 'Parfums et cosmétiques en Tunisie'.

7 Al-Ghazāli, *Iḥyā*, vol. I, p. 130.
8 Cf. *Fatāwā*, vol. V, p. 327ff. and p. 363ff.
9 Al-Ghazāli, *Iḥyā*, vol. I, also p. 137ff.
10 'Uqbāni, p. 268; cf. also le *Traité de Hisba by Ibn Abderraouf, Hesperis*, vol. I–III, fasc. III, 1966, pp. 367–70.
11 *Ibid.*, p. 269: 'lā siyyamā mā yad'ū ilaihi ittilā'u ba'ḍi-l-fāsiqāti 'alā mahāsini-l-ukhrā min taḥarruqi shahwati-l-tafā'uli alladhi yakhtāru ba'ḍuhunna ladhdhatahu 'an mujāma'ati lrajuli.'
12 Cf. H. Pérès, *La Poésie andalouse*, p. 34; A. Amīn, *Qamus*, p. 179.
13 Oum El Khir, 'Le hammam', chronique de la revue *Faiza*, no. 9, novembre 1960.
14 Ahmad Sefrioui, *La Boîte à merveille*, pp. 11–14, Paris, Le Seuil, 1954.
15 'Tale of Sard Ben Ward'.
16 *The Thousand and One Nights*, Arabic text, 790th Night, vol. II, pp. 12–17.
17 Quoted by J. Carcopino, *op. cit.*, p. 304. 'Baths, wine and lust may corrupt our bodies, but they make life worth living.'
18 Ibn Khaldūn, *Muqaddinia*, Arabic text, ed. Cairo, undated, p. 86.
19 A. Amīn, *Qamus*, p. 187.
20 *Fatāwā Hindiyya*, vol. V, p. 356.
21 Moslem, vol. I, p. 34ff; Tabari, *Annales*, I, 154; Gaudefroy-Demombynes, p. 63; Muhammad Essad Bey, *Mahomet*, p. 55.
22 *Iḥyā*, vol. I, p. 132.
23 *Fatāwā*, vol. V, p. 357.
24 *Ibid.*, p. 357.
25 *Fatāwā Qadhi-Khan*, vol. III, p. 409.
26 Quoted by Ghazāli, *Iḥyā*, vol. I, p. 132.
27 A. Mazahéri, *La Vie quotidienne des musulmans*, p. 47.
28 C.-A. Julien, *Histoire de l'Afrique du Nord*, p. 92.
29 Ah'mad Amīn, *Qamus*, p. 187.
30 *Dictionnaire de sexologie*, p. 321.
31 Genesis, 17, 9–14.
32 Cf. *Dictionnaire des religions*, p. 84.
33 The origin of circumcision, according to Frazer, in *Oeuvres* of Marcel Mauss, vol. I, p. 142.
34 Exodus, 4, 24–6.
35 P. Gordon, *L'Initiation sexuelle et l'évolution religieuse*, p. 68.
36 Maryse Choisy, *Moïse*, p. 91.
37 *Ibid.*, p. 92.
38 *Ibid.*, p. 94.
39 *Ibid.*, p. 96.
40 Galatians, 6, 12–15.

41 Ghazāli, *Iḥyā*, vol. I, p. 132.
42 In addition to personal experience, my main sources here are: Salah al-Rizgui, *Al-Aghāni al-Tūnusiyya*, pp. 171–5; Aḥmad Amīn, *Qamus*, pp. 187–9.
43 My translation here is from the version given by Salah Rizgui, *loc. cit.*, p. 187: 'Ulik mṭahhar wu 'qābiq 'arās wu ḥsānik ywalwal mā bīn l-ghrūs.
– Ulik mṭahhar wu 'qa biq shbāb wu ḥsānik ywalwal mā bin l'uzzah.
– Winī um l-maṭahhar, wīnī khāltu tjī tarmī drāhim 'alā 'ammārtū.'
44 Yussef al-Masry, *Le Drame sexuel de la femme dans l'Orient arabe*, p. 67.
45 *Ibid.*, p. 110ff; cf. also Aḥmad Amīn, *Qamus*, pp. 188–9.
46 *L'Érotisme des Mille et une Nuits*, p. 125.
47 *The Thousand and One Nights*, vol. I, p. 516.
48 *Ibid.* Cf. Marie Bonaparte, *La Sexualité de la femme*, p. 321.
49 Rachid Boujedra, *La Répudiation*, p. 71.
50 P. Gordon, *L'Initiation sexuelle*, pp. 10–11.
51 P. 389.
52 Quran, 'Women', IV, 3–4, p. 72 and 28–31, p. 76; 'The Believers', XXIII, 5 and 6, p. 343; 'The Stairways', LXX, 29–31, p. 607.
53 Quran, 'Light', XXIV, 33, p. 356.
54 Cf. Tabari, *Tafsīr*, vol. XVII, 88; Razi, vol. VI, pp. 308–9.
55 For these forms of pre-Islamic *nikāḥ* I have referred to 'Ainī, who comments on one of Aysha's hadiths, vol. IX, pp. 414–15.
56 'Ainī, vol. III, p. 230: 'wa la siyyama nis-u miṣra fa inna fihinna biḍ'an la tūsafu wa munkarātun la tumna'u.'
57 *Ibid.*, p. 230.
58 Cf. Maqrīzi, *Khitat*, vol. I, p. 89.
59 M. Mazahéri, *La Vie quotidienne des musulmans au Moyen Age*, p. 64.
60 *Ibid.*, p. 65.
61 *Ibid.*, p. 65.
62 J. Berque, *Le Maghreb d'hier à demain*, p. 326.
63 *Ibid.*, p. 326.
64 These paragraphs were written after carrying out an investigation in the 'field'; I have also used an unpublished report by Othman Larifi, *La prostitution réglementée dans la capitale* (Tunis).
65 Two sources confirm one another: Najib Maḥfūdh's *Qasr-al-shauq*, pp. 393–4 and Rachid Boujedra, *La Répudiation*, pp. 152–4.
66 Cf. Sylvestre de Sacy, *Christomathie arabe*, vol. I, p. 104ff.
67 Cf. Ibn 'Udhara, 'Al-bayān al-mughrib fi akhbār al-maghrib', vol. I, p. 126, Leiden, ed. Dozy, 1859.
68 Many examples could be cited. Two particularly good ones are: Muhammad Abdel'Adhim Azirquāni, 'Albighā' in *Alhidāya al islamia*, vol. IV, 1353h., p. 195ff; Mustapha Abdelwahid, *Al-Islām wal mushkila ṭūl jinsiyya*, p. 87ff.
69 Othman Larifi, *loc. cit.*
70 Enver Dehoï, *L'Érotisme des Mille et une Nuits*, p. 177.
71 In Najib Maḥfūdh, *Qasr al-shauq*, p. 396.

72 In 'Le teste du dessin chez les prostituées', by Sami Ali, in *Al majalla al jinā-iyya al qaumiyya*, vol. I, no. 2, juillet 1958, p. 103.
73 In the same number, 'Abdelmonem al-Meligī, 'La représentation de l'être humain chez les prostituées d'après le test du Rorschach'. Cf. also the study of prostitution in Cairo, published by the Egyptian National Centre, 'Al bighā fil qāhira', 1961.
74 *Loc. cit.*, p. 266.
75 *Loc. cit.*, p. 264, introduction by A. Chenoufy, pp. 149–50.
76 *Ibid.*, p. 262.
77 *Ibid.*, p. 261.
78 *Ibid.*, p. 264.
79 *Ibid.*, p. 264.
80 *Kitāb al fisāl fi l milal wal aḥwā wa lniḥāl*, Cairo, 1317h., 2 vols; cf. vol. I, p. 135 and vol. II, p. 114.
81 *Kitāb naqt al-'arūs fi tawārīkh al-khulafā*, Cairo, 1951, pp. 72–3.
82 *Kitāb al-akhlāq wa l siyar*, Beirut, 1961, trans. N. Tomiche, p. 58.
83 *Ibid.*, p. 59.
84 *The Thousand and One Nights*, vol. I, p. 347ff.
85 *Ibid.*, vol. II, p. 1ff.
86 *Ibid.*, vol. I, p. 66ff.
87 Chemseddine, *Hanifa, Mahbouba et moi*, Tunis, undated (probably about 1920).
88 *La Répudiation*, p. 71.
89 *Ibid.*, p. 179.
90 *Ibid.*, p. 57.
91 *Ibid.*, p. 134.
92 *Ibid.*, p. 136.
93 *Ibid.*, p. 137.
94 *Ibid.*, p. 168.
95 *Ibid.*, pp. 106–7. Cf. also an attempted seduction in an oven (p. 241) and a scene in which the mother surprises her son in the middle of sexual intercourse with a boy of his own age (p. 242).
96 *Ibid.*, p. 241.
97 *Ibid.*, p. 241.
98 Abu Nawās, *Diwān*, p. 116; cf. Jamel Ben Cheikh, 'Poésies bachiques d'Abu Nawās', in *Bulletin d'études orientales*, vol. X, VII, 1963–4, p. 60ff. Cf. also Abu Nawās, *Diwān*, pp. 242–572. In *The Thousand and One Nights* the tale of the Sea Rose (vol. IV, p. 405ff) tells of a veritable change of sex caused by magic. Cf. Enver Dehoï, *loc. cit.*, p. 208 and Habib Ezzayat, *La Femme garçonne en islam*.
99 Salaheddin al-Munajjid, *Jamāl al-marāti 'inda al arab*, p. 71.
100 *Dictionnaire de sexologie*, article 'Fesse', p. 167.
101 *Ibid.*
102 Cf. *Diwān al Sabāba*, p. 31.
103 Abu Nasr al-Hamadhāni, *Kitāb al-sab'iyyāt*, p. 174.
104 *L'Etre et le néant*, p. 667; *Being and Nothingness*, trans. Hazel E. Barnes, London, Methuen, 1958, p. 578.
105 *Ibid.*, p. 668; *Ibid.*, p. 579.
106 *Dictionnaire de sexologie*, p. 352.

107 *L'Être et le néant*, pp. 471–2; *Being and Nothingness*, pp. 400–2.
108 Cf. Aḥmad Amīn, *Qamus*, p. 87.
109 Cf. *Fatāwā*, vol. V, p. 327ff.
110 *Dix contes tunisiens pour enfants.*
111 Cf. P. Saint-Yves, *L'éternuement et le baillement dans la magie, l'ethnographie et le folklore médical*, 1921. I have also learnt much from Claude Gaignebet's thesis for the doctorat du 3e cycle 'on *Le Folklore obscène des enfants français.*'
112 *Loc. cit.*, p. 45.
113 Especially in the tale 'Danse, danse mon gourdin'.
114 Cf. Paul Germain, 'La musique et la psychanalyse', in *Revue française de Psychanalyse*, 1928, no. 4.
115 Goodland's *Bibliography of Sex Rites* provides full and valuable information on this point. It is a mine of historical reference.
116 Cf. E. Dermenghem, *Le Culte des saints au Maghreb.*
117 Aḥmad Amīn, *Qamus*, p. 288.
118 Cf. H. Renault, 'Les survivances des cultes de Cybèle, Vénus et Bacchus Aissaoua, Ouled Nail, Karakous' in *Revue tunisienne*, 1917, p. 150ff.

Chapter 13 In the kingdom of the mothers

1 Helene Deutsch, *The Psychology of Women*, London, Research Books, 1947, vol. II, p. 257.
2 One of the Prophet's well-known hadiths: 'The vaginal bond is an excess of existence.'
3 Cf. al-Qudūri, *Mukhtaṣar*, trans. Bousquet and Bercher, p. 68.
4 *Ibid.*, note p. 5.
5 *Ibid* Cf. also *Fatāwā*, vol. I, p. 544ff.
6 *Arabian Nights*, trans. Lane, vol. IV, p. 298. Compare with *The Thousand and One Nights*, trans. Mardrus and Mathers, vol. IV, p. 531.
7 Mouloud Feraoum, 'Le désaccord', in *Soleil*, no. 6, Alger, 15 juin 1951, p. 11
8 Cf. al-Bahy al-Khūli, *Al-Mar-ah*, p. 133.
9 Sleim Ammar, 'Les troubles "psycho-organiques" de la grossesse, de l'accouchement, et de l'allaitement en Tunisie', in *La Tunisie médicale*, no. 1–2, janvier-février 1962. Cf. also a more recent work that reaches the same conclusions: J.-P. Fievet, *A partir de l'Observation des manifestations hystériques en milieu tunisien, étude des relations entre l'hystérie et la culture*, thèse pour le doctorat en médicine, Paris, 1970. See especially the second chapter.
10 J. Lacan, *Écrits*, p. 182.
11 Quoted by J. Berque, *Les Arabes d'hier à demain*, p. 163. Cf. also Nāsir al-Ḥanī's *Muḥādharāt 'an Jamīl al Zahāwi*, p. 114ff and p. 132ff. Cf. also *Diwān*, II, pp. 168, 241, 265.
12 Cf. *Dix contes tunisiens pour enfants.*

13 *Loc. cit.*, p. 43.
14 'Entretiens avec Rachid Boujedra', in *Le Monde*, supplément littéraire 24 janvier 1970.
15 H. Bourguiba, speech of 13 August 1965.
16 C. G. Jung, 'The relations between the ego and the unconscious', *Collected Works*, vol. 7, tr. R. F. C. Hull, London, Routledge & Kegan Paul, 1953, p. 195.
17 *Ibid.*, p. 196.
18 Ghālī Shukrī, *Azmat al-jins*, p. 69.
19 Najib Maḥfūdh, *Baina al-qaṣrain*, pp. 49, 353, 387; *Qasr al-shauq*, pp. 402–5; *Al-Sukkariyya*, pp. 139–362.
20 C. G. Jung, *op. cit.*, p. 196.
21 *The Thousand and One Nights*, vol. II, p. 554ff.
22 *Ibid.*, vol. II, p. 568.
23 C. G. Jung, *op. cit.*, p. 196.
24 Roger Bastide, *Sociologie et psychanalyse*, p. 277.
25 *Al-Majānī al-ḥaditha*, vol. III, p. 126. Cf. Elyas Selim al-Ḥāwi, *Ibn Rūmi*, an excellent analysis of Ibn Rūmi's vision of nature, p. 33ff.

Conclusion

1 J. Berque, *Les Arabes d'hier à demain*, p. 155.
2 *Ibid.* Cf. also *Le Maghreb entre deux guerres.*
3 There is a rich bibliography on this subject. Reference might be made to: Durriyya Shafiq, *al mar-at al misriya*, Cairo, 1955; Ibrahim Abdallah Māhī, *Mushkilat almar-a fil bilād al 'arabiyya*, Baghdad, 1957; Ghālī Shukrī, *Azmat al jins fil qiṣṣat-al 'arabī*, Beirut, 1962.
4 Laila Ba'alabakki, *Anā Aḥyā*, 1st ed. Beirut, 1950. I quote from the second edition of 1963.
5 *Ibid.*, p. 288.
6 *Faiza*, no. 56, mars-avril 1956.
7 *La Presse de Tunisie*, 27 juillet 1970.
8 *La Presse de Tunisie*, 19 septembre 1971.
9 *La Presse de Tunisie*, 23 avril 1967.
10 *La Presse de Tunisie*, 16 aout 1968.
11 *Faiza*, no. 36, octobre-novembre 1963.
12 On the situation of Tunisian women in the years prior to the Second World War one might consult with profit the 'reportage' by Lucie-Paule Marguerite, *Les Tunisiennes*, published in 1937 in Paris, by Editions Denoël. Cf. also the study by Henri de Montety, *Le Mariage musulman en Tunisie*, published in Tunis, SAPI, 1941.
13 *Leila*. Cf. L.-P. Marguerite, *op. cit.*, pp. 30–1.
14 Sleim Ammar and Ezzedine Mbarek, 'L'hystérie chez la jeune fille et la femme tunisienne', in *La Tunisie médicale*, no. 4, juillet-avril 1961, p. 7.
15 Cf. the translation given by Aziz Lahbabi, *Florilège poétique arabe et berbère*, p. 74.

16 Ghālī Shukrī, *Azmat al-Jins*, p. 263.
17 Laila Ba'alabakki, *Al-aīliha al-mamsūkha*, Beirut, 1966, p. 47.
18 Laila Ba'alabakki, *Ana Aḥyā*, p. 312.
19 *Ibid.*, p. 276.
20 *Ibid.*, p. 296 (a'ṭī idhan anā aḥya).
21 *Dictionnaire de sexologie*, Supplément, pp. 354–5.
22 Ghālī Shukrī, *op. cit.*, p. 114.
23 *Bain al-qasrain*, p. 49.
24 *Ibid.*, p. 288.
25 *Quạsr al-shauq*, pp. 396–7.
26 *Dictionnaire de sexologie*, p. 150.
27 Henry Winthrop, 'L'avenir de la révolution sexuelle', in *Diogène*, no. 70, avril-juin 1970, p. 90.
28 J. Berque, *Les Arabes d'hier à demain*, chap. 1.
29 G. Bachelard, *La Poétique de l'espace*, p. 200; *Poetics of Space*, tr. Maria Jolas, Boston, Beacon Press, 1964, p. 222.

Bibliography

A. *Primary sources*

Quran, Vulgate, ed. Ottoman, Istanbul, 1309h. Ed. Flugel, Leipzig, 1837.

Translation of the Quran:
The Quran, trans. Arthur J. Arberry, Oxford University Press, 1983.

Commentaries on the Quran

Abu Ḥayān al-Andalusī, *Tafsīr al baḥr al-muḥīṭ*, Cairo, 1328h., 9 vols.
Baydhawi, *Anwar at tanzīl*, Leipzig, 1846.
Qotb Said, *Fi dhilāl al-Qurān*, Beirut, 1973, 6 vols.
Razi Fakhreddin, *Al Tafsīr al-Kabīr*, Bulaq, 1270h.-1289h., 8 vols.
Riḍha Raschid, *Tafsīr al-Manār*, Cairo, 1948, 12 vols.
Tabari, *Jamā' al-bayān fi tafsīr al-Qurān*, Cairo, 1321h., 30 vols.

Hadiths

Boukhāri, *Ṣaḥīḥ*, official edition of the sultan Abdulhamid II, Cairo, 1312h., 9 vols.
Moslem, *Saḥīḥ*, 1st ed., 1328h., Cairo, 7 vols.
Nawawi, *Al-arba'īn al-nawawiyya*, ed. Taftazani, Tunis, 1295h.
Qastallāni, *Irshād al sāri, sharḥ saḥīṇ al-Bukhāri*, Bulaq, 1304h., 9 vols.
'Ainī, *'Umdat al qāri shar'iḥ al-Bukhāri*, Istanbul, 1308h., 11 vols.
Al-Fatāwā al-Hindiyya, ed. Bulaq, 1310h., 6 vols.
Al-Ghazali, *Iḥyā'ulūm al dīn*, Cairo, 1302h., 4 vols.
Abu Ḥanīfa, *Kitāb al-fiqh al-akbar*, Lucknow, 1926.
Abu Ḥanīfa, *Al-Musnad*, Lahore, 1889.
Ibn Ḥanbal, *Al-Musnad*, Cairo, 1327h., 16 vols.
Malik, *Al-Muwaṭṭa*, Cairo, 1313h.
Shāfi'i, *Kitāb al-umūr*, Cairo, 1321–5h., 7 vols.
Shāfi'i, *Risala fi uṣūl al-fiqh*, Cairo, 1312h.

Bibliography

Lexicography

Ibn Manḏhūr, *Lisān al'arab*, Bulaq, 1300h, 20 vols.
Shirazi Firuzabadi, *Al-Qāmūs al-muḥīt*, Bulaq, 1301h., 4 vols.
Ridha Muhammad, *Matn al lugha al'arabiyya*, Beirut, 1958, 5 vols.

Other general references

Amīn Aḥmad, *Qamus al'ādāt wa altaqālīd wal-ta'ābīr al-maṣriyya*, Cairo, 1953.
Dictionnaire de sexologie, Paris, 1962; Supplément, Paris, 1965.
Encyclopédie de l'Islam, Paris, 1954.
Goodland, Roger, *Bibliography of Sex Rites*, London, 1931.
Pearson, J. D., *Index Islamicus*, Cambridge, 1954 and 1962.
Sarkis A., *Mu'jam al-matbū'at al' 'arabiyyah wal mu'arraba*, Cairo, 1928–9.
Vajda, G., 'Notes de bibliographie maghrébine', in *Hesperis*, 37, 1950, and 41, 1951.
Vajda, G., *Répertoire des catalogues et inventaires de manuscrits arabes*, Paris, 1955.

B. *Works in Arabic*

Abd al Baqi Fuad, *Al-Mu'jam al-Mufahras li alfadhi i qur'ān al-karīm*, Cairo, undated.
Abdelwahid Mustafa, *Al-Islām wal mushkila ṭūl jinsiyya*, Cairo, 1961.
Abu Nawās, *Diwān*, Beirut, undated.
Al-Abshihi Shihāb alldin, *Al-Mostaṭraf*, Cairo, 1292h., French trans. Rat, Paris, 1899–1902.
Al'Aḍm Ṣādiq Jalāl, *Fil ḥubb wal ḥubb l'udhri*, Beirut, 1968.
Al'amil Husain Makki, *Al-Mut'atu' fil-islam*, Beirut, 1962.
Alf laila wa laila (*The Thousand and One Nights*). Many editions. The least unsatisfactory, Cairo, 1969. (Translator's note: There appears to be no recent English translation of *The Thousand and One Nights*. Our nineteenth-century ones are often marred by a prudish desire to protect the reader's susceptibilities. The Preface (1906) to Lane's Everyman's Library Version declares quite unshamefacedly: 'With regard to the omissions, Lane's translation is intended for the general public of both sexes, and it was absolutely necessary to excise a number of words, phrases, and passages on the score of decency. Even a few complete tales had to be omitted, because they could not be purified without destruction.' Clearly, such a version would be of little use as a reference for a book on Islam and sexuality! The most recent and, to my mind, best version is Mathers' retranslation of Mardrus's French translation: *The Thousand and One Nights*, trans. Powys Mathers, in 4 vols. London, Folio Society, 1958.)
Alūsi, Zādeh, *Ghāliyyāt al-mawā'idh*, Cairo, 1911.
Alwi, Abd alḥamīd, *al-Zauj al-marbūṭ*, Baghdad, 1964.

Amīn, Aḥmad, *Fajral-islam*, Beirut, 10th ed., 1969.
Amīn, Aḥmad, *Ḍuha-al-Islām*, Beirut, 10th ed., 1969.
Amīn, Aḥmad, *Ḍhuhral-islam*, Beirut, 10th ed., 1969.
Anṣāri, Shamsaldin, *Kitāb al siyāsa fi'ilmal firāsa*, Cairo, 1882.
Antaki, Daud, *Tazyīn al-aswāq bi tafṣīl ashwāq al-'ushshāq*, Cairo, 1308h.
'Aqqād 'Abbās Maḥmūd, *Iblis*, Beirut, 1969.
'Aqqād 'Abbās Maḥmūd, *Faṭimatu-z-zahrā*, Beirut, 1967.
Aṣfaḥāni, Abulfaraj, *Kitāb al aghāni*, 20 vols., Cairo, 1323h.
Asma'i (al)-Abdaljawad, *Abul faraj al aṣbaḥāni wa kitābuhual-Aghānī*, Cairo, 1951.
Ba'alabakki, Laila, *Anā Aḥya* (novel), 2nd ed., Beirut, 1963.
Ba'alabakki, Laila, *Al-Āliha al-mamsūkha* (novel), Beirut, 1966.
Barra (al), Zakaria, *Aḥkāmal walad fil islam*, Cairo, 1964.
Bashshar, Ibn Burd, *Diwān*, Beirut, 1963.
Ben 'Ashur Tahar, *Uṣūl al-niḍhām al-ijtimā'i fil islām*, Tunis, 1964.
Bent al-Shati, 'Āisha, *Nisā-al-nabi*, Beirut, undated.
Bent al-Shati, 'Āisha, *Banāt-al-nabi*, Beirut, undated.
Bouhdiba, Abdelwahab, *Khawāṭir ḥaul al-dīn*, in review *Al-Fikr*, June 1966.
Bouhdiba, Abdelwahab, *Al ḍamīr aldīnī wal mujtama' al ḥadīth*, Tunis, 1965.
Busiri, *Burda*, Tunis, 1327h. (French trans. by R. Basset, Paris, 1907.)
Dabbagh, Abdelaziz, *Kitāb al-ibrīz*, Cairo, 1306h.
Damiri, Kamaluddin, *Kitāb ḥāyāt al-ḥayawān*, Cairo, 1284h.
Fashni, Ahmed, *Kitāb al-majālis al-sanya, sharḥ' al-araba'ın al-nawawiyya*, Cairo, 1299h.
Ghazāli (al), Abu Ḥāmid, *Iḥya'ulūm al-dīn*, Cairo, 1302h. 4 vols.
Ghazāli (al), *Al durrat al fākhira fi kashfi 'ulūm al-akhira*, Geneva, 1878.
Guiga, Abderrahman, *Min aqāsīs, banī hilāl*, Tunis, 1963. (French trans. by T. Guiga, *La Geste hilalienne*, Tunis, 1968.)
Ḥaddād (al), Ṭahar, *Imra-atuna iza al sharī'a wal mujtama'*, Tunis, 1930.
Ḥalbi (al), Ibrāhīm, *Multaqa al-Abḥur*, Istanbul, 1296h.
H'allāj (al), al-Hasayn, *Dīwān*, ed Massignon, new ed., Paris, 1955.
Hamadhani (al), Abderrahman, *Kitāb al-sab'iyyāt*, Cairo, 1299h.
Husari (al), Ibrahim, *Dhail Azhār al-adab*, Cairo, 1353h.
Ibn Abdu Rabbihi, Shihāb al dīn, *Al'iqd al farīd*, Cairo, 1305h.
Ibn al-Arabi, Mohieddin, *Shajarat al-kaun*, Cairo, 1310h.
Ibn al'Arabi, Mohieddin, *Diwān*, Bulaq, 1855.
Ibn al'Arabi, Mohieddin, *Al futūḥat al-maqiya*, 2 vols, Bulaq, 1270h.
Ibn al-Faridh, Omar, *Dīwān*, Beirut, 1887 and Cairo, 1289h.
Ibn Ḥajla, al-Maghrabi, Shihāb al dīn, *Dīwan al sabāba*, Cairo, 1308h.
Ibn Ḥazm, *Kitāb al-akhlāq wal siyar*, Beirut, 1961 (with French translation by Nadia Tommiche).
Ibn Ḥazm, *Tauq al ḥamāma*, Algiers, 1949 (with French trans. by Léon Bercher, *Le Collier du pigeon*).
Ibn Ḥazm, *Naqṭ al'arūs fi tawārīkh al khulafa*, Cairo, 1951.
Ibn Kamal Basha, *Rujū al-shaikh ilā ṣibāh*, Cairo, 1273h.
Ibn Khaldūn, Abderrahman, Al-Muqaddinia, Bulaq, 1274h. (French trans. by V. Monteil, Beirut, 1967–8.)

Ibn Najim, Zain al'ābidīn, *Al-Ashbāh wal naḍhā-ir*, Cairo, 1322h.
Ibn al-Qayyim al-Jawzia, *Akhbār al-nissā*, Beirut, 1964.
Ibn al-Qayyim al-Jawzia, *Alṭibb alnabawi*, Beirut, 1958.
Ibn Sirin, Muhammad, *Ta bīr al-ru-yā*, Tunis, 1368h.
Ibn Sirin, Muhammad (attributed to), *Muntakhab al-kalām fi tafsīr al-aḥlām*, Cairo, 1301h.
Ibn Thābit, Hasan, *Dīwān*, Beirut, 1966.
Ibn al-Wardi Zin-Eddin, *Lāmiyyāt*, Tunis, 1342h. (French trans. by Issac Cattan, *Bulletin de l'Institut de Carthage*, Tunis, juillet 1900.)
Jāḥidh 'Amr Abu 'Uthmān, *Kitāb al ḥayawān*, Cairo, 1284h.
Jāḥidh 'Amr Abu 'Uthmān, *Kitāb al-bukhalā*, Cairo, 1938. (French trans. C. Pellat, Paris, 1962.)
Jāḥidh 'Amr Abu 'Uthmān, *Kitāb al-Tarbi 'wal tadwīr*, Damascus, 1952.
Jāḥidh 'Amr Abu 'Uthmān, *Mufākharat al-jawāri wal ghilwān*, Beirut, 1964.
Jamil Buthaina, *Dīwān*, Beirut, 1966.
Jilani, Abdelqader, *Al-insān al-kāmil*, Cairo, 1300h.
Khafaji, Shihab aldīn, *Ṭurrāz al-majālis*, Cairo, 1283h.
Khairuddin, Ahmad, *Aghāni*, Tunis, 1968.
Khalaf, Muhammad Aḥmad, *Al jann al quṣuṣi fil Qurān*, Cairo, 1954.
Khalaffalah, Muhammad (*et al.*), *Althaqāfat al-islāmiyya wal ḥayāt al-mu'āṣira*, Cairo, 1955.
Khan, Muhammad Sadiq Hassan, *Nashwat al-sakrān*, Constantinople, 1296h.
Khuli (al) al-Bahī, *Al-mar-ah bain al bait wal mujtama'*, Cairo, undated.
Maarri (al), Abul'ala, *Risālatul-ghufrān*, Cairo, 1950.
Maarri (al), Abul'ala, *Saqt al-zand*, Beirut, 1963.
Maḥfūdh, Najib, *Bain al-qaṣrain* (novel), 5th ed., Cairo, 1964.
Maḥfūdh, Najib, *Qaṣr al-shauq* (novel) 6th ed., Cairo, 1966.
Maḥfūdh, Najib, *Al-Sukkariyya* (novel), 5th ed., Cairo, 1964.
Maqqari, al-Lissan aldin, *Naf'ah'tīb*, Cairo, 1302h.
Marqaz (al), al-Qaumi Lil Ŭuh'ūth al itima' iyya, *al Bighā fil Qāhira*, Cairo, 1961.
Marzuqi (al), Mhamed, *Al-Adab al-sha'bi*, Tunis, 1967.
Meligi (al), Ahmed, Ṣuwar al insān fi adhānil-baghyā, in *Majallat al jināya al qaumiyya*, Cairo, vol. I, no. 2, July 1968.
Munajjid (al), Ṣalāḥ aldin, *Al-Ḥayāt al-jinsiyya 'ind al 'arab*, Beirut, 1958.
Munajjid (al), Ṣalāḥ aldin, *Jamāl al-mar-aht 'indu ul'urub*, Beirut, 1957.
Nefzāwi, Muhammad, *Al-Rauḍ al'āṭir fi nuzhat al-khāṭir*, Tunis, undated. (French trans. by Isidore Liseux; new ed., Paris, 1960.)
Nazli (al), Muhammad, *Khazīnat al-asrār*, Cairo, 1306h.
Qāḍi (al), Abderrahim, *Daqā-iq al-akhbār al-kabīr*, Tunis, undated.
Qāḍi Khan, *Fatāwā*, in *Fatāwā Hindiyya*, Bulaq, 6 vols, 1310h.
Qalamawi (al), Suhayr, *Alf laila wa laila*, Cairo, 1966.
Qanawi (al), Mas'ūd, *Sharḥ lāmiyyat ibn al-wardi*, Cairo, 1310h.
Qudūri (al), *Mukhtaṣar*, Tunis, undated (with French trans. by G.-H. Bousquet and L. Bercher).
Raghib (al), Aḥmad, *Safīnat al rāghib wa dafīnat al maṭālib*, Istanbul, 1255h.

Rizqi (al), Salah, *Al-Aghāni al-tūnusiyya*, Tunis, 1967.
Safadi Salahedin, *Al-Ghaith al-musajjam fi sharḥ lāmiyyat al'ajam*, Cairo, 1305h.
Sandubi Ḥasan, *Tārīkh al iḥtifāl bilmaulid al-nabawi*, Cairo, 1948.
Sarraj (al), *Maṣārī' al'ushshāq*, Istanbul, 1301h.
Sharāra, Abdellatif, *Falsafat al-ḥubb 'ind al'arab*, Beirut, 1960.
Shibli (al), Badredin, *Akām al-marjān fi aḥkam al-Jān*, Cairo, 1326h.
Shukri, Ghali, *Azmat al-jins fil qiṣṣat al'arabiyya*, Beirut, 1962.
Suyūtī (al), Jalaleddīn, *Kitāb al-īdhāh'fi 'ilmil nikāh*, Tunis, undated.
Suyūtī (al), Jalaleddīn, *Kitāb al raḥma*, Cairo, undated.
Taftazani (al), Sa'adaldin, *Sharh al-arba-'īn al-nawawiyya*, Tunis, 1295h.
Tahir (al), Abdeljalil, *Albadw wal'ashā-ir fil biladil 'arabiyya*, Beirut, 1955.
Tawhidi, Abu Hayan, *Al im-tau' wal mu-ānasa*, Beirut, undated.
Uqbani (al), Muhammad, 'Tuḥfat al-nāḍhir wa ghunyat al-dhākir', in *Bulletin d'études orientales*, vol. XIV, 1965–6.
Zahawi, J. S., *Dīwān* (3 vols), Cairo, 1955.
Zayla'i, Fakhruddin, *Tabīn al ḥaqā-īq, Sharḥ Kanz al-daqā-iq*, Bulaq, 1313h.
Zayyat (al), Ḥabīb, *Al-Mar-at al ghulāmiyya fil islām*, in review *Mashriq*, no. 50, Beirut, 1956.
Zayyat (al), Ḥabīb, *Al-liḥī islām*, in review *Mashriq*, no. 50, Beirut, 1956.

C.1 *Sociology and history of religions*

Allendy, R., *Le Symbolisme des religions*, Paris, Chacornac, 1948.
Balandier, G., 'Sociologie, ethnologie, ethnographie', in *Traité de sociologie*, by G. Gurvitch, Paris, PUF, vol. I, pp. 99–113.
Balandier, G., *Sociologie actuelle de l'Afrique noire*, Paris, PUF, 1955.
Bastide, R., 'L'Homme africain à travers sa religion traditionnelle', *Présence africaine*, 1962, vol. I, pp. 32–43.
Bastide, R., *Sociologie et psychanalyse*, Paris, PUF, 1952.
Bastide, R., *Eléments de sociologie religieuse*, Paris, A. Colin, 1935.
Bastide, R., *Les Religions africaines au Brésil*, Paris, PUF, 1960.
Bastide, R., *Le Condomblé de Bahia*, The Hague and Paris, Mouton, 1960.
Bastide, R., *Anthropologie appliquée*, Paris, Payot, 1971.
Bloch, M., *Les Rois thaumaturges*, Paris, A. Colin, 1961.
Caillois, R., *Le Rêve et les sociétés humaines*, Paris, Gallimard, 1968.
Caillois, R., *L'Homme et le sacré*, Paris, Gallimard, 1950.
Cazeneuve, J., *Les Rites et la condition humaine*, Paris, PUF, 1958.
Charles, Henri, 'Les formes élémentaires de l'intercommunion', *Rev. Hist. Phil. Rel.*, Paris, 1950, pp. 100–18.
Desroche, H., *Marxisme et religions*, Paris, PUF, 1962.
Diel, P., *La Divinité*, Paris, Payot, 1950.
Diel, P., *Le symbolisme dans la mythologie grecque*, 2nd ed., Paris, Payot, 1966.
Dieterlen, G., *Essai sur la religion Bambara*, Paris, PUF, 1951.

Dufrenne, M., *La personnalité de base*, Paris, PUF, 1953.

Duméry, H., 'Quelques alibis du croyant', in *Esprit*, 1952, pp. 952–72.

Durkheim, E., *Les Formes élémentaires de la vie religieuse*, Paris, PUF, 1913.

Durkheim, E., *The Elementary Forms of the Religious Life*, tr. J. W. Swain, London, Allen & Unwin, 1976.

Eliade, M., *Aspects du mythe*, Paris, NRF, 1963.

Eliade, M., *Le Sacré et le profane*, Paris, Gallimard, 1965.

Eliade, M., *Traité d'histoire des religions*, Paris, Payot, 1948.

Frazer, J., *The Golden Bough*, 3 vols, London, Macmillan, 1900.

Gernet, L., *Le génie grec dans la religion*, Paris, Albin Michel, 1932.

Gordon, P., *L'Initiation sexuelle et l'évolution religieuse*, Paris, PUF, 1946.

Gurvitch, G., *La vocation actuelle de la sociologie*, 2nd ed., 2 vols, Paris, PUF, 1957.

Guzzo, Augusto, *La religione, fenomenologia e filosofia dell'experienza religiosa*, Torino, Academia della sciencia, 1963.

Harrington, W., *The Promise to Love: A Scriptural View of Marriage*, London, 1968.

Hertz, R., *Mélanges de sociologie religieuse et folklore*, Paris, Alcan, 1928.

Hyppolite, J., *Logique et existence*, Paris, PUF, 1953.

Lanternari, H., *Les Institutions religieuses des peuples opprimés*, Paris, Maspero.

Leenhardt, M., *Do Kamo*, Paris, Gallimard, 1947.

Lévi-Strauss, C., *Tristes Tropiques*. Paris, Plon, 1954; *Tristes Tropiques*, trans. J. and D. Weightman, London, 1973.

Lévi-Strauss, C., 'Le sorcier et sa magie', in *Les Temps modernes*, 1949, 14, pp. 3–24.

Lévi-Strauss, C., *Les Structures élémentaires de la parenté*, Paris, PUF, 1949; *Elementary Structures of Kinship*, trans. Bell, von Sturmer, Needham, London, Eyre & Spottiswoode, 1969.

Lévy-Bruhl H., *Le Surnaturel et les dieux*, Paris, PUF, 1931.

Lévy-Bruhl, H., *Mythologie primitive*, Paris, PUF, 1935.

Lévy-Bruhl, H., *Expériences mystiques et les symboles chez les primitifs*, Paris, PUF, 1938.

Lévy-Bruhl, H., *Carnets posthumes*, Paris, PUF, 1949.

Martino, E. de, *La Terre des remords*, Paris, Gallimard, 1966.

Mauss, M., *Sociologie et anthropologie*, Paris, PUF, 1950.

Mauss, M., *Manuel d'ethnographie*, Paris, Payot, 1947.

Mauss, M., *Oeuvres*, Les fonctions du sacré, Paris, Ed. de Minuit, 1968.

Mauss, M., 'La parenté à plaisanterie', *Ann. ec. Pr. H.E.*, 1927, pp. 283–328.

Mead, Margaret, *Male and Female: a study of the sexes in a changing world*, London, 1949.

Naville, P., *De l'Aliénation à la jouissance. La genèse de la sociologie du travail chez Marx et Engels*, Paris, Rivière, 1957.

Nodet, C.-H., 'Considérations psychologiques à propos des attraits nevrotiques pour la vocation religieuse', in *Vie spirituelle*, 1950, pp. 279–306.

Nuttin, Joseph, *Psychanalyse et la conception spiritualiste de l'homme*, Paris, J. Vrin, 1950.
Osborn, R., *Marxism and Psycho-Analysis*, London, Octagon, 1972.
Otto, Rudolf, *The Idea of the Holy*, trans. J. W. Harvey, Oxford, 1923.
Parsons, Talcott (ed.), *Towards a General Theory of Action*, Cambridge, Mass., Harvard University Press, 1951.
Ramnoux, C., *La Nuit et les enfants de la nuit dans la tradition grecque*, Paris, Flammarion, 1959.
Van Der Leeuw, G., and Martin, J., *La Religion dans son essence et ses manifestations*, Paris, Payot, 1948.
Wach, J., 'Problématique et typologie de l'expérience religieuse', *Arch. Soc. Rel.*, no. 16, pp. 35–77.
Wach, J., *Sociologie de la religion*, Paris, Payot, 1955.

C.2 *Psychology, psychoanalysis and sexology*

Abraham, K., *Clinical Papers and Essays on Psycho-Analysis*, trans. H. C. Abraham and D. R. Ellison, London, Hogarth, 1955.
Allendy, R. and Y., *Capitalisme and sexualité*, Paris, Denoël, 1932.
Bachelard, G., *La Psychanalyse du feu*, Paris, Gallimard, 1949.
Bachelard, G., *L'Eau et les rêves*, Paris, José Corti, 1948.
Bachelard, G., *L'Air et les songes*, Paris, José Corti, 1950.
Bachelard, G., *La Terre et les rêveries de la volonté*, Paris, José Corti, 1948.
Bachelard, G., *La Terre et les rêveries du repos*, Paris, José Corti, 1948.
Bachelard, G., *La Poétique de l'espace*, Paris, PUF, 1957; *The Poetics of Space*, tr. Maria Jolas, Boston, Beacon Press, 1964.
Bachelard, G., *La Poétique de la rêverie*, Paris, PUF, 1961.
Bachelard, G., *La Flamme d'une chandelle*, Paris, PUF, 1961.
Bastide, R., *Sociologie et psychanalyse*, in vol. II, *Traité de sociologie* by Georges Gurvitch, Paris, PUF, 1960, pp. 402–19.
Bastide, R., *Sociologie et psychanalyse*, Paris, PUF, 1950.
Bataille, G., *L'Erotisme*, Paris, Ed. de Minuit, 1957.
Bandouin, Ch., *Psychanalyse du symbole religieux*, Paris, A. Fayard, 1957.
Baudouin, Ch., *L'Oeuvre de Jung*, Paris, Payot, 1963.
Benedict, R., *Echantillons de civilization*, Paris, Gallimard, 1949.
Berguer, G., *Traité de psychologie de la religion*, Paris, Payot, 1946.
Bonaparte, M., *Psychanalyse et anthropologie*, Paris, PUF, 1952.
Boullet, J., *Symbolisme sexuel*, Paris, J.-J. Pauvert, 1961.
Cetremon, G. de, *Religions et sexualisme*, Paris, Ed. de 'L'idée libre', 1928.
Choisy, M., *Moïse*, Geneva, Ed. Mont-Blanc, 1966.
Choisy, M., *La Survie après la mort*, Paris, Labergerie, 1967.
Choisy, M., *L'Etre et le silence*, Geneva, Ed. Mont-Blanc, 1962.
Choisy, M., *Psychanalyse et catholicisme*, Paris, L'Arche, 1950.
David, Ch. and Fain, M., 'Aspects fonctionnels de la vie onirique', in *Rev. fr. de psychanalyse*, numéro spécial, 1963.
Dollar, J., *Frustration and Aggression*, London, Kegan Paul, 1944.

Ferenczi, S., *Thalassa: a theory of genitality*, trans. H. A. Bunker, New York, 1968.
Flugel, S. C., *The Psychology of Clothes*, London, Hogarth, 1930.
Freud, S., *New Introductory Lectures on Psycho-Analysis*, Standard Edition, London, Hogarth, 1962, vol. XXII, p. 3.
Freud, S., *An Outline of Psycho-Analysis*, Standard Edition, London, Hogarth, 1969, vol. XXIII, p. 141.
Freud, S., *Totem and Taboo*, Standard Edition, vol. XIII, London, Routledge & Kegan Paul, 1950, p. 1.
Friedmann, H., 'Psychanalyse et sociologie', *Bull. Psychol.*, 1956, no. 1, pp. 12–23.
Fromm, E., *The Forgotten Language*, London, 1952.
Glover, E., *Freud or Jung*, London, 1950.
Graham-Cole, W., *Sex and Love in the Bible*, London, 1959.
Hanry, P., *Erotisme africain*, Paris, Payot, 1970.
Havel, J.-E., *La Condition de la femme*, Paris, Colin, 1961.
Held, R., 'Contribution à l'étude psychanalytique du phénomène religieux', in *Rev. fr. de Psychanalyse*, mai-juin 1969, nos. 2–3.
Hesnard, A., *Morale sans péché*, Paris, PUF, 1954.
Horney, K., *New Ways in Psycho-Analysis*, London, 1918.
James, E. O., *The Beginnings of Religion*, London, 1948.
Jaspers, K., *General Psychopathology*, trans. J. Hoenig and M. W. Hamilton, Manchester, 1963.
Jeannière, A., *Anthropologie sexuelle*, Paris, Autier, 1964.
Jung, C. G., *Collected Works*, tr. R. F. C. Hull, London, Routledge & Kegan Paul, various dates.
Kent, C., 'Les ressources cachées de l'homme', in *Rev. fr. de Psychanalyse*, 1962, no. 1.
Klein, M., *Contributions to Psycho-Analysis*, London, Hogarth, 1950.
Konig, R., *La Mode*, Paris, Payot, 1967.
Kouretas, D., 'Aspects modernes des cures psychothérapiques pratiquées dans les sanctuaires de la Grèce antique', in *Rev. fr. de Psychanalyse*, 1963, nos. 2–3.
Lacan, J., *Écrits*, Paris, Seuil, 1966; *Ecrits: a Selection*, tr. Alan Sheridan, London, Tavistock, 1977.
Lo Duca, *Technique de l'érotisme*, Paris, Pauvert, 1962.
Malinowski, B., *Sex and Repression in Savage Society*, London, 1927.
Marcuse, H., *Eros and Civilization*, London, 1970.
Masson-Oursel, 'La sociologie de Durkheim et la psychanalyse', *Psyché*, 1947, II, 13–14.
Mauco, G., 'Psychologie du primitif et psychologie de l'inconscient', *Psyché*, no. 5, mars 1947.
Michel, A., *Psychanalyse de la musique*, Paris, PUF, 1951.
Michelet, J., *La Sorcière*, Paris, 1862.
Morin, E., *Les Stars*, Paris, Seuil, 1961.
Neesser, M., *Les Principes de la psychologie de la religion et la psychanalyse*, Neuchâtel, 1920.
Nefzāwi, M., *Le Jardin parfumé*, tr. Isidore Liseux, Paris, 1886 (new edn 1906).

Nefzāwi, M., *Le Jardin enchanté*, tr. Leopold Blondeau, Paris, 1960.
Nygren, A., *Agapé and Eros*, 3 vols, trans. A. G. Herbert, London, 1932–9.
Osborn, R., *Marxism and Psycho-Analysis*, London, Octagon, 1972.
Paris, R., 'Psychanalyse, culture et néoténie', in *Rev. fr. de Psychanalyse*, 1962, no. 1.
Pesch, E., *La Psychologie collective*, Paris, Bordas, 1947.
Piper, O., *L'Evangile et la vie sexuelle*, Geneva, Delachaux & Niestlé, 1955.
Ramnoux, C., 'Sur une page de "Moïse et le monothéisme" ', in *La Psychanalyse*, 1957, vol. 3, p. 165ff.
Rank, O., *The Trauma of Birth*, New York, 1973.
Ricoeur, P., Numéro spécial de la revue *Esprit*, conçu et présenté par P. Ricoeur, sur la sexualité, novembre 1960, pp. 1665–1964.
Sarano, D., *La Culpabilité*, Paris, A. Colin, 1957.
Schelsky, H., *Sociologie de la sexualité*, Paris, Gallimard, 1966.
Selbie, W. S., *The Psychology of Religion*, Oxford University Press, 1924.
Shentoub, S. A., 'Psychanalyse, ethnologie et ethnologie psychanalytique', in *Rev. fr. de Psychanalyse*, 1964, no. 3.
Stoetzel, J., *La Psychologie sociale*, Paris, Flammarion, 1963.
Taylor, G. R., *Sex in History*, rev. ed., London, 1965.
Villeneuve, R., *Le Diable, erotologie de Satan*, Paris, Pauvert, 1962.
Winthrop, H., 'L'avenir de la révolution sexuelle', in *Diogène*, 1970, no. 70, pp. 65–94.

C.3 *Studies of the Arabo-Muslim societies*

Akrout, A., *Les Pratiques de la prière et l'hygiène chez les musulmans*, thèse médecine, Paris, Jouve, 1936.
Amar, E., 'Alchimie arabe', *RT*, 1904, p. 8; 1905, pp. 152–65.
Ammar, A., *Growing up in an Egyptian village*, London, Routledge & Kegan Paul, 1954.
Ammar, S., 'Les troubles "psycho-organiques" de la grossesse, de l'accouchement et de l'allaitement en Tunisie', *Tunisie médicale*, 1962, nos. 1–2, pp. 1–11.
Ammar, S., and M'Barek, E., 'L'hystérie chez la jeune fille et la femme tunisiennes', *Tunisie médicale*, 1961, no. 4, pp. 12–27.
Anderson, J. N. D., 'Law and Custom in Muslim Areas in Africa; recent developments in Nigeria', *Civilizations*, 7, 1957, pp. 17–31.
Bairam, B., 'Les sports équestres à Tunis au XIXᵉ siècle', *IBLA*, 1957, pp. 31–6.
Baron, A. M., 'Mariages et divorces à Casablanca', *Hesperis*, 40, 1953, pp. 419–40.
Bates, E., 'Ethnographic notes from Marsa matruh', *The Journal of the Royal Asiatic Society*, London, 1915, pp. 727–85.
Bel, A., 'La 'Ansra: jeux et rites du solstice d'été en Berbérie', *Mélange Gaudefroy-Demombynes*, 1935–45, pp. 49–83.

Bel, A., *La Religion musulmane en Berbérie*, vol. I, Paris, Geuthner, 1938 (SG 285).
Bel, A., 'Survivance d'une fête du printemps à Tunis', *RT*, 1934, pp. 337–61.
Bencheneb, S., 'Survivance païenne: l'éternuement', in *BEA*, 11, 1951, pp. 99–108.
Bercher, L., 'L'apostasie, le blasphème et la rébellion dans le droit musulman malékite', *RT*, 1923, pp. 115–29.
Bercher, L., 'La censure des moeurs selon Al Ghazali', *IBLA*, vol. XVIII, 1955, pp. 313–21 and vol. XXI, 1958, pp. 389–407.
Berque, Jacques, *Les Arabes d'hier à demain*, Paris, Seuil, 1960.
Berque, Jacques, *Le Maghreb entre deux guerres*, Paris, Seuil, 1962.
Berque, J. and Charnay, J.-P., *Normes et valeurs dans l'islam contemporain*, Paris, Payot.
Bertherland, E. L., *Médecine et hygiène des Arabes*, Paris, 1855.
Berthier, A., 'Les Berbères entre l'Islam et l'Occident', *Population*, 2nd year, no. 1, 1947.
Biron, A., 'Art sacré islamique', *Diogène*, no. 24, oct.-dec. 1958.
Bishr, F., 'Philosophie et jurisprudence illustrées par les Arabes', *Mél. L. Massignon*, II, 1957, pp. 77–109.
Blachère, R., *Le problème de Mahomet*, Paris, PUF, 1952.
Bouhdiba, A., *A la Recherche des normes perdues*, Tunis, MTE, 1973.
Bouhdiba, A., *Criminalité et changements sociaux en Tunisie*, Tunis, 'Les mémoires du CERES', 1960.
Boujedra, R., *La Répudiation* (novel), Paris, Denoël, 1970.
Bousquet, G.-H., *L'Ethique sexuelle de l'islam*, Paris, Maisonneuve, 1966.
Boussen, Abdelhamid, *Contribution à l'étude du jeûne dans l'islam*, thèse médecine, Paris, Imprimerie Arnette, 1942.
Brunot, L., 'Cultes naturistes à Sefrou', *Arch. berbères*, 3, 1918.
Brunschwig, R., *La Berbérie orientale sous les Hafsides*, 2 vols, Paris, IAOAM, 1940, 1947.
Browne, E., *Arabian Medicine*, Cambridge, 1921.
Burckhardt, T., *Du soufisme, Introduction au langage doctrinal du soufisme*, Alger, Messerchmitt, 1951.
Cahen, C., 'Mouvements et organisations populaires dans les villes de l'Asie musulmane au Moyen Age', *Recueil Soc. J. Bodin*, 7, 1955, pp. 273–88.
Calverley, E. J., 'Beauty for Ashes', *Muslim World*, 10, 1920, pp. 39–40.
Camilleri, C., 'Les jeunes Tunisiens cultivés face au problème de la mixité', *Confluent*, no. 20, pp. 262–87.
Carcopino, J., *La Vie quotidienne à Rome*, Paris, Hachette, 1951.
Carton, L., 'Tatouages africains', *Revue tunisienne*, 1913, pp. 676–95.
Certeux (1834–1904), *Contributions au folklore des Arabes*, Paris, Maisonneuve, 1884.
Charles, R., *L'Âme musulmane*, Paris, Flammarion, 1959.
Chelhod, J., 'Les attitudes et les gestes de la prière rituelle dans l'Islam', *Revue d'Hist. des Religions*, oct.-dec. 1959.
Chelhod, J., *Introduction à la sociologie de l'Islam de l'animisme à l'universalisme*, Paris, Besson-Chantemerle, 1953.

Chelhod, J., *Les Structures du sacré chez les Arabes*, Paris, Maisonneuve, 1964.

Chénier, Louis, *Recherches historiques sur les Maures et histoire de l'Empire du Maroc*, 1787, 3 vols.

Cohen, C. K., 'Le lévirat dans le droit hébraïque', *RT Droit*, 4, 1954, pp. 16–21.

Communaux, V., 'Rapport sur le droit des pauvres en Tunisie', *Rev. Tun.*, 1898, pp. 255–69.

Cuisenier, J., *L'Ansarine*, Paris, Publ. Université de Tunis, 1960.

Darmon, R., *La Situation des cultes en Tunisie*, Tunis, La Rapide, 1930.

De Ambrogio, 'Législation et coutumes des Berbères du Sud tunisien', *RT*, 1903, pp. 27–39.

Dehoï, E. F., *L'érotisme des Mille et une Nuits*, Paris, J.-J. Pauvert, 1961.

Delafosse, M., 'Coutumes et fêtes matrimoniales chez les musulmans soudanais', *RMM*, 11, 1910, pp. 405–21.

De La Salle, 'Sur le folklore tunisien', *Rev. afr.*, 74, 1944; 99, 1946.

Del Mares, 'Sortilèges, pratiques à Mazagan pour préserver les jeunes épouses d'une maternité trop précoce', *Rev. Anthropol.*, 43, 1933, pp. 477–8.

Dermenghem, E., *Au Pays d'Abel*, Paris, 1942.

Dermenghem, E., 'Les confréries noires en Algérie (Diwans de Sidi Blal)', *Rev. afr.*, 97, 1953, pp. 314–67.

Dermenghem, E., 'Le mythe de Psyché dans le folklore nord-africain', in *Rev. afr.*, 1er–2e trim., 1945, pp. 41–81.

Dermenghem, E., *Mahomet*, Paris, Seuil, 1957.

Dermenghem, E., 'Le culte des saints au Maghreb', *Rev. afr.*, 1936, pp. 135–61.

Diague, 'A propos des Aïssaouas', *Afrique et Asie*, 1960, pp. 3–12.

Donaldson, B. A., 'The Koran as magic', in *Muslim World*, 1937, no. 27, pp. 254–66.

Donaldson, D. M., 'Temporary marriage in Islam', *Muslim World*, no. 26, 1936, pp. 358–64.

Doutte, E., *Magie et religion en Afrique du Nord*, Algiers, 1909.

Dozy, A., *Essai sur l'histoire de l'islamisme*, Leiden-Paris, 1879.

Dubouloz-Laffin, M.-L., *Le Bou-Mergoud, folklore tunisien*, Paris, Maisonneuve, 1946.

Ehrenfels, V. R., 'Ambivalent attitudes to woman in Islamic society', *Islamic Culture*, 26, 1951, pp. 73–88.

Elisseeff, Nikita, *Thèmes et motifs des 'Mille et une Nuits'*, Beirut, Ed. Institut français de Damas, 1946.

Erlanger, R. d', *Histoire de la musique arabe*, Paris, Gueuthner, 6 vols, 1930–59.

Esenkova, P., 'La femme turque contemporaine, education et rôle social', *IBLA*, 1951, vol. XIV, pp. 255–77.

Esin, Emel, *La Mecque, ville bénie, Médine, ville radieuse*, Paris, Albin Michel, 1963.

Essad, Bey Mohammed, *Allah est grand*, Paris, Payot, 1937.

Ettinghausen, R., *La Peinture arabe*, Paris, Skira, 1962.

Evans-Pritchard, E. E., 'The Sanusi of Cyrenaica', *Africa*, 15, 1945, pp. 61–79.
Farmer, H. G. A., 'The religious music of Islam', *Journal of Royal Asiatic Society*, 1952, pp. 60–5.
Fauvelle, *Le peuple d'Allah*, Paris, Levrault, 1958.
Feghali, Joseph, 'La conception coranique du mariage et celle du droit canonique', *Ann. ec. Legisl. Rel.*, 2, 1951–2, pp. 58–64.
Feraoun, M., 'Le désaccord' (story), in *Soleil*, no. 6, 1951, pp. 36–58.
Flaux, A., *La Régence de Tunis au XIXe siècle*, Paris, 1865.
Gabrieli, F., *Les Arabes*, Paris, Buchet-Castel, 1963.
Gabrieli, F., and Walter, G., *Mahomet*, Paris, Albin Michel, 1963.
Gardet, L., *L'Islam, religion et communauté*, Paris, Desclée de Brouwer, 1970.
Gary, M., 'Magie et sorcellerie en Afrique du Nord', *Bull. Eco. Pub. Mar.*, no. 230, 1954.
Gaudefroy-Demombynes, M., *Le pèlerinage à La Mecque*, Paris, Gauthier, 1923.
Gaudefroy-Demombynes, M., *Les Institutions musulmanes*, Paris, Flammarion, 1921.
Gaudefroy-Demombynes, M., *Mahomet*, Paris, Albin Michel, 1957.
Gaudry, M., *La Femme chaouia de l'Aurès*, Paris, 1929.
Gautier, E.-F., *Le Passé de l'Afrique du Nord: Les siècles obscurs*, Paris, Payot, 1937.
Germain, G., 'Le culte du bélier en Afrique du Nord', *Hespéris*, 35, 1948, pp. 93–124.
Gibb, H., *Mohammedanism: An Historical Survey*, London, 1949.
Gobert, E.-G., 'Essai sur la litholâtrie', *Rev. afr.*, 1948, no. 92, pp. 24–110.
Gobert, E.-G., 'La chguiga ou amulette en bois d'éthedra', *Revue tunisienne*, 1940, no. 5, pp. 1–5.
Gobert, E.-G., 'Note sur les tatouages indigenes dans la région de Gafsa', *Revue tunisienne*, 1911, pp. 32–51.
Gobert, E.-G., 'Les réferences historiques des nourritures tunisiennes', *Cahiers de Tunisie*, 3, 1955, pp. 501–42.
Gobert, E.-J. de, 'Le pudendum magique et le problème des cauris', *Rev. afr.*, 1951, no. 95, pp. 5–62.
Goeje, M.-J. de, 'L'encensement des morts chez les anciens Arabes', *Actes XIVe Congr. int. d'orientalisme*, 1905, section 1, p. 37.
Goichon, A.-M., 'La conservation du groupe mozabite et la religion de ses femmes', *Rev. de Philosophie*, 33, 1926, pp. 290–321.
Goichon, A.-M., *La Femme dans le milieu familial à Fez*, Paris, 1929, pp. 285–91.
Goichon, A.-M., *La Vie feminine au Mzab*, Paris, Gueuthner, 1951.
Goldziher, J., *Le Dogme et la loi de l'Islam*, Paris, Gueuthner, 1958.
Golvin, L., 'Notes sur deux procédés de divination en Afrique du Nord', in *Ann. I.E. Alg.*, 12, 1954.
Grunebaum, G. E., *Classicisme et déclin culturel dans l'histoire de l'islam*, Paris, Besson & Chantemerle, 1957.

Grunebaum, G. E., 'Idéologie musulmane et esthétique arabe', *Studia islamica*, 1955.
Hayck, Michel, *Le Mystère d'Ismaïl*, Tours, 1964.
Herger, J., 'Le mensonge et la feinte prophylactique au Maroc', *RHR*, 1933, 108, pp. 229–45.
Herger, J., 'Tatouages', various articles in *Hespéris*, 1921, 1929, 1948.
Himes, N. E., *Medical History of Contraception*, New York, 1963 (2nd edn).
Hinningh, Joseph, 'Les fêtes du printemps chez les Arabes et leurs implications historiques', *Revista do mesen Paulista*, São Paulo, NS, 4, 1950, pp. 389–432.
Hunke, S., *Le Soleil d'Allah brille sur l'Occident*, Paris, Albin Michel, 1963.
Idris, H. R., *Les Manaquibs d'Abou Ishaq al Gabanyani et de Muhriz b. Khalaf (Sidi Mahrez)*, thèse complémentaire, Fac. Lettres, Paris, 1959.
Ikbal, A. Sh., *Islamic Sufism*, London, 1933.
Ivanow, W., 'Peinture et poésie en Orient', *Orient*, 4, 1957, pp. 7–14.
Jacquot, L.-M., 'Contribution au folklore de l'Algérie', *Revue des traditions populaires*, Paris, no. 6, 1912.
Jacquot, L.-M., 'Coutumes de Savoie et de Tunisie concernant les femmes stériles et les femmes enceintes', *Revue des traditions populaires*, déc. 1912.
James, E. D., *Mythes et rites dans le Proche-Orient ancien*, Paris, Payot, 1960.
Jomier, J., 'La place du Koran dans la vie quotidienne en Egypte', *IBLA*, vol. XV, 1952, pp. 131–65.
Jonin, J., 'Chants et jeux maternels à Rabat', *Hespéris*, 37 (1950), pp. 137–56.
Jonin, J., 'Valeur symbolique des aliments et rites alimentaires à Rabat', *Hespéris*, 1957, 3e–4e trimèstre, pp. 299–327.
Lacoste, Camille, *Légendes et contes merveilleux de Grande Kabylie*, Paris, Gueuthner, 1965, 2 vols.
Lacouture, J. and S., *L'Egypte en mouvement*, Paris, Seuil, 1956.
Laoust, H., *Mots et choses berbères*, Paris, 1920.
Lecoeur, C., *Le Rite et l'outil*, 2nd ed., Paris, PUF, 1971.
Lecomte, G., 'Le livre des règles de conduites des maîtres d'école par Ibn Sahnūn', *R. Et. islamiques*, 21, 1953, pp. 77–105.
Lelong, M., 'Femmes tunisiennes d'aujourd'hui', *IBLA*, vol. XXII, 1959, pp. 354–7.
Lelong, M., 'La jeune fille de demain en Tunisie (une enquête de la revue "Al Ilham")', *IBLA*, vol. XVIII, 1955, pp. 357–62.
Lelong, M., 'La personnalité de la femme tunisienne', *IBLA*, vol. XIX, 1956, p. 423.
Lemanski, D., 'Hypnotisme et Aissaouas', *RT*, 1898, pp. 327–33.
Lemanski, D., 'Psychologie de la femme arabe', *RT*, 1900, p. 87.
Lesourd, M., 'Les femmes d'In Salla mangeuses de chats à l'occasion de la fête d'Es-Sabāa', *J. Soc. Afr.*, 7, 1937, pp. 33–5.
Letellier, G., 'Devoir et structure mentale: Contribution à l'étude

psycho-sociale des milieux nord-africains', *IBLA*, 15, 1952, pp. 303–6.
Letellier, G., 'La religion musulmane en Berbérie', *IBLA*, 3, 1939, pp. 377–85.
Lévi-Provençal, E., 'Un chant populaire religieux du Djebel marocain', *RA*, 59, 1918, pp. 215–48.
Lévy, R., *An Introduction to the Sociology of Islam*, 2 vols, London, 1933.
Lewicki, T., 'Culte du bélier dans la Tunisie musulmane', *REI*, 9, 1935, pp. 195–200.
Lewicki, T., 'Culte du bélier dans la Tunisie musulmane', cf. *RT*, 1935, pp. 195–200, 1936, pp. 484–92.
Lori, A., 'Aissaouas charmeurs de serpents', *RT*, 1900, pp. 142–279.
Lori, A., 'La circoncision chez les indigènes israélites et musulmans de Tunis', *RT*, 1900, pp. 54–62.
Loti, P., *Les Désenchantées* (novel), Paris, Calmann-Levy, new ed., 1966.
Macdonald, J., 'Joseph in the Qur'an and Muslim commentary', *Muslim World*, 46, 1956, pp. 113–31 and 207–24.
Marçais, G., *L'église et la mosquée*, Paris, Cahiers du Sud, 1947, pp. 174–9.
Marçais, G., *La Berbérie musulmane et l'Orient du Moyen Age*, Paris, Montaigne, 1946.
Margoliouth, D., 'Muhammadan circumcision', in *Encyclopedia of Religion and Ethics*, vol. II, p. 678.
Marguerite, L.-P., *Les Tunisiennes*, Paris, Denoël, 1937.
Marty, G., 'Les chants lyriques populaires du Sud tunisien', *RT*, 1936, pp. 93–135 and 256–95; 1937, pp. 138–77 and 434–61.
Masry (al), Y., *Le Drame sexuel de la femme dans l'Orient arabe*, Paris, Laffont, 1962.
Massignon, L., 'La "Futuwwa" ou pacte d'honneur artisanal entre travailleurs musulmans au Moyen Age', in *Nouvelle Clio*, 1952, pp. 171–98.
Massignon, L., *La passion d'al-Hallaj*, Paris, 1922.
Massignon, L., 'Le rite islamique du Hajj', *Actes du VII*e *Congrès hist. rel.*, 1951, pp. 146–58.
Massignon, L., 'Les sept dormants d'Ephèse', *Rev. Et. islam*, 22, 1954, cont. in 1955, pp. 93–104.
Massignon, L., *Essai sur les origines du lexique technique de la mystique musulmane*, new ed., Paris, Vrin, 1968.
Massignon, L., 'Sur la Futuwwa', *XXII*e *Congrès orientaliste*, 1951, 11, pp. 277–9.
Massignon, L., 'Thèmes archétypiques en onirocritique musulmane', *Eranos*, 12, 1945, pp. 241–57.
Maunier, R., 'La femme en Kabylie', *Memorial H. Basset*, vol. II, 1928, pp. 131–7.
Maunier, R., *Mélanges de sociologie nord-africaine*, Paris, Alcan, 1930.
Maunier, R., 'L'ordre social nord-africain. Tribu, Cité, État', *Mélanges Mechaim*, 1935, vol. I, pp. 339–49.
Maunier, R., 'Recherches sur les échanges rituels en Afrique du Nord', Am. Soc., nouv. série, vol. II, 1924–5.

Mazahéri A., *La Vie quotidienne des musulmans au Moyen Age*, Paris, Hachette, 1947.
Menouillard, H., 'Moeurs indigènes: mejnoun', *RT*, 1905, pp. 477–89.
Menouillard, H., 'Une noce à Zarzis: la danse des chevaux', *RT*, 1905, pp. 3–12.
Menouillard, H., 'Pratiques pour solliciter la pluie', *RT*, 1910, pp. 302–11.
Michaux-Bellaire, E., 'Quelques aspects de l'Islam chez les Berbères marocaines', *RMM*, 2, 1907, 347–55.
Michaux-Bellaire, E., 'Une histoire de rapt', *Arch. marocaines*, 5, 1905, pp. 436–42.
Milliot, L., *La Femme musulmane au Maghreb*, Paris, Roussel, 1909.
Mole, M., *Les Mystiques musulmans*, Paris, PUF, 1965.
Monteil, Vincent, *L'islam noir*, Paris, Seuil, 1964.
Montgomery Watt, W., *Mohammad, Prophet and Statesman*, Oxford, 1961.
Montety, H. de, *Le mariage musulman en Tunisie*, Tunis, SAPI, 1941.
Moubarac, Y., *Abraham dans le Coran*, Paris, Vrin, 1958.
M'Rabet, F., *La Femme algérienne*, Paris, Maspéro, 1964.
Neila, 'La femme kairouannaise', *IBLA*, vol. IV, 1941, pp. 349–58.
Neila, 'Questions féminines', *IBLA*, 5, 1942, pp. 78–85 and 408–14.
Nores, E., 'Étude sur le don "mouta'a", ou don de consolation', *Rev. algérienne*, 1928, part I, pp. 1–13.
Pellat, C., *Le Milieu basrien et la formation de Jahiz*, Paris, 1953.
Pérès, H., *La Poésie andalouse en arabe classique au XI*[e] *siècle*, Paris, Maisonneuve, 1953.
Pérès, H., 'Poésie à Fès sous les Almaravides et les Almohades', *Hespéris*, 1934, vol. XVIII, pp. 37–59.
Pérès, H., *Le siècle d'Ibn Khaldoun*, Algiers, La Maison des Livres, 1960.
Peron, Dr N., *Femmes arabes avant et depuis l'islamisme*, Paris, Librairie nouvelle, 1858.
Peron, Dr N., *La médecine du prophète*, French trans. from Arabic by Slimane B. Daoud, Paris, Tissier, 1860.
Pesle, O., *La femme musulmane dans le droit, la religion et les moeurs*, Casablanca, Laporté, 1946.
Planhol, X. de, *Le monde islamique*, Paris, PUF, 1957.
Planhol, X. de, 'Le paysage urbain de l'Islam', *Table ronde*, 126, 1958, pp. 121–32.
Probst-Biraben, J.-H., 'Le Djinn-Serpent dans l'Afrique du Nord', in *En Terre d'Islam*, 1947, fasc. 38 and 39.
Probst-Biraben, J.-H., 'La main de Fatma et ses antécédents symboliques', *Revue anthropologique*, 43, 1933, pp. 370–5.
Probst-Biraben, J.-H., 'Prêtresses', *Revue anthropologique*, 45, 1935, pp. 257–64.
Probst-Biraben, J.-H., 'Le serpent: persistance de son culte en Afrique du Nord', *J. Soc. Afr.*, 3, 1933, pp. 289–95.
Renan, E., *L'islamisme et la science*, Paris, Calmann Lévy, 1883.
Renan, E., *De Moise à Mohammed*, Paris, Calmann Lévy, 1955, 2 vols.

Renault, H., *Les Survivances des cultes de Cybèle, Venus, Bacchus (Aïssaoua, Ouled Naïl, Karabouz), RT*, 1917, pp. 150–8.
Robson, J., 'Magic Cures in Popular Islam', *Muslim World*, 24, 1934, pp. 33–43.
Roche, M. H., 'The Muslim women in North Africa', *Muslim World*, 23, 1933, pp. 262–74.
Rodinson, M., *Islam et capitalisme*, Paris, Seuil, 1967.
Salinger, G., 'Was the futuwwa an oriental chivalry?', *Proc. Amer. Philos. Soc.*, 94, 1950, pp. 481–93.
Salmon, G.-H., 'Les Bdadoua', Archives marocaines, Paris, 1905, vol. II, pp. 362–81.
Schacht, J., *Esquisse d'une histoire au droit musulman*, Paris, Librarie Orientale et Américaine, 1953.
Schacht, J., 'Notes sur la sociologie du droit musulman', *Revue africaine*, 1952, pp. 311–37.
Selima, R., *Harems et musulmanes d'Egypte*, Paris, 1902.
Serradj, M. B., 'Quelques usages féminins populaires a Tlemcen', *IBLA*, vol. XIV, 1951, pp. 279–89.
Smith, W. C., *Kinship and Marriage in Early Arabia*, London, 1903.
Sugier, C., 'Les jeunes filles tunisiennes d'aujourd'hui', *IBLA*, vol. XIX, 1956, pp. 233–89.
Sureau, 'Aïn Barouta', *Rev. tun.*, 1915, pp. 297–301.
Sureau, 'Le tapis sacré', *Rev. tun.*, 1915, pp. 70–5.
Tharaud, J. and J., *Les mille et un jours de l'islam*, Paris, Plon, 1941.
Thévenot, Jean, *Relation d'un voyage fait au Levant*, Paris, 1664.
Tillion, G., *Le harem et les cousins*, Paris, Seuil, 1966.
Torabi, A., *Étude sociologique: les séquelles du soufisme dans l'âme persane*, thèse lettres, Paris, 1959.
Vadet, J.-C., *L'esprit courtois en Orient dans les cinq premiers siècles de l'Hégire*, Paris, 1968.
Westermarck, E., *Survivances païennes dans la civilisation mahométane*, Paris, Payot, 1935.
Wiet, G., *Grandeur de l'Islam*, Paris, Table ronde, 1961.
Wiet, G., *Introduction à la littérature arabe*, Paris, Maisonneuve et Larousse, 1966.

C.4 *Philosophical references*

Alain, *Système des beaux-arts*, Paris, Gallimard, 1926.
Alain, *Entretiens aux bords de la mer*, Paris, Gallimard, 1930.
Alain, *Propos sur la religion*, Paris, Rieder, 1938.
Alain, *Les Aventures du coeur*, Paris, Harthrann, 1945.
Bergson, H., *Les deux sources de la morale et de la religion*, 48th ed., Paris, PUF, 1946; *The Two Sources of Morality and Religion*, trans. R. A. Audra and C. Brereton, London, 1935.
Hyppolite, J., 'Bachelard ou le romantisme de l'intelligence', *Rev. Philos.*, janv-mars 1954, pp. 93–104.

Jankélévitch, V., *Traité des vertus*, 1st ed., Paris, Bordas, 1947 (2nd ed., in 3 vols: I *Le sérieux et l'intention*, 1968; II *Les vertus et l'amour*, 1970; III *La méchanceté et l'innocence*, 1972).
Kierkegaard, S., *Either/Or*, trans. D. F. and L. M. Swenson, 2 vols, Princeton, New Jersey, Princeton University Press, 1971.
Kierkegaard, S., *Fear and Trembling*, trans. W. Lowrie, Princeton, New Jersey, Princeton University Press, 1941.
Lahbabi, M. A., *Du clos à l'ouvert*, Casablanca, Dar al-Kitāb, 1961.
Lahbabi, M. A., *De l'Etre à la personne: essai de personnalisme réaliste*, Paris, PUF, 1954.
Lahbabi, M. A., *Le Personnalisme musulman*, Paris, PUF, 1964.
Merleau-Ponty, M., *Phénoménologie de la perception*, 8th ed., Paris, Gallimard, 1945; *Phenomenology of Perception*, trans. Colin Smith, London, Routledge & Kegan Paul, 1962.
Nietzsche, F., *The Genealogy of Morals*, trans. W. Kaufmann and R. J. Hollingdale, New York, Vintage Books, 1969.
Nietzsche, F., *The Birth of Tragedy*, trans. W. Kaufmann, New York, Random House, 1967.
Sartre, J.-P., *L'Être et le néant*, Paris, Gallimard, 1943; *Being and Nothingness*, trans. Hazel E. Barnes, London, Methuen, 1958.
Plato, *The Symposium*, trans. W. Hamilton, Harmondsworth, Penguin, 1951.
Ricoeur, P., *Histoire et vérité*, Paris, Seuil, 1953; *History and Truth*, trans. C. A. Kelbley, Evanston, Ill., Northwestern University Press, 1965.
Ricoeur, P., *De l'Interprétation: essai sur Freud*, Paris, Seuil, 1965.